Brain   Development
and
Behavior

Contributors

Anthony M. Adinolfi

Joseph Altman

David W. Caley

Walter B. Essman

Edward Geller

Albert Globus

Toke Hoppenbrouwers

Yoshiaki Iwamura

Richard N. Lolley

Dennis J. McGinty

David S. Maxwell

Dietland Müller-Schwarze

Dominick P. Purpura

Austin H. Riesen

Guenter H. Rose

Mortimer G. Rosen

Shawn Schapiro

Arnold B. Scheibel

Madge E. Scheibel

M. B. Sterman

Richard E. Whalen

Arthur Yuwiler

Brain Development and Behavior

Edited by

M. B. Sterman

Neuropsychology Research Laboratory
Veterans Administration Hospital
Sepulveda, California
and
Department of Anatomy
University of California
Los Angeles, California

Dennis J. McGinty

Neuropsychology Research Laboratory
Veterans Administration Hospital
Sepulveda, California
and
Department of Psychology
University of California
Los Angeles, California

Anthony M. Adinolfi

Neurocytology Research Laboratory
Veterans Administration Hospital
Sepulveda, California
and
Department of Anatomy
University of California
Los Angeles, California

1971 **ACADEMIC PRESS**
New York and London

LKN KIMI HH

ACADEMIC PRESS, INC.
111 Fifth Avenue, New York, New York 10003

United Kingdom Edition published by
ACADEMIC PRESS, INC. (LONDON) LTD.
Berkeley Square House, London W1X 6BA

LIBRARY OF CONGRESS CATALOG CARD NUMBER: 70 - 165472

PRINTED IN THE UNITED STATES OF AMERICA

Dedication

In late July of 1970, Dr. Shawn Schapiro rushed into our office with the final modified draft of his contribution entitled "Hormonal and environmental influences on rat brain development and behavior." Shawn was relieved to have his chapter finished, both because it represented the most complete and integrated expression of an enormous research and conceptual effort over the past several years, and because it had constituted the last major distraction from his growing excitement over an upcoming trip to the Endocrine Meeting at Sao Paulo, Brazil. He had previously considered traveling together with one of us to the International Congress of Anatomy in Leningrad, USSR, but the opportunity to visit the South American continent and to explore its anthropological mysteries had captured his imagination and caused him to change his plans. It was decided to exchange notes after returning from our respective scientific and cultural adventures. We were denied that opportunity. On August 9, 1970, Dr. Shawn Schapiro and his wife Lorraine died in an airplane crash outside of Cuzco, Peru.

Shawn Schapiro was dedicated to a broad, energetic, and imaginative approach to the study of the developing nervous system. Few scientists that one can think of so aptly epitomized the scientific philosopy within which this text was conceived. In sadness and with this in mind, we wish to dedicate this book to his memory. We wish, also, to share with our readers some of the intimate thoughts of his close friend and fellow participant in this volume, Dr. Arthur Yuwiler.

In a sense every textbook is a graveyard and every sentence the epitaph and summation of a man's life. In a compendium such as this, the summations are broader and the man emerges somewhat more clearly. Shawn Schapiro's chapter in this volume reveals much of the man, but it is only an outline—a shadow—and not the man himself.

Everything about Shawn was unique and quixotic. The whimsical paradox of his name—Shawn Schapiro—was symbolic of the whimsical paradox of the man himself. Even so prosaic and uniform a thing as a curriculum vitae took on a unique flavor in his case. A New Yorker by birth and inclination, he went to Berkeley for a B.S. in biochemistry and to the University of Southern California for his doctorate in physiology. During and after his graduation he bounded about doing research and teaching at the San Fernando Valley State College, the University of Southern California Medical School, the University of California at Los Angeles, the

Institute for Medical Research at the Cedars of Lebanon Hospital, the Veterans Administration, and the Karolinska Institute of Sweden, where he was a postdoctoral fellow with U. S. Von Euler. Each place was a journey and an exploration of new mysteries to supplement his developing picture of ontogeny, and at each place he left part of himself with his colleagues and, in turn, incorporated part of them into his being. Even when he finally settled as Chief of the Developmental Neuroendocrinology Laboratory at the Veterans Administration in San Fernando, it was a bouncy settling, and by person, phone, and correspondence his bubbling ideas bounded back and forth among colleagues over the world.

Shawn's mind was imaginative and creative, a compounding of the synthetic and analytic. The particular was the interest of the moment, but it was always seen in the context of the general, as a member of the class and as a definer of the rule. A journey with Shawn, whether conceptual or actual, was an exhilarating and exasperating concatenation of detours at every historical monument, every side road that looked exciting, every strange rock or peculiarly twisted tree. Yet he always arrived at his destination infinitely richer and more knowledgeable than those who took the straight, simple road. Shawn's universe was full of marvels to be arranged and rearranged into patterns just as shapes and colors are arranged by a master painter into an interlocking and self-consistent whole. His interweaving of fact and concept, finding and framework is reflected in his writings. The goal is marked, the highway leading to it thinly or thickly drawn in accordance with the data, and the intriguing side roads pointed to and remarked upon.

Archaeology was history and passion frozen in stone, and Shawn and Lorraine went to view that history at Machu Picchu, the home of the mighty Inca, and Cuzco, the seat of this empire, and the plane crashed and they were dead. They changed their plans and went early to be with students and to vociferously argue history and politics and sociology and art. They died as they lived, in pursuit of beauty and understanding, and in the midst of young, excited, and eager minds.

Contents

Part II.   The Emergence of Structure and Function

Chapter 5.   **The Postnatal Development of Synaptic Contacts in the Cerebral Cortex**

Anthony M. Adinolfi

Chapter 6.   **Ultrastructure of Developing Cerebral Cortex in the Rat**

David W. Caley and David S. Maxwell

Chapter 7.   **Postnatal Neurochemical Development of the Retina: A Prototype of Regional CNS Ontogeny**

Richard N. Lolley

Chapter 8.   **Development of Supraspinal Modulation of Motor Activity during Sleep and Wakefulness**

Yoshiaki Iwamura

Part III.   Environment as the Sculptor

Chapter 19.   **Nutritional Deprivation and Neural Development**

Joseph Altman

List of Contributors

Number in parentheses indicate the pages on which the authors' contributions begin.

ANTHONY M. ADINOLFI (71), Neurocytology Research Laboratory, Veterans Administration Hospital, Sepulveda, California, and Department of Anatomy, University of California, Los Angeles, California

JOSEPH ALTMAN (359), Department of Biological Sciences, Laboratory of Developmental Neurobiology, Purdue University, Lafayette, Indiana

DAVID W. CALEY (89), Department of Anatomy, School of Medicine, University of Virginia, Charlottesville, Virginia

WALTER B. ESSMAN (265), Department of Psychology, Queens College of the City University of New York, New York, New York

EDWARD GELLER (277), Neurobiochemistry Laboratory, Veterans Administration Center, and Department of Psychiatry, University of California School of Medicine, Los Angeles, California

ALBERT GLOBUS (253), Curriculum of Human Morphology and Department of Psychobiology and Human Behavior, University of California, Irvine, California

TOKE HOPPENBROUWERS (203), Veterans Administration Hospital, Sepulveda, California, and Department of Psychology, University of California, Los Angeles, California

YOSHIAKI IWAMURA (129), Department of Neurophysiology, Brain Research Institute School of Medicine, University of Tokyo, Tokyo, Japan

RICHARD N. LOLLEY (107), Neurochemistry Laboratories, Veterans Administration Hospital, Sepulveda, California, and Department of Anatomy, University of California, Los Angeles, California

DENNIS J. McGINTY (335), Neuropsychology Research Laboratory, Veterans Administration Hospital, Sepulveda, California, and Department of Psychology, University of California School of Medicine, Los Angeles, California

DAVID S. MAXWELL (89), Department of Anatomy, University of California School of Medicine, Los Angeles, California

DEITLAND MÜLLER-SCHWARZE (229), Ecology Center, Utah State University, Logan, Utah

DOMINICK P. PURPURA (23), Rose F. Kennedy Center for Research in Mental Retardation and Human Development, Albert Einstein College of Medicine, Yeshiva University, Bronx, New York

AUSTIN H. RIESEN (59), Department of Psychology, University of California, Riverside, California

GUENTER H. ROSE (145), Laboratories of Development Psychology, Nebraska Psychiatric Institute, Omaha, Nebraska

MORTIMER G. ROSEN (185), Department of Obstetrics-Gynecology, University of Rochester, School of Medicine and Dentistry, Rochester, New York

SHAWN SCHAPIRO (307),* Developmental Neuroendocrinology Laboratory, Veterans Administration Hospital, San Fernando, and Department of Psychiatry, University of California, Los Angeles, California

xiii

*Deceased.

ARNOLD B. SCHEIBEL (1), Departments of Anatomy, Psychiatry and Brain Research Institute, University of California, Center for the Health Sciences, Los Angeles, California

MADGE E. SCHEIBEL (1), Departments of Anatomy, Psychiatry and Brain Research Institute, University of California, Center for the Health Sciences, Los Angeles, California

M. B. STERMAN (203), Neuropsychology Research Laboratory, Veterans Administration Hospital, Sepulveda California, and Department of Anatomy, University of California, Los Angeles, California

RICHARD E. WHALEN (297), Department of Psychobiology, University of California, Irvine, California

ARTHUR YUWILER (43), Neurobiochemistry Laboratory, Veterans Administration Center, and Department of Psychiatry, University of California School of Medicine, Los Angeles, California

Preface

This volume attempts to present and unify a broad spectrum of technical and conceptual approaches to the study of the developing mammalian nervous system. In recognition of the need for interdisciplinary perspective by both the novice and the more experienced investigator, we have attempted to bring together scientific contributions which reflect problems and methods in developmental research and which represent most disciplines in the neurosciences.

The text is divided into three sections which provide an overview, a description of emerging structural-functional relationships, and a consideration of the impact of environment on neural development. Each of these sections includes contributions from neuroanatomy, neurophysiology, neurochemistry, and neuropsychology. Complete success in any effort to integrate these diverse data is difficult to achieve at the present time. Hopefully this compendium will facilitate multidisciplinary research which will promote further unity in the future.

Some of the contributions are expansions of papers presented at a symposium on neural ontogeny which convened at the Second Annual Winter Conference on Brain Research held at Snowmass-at-Aspen, Colorado, in January of 1969. We appreciate the willingness of those authors to update and revise their presentations for publication.

We wish to express our appreciation to all the contributors and to especially thank Miss Margaret McCabe for her technical assistance. As can be seen from the list of contributors, the Veterans Administration deserves recognition for supporting research in neural development toward the goal of a true preventive medicine in neurology and psychiatry.

M. B. Sterman
D. J. McGinty
A. M. Adinolfi

PART I   OVERVIEW

CHAPTER 1 Selected Structural-Functional Correlations in Postnatal Brain

Madge E. Scheibel and Arnold B. Scheibel

I. INTRODUCTION

It is our purpose in the following chapter to review briefly several groups of data on brain maturation, structural and functional, which we have gathered over the past few years. We have purposely limited ourselves to observations gathered with techniques of rather coarse grain in order to maintain a broad view of certain developmental problems. The chrome-silver method of Golgi and its modifications reveal virtually the entire external morphology of neurons and their processes, neuroglia, and on occasion, the vascular stroma. Golgi stains performed sequentially on brain tissue of littermates provide a powerful running commentary on the structural aspects of maturation for all neural structures greater than 0.3 to 0.5 μ in size. Similarly, "gross" electrodes (effective recording tips of greater than 250 μ), depth-implanted in pairs and trios in the immediate postnatal period and recorded electroencephalographically, provide adequate information about local events in neural domains of at least 1 mm^3 in size and 10 msec or more in duration. When data gleaned through these two techniques are examined and interpreted within the frame of the mobile responding neonate, a number of first-order correlations can be attempted; these correlations are then susceptible of further analysis with techniques of higher resolution.

In this report we are concerned in particular with the progressive development of cortical and subcortical electrical activity, and with the maturation of cortical synchronizing and desynchronizing mechanisms. The physical appearance of dendrites and axons are considered in some detail since these form a significant portion of the neural ground in which the functional drama is played out.

1

II. STRUCTURAL MATURATION

A. Basilar Dendrites

Figure 1 illustrates certain aspects of the maturational process visible in the vicinity of the pyramidal cell body during the postnatal period. The cells shown in Fig. 1A already bear a well-developed apical shaft, and the basilar branches are beginning to develop. This would correspond to the immediate perinatal period for medial orbito-frontal and visual cortices, and to a period perhaps 7 to 10 days before term in the sensorimotor area in kittens. Presumptive basilar dendrite branches spread out from the soma at a number of places along its surface, often around the entire periphery of the still ovoid cell body. When this appearance is compared with elements in Fig. 1b and 1c, it becomes clear that the majority of these early branches are lost or resorbed since final basilar branch patterns are generally restricted to the area of the two base angles of the more fully developed pyramidal cell silhouette. At the initial stage shown in Fig. 1a, most of these protobranches are not longer than 5 to 20 μ and are in almost all cases capped by irregular enlargements resembling growth cones. The short protobranches are also studded with beadlike enlargements bearing secondary

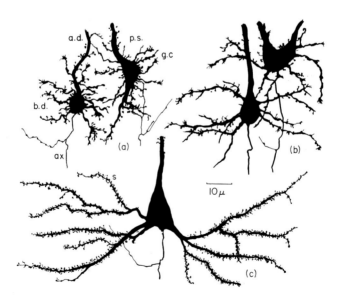

FIG. 1. Cell bodies and basilar dendrites of primary visual cortex pyramids in kittens at three postnatal epochs: a, 1 to 2 days; b, 7 to 10 days; c, 90 days; ax, axon; b.d., basilar dendrites; a.d., apical dendrites; p.s., pseudospines; s, spines; g.c., growth cones. Drawn from rapid Golgi material. 300X.

hairlike projections. The highly variable appearance of this aspect of the developing pyramid marks it as the most rapidly changing portion of the neuron at this epoch.

In addition, the surface of the cell bodies and presumptive basilar branches bear many hairlike projections of variable size and shape, seldom more than 2 to 4 μ in length. Some of these resemble simple stalks, some bear tiny bulbs or enlargements, and a few are bifurcated or multiply branched. They superficially resemble, and are of approximately the same size as, the dendritic spines or thorns which will appear somewhat later in the final maturative sequences of cell growth. In the mature element, spines are ordinarily not found on somata except in certain regional nuclei (Scheibel and Scheibel, 1968), nor on the first 50 to 100 μ of primary dendrite shafts (Ramón y Cajal, 1909). However, in the newborn, the distribution is not selective and these heteromorphic protospines may be found in relatively light concentrations (0.1 to 0.2/μ) almost anywhere along the surface of the neuron. Most of these appear to be resorbed and replaced by true spines which are of regular appearance and more densely packed (0.3 to 0.5/μ) (Globus and Scheibel, 1967b). Although there is now abundant evidence to support the position that spines represent preferential synaptic sites along the psotsynaptic membrane (see Globus, Chapter 13; Gray 1959, Scheibel and Scheibel, 1968, for review), the role of protospines is not clear.

Figures 1b and 1c document the progressive paring down process by which relatively large numbers of short, soma-derived dendrites disappear while a restricted number arising at or near the base angles of the developing pyramidal cell begin to lengthen and branch. The full spread of the basilar complement may not be reached in kittens for 3 to 6 months. True spines begin to appear between the tenth and twentieth day, however, and appear relatively mature in morphology and distribution within 4 to 6 weeks.

B. Apical Dendrites

Apical dendrite shafts are invariably present and relatively well advanced by the time of birth in the kitten. Conel's study (1939) has indicated the variation in degree of development among apical dendrites of selected cortical areas in the human neonate. Similar degrees of variation are seen in the kitten where the apical arches of sensorimotor cortex seem farthest along in development. In other areas such as primary visual and medial orbito-frontal cortices, many apical shafts, especially those of more deeply lying pyramids, are only reaching the vicinity of the first layer in the neonatal period. Figures 2a through d illustrate a typical sequence of maturation where the spreading of the apical arch has just begun at birth. The dendrite tips usually bear irregular enlargements which we assume to be growth cones while the dendritic branches themselves are richly beaded, each excrescence often carrying a small group of hairlike extensions. Unlike the dendritic area surrounding the cell body, most of the dendritic membrane is totally devoid of spinelike extensions, and will not begin to develop them for at least 7 to 10 days. It is not yet clear whether this means that no functionally meaningful presynaptic contacts exist at this point. If such were indeed the case, we might assume by the same reasoning that the presence of protospines on dendrite surfaces near the pyramidal cell body indicate an at least temporary assemblage of proximal axodendritic, and possible axosomatic synapses for primitive transfer and control purposes during the early days of life. With increasing maturation of the apical arch, it is obvious that increasing lengths of apical dendrite membrane come to occupy space in the first cortical layer. Because of the partial nature of most Golgi impregnations, we are seldom fully aware of the density and degree of overlap of apical arches in the mature neocortex. Figure 3 gives some idea of the nature of such dendritic neuropil in newborn and in almost mature cats. Even without those synaptic specializations peculiar to pre- and postsynaptic membranes which we now consider pathognomonic of chemogenic synapses, it is easy to conceive of a number of interactive mechanisms operative in such a matrix. (See Section IV.)

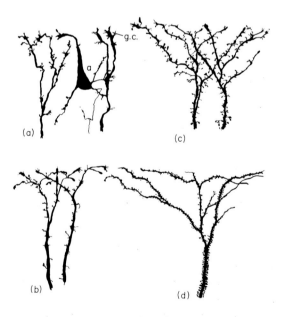

FIG. 2. Apical dendrite systems of primary visual cortex pyramids in kittens at four postnatal epochs: a, 1 to 2 days; b, 7 to 10 days; c, 30 days; d, 90 days. a, small pyramid of layer 2; g.c., growth cone. Drawn from rapid Golgi material. 150X.

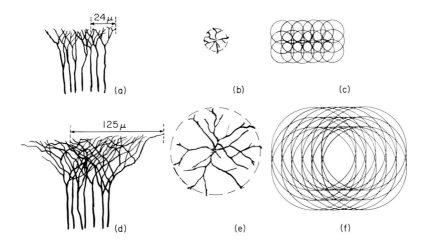

FIG. 3. The growth of apical arches of pyramidal cell dendrites in kitten visual cortex. a and d compare the spread of the apical arch system at 2 and at 90 days. b and d are drawn from tangential sections through the pial-glial surface to show the approximate size of the two domains, while c and f show schematically how the domains interpenetrate each other at the two epochs. a and d are based on rapid Golgi material. 100X.

C. Efferent Axons

At birth, the axons of the major corticifugal elements appear relatively well developed and, in most cases, have already reached their termini. However, we have noticed that in the case of many layer 2 and 3 neurons bearing the usual stigmata of young pyramids, the axons are just beginning to grow (Fig. 4d). We suggest that these pyramids may largely be concerned with the generation of cortico-cortical systems, although there is, as yet, no compelling evidence to support this inference.

Another component whose strictly intracortical distribution is well documented is the recurrent collateral ensemble which appears to develop upon the vast majority of corticifugal axons during their initial trajectory. In adult preparations these components can be followed easily in Golgi stains (Ramón y Cajal, 1911; Globus and Scheibel, 1968; Scheibel and Scheibel, 1969) with or without preceding experimental manipulation. Some of our experimental data (Globus and Scheibel, 1968) indicate that such axons ascend obliquely through the cortex, terminating preferentially on basilar dendrites and apical arches of pyramids, for a radial distance of at least 2 mm.

The majority of these fibers appear to develop in the immediate postnatal phase. The majority of our sections taken from kittens during the first few weeks of life contain abundant examples of such recurrent collaterals ranging from a few to several hundred microns in length, frequently beaded along their course, and usually terminating in a single beadlike growth bud or cone (Fig. 4c). In tissue beyond 4 to 6 weeks of age, it becomes progressively more rare to find such axons in the "unfinished" state, i.e., without their terminal elaboration and/or synaptic apparatus, whether the postsynaptic receptive element is stained or not.

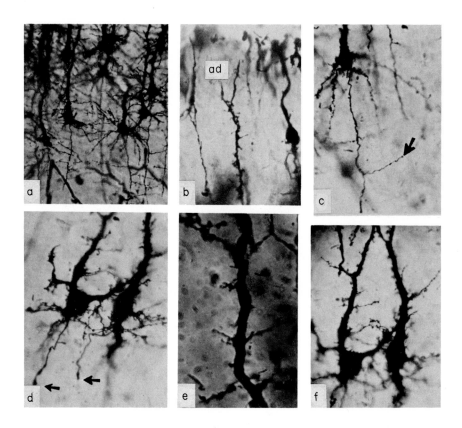

FIG. 4. Visual cortex of the kitten of 2 days of age: a, general view of layer 5 pyramidal cells; b, simple terminal arch crowning the apical dendrite, ad, of a layer 5 pyramid; c, developing recurrent collateral on the axon of a layer 5 pyramid (arrow points to terminal growth cone); d, layer 3 pyramids showing the late development of the axons with terminal growth cones (arrows) still only about 50 μ from the cell body. The generally hairy appearance of the somata is due to a combination of protospines and larval basilar dendrites sprouting at a number of points: e, apical dendrite of layer 5 pyramid showing protospines and developing oblique dendrite branches; f, another view of the two pyramids in d shown at different focus to reveal the protospines and larval oblique dendrites. All photos from Golgi-stained sections of 1.5-day kitten. Magnifications: a and b, 100X; c, 150X; d and f, 200X; e, 400X.

The local circuit (type 2, short-axoned, Golgi II) cells of cerebral cortex represent a complex problem in description. The group is extremely heterogeneous with wide variations in the nature of the dendritic domains, axonal paths, and especially, connective patterns. In earlier communications we have stressed that some of these elements, particularly those in layer 4 of the primary sensory receptive fields, were scarcely beyond the bipolar spongioblast stage at birth, and therefore incapable of providing functionally relevant postsynaptic membrane for axonal presynaptic terminals (Scheibel and Scheibel, 1964). However, other cell types within this general group have unquestionably undergone more extensive development by this time and offer an at least minimum amount of dendritic surface area to presynaptic terminals. Anatomically (Golgi) controlled single unit analyses will undoubtedly be necessary before meaningful statements can be made as to the role of these cells in both immature and mature cortex.

D. Afferent Axons

In previous papers (Scheibel and Scheibel, 1963, 1964) we have briefly described the developmental morphology of the major types of corticipetal afferents; specific sensory, and nonspecific fibers derived from the axial core, and we shall only briefly review that material here.

1. Specific afferents can be identified in most primary receptive areas (somatosensory, visual, auditory) by their already complexly patterned terminals present through the central reaches of cortex (laminae 3 and 4). Figure 5 shows that the arborizations become very much more complex during the ensuing postnatal phase, although we have not yet established to our own satisfaction when this process is complete. There is, indeed, the possibility that such a process may never be entirely complete, maintaining a plastic potentiality for growth in response to unusual sensory challenges in later life. We have determined in previous studies (Globus and Scheibel, 1967a and b) that the single most important recipient element for these presynaptic termini is the central portion of the shafts of lamina 5 pyramids, at least in visual cortex of rabbits. It is probable that pyramidal elements in layer 3 may also be supplied, possibly on their basilar shafts. It also seems likely that their synaptic articulations may have to await the development of spines during the second postnatal week. In the rabbit, at least, most of the synaptic connections appear to have been effected by the end of the first month of life. This process may well take somewhat longer in the kitten—a more slowly maturing organism.

2. Nonspecific afferents can be identified at birth in most cases as long ascending fibers bearing small buds or nascent side branches while traversing cortex in a direction perpendicular to the surface. As pointed out by us in earlier papers, we have had the greatest difficulty in recognizing evidence of synaptic connections between this fiber group with any cortical elements during the immediate postnatal phase. However, approximately 10 days to 2 weeks after birth, at a time when spindle bursts are beginning to appear in spontaneous sleep recordings (see below), and spines are becoming identifiable in considerable numbers along the apical dendrite shafts, it becomes possible to see examples of axodendritic contacts between such fibers and the apical shafts with which they have, until now, run parallel to but apart from. The principal pattern of contact appears to consist of repetitive series of axodendrite contacts wherein individual dendritic spines are in direct contact with the ascending preterminal fiber or with very short side branches. These presumed nonspecific fibers "follow" the apical shafts as they form multiple branched dendritic arches, thereby contributing also to the complex neuropil of the first cortical layer.

III. FUNCTIONAL MATURATION

A. Spontaneous Cortical Activity

An abundant literature (Lindsley, 1936; Jasper *et al.*, 1937; Flexner *et al.*, 1950; Crain, 1952; Charles and Fuller, 1956; Schade, 1959; etc.) supports the

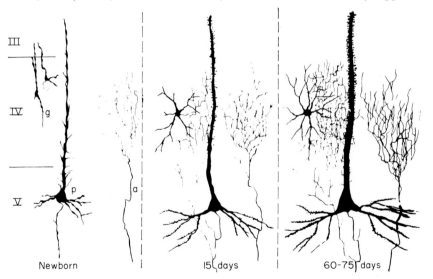

FIG. 5. Certain aspects of development in cortical layers 3, 4, and 5. The short-axoned cells (stellate or Golgi II), g, first appear as primitive bipolar components at birth, then develop increasingly complex axonal and dendritic plexuses reaching maturity between 60 and 90 days. During this period, the terminal arbors of specific afferent fibers, a, are also reaching maturity as are the pyramids. Based on rapid Golgi material. 200X. (From Scheibel and Scheibel, 1964.)

maturative progression of cortical activity from slow, relatively disorganized electrical rhythms characteristic of the perinatal period to the more rapid, regular rhythms of maturity. These patterns are seen with great clarity in cerebral and cerebellar cortices and will be reviewed only briefly since the details are generally available.

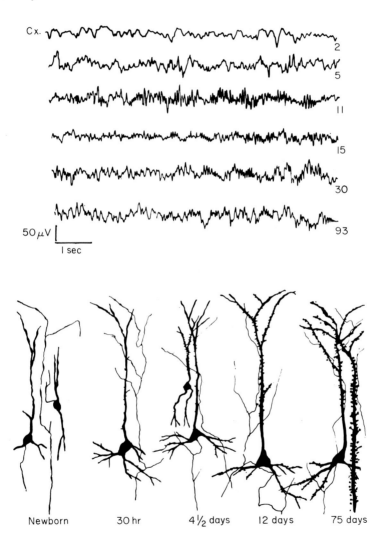

FIG. 6. Some structural and functional correlates of cortical maturation. Upper series of EEG traces follows development from 2 to 93 days with the appearance of spindle bursts (day 11) and the appearance of increasingly mature alpha-rich records by day 30. Record is indistinguishable from the adult by day 93. The lower series of drawings from Golgi material summarizes the maturation of somata, dendrites, and axons. See text. 100X. (From Scheibel and Scheibel, 1964.)

Records of electrocortical activity in the newborn kitten are generally similar to those reported for the human neonate (Lindsley, 1936), the rat (Crain, 1952), the rabbit (Schade, 1959), the dog (Charles and Fuller, 1956) etc. Tracings of the first 2 to 3 days following birth at term consist largely of irregular 4 to 6/sec. rhythms alternating with slower patterns of unpredictable frequency and duration. Amplitudes are variable but seldom exceed 50 μV. By the end of the first week, there is perceptible increase in the frequency spectrum although specific amplitude and frequency patterns remain highly variable. Between the fifth and tenth day of age, isolated spindle bursts begin to appear and by the end of the second week, appreciable lengths of the electrocortical tracing are occupied by intermittent and sometimes continuous spindling (Fig. 6). By comparison, clear spindles are observed in the human infant at about 30 days, as reviewed in Chapter 10. Progressive enhancement in resting frequency and in the development of well-formed spindle bursts appear to constitute two of the most obvious signs of maturation. Similar conclusions have been drawn by Schade in the rabbit (1959). Alpha activity, appearing first over posterolateral (primary visual receptive) cortical stations follows onset of spindling by 2 or 3 days and is usually coeval with opening of the eyes. The record appears essentially mature as early as 1 month of age although final organization of sleeping and waking patterns may not be achieved for another 4 to 6 weeks. Detailed analyses of the development of sleeping states are presented in Chapters 11 and 18 of this volume.

B. Cerebellar Activity

A somewhat similar progression can be found in cerebellar cortex, as summarized in Fig.7. At birth, rhythms are very slow and irregular with frequencies of 2 to 5 cycles predominating although, at times, the record may appear virtually isopotential. Frequencies increase quite rapidly during the initial 2 weeks of postnatal life and approximate 10 to 30 cycles at 15 days. After 3 months, the record is indistinguishable from that of the adult and is characterized by fast rhythms which reach the limit of resolution of the pen recorder (50 to 80 Hz). Analysis of these rhythms by means of the oscilloscope shows that there are, in fact, much faster components reaching 100 Hz and beyond. As in the case of the cerebral cortex, the progressive development of cerebellar electrocortical rhythms can be related to the maturation of the major histological elements. Limitations of space prevent detailed analysis of this process which was first described from the histological point of view by Ramón y Cajal (1911). Suffice it to say, the maturation of the Purkinje cell dendritic apparatus and the axon systems furnishing its presynaptic input are temporally correlatable with the sequential development of electrocortical activity recordable from the surface of the cerebellum. Correlative aspects of synaptogenesis in the cerebellar cortex are discussed in greater detail by Purpura in Chapter 2.

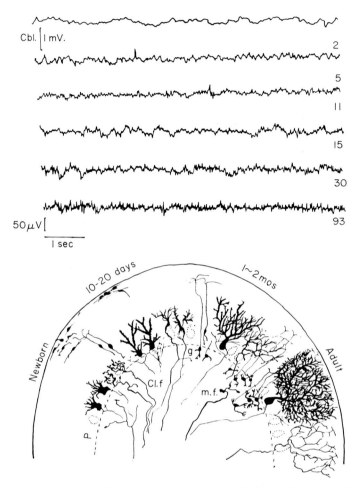

FIG. 7. Some structural-functional correlates of cerebellar cortical maturation. Upper series of traces show progressive maturation toward the adult >100/sec rhythm reached by the third month. The drawing at the bottom epitomizes the growth sequence of histological components of cerebellar cortex including Purkinje cells (P), granule cells (g), climbing fibers (Cl. f.), and mossy fibers (m.f.). The drawings are based on Golgi-stained material. 100X. (From Scheibel and Scheibel, 1964.)

C. Activity of the Reticular Formation

A somewhat different problem is mirrored in the development of the brain stem reticular core. Here, most structural elements appear relatively mature at birth. Major reticular dendritic domains already appear in an essentially adult state, as do some of the input and output systems. It also seems likely that a sizable fraction of reticulo-reticular circuitry is already present and functional to support those integrative mechanisms necessary for complex sequencing in respiration, cardiovascular control, suckling and deglutition, vocalization, and grossly patterned movements of extremities. However, the remote projections of reticular elements to cortical, subcortical, and spinal levels are incomplete, both in terms of presynaptic terminals and the postsynaptic ensembles upon which they play. Accordingly, the most effective measure of reticular development, structurally and functionally, must be sought far from the core itself. One sensitive index to the complex maturational process undergone by such pre- and postsynaptic structures is the development of synchronogenic and desynchronogenic (activation) mechanisms at the cortical level. These will be examined below.

The development of electrical rhythms indigenous to the pontomesencephalic (reticular) tegmentum is summarized in Fig. 8. Despite the relatively mature appearance of the intrareticular structures, the electrical patterns initially appear slow and irregular, and their development appears to mirror that of the overlying cerebellar cortex, at least for the first 6 to 8 weeks of life. Thereafter, the increase in frequency spectrum is less marked with 30 to 35/sec waves appearing to represent ceiling values from the second month on. It may be that the

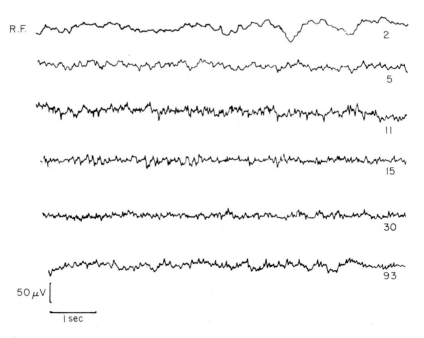

FIG. 8.   Maturation of electrical activity in the mesencephalic tegmentum of the kitten from 2 to 93 days of age. (See text.)(From Scheibel and Scheibel, 1964.)

increasing differences between reticular core and cerebellum beyond the second week of life reflect the increasing maturation of specialized elements in cerebellar cortex capable of generating more rapid intrinsic rhythms.

D. Evoked Cortical Activity

The cortical evoked response has proven a powerful measure of the degree of maturation in the central nervous system since the study of Ulett *et al.* (1944). While typical triphasic strychnine spikes can be demonstrated in the rabbit at birth (Bishop, 1950) and well before birth in the guinea pig (Flexner *et al.*, 1950), cortical responses to specific sensory stimuli and to electrical shocks administered in afferent tracts show greater variability, depending on species and on the cortical site examined. A detailed examination of prenatal sensory evoked potentials in the guinea pig is presented by Rosen in Chapter 10 of this volume. In general, the evoked response of immature cortical tissue is characterized by an initial negative deflection of long latency (150 – 200 msec) which can be derived over rather broad areas of cortex. By the end of the second week, a larval positive response of much shorter latency has appeared. The latter component grows rapidly in amplitude, culminating in the mature evoked positive-negative complex which is dominated by the initial positive component. Its derivation is now quite rigorously limited to the appropriate sensory receptive area. Since this phenomenon will be considered in detail by Rose (Chapter 9 in this volume), we will only mention a single aspect of the phenomenon which develops with repetition of flash-evoked responses from visual cortex. As indicated in Fig. 9, when a series of 16 strobe flashes are presented to a 1 and 1/2-day kitten at intervals of 2 to 10 sec each, the initial cortical response shows the expected predominantly surface-negative configuration. With repeated exposure to the stimulus, a late-appearing positive component becomes increasingly obvious and at the end of the series, constitutes the initial deflection. At this time, the entire complex is quite similar to that of mature visual cortex. It should be noted that these results do not coincide with those of a similar study of visual evoked potentials in kittens by Ellingson and Wilcott (1960). However, these workers were using nembutalized preparations so the series cannot be considered entirely comparable. The mechanism underlying this change in evoked potential configuration with repetition is presently under investigation.

E. Cortical Desynchronization

Desynchronization of cortical electrical activity is readily obtained in the adult preparation by relatively high frequency stimulation (100 – 300/sec) in the brain stem reticular core (Moruzzi and Magoun, 1949). Furthermore, the effect can be repeated many times over up to the point of habituation, so long as

a nonalert (at least partly synchronized) cortical background is available. However, in the newborn kitten, usual stimulus frequencies appear relatively less
effective than slow (7 − 10/sec) stimuli administered to the reticular core.
Furthermore, the effect can seldom be obtained more than once or twice
without a very prolonged 'rest' period (4 − 12 hr). In Fig. 9, the first three

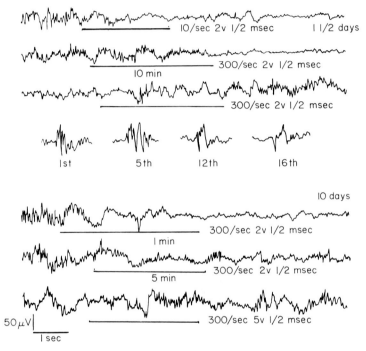

FIG. 9. The first three traces summarize the problem of cortical activation in very
young cats. A 10/sec, 2 V tegmental stimulation desynchronizes record on first attempt but
not on second (second trace not shown). Some time later, 300/sec 2 V tegmental stimulation appears capable of desynchronizing the record after several seconds' latency, but on
the second trial, 10 min later, proves ineffective. At 10 days of age, 300/sec stimulation is
relatively more effective on the first attempt (desynchronization develops more rapidly).
However, the stimulus is almost entirely ineffective when repeated 1 min later, and equally
so, 5 min later. In the middle of the figure are four representative responses from a series of
evoked cortical responses to light flash administered at 10-sec intervals to the 1.5-day kitten.
The initial deflection is characteristically surface-negative but with repetition, an early
surface-positive component appears. (From Scheibel and Scheibel, 1964.)

traces summarize problems of cortical activation in the 1.5-day old cat. Ten/sec
2 V tegmental stimulation activates the EEG once only (second trace not
shown). In this case, 300/sec stimulation delivered through the same probe is
also effective once, but not again even after a lapse of 10 min. In the lower half
of the record, stimulation at usual activating frequencies in the same kitten at 10

days of age is still effective only once. In Fig. 10, illustrating the situation in another cat at 16 days of age, 10/sec tegmental stimulation still produces a desynchronized record on the first trial but is virtually without effect the second time. In the lower pair of traces, a rather typical effect is noted. High frequency stimulation (300/sec) remains entirely ineffective, producing no obvious flattening of the cortical record at 2 or at 5 V. These two figures indicate the variability in response of very young kitten cortex to tegmental stimulation. Nevertheless, in an experience of approximately 65 chronically implanted neonatal kittens, the vast majority have shown cortical desynchronization to slow stimulation only, during the first 15 to 20 days of life. After this, classical activation frequencies gradually become more effective, and slow stimuli administered to the upper half of the core increasingly produce cortical synchronization. It must be assumed that the evanescent nature of the activation response is due to immaturity of the synaptic systems involved with rapid exhaustion of mediator substances and their slow resynthesis.

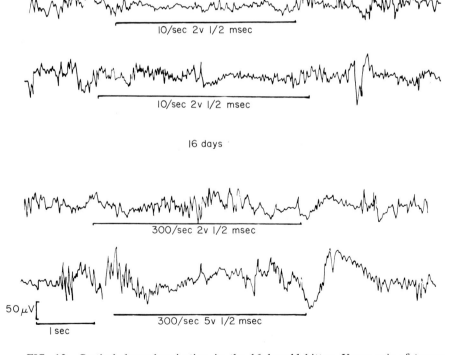

FIG. 10. Cortical desynchronization in the 16-day-old kitten. Upper pair of traces: 10/sec, 2 V tegmental stimulation produces desynchronization on the first trial but is ineffective on the second. Lower pair of traces: 300/sec stimulation to tegmentum is ineffective in this animal both at 2 V and at 5 V. (From Scheibel and Scheibel, 1964.)

F. Cortical Synchronization

Although neonatal cortex seems capable of generating some degree of desynchronization to slow stimulation, it seems peculiarly ill-equipped to follow slowly repetitive stimuli (5 − 10/sec) whether administered directly to the brain stem or via sensory receptors. This apparent inability to develop synchronous patterns of electrical activity is illustrated in Figs. 11 and 12. At 1.5 days, kitten cortex is apparently too immature to generate synchronous wave-following responses to 10/sec stimulation of the tegmentum. Instead, the response to both 10/sec and 300/sec stimulation is desynchronization. Similarly, 10/sec flicker produces only desynchronization of visual cortex. At 4 days of age, however, some kittens have reached a state of cortical maturity such that, under certain circumstances, some cortical following of iterative stimuli can be seen. In the first two pairs of traces in Fig. 12, trains of light flashes or clicks at 10/sec produce larval bursts of synchronous waves in neocortex at approximately 10/sec. In the third pair of traces, a combination of clicks and flashes at 10/sec shows more prolonged periods of synchrony. In the final pair of traces, 5 V, 10/sec stimulation of the tegmentum is effective in producing obvious, if

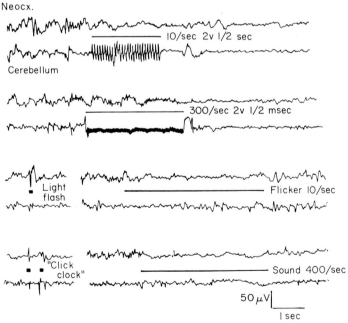

FIG. 11. Attempts to produce cortical synchronization in 1.5-day kitten. First two pairs of traces show cortical desynchronization to tegmental stimulation at 10/sec and 300/sec. Second two pairs show response to single stimuli (flash and click) and to 10/sec flicker and 400/sec sound stimuli. In each case, some degree of cortical desynchronization develops. (From Scheibel and Scheibel, 1964.)

somewhat erratic cortical synchrony although 2 V, 10/sec stimulation at the same point (record not shown) produced only cortical desynchronization.

Several physiological criteria of cortical maturation have appeared in the above material. Among them, the shift in polarity of the cortical evoked response from an essentially surface-negative to a surface-positive configuration, the development of spindling and the capacity to generate synchronous waves to an appropriately slow stimulus appear most significant in conjunction with the general and progressive enhancement of spontaneous cortical rhythms.

IV. CORRELATION OF STRUCTURE AND FUNCTION

The structural substrates underlying these maturative phenomena can only be suggested at present. To be completely successful, any such attempt will

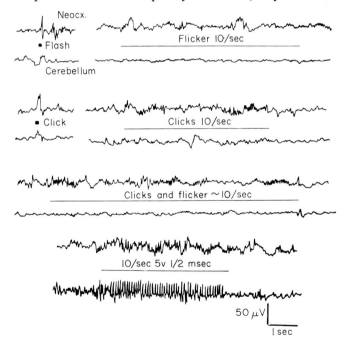

FIG. 12. Initial development of cortical synchronization in 4-day-old kitten. First two pairs of traces show response to single stimuli (flash and click) and to 10/sec flicker and clicks. Larval bursts of sharp waves at roughly 10/sec frequency can be seen with flicker and a little more clearly with clicks. Combination of the two stimuli (third pair of traces) shows more effective following in longer bursts. In this animal, 10/sec 5 V tegmental stimulation was effective in producing bursts of sharp waves following the stimulation. However, the same stimulus at 2 V (not shown) was still ineffective and produced only cortical flattening. (From Scheibel and Scheibel, 1964.)

eventually have to integrate phenomena at the level of the individual membrane plus the entire range of neurochemical factors, so many of which still elude us. A number of attempts have been made to explain the change in polarity and distribution of the cortical evoked potential. Purpura (1960) has indicated that the postnatal development of pyramidal cell basilar dendrite systems and their attendant presynaptic ensemble cause a significant change in intracortical current distribution. The deep current sink provided by this newly developed synaptic system results in a source at the cortical surface recorded as the primary positive deflection. Further details on the findings of Purpura and his colleagues are discussed in Chapter 2. Our own studies (Scheibel and Scheibel, 1963, 1964) led us to emphasize the importance of maturation of axonal and dendritic neuropil in the fourth cortical layer. Of special interest to us was the development, almost *ab initio,* of the stellate (local circuit) cell systems of this layer and their partial insertion into the receptive cortical circuitry at this level. This rapidly growing synaptic field was conceived as generating, with time (2 − 4 weeks), the initial locus for an intensive and relatively persistent depolarization, reflected ultimately as a surface-positive disturbance. Both of these models depend on localization of the initial depolarization of afferent terminals in cortex.

A somewhat different approach was used by Rose and Lindsley (1965, and Rose, Chapter 9, this volume) and Kovar (1968) who have indicated that the ontogenetically early-appearing long latency negative wave is a manifestation of activity in the nonspecific corticipetal radiation whereas the ontogenetically later-appearing positive wave has a specific sensory system (lateral geniculate) origin. Although each model of the mechanism involved has appealing features, further investigation is clearly indicated.

The development of spontaneous cortical spindling, the capacity for slow wave sleep, and the generation of cortical synchrony secondary to slow stimulation of the axial core, all represent challenging problems for structure-function correlation. In previous communications, we have suggested that these phenomena, all presumed evidences of upper brain stem pacemaker control over cortical activity, might be causally bound to the developing relations between intracortical terminals of nonspecific fibers and apical shafts of pyramids (Scheibel and Scheibel, 1963, 1964). At birth, most apical dendrites are either devoid of dendrite spines or bear numbers of erratically distributed heteromorphic pseudospines. At this epoch, it has been difficult or impossible in our experience to find any nonspecific corticipetal fibers in axodendrite apposition with the shafts. Within a week or 10 days, however, the situation has changed appreciably. Many of these dendrites are now beginning to show ensembles of spines, similar in shape and distribution to those of the adult. And simultaneously with this, a number of examples of axodendritic contact between the nonspecific corticipetal fibers and apical shafts can be seen in virtually every Golgi section (see lower part of Fig. 6). It is tempting to theorize, though certainly unproven, that

with the onset of development of the definitive spine system, the axons previously running parallel to the apical shafts now migrate slightly laterally under
some type of neurobiotactic-like force to effect multiple contacts with the spine
tips. In view of what is now known about the impressive degree of plasticity in
the neonatal nervous system, movements of this nature through the as-yet-
considerable amounts of extracellular space do not seem unthinkable.

We have referred above to the extensive lateral growth of apical arches during
the critical period from birth to about 3 months of age. In Fig. 3 we compared
the arch systems of kittens at 2 and at 90 days of age respectively, a period
during which the total average spread increased by a factor of 5 times or more.
Since the terminal arch of each apical shaft expands by approximately the same
order of magnitude while the distance between the parent apical shafts does not
change, it is obvious that each terminal arch system penetrates into a considerable number of adjacent systems. This mutual interpenetration of domains and
the increasingly rich branching pattern of each dendrite radical contributing to
the domain, results in extremely dense dendritic neuropil. Well-impregnated
Golgi sections bear this out and, in fact, produce a field so completely filled with
the criss-crossed silver-stained branches that photography has proven almost
impossible. Although reliable dendrite counts in this region of maximal density
(cortical layer 1) are difficult to obtain because of the partial nature of the Golgi
impregnation, examination of hundreds of well-stained neocortical preparations
convince us that the dendritic density per unit volume here exceeds even that of
the hippocampus.

In the case of the latter, Green (1958, 1964) has hypothesized that the dense
packing of hippocampal elements and the limited extraneural space between
dendrites may provide a satisfactory matrix for development of the hypersynchrony to which the hippocampus is prone. Presumably, the high concentrations
of potassium which rapidly accumulate following initial hippocampal dendrite
activity encourage massive recurrent depolarizing episodes. The resultant cortical
spiking activity spreads progressively across the dendrite fields, recruiting progressively greater masses of neural tissue into hypersynchrony.

The dense matrix of apical arches which characterizes the first layer of
cerebral neocortex in the 2- to 3-month-old cat may provide a similar substrate,
and one that is essentially absent in newborn cortex. We suggest this as one
possible reason why it is so difficult to produce, or detect, any form of cortical
synchrony in the newborn, and why various types of synchronous activity
gradually become evident after the seventh to tenth day of life. In this regard, it
is interesting to recall that several investigators (Spencer and Brookhart, 1961;
Calvet et al., 1964; etc.) have concluded from laminar analysis of cortical
synchronous waves that spindling, especially that associated with recruitment
phenomena, is related to activity initiated in the distal portions of the apical
shafts. Similarly, those synchronous waves characterized by a positive-negative
diphasic profile appear characterized by maximal initial activity (sink formation)

at intermediate cortical depths (layers 3 and 4) where basilar dendrite systems and axo-dendritic articulations are maturing. It should be added that single unit analysis of immature cortex, though not included in the present report, suggests additional mechanisms which require consideration and integration into any proposed model of the maturative process. The capability of immature dendritic membrane to support regenerative responses (i.e., dendritic spiking) as suggested by D. P. Purpura *et al.* (1967) is certainly one of these.

V. CONCLUSION

The process of maturation in the brain is enormously complex. Changes occur simultaneously at all levels from that of the total organ to the molecule. Techniques are not yet available which can allow analyses of the process at each of the many levels of resolution required. And if the grain of our enquiry eventually proves to be of scope sufficient to encompass all the necessary levels and processes, we would still be confronted by the challenge of weighing the relative import of each. Perhaps the only virtue of the present analysis lies in the fact that we have restricted it to several items at the coarsest level of grain in the investigative spectrum. This position allows some degree of overview and with it, the presentation of problems of a rather general nature. Their eventual resolution depends on techniques with shorter focal depths and progressively finer grain, as each of the succeeding chapters demonstrates.

ACKNOWLEDGMENT

The studies reported here were supported by U.S. Public Health Service Grants NB 01063 and HD 00972.

REFERENCES

Bishop, E. J. (1950). *Electroencephalogy. Clin. Neurophysiol. 2.,* 309.
Calvet, J., Calvet, M. C., and Scherrer, J. (1964). *Electroencephology. Clin. Neurophysiol. 17,* 109.
Charles, M. S., and Fuller, J. L. (1956). *Electroencephology. Clin. Neurophysiol. 8,* 645.
Conel, J. L. (1939), "The Postnatal Development of the Human Cerebral Cortex", Vols. 1 et seq. Harvard Univ. Press, Cambridge, Massachusetts.
Crain, S. M. (1952). *Proc. Soc. Exp. Biol. Med. 81,* 49.
Ellingson, R. J., and Wilcott, R. C. (1960). *J. Neurophysiol. 23,* 363.
Flexner, L. B., Tyler, D. B., and Gallant, L. J. (1950). *J. Neurophysiol. 13,* 427.
Globus, A., and Scheibel, A. B. (1967a). *Exp. Neurol. 18,* 116.
Globus, A., and Scheibel, A. B. (1967b). *J. Comp. Neurol. 131,* 115.
Globus, A., and Scheibel, A. B. (1968). Unpublished data.
Gray, E. G. (1959). *J. Anat. 93,* 420.

Green, J. D. (1958). *In* "Temporal Lobe Epilepsy" (M. Baldwin *et al.,* eds.) pp. 58-68. Thomas, Springfield, Illinois.

Green, J. D. (1964). *Physiol. Rev. 44,* 561.

Jasper, H. H., Bridgman, C. S., and Carmichael, L. (1937). *J. Exp. Psychol. 21,* 63.

Kovar, C. W. (1968). Doctoral Thesis, University of California, Los Angeles, California.

Lindsley, D. B. (1936). *Science 84,* 354.

Moruzzi, G., and Magoun, H. W. (1949), *Electroencephology Clin. Neurophysiol. 1,* 455.

Purpura, D. P. (1960). *In* "The Central Nervous System and Behavior," 3d conf. (M. A. B. Brazier, ed.), p. 253. Josiah Macy, Jr. Found., New York.

Purpura, D. P., Shofer, R. J., and Scarff, T. (1967). *In* "Regional Development of the Brain in Early Life," p. 297. Davis, Philadelphia, Pennsylvania.

Ramón y Cajal, S. (1909). "Histologie du système nerveux de l'homme et des vertébrés" (L. Azoulay, transl.), Vol 1. Maloine, Paris.

Ramón y Cajal, S. (1911). "Histologie du système nerveux de l'homme et des vertébrés" (L. Azoulay, transl.), Vol. 2. Maloine, Paris.

Rose, G. H., and Lindsley, D. B. (1965). *Science 148,* 1244.

Schade, J. P. (1959). *J. Neurophysiol. 22,* 245.

Scheibel, M. E., and Scheibel A. B. (1963). *Electroencephology Clin. Neurophysiol.* Suppl. *24,* 235.

Scheibel, M. E., and Scheibel, A. B. (1968). *In* "Communications in Behavioral Biology," Part A, Vol. 1, No. 4, p. 231. Academic Press, New York.

Scheibel, M. E., and Scheibel, A. B. (1969). Unpublished data.

Spencer, W. A., and Brookhart, J. M. (1961). *J. Neurophysiol. 24, 26, 50.*

Ulett, G., Dow, R. S., and Larsell, O. (1944). *J. Comp. Neurol. 80,* 1.

CHAPTER 2 Synaptogenesis in Mammalin Cortex Problems and Perspectives

Dominick P. Purpura

I. INTRODUCTION

The central dogma of developmental neurobiology can be summarized in the widely held article of faith that despite considerable specificity in the establishment of neuronal macro- and microcircuitry a variable degree of plasticity must obtain in the elaboration of different synaptic organizations to allow for the dynamic expression of individuality in behavior. The fact that the implications of this view are far more impressive than the data available to support it need not detract from its universal appeal. The possibility that external or internal environmental perturbations may significantly modify the development of brain structure and function is of global concern to an aroused social consciousness that has little patience with trivial details of "nature-nurture" polemics. Nonetheless, it falls to the developmental neurobiologist to resolve the chief problem of providing fundamental information on factors influencing the development of brain and behavior. Indeed, much energy has already been expended in attempts to demonstrate changes in development of brain structure and function by one or another environmental manipulation. Unfortunately in many instances what has been gained by this is entropy rather than clarification. What is required at this stage in the dramatic growth of developmental neurobiology is a detailed examination of the adequacy of experimental designs and methods employed in studies of different parameters of brain development, definition of what is known from these studies and perhaps more importantly, what is *not* known. This effort will undoubtedly require the cooperative attention of neurophysiologist, morphologist, neurochemist, and psychologist alike to the details of developmental processes and their interrelations. Few areas of neurobiological research can offer the opportunity for more fruitful interdisciplinary investigation than that concerned with the maturation of brain and behavior. And none can provide more significant clues to the operation of complex neuronal organizations than developmental studies in which *growth and change* become critical parameters for structure-function correlations.

The past decade has witnessed a number of concerted attempts to effect structure-function correlations in the immature mammalian brain. While these investigations have elucidated some of the elementary operations of immature neuronal organizations, they can be considered little more than preludes to studies of developmental patterns of behavior. It is self-evident that data obtained in electrophysiological and morphological investigations of developing neuronal systems must be interfaced with findings from experimental psychology if the objective of elucidating the basic mechanisms of the development of behavior is to be attained. However meager the basic information may be on the postnatal maturation of neuronal organizations in the mammalian brain, it is sufficient to permit the first steps in this direction. Some of the data obtained in recent years in studies of the author and his collaborators may serve as focal points for illuminating problems of effecting meaningful structure-function relationships in the developing mammalian brain, particularly in respect to the critical problems of postnatal synaptogenesis. Inasmuch as the intention here is to indicate special areas of personal concern, the reader is encouraged to consult the reports cited for details of specific investigations as well as references to works of others omitted from consideration.

II. POSTNATAL SYNAPTOGENESIS IN CEREBRAL NEOCORTEX

The postnatal differentiation of neurons in the mammalian cerebral cortex was sketched in broad outlines in the initial studies of Cajal and subsequently confirmed by many workers (cf. Purpura, 1969; see also Scheibel and Scheibel, Chapter 1). It has been established that pyramidal neurons of the feline neocortex exhibit well-developed apical dendrites which extend into the molecular layer where they come into synaptic relation with axonal terminals from different sources (Fig. 1) (Noback and Purpura, 1961). In view of the relatively poor development of basilar dendrites of pyramidal neurons in the neonatal kitten, it is not surprising that the earliest synaptic relations between pyramidal neurons and other elements at this stage are effected via axodendritic synapses that occupy largely the trunks of apical dendrites (Voeller *et al.,* 1963). Only later in the postnatal period, i.e., by the end of the first and during the second week are axosomatic synapses elaborated as well as axodendritic spine synapses. Thereafter a further increase in the complexity of dendritic and axoncollateral branching occurs along with a proliferation of all varieties of synapses. It is remarkable that in the kitten the end of the third postnatal week signals the completion of neuronal morphogenesis in the neocortex as judged by electron microscopic observations. But it is during and after this period that glial elements undergo their maximum phase of elaboration which is reflected in part in myelination of corticospinal, interhemispheric, and intrahemispheric projection systems. Thus from the standpoint of defining maturational sequences in neocortex, myelination must be considered a relatively late ontogenetic event compared to neuronal and synaptic development (Purpura *et al.,* 1964).

The fact that synapses with fine structural characteristics identical to those observed in mature feline neocortex are detectable on superficially located apical dendrites of neonatal kittens (Fig. 1) raises several questions, not the least of which is the question of functional significance. There can be no doubt that such synapses are involved in the generation of the negative phases of most varieties of evoked potentials recorded in the neonatal period (Purpura, 1961). In fact, the finding that local cortical stimulation in the newborn or near-term fetal kitten is capable of eliciting a graded surface-negativity entirely similar to that observed in the adult animal (Fig. 1) has served to clarify the nature of this superficial cortical response as well as its morphological substrate (Purpura *et al.,* 1960). Thus axodendritic synapses that participate in the elaboration of this response have attained a degree of morphophysiological maturation comparable to that of the adult animal. Evidently the maturation of these synapses proceeds to completion antenatally, unlike axosomatic and axodendritic spine synapses which have a programmed developmental phase coinciding with the early postnatal period. One of the major problems for future consideration is whether the pattern of synaptogenesis summarized above is indicative of a changing mode of information processing in neocortical neuronal organizations in the early postnatal period. This has already been suggested in respect to the changing electrographic characteristics of primary evoked responses (Purpura, 1961), but comparative microelectrode studies of patterns of unit responses in primary sensory projection cortex in neonatal and 1-month-old kittens might be more illuminating in this regard. Data are already available on receptive fields (Hubel and Wiesel, 1963) and the properties of immature neurons and synapses which should be of value in the design of such studies. Some of these data will be considered briefly from the standpoint of their relationship to the foregoing morphological observations on neocortical synaptogenesis.

III. DIFFERENTIAL MATURATION OF EXCITATORY AND INHIBITORY SYNAPTIC ELECTROGENESIS IN CEREBRAL CORTEX

Considerable difficulty has been experienced in attempts to obtain satisfactory intracellular recordings from neurons in the immature feline brain. Nonetheless it must be recognized that the valuable information derived from

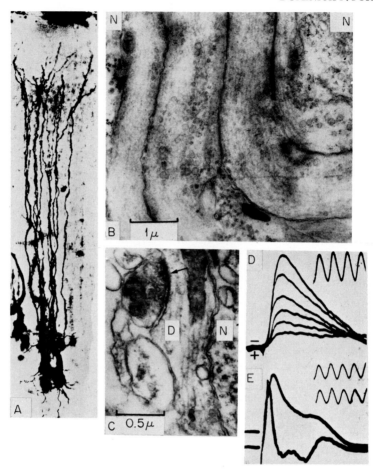

FIG. 1. A. Golgi-Cox preparation of pyramidal neurons in neocortex of newborn kitten. Note well-developed apical dendrites and absence of basilar dendrites. Dendritic spines are not observed at this stage and tangential spread of dendrites in the molecular layer is less than 50 μ. The apical dendrites are about 0.3 mm in length in this photomicrograph. (From Purpura *et al.*, 1960). B. Electron micrograph of elements in superficial regions of neocortex of near-term fetal kitten. N, two neuron cell bodies with 4-6 dendrites packed between them. Note absence of glial processes between neural elements at this developmental stage and indistinct appearance of dendritic tubules. (From Voeller *et al.*, 1963). C. Axodendritic synapse from the superficial neuropil of newborn kitten. D, dendrites. N, neuron cell body. Arrow indicates region of postsynaptic thickening. The presynaptic axon terminal exhibits clusters of synaptic vesicles and mitochondria (from Purpura, 1962). D. Characteristics of long duration graded superficial cortical responses recorded 1.5 mm from stimulating electrodes on suprasylvian gyrus of a near-term kitten. Stimulus frequency 0.5/sec. Six superposed responses at different stimulus strengths. cal 100 cps; 0.1 mV. E. Comparison of superficial cortical responses recorded at 1.5 mm with a large (0.5 mm) ball-tipped electrode (upper channel) and response recorded at the site of stimulation with a 0.1 mm wire electrode in newborn kitten. Cal. 100 cps; 0.1 mV. (From Purpura *et al.*, 1960.)

transmembrane recording amply compensates for the paucity of data obtained per experimental day.

It can now be stated unequivocally that resting membrane potentials of immature cortical neurons do not differ significantly from mature cortical neurons (Purpura *et al.,* 1965, 1968). Thus claims to the effect that immature neurons have low membrane resting potentials (Deza and Eidelberg, 1967) and by implication different ionic gradients compared to mature neurons must be dismissed on technical grounds. This is not to say that electrogenic mechanisms of immature neurons do not exhibit some fundamental differences from mature neurons. Characteristically, neurons in kitten cortex, especially in the immediate neonatal period, rarely exhibit spontaneous discharges (Huttenlocher, 1967). Elements in sensorimotor cortex are readily excited by thalamic stimulation but even when such stimulation elicits large excitatory postsynaptic potentials (EPSPs) the latter generally trigger one, or at the most, two spike potentials (Fig. 2) (Purpura *et al.,* 1965). These observations taken together with other findings

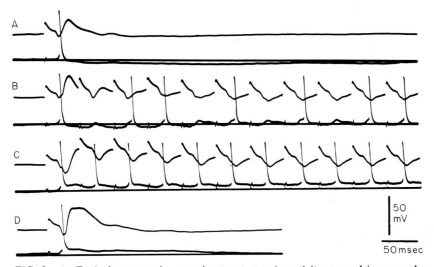

FIG. 2. A. Evoked response in sensorimotor cortex (negativity upward in upper chan-nel records) is associated with an EPSP and spike potential in a neuron from a 6-day-old kitten (stimulation in ventrolateral thalamus at 0.5/sec). Resting membrane potential baseline indicated by third beam which was superimposed in intracellular trace prior to stimulation. The spike potential is succeeded by a prolonged IPSP. B. Repetitive thalamic (20/sec) results in marked attenuation of surface negativity and prolongation of surface-positive component of evoked response. IPSP elicited by first stimulus is curtailed by successively evoked EPSPs some of which exhibit late components which trigger discharges. C. 20 sec after B. Repetitive stimulation produces summation of EPSPs and one-to-one cell discharge. D. 10 sec after C. Single-shock stimulation evokes augmented and prolonged EPSP and associated cell discharge rather than the late IPSP seen prior to repetitive stimulation. These data emphasize that transitions from inhibitory to exhibitory activities in postactivation facilitation phases can be observed in complex synaptic interactions in cortical neurons of very young kittens. (From Purpura *et. al.,* 1965.)

indicate that ionic mechanisms underlying the spike potential and its sequelae in immature cortical neurons differ in some obscure fashion from those operating in mature cortical cells.

Perhaps the most important data obtained with intracellular recording and stimulation relates to the nature of the synaptic events observed in immature cortical neurons. Mention has already been made of the fact that immature cortical neurons generally display prominent EPSPs in response to afferent stimulation of neocortex (Fig. 2). Additionally, such EPSPs also exhibit relatively slow rise times and prolonged falling phases (Purpura *et al.*, 1965). These EPSP characteristics may reflect the relatively high input impedance of immature cortical neurons, the dendritic location of excitatory synapses and/or prolonged transmitter action. Further characterization of excitatory synaptic activities in immature neocortex awaits more detailed studies. There are suggestions that many cortical neurons, particularly in the hippocampus (Purpura *et al.*, 1968), are not subjected to the powerful excitatory drives observed in mature neurons. However, the same cannot be said for inhibitory synaptic activities which are well developed in cortical neurons, even in the immediate neonatal period.

The finding that neocortical (Fig. 2) and hippocampal neurons (Figs. 3 and 4) may exhibit prominent and prolonged IPSPs in the immediate neonatal period has raised the relevant question of the nature of the synaptic pathways gener-

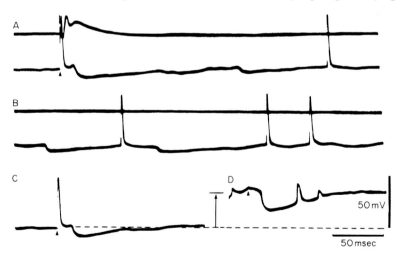

FIG. 3. Intracellular records obtained from a hippocampal pyramidal neuron in a 3-day-old kitten. Upper channel records, responses recorded from the surface of the hippocampus at the hippocampalfimbrial junction following fimbrial stimulation. A. Fimbrial stimulation elicits a subthreshold EPSP and a prolonged IPSP. Note spontaneously recurring IPSP in B, C, and D. Comparison of evoked IPSPs before and after partial depolarization of the neuron as indicated by the loss of membrane potential as shown by arrow. (From Purpura *et al.* 1968.)

ating these IPSPs. To obtain an adequate answer to this has required detailed examination of the morphological characteristics of neurons and synpatic relations of hippocampal neurons at various postnatal developmental stages. Again, this emphasizes the necessity for correlative light and electron microscope studies to complement electrophysiological investigations at the single unit level in programs of research on the developing nervous system.

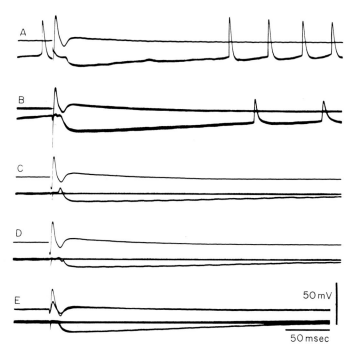

FIG. 4. Series of intracellular recordings from five different neurons impaled in the hippocampus during the same experiment in a 6-day-old kitten. In all instances fimbrial stimulation evokes a prolonged (300 msec) IPSP with essentially similar characteristics in all neurons. Third beam in C, D, and E indicates baseline membrane potential level. Cells in A and B exhibit spike potentials but the bottom three elements have been depolarized by the impalement. E. The IPSP evoked by a threshold fimbrial stimulus is unchanged by a stronger stimulus. (From Pupura *et al.*, 1968.)

Examination of Golgi-Cox preparations of neonatal kitten hippocampus has revealed pyramidal neurons with well-developed apical and basilar dendrites, many of which exhibit numerous spines (Purpura, 1964; Purpura and Pappas, 1968). Additionally it has been demonstrated that basket-pyramids of the stratum radiatum are also well developed at birth. Axons of these elements can be traced to the pyramidal layer where they bifurcate. An ascending branch distributes along apical dendrites and a descending branch distributes within the field generated by basilar dendrites of pyramidal neurons (Fig. 5).

Electron microscopical studies (Schwartz *et al.*, 1968) have confirmed earlier observations on immature neocortex (Voeller *et al.*, 1963) in showing a paucity of axosomatic synapses and a differential development of axodendritic synapses

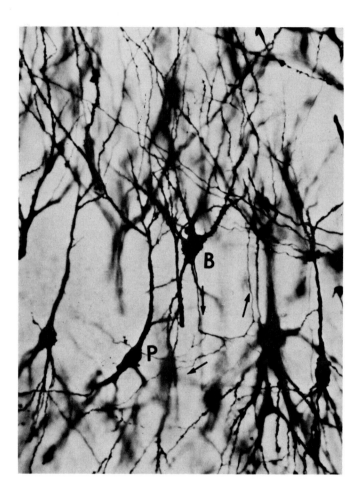

FIG. 5. Golgi-Cox preparation showing pyramidal and nonpyramidal neuron relations in hippocampus of 3-day-old kitten. P, Pyramidal neurons in superficial parts of stratum pyramidale; basilar dendrites and spines on apical and basilar dendrites are detectable. B, A modified basket-pyramid neuron of the stratum radiatum can be seen. Dendrites from the superior pole of this neuron are thick, covered with prominent spines, and distribute in the stratum moleculare. Dendrites from inferior pole course downward. Cell body of neuron also exhibits prominent spines. The main stem axon descends to the stratum pyramidale and bifurcates. One branch ascends along apical-dendritic shafts of hippocampal neurons; the other descends along basilar dendrites of pyramidal neurons. (From Purpura and Pappas, 1968.)

in the neonatal kitten hippocampus. However, in contrast to immature neocortex, dendrites of hippocampal pyramidal neurons exhibit many more trunk synapses and large numbers of spine synapses in the immediate neonatal period. The precocious elaboration of axodendritic spine synapses in the immature hippocampus is additional evidence that elements of the archicortex attain a level of maturation in the newborn kitten that is not observed until the second postnatal week for neocortical neurons (Purpura, 1964). But it must be emphasized that despite the extraordinary differential development of axodendritic synapses on immature hippocampal pyramidal or nonpyramidal neurons, it is rare indeed to encounter axosomatic synapses until the second postnatal week. In view of intracellular data indicating the operation of powerful inhibitory pathways in the neonatal kitten hippocampus (Figs. 2 and 4), it follows that the prolonged IPSPs elicited in hippocampal pyramidal neurons by fimbria or subiculum stimulation are generated predominantly if not exclusively at axodendritic synapses (Purpura *et al.,* 1968). These morphophysiological findings in the immature hippocampus are not in accord with the "basket cell-axosomatic inhibition" hypothesis of Andersen, Eccles, and Løyning (1964), but they do not necessarily refute the hypotheses of the latter workers who carried out their studies on mature preparations. A possible explanation of the discrepancy in findings is that while inhibition of hippocampal pyramidal neurons may be effected in immature animals by cells such as those illustrated in Fig. 5, maturation of the hippocampus may be associated with a translocation of inhibitory synapses from proximal dendrites to the soma (Purpura, 1969). Progressive elaboration of inhibitory axosomatic synapses could also occur, although the appearance of many axosomatic synapses by the third postnatal week may also reflect an increase in excitatory synaptic drives evident at this time (Purpura *et al.,* 1968) as well as an augmentation of axosomatic inhibitory input from basket cells.

The precocious development of inhibitory activities in immature neocortex and hippocampus has implications for developmental neurobiology and psychobiology which extend well beyond the problem of the nature of the pathways generating IPSPs in these structures. Heretofore it has been assumed that observations on the morphological characteristics of cortical neurons and fiber pathways or biochemical and EEG studies provided adequate criteria for assessing the relative degree of maturation of the mammalian brain. While these criteria serve a useful purpose in providing data for longitudinal studies of brain maturation, from the standpoint of physiological operations of the immature brain, they have major deficiencies. The immature neocortex and hippocampus are by no means *immature* as regards the differential development of inhibitory synaptic activities. In fact, insofar as *inhibition* is concerned it must be allowed that the cerebral cortex of the neonatal kitten is virtually as "mature" as it will ever be! If, then, there is any problem that requires the immediate attention of neurobiologists interested in the development of behavior, it is the problem of

defining the functional significance of the precocious and differential development of inhibition in immature cerebral cortex. Evidently the maturation of
many cortical inhibitory elements and their synaptic pathways is complete by
the neonatal period. In this connection it should be recalled that maturation of
cortical neurons is associated with an intensification of their metabolic activities
as reflected in changes in intracytoplasmic organelles (Purpura, 1964; Voeller *et
al.*, 1963; Schwartz *et al.*, 1968). If it is assumed that inhibitory neurons
exhibiting a precocious development have a greater requirement for aerobic
modes of metabolism than immature excitatory neurons, then it is not unlikely
that some inhibitory elements may be preferentially susceptible to circulatory,
respiratory, metabolic, or traumatic insults. It is not difficult to envision the
consequences of the loss of inhibitory input to cortical neuronal organizations in
early phases of cortical maturation. If a high degree of inhibitory synaptic
activity is required to ensure the orderly sculpturing of neuronal connectivity
patterns, it can be expected that even relatively minor disturbances in inhibitory
neuron function may have cataclysmic repercussions for the development of
those behavioral activities uniquely related to neocortical and hippocampal
operations.

IV. FUNCTIONAL PROPERTIES OF DENDRITES OF IMMATURE CORTICAL NEURONS

Intracelluar recording from immature neocortical and hippocampal neurons
has disclosed features of spike potentials which are rarely encountered in studies
of mature cortical neurons (Purpura, 1967). In several instances spontaneous
spikes recorded from immature cortical neurons may exhibit several discontinuities on their rising or falling phases that are indicative of multiple sites of
impulse origin (Purpura *et al.*, 1965, 1968). It is of particular interest that under
conditions of spontaneous or induced membrane hyperpolarization evoked
spikes may lack depolarizing prepotentials (Fig. 6) or exhibit fast prepotentials
(Fig. 7). Evidence has been reviewed elsewhere supporting the hypothesis that
such spikes arise at one or more sites in dendrites and either propagate into the
soma in an all-or-none fashion or block somewhere in the dendritic tree (Purpura, 1967). Figure 8 summarizes the probable sequence of events in immature
cortical neurons during the transition from normally evoked spikes to spikes of
dendritic origin. It is of importance to emphasize that whereas IPSPs effectively
suppress impulse initiation in cells exhibiting only one impulse trigger site,
usually at initial-segment-soma regions, such IPSPs may not suppress spikes of
dendritic origin. Paradoxically, IPSPs developing in or close to the soma may
facilitate the development of dendritic spikes in immature neurons subjected to
intense excitatory axodendritic activation. This extraordinary circumstance may

be a result of the relatively undifferentiated electrogenic properties of dendrites of some immature cortical neurons. Thus dendritic membrane, like axon-soma membrane, would appear to be capable of supporting spike electrogenesis in early developmental periods but this property is not observed in normal mature cortical neurons (Purpura, 1967).

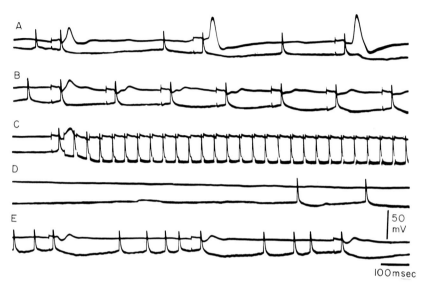

FIG. 6. Alteration in firing level of a neuron from sensorimotor cortex of a 2-week-old kitten during summation of IPSPs evoked by repetitive ventrolateral thalamic stimulation. A. Stimulation at 2/sec elicits prominent long-lasting negative cortical surface responses (upper channel records). Evoked spike potential is succeeded by an IPSP. B. During 5/sec stimulation each evoked spike is initiated by a slow EPSP. C. Stimulation at 20/sec. The first stimulus elicits a normal spike triggered by an EPSP. Successive stimuli result in summation of IPSPs and generation of spikes which arise without depolarizing prepotentials and from a level of increased membrane potential. D. Several seconds following cessation of stimulation, membrane potential decreases to a level where spontaneous spikes arise from slow depolarizing potentials. E. EPSPs trigger normal spikes again as in A. Note also marked depression of negative phase of evoked potential.

The potentiality of dendrites of immature cortical neurons to exhibit spike electrogenesis has raised several important but unresolved questions. There is of course the intriguing possibility that during maturation of cortical neurons mechanisms of dendritic electrogenesis are modified to "suppress" spike potential generation and propagation. A functional change in the biophysical properties of dendritic membrane during postnatal development could be brought about by an increase in synaptic contacts which might operate to "suppress" spike electrogenesis in nonsynaptic dendritic membrane. This implies a trophic function of axodendritic synapses apart from their involvement in excitatory and inhibitory synaptic transactions. Another question which arises relates to the mode of integration of synaptic activities in immature cortical neurons. Allowing for multiple sites of impulse initiation, it follows that locally generated PSPs in dendrites could exert profound effects on the excitability of immature neurons; effects which are usually attenuated by the necessity for electrotonic propagation to soma-initial segment regions in mature neurons (Rall *et al.*, 1967). Clearly the factors contributing to excitability properties of immature

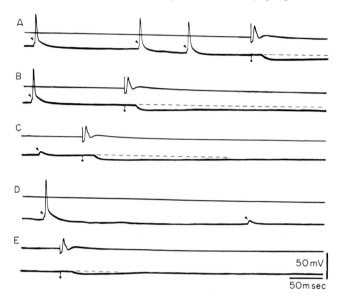

FIG. 7. Some consequences of a spontaneously developing increase in membrane potential in a hippocampal pyramidal neuron in 9-day-old kitten. A-E, from continuous record. Arrowheads indicate inflection between fast prepotential (FPP) and spike in this element. A. Fornix-evoked IPSP is prominent at a time when spike potential is about 40 mV. B and C, evoked IPSP becomes "smaller" as membrane potential increases and spike potential augments in amplitude. FPP dissociated from spikes shown in C and D. E, IPSP is attenuated as membrane potential increases further. (From Purpura *et al.*, 1968.)

neurons are extremely complex (Purpura, 1969) and not likely to be critically dependent solely on the potentiality of dendritic spike electrogenesis. Nevertheless this property of immature cortical neurons must be taken into consideration in any attempts to analyze modes of information transfer in immature cortical neuronal organizations. The problem is one that is not likely to be solved by application of the standard spinal motoneuron model to the situation encountered in neurons of immature cortex.

The chief reason for introducing the problem of the changing properties of dendrites of immature cortical neurons is to emphasize that factors influencing maturation of *gross* features of cortical neurons may also exert profound effects on more subtle aspects of maturational processes such as those affecting dendritic membrane properties. Thus in addition to changes occurring in overt neuronal morphology, neuron-glia relations and synaptic interrelations, developmental processes would appear to operate at the membrane level to alter electrogenic mechanisms, increasing the excitability of some components of the

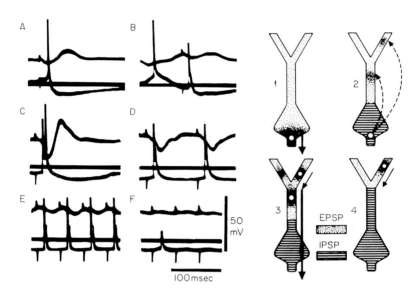

FIG. 8. Impulse initiation and propagation in dendrites of a neuron from a 21-day-old kitten. Upper channel record, cortical surface evoked response to ventrolateral thalamic stimulation. Third beam of oscilloscope was placed at resting membrane potential level established in absence of stimulation. A. Single-shock thalamic stimulus evokes small EPSP which triggers a normal spike potential. Latter is succeeded by an IPSP. B. Spontaneous discharge initiated by slow EPSP precedes stimulus. When stimulus occurs on small succeeding IPSP, evoked spike is smaller in amplitude and arises from a lower firing level. C. Early phase of 5/sec thalamic stimulation during which IPSP summation leads to sustained membrane hyperpolarization. Spike potential is evoked with shorter latency than in A. Spike arises directly from baseline and exhibits rapid rise time. Note second component on shoulder of first spike. D and E, increase in stimulus frequency results in reduction of second component and finally in F, failure of all-or-none spikes and appearance of partial response whose latency is similar to second component of spikes in E. Diagrams to the right show (1) original condition similar to that in A, when EPSPs trigger impulse at normal spike initiation site (white dot). (2) IPSPs produce transitory shift in impulse trigger sites to dendrites. (3) Repetitive stimulation as in C, through E, leads to depression of primary impulse trigger site by IPSPs and activation of dendritic loci by axodendritic EPSPs. Large arrow indicates all-or-none propagating spike. Small arrow represents partial spike. (4) Conditions such as those in F, at a stage when partial response arising in distal dendritic site is incapable of initiating conducted dendritic spike. (Modified from Purpura *et al.*, 1965.)

neuron, i.e., cell body and axon, while "suppressing" spike electrogenesis in most of the dendritic system. The extent to which this reciprocal alteration in the excitability of different parts of cortical neurons during postnatal ontogenesis occurs in other elements is unknown. Its detection, however, will require application of microphysiological techniques by workers willing to expend the extraordinary efforts required to obtain satisfactory intracellular recordings from neurons of the immature mammalian brain.

V. PROBLEMS IN STUDIES OF SYNAPTOGENESIS IN CEREBELLAR CORTEX

The mammalian cerebellar cortex undergoes the most protracted period of postnatal maturation of all brain structures. In the cat the final elaboration of Purkinje cell dendrites and their parallel fiber system, which is derived largely from differentiation and inward migration of external granule cells, occurs by the end of the second postnatal month (Purpura *et al.,* 1964). The dependency of Purkinje cell dendritic differentiation upon the integrity of the parallel fiber system, which provides the major input to Purkinje dendrites, has been shown in studies involving radiation-induced destruction of external granule cells in the neonatal period (Shofer *et al.,* 1964). Under these conditions Purkinje cell dendrites fail to attain their full maturation and may exhibit bizarre growth distortion. Additionally, Purkinje cells may be displaced from their normal position in the cerebellar cortex. The demonstration of Purkinje cell dendritic growth retardation following attenuation of presynaptic inputs represents a clear example of the trophic influence of presynaptic pathways in determining the growth and elaboration of postsynaptic dendritic elements. It is necessary to distinguish here between loss of synapses when a presynaptic pathway is interrupted and frank growth retardation or distortion following failure of development of the presynaptic pathway. In the preceding chapter examples were cited of loss of dendritic spines of cortical neurons following functional or surgical interruption of afferent pathways. In this context it should be recalled that complete subpial isolation of a large slab of neocortex in the neonatal kitten does not significantly alter the time course of elaboration of intracortical neuronal dendritic systems in the isolated region (Purpura and Housepian, 1961). As a matter of fact, such isolation, which interrupts main stem axons in the white matter, leads to an augmentation in excitability of the isolated slab of immature neocortex as a result, in part, of proliferation of intracortical axon collaterals of pyramidal neurons. In the case of immature cerebellar cortex, failure of the parallel fiber-axodendritic system to develop following radiation-induced destruction of external granule cells not only leads to profound retardation of Purkinje cell dendritic growth, but there is some suggestion that such dendrites stripped of synaptic contacts have an augmented excitability to electrical stimulation (Shofer *et al.,* 1964). This illustrates the important influence that presynaptic pathways may exert on the growth and functional properties of postsynaptic elements during their postnatal ontogenesis.

A vast literature has accumulated in recent years on structure-function correlations in the cerebellum of mammals (Eccles *et al.,* 1967) and submammalian species (Llinas, 1969). The cerebellum is now one of the most completely studied structures from the standpoint of its internal circuitry, distribution of input and output pathways and functional nature of its intrinsic elements. It is to be expected that ontogenetic studies of the mammalian cerebellum will provide important models for analyzing the differential development and functional properties of intrinsic excitatory and inhibitory pathways as indicated in earlier investigations (Purpura *et al.,* 1964; Shofer *et al.,* 1964). Already the direction of these ontogentic studies is clear from the results published in a recent symposium on the subject (Llinas, 1969). Studies in our laboratory by Shofer and his associates (Shofer *et al.,* 1969) have demonstrated that prior to the fourth week spontaneous or evoked unit discharge in the kitten cerebellum is minimal and rarely shows the sustained pattern of mature animals (Fig. 9). Nevertheless in 2-week-old kittens Purkinje cells are capable of following rapid repetitive stimulation of juxtafastigial pathways, but this repetitive responsiveness is not as prominent following stimulation of climbing fiber inputs to the

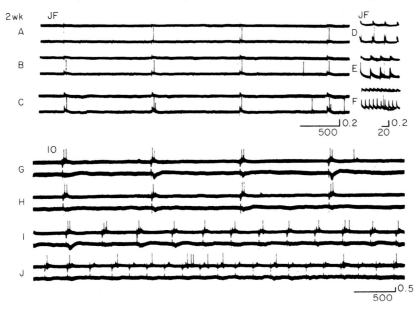

FIG. 9. Excitatory responses of cerebellar unit activity evoked by juxtafastigial (JF) and inferior olive (IO) stimulation in a 2-week-old kitten. A-F. Gross surface recordings and evoked single unit activity in an 11-day-old kitten. A solitary spike follows each slow (1/sec) JF stimulus of graded intensity. Occasional "spontaneous" discharges to be noted in C and D. Examples of unit firing in response to increasing stimulus rates (30, 40 and 100/sec) are seen in D-F. Unit responses following up to 30/sec are to be noted. G-J. 14-day-old kitten. IO stimulation at increasing stimulus rates results in considerably less responsiveness than that usually observed following JF stimulation. (From Shofer *et al.,* 1969.)

A

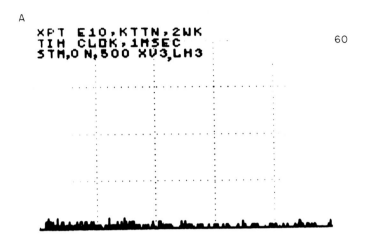

B

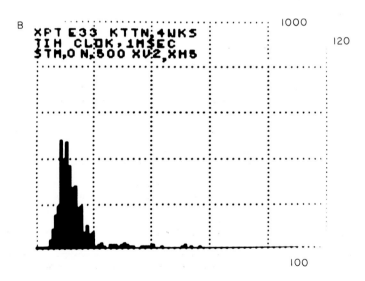

FIG. 10. Interspike internal histograms of cerebellar unit activity in the second and fourth postnatal weeks. The scale values of the ordinate and abscissa in each record indicate the full scale value for time (msec) and for the number of spikes per unit time (bin width). N, the number of bins for each record is 500 and the bin width is 2 msec and 1 msec in A and B, respectively. Differences in both the incidence and regularity of firing are seen at the two stages of postnatal development. The relatively short interspike intervals in the 2-week-old animal can be attributed to the irregular occurrence of double spikes during spontaneous activity rather than the more sustained high-frequency burst firing seen at the later developmental stage. (From Shofer, 1970.)

cerebellum. Other lines of investigation have suggested that olivary stimulation in 4-week-old kittens elicits more typical climbing fiber responses. Following strong olivary stimulation, significant inhibition of cerebellar unit activity is observed, as would be expected if such stimulation activated climbing fibers whose collaterals engage inhibitory interneurons synaptically related to Purkinje cells (Shofer *et al.,* 1969). These data point to the operation of inhibitory pathways in the immature cerebellum at a development stage in which many of the excitatory inputs to Purkinje cells are poorly differentiated. Thus, as in immature neocortex and hippocampus, inhibitory elements may undergo a preferential precocious development in the immature cerebellar cortex. Suitable experimental designs employing intracellular recording techniques should permit further testing of this hypothesis in the immature cerebellum.

Finally, mention should be made of preliminary results of quantitative analysis of spontaneous and evoked unit activity in immature cerebellar cortex (Shofer, 1970). For example, it has been shown that prior to the second postnatal week, interval histograms emphasize the irregularity and paucity of spontaneous discharges (Fig. 10A). In slightly older kittens interspike interval analysis demonstrates less dispersion of intervals, a reflection of the increase in regularity and organization of spontaneous firing (Fig. 10B). Applications of such quantitative methods to studies of changing patterns of unit activities to different inputs during postnatal ontogenesis should complement continuing intracellular studies of developing synaptic organizations in the cerebellum as well as other neuronal subsystems of the immature mammalian brain. In this connection it should be noted that considerable information is now available on the synaptic mechanisms subserving a variety of operations and processes in thalamic and related neuronal subsystems in mature animals (Purpura, 1970). Such data on neuronal synchronization, desynchronization, parallel processing, gating, filtering, etc., should provide a suitable basis for comparative studies of the development of integrative activities within different neuronal subsystems.

VI. COMMENT AND CONCLUSION

The preceding survey of problems concerning synaptogenesis and the development of neuronal properties in the immature cerebral and cerebellar cortex has focused on several principles as well as a few suggestions as to possibly fruitful directions for future research in developmental neurobiology. The principles of cortical synaptogenesis elucidated can be recapitulated as follows:

1. Axodendritic synapses exhibit a differential rate of maturation in the mammalian cerebral cortex. Those related to dendritic trunks develop in the antenatal period prior to the onset of obvious cortical function. Proliferation of axodendritic synapses including spine synapses occurs in the postnatal period along with the elaboration of axosomatic synapses.

2. Inhibitory synaptic pathways are relatively well developed compared to excitatory synaptic pathways in the neonatal kitten neocortex, hippocampus, and probably also in the cerbellar cortex.

3. The effectiveness of cortical excitatory synapses in young kittens is limited by the relatively low level repetitive responsiveness of immature neurons. This decreased excitability is probably an intrinsic membrane property of immature neurons during the early postnatal period. However, in some elements this reduced excitability is counteracted by an augmented responsiveness of dendrites to excitatory synaptic inputs. This may result in spike generation and propagation in dendrites, especially under conditions in which depression of primary impulse trigger sites occur as a consequence of IPSPs generated in or close to the soma.

The patterns of synaptogenesis summarized above provide evidence that in the early postnatal period thalamocortical afferent pathways distribute activity in immature cortex in a manner that is fundamentally different from that observed in mature cortex. It follows from this and observations on patterns of spontaneous and evoked unit discharges that information processing in immature cortical neuronal organizations is likely to be *qualitatively* as well as quantitatively different from that in mature organizations. The problem of defining how such differences might be influenced by internal and external environmental manipulations and perturbations is of no little importance in this regard. As indicated elsewhere in this volume, there are strong *suggestions* that patterns of dendritic development and synaptogenesis may be significantly altered by a variety of such manipulations. Suffice it to say that if these suggestions are to be upgraded to the level of facts it will be necessary to develop quantitative methods for evaluation of developmental morphophysiological processes whose complexity has only recently been appreciated.

REFERENCES

Andersen, P., Eccles, J. C., and Løyning, Y. (1964). *J. Neurophysiol. 27,* 608.

Deza, L., and Eidelberg, E. (1967). *Exp. Neurol. 17,* 425.

Eccles, J. C., Ito, M., and Szentagothai, J. (1967). "The Cerebellum As A Neuronal Machine." Springer, Berlin.

Hubel, D. H., and Wiesel, T. N. (1963). *J. Neurophysiol. 26,* 994.

Huttenlocher, P. R. (1967). *Exp. Neurol. 17,* 247.

Llinas, R. (1969). "Neurobiology of Cerebellar Evolution and Development." Am. Med. Assoc., Chicago, Illinois.

Noback, C. R., and Purpura, D. P. (1961). *J. Comp. Neurol. 117,* 291.

Purpura, D. P. (1961). *Ann. N. Y. Acad. Sci. 94,* 604.

Purpura, D. P. (1962). *World Neurolo. 3,* 275.

Purpura, D. P. (1964). *In* "Neurologic and Electroencephalographic Correlative Studies in Infancy" (P. Kellaway and I. Petersén, eds.), pp. 117-154, Grune & Stratton, New York.

Purpura, D. P. (1967). *In* "The Neurosciences. A Study Program" (G. C. Quarton, T. Melnechuck, and F. O. Schmitt, eds.), pp. 372-393, Rockefeller Univ. Press, New York.

Purpura, D. P. (1969). *In* "Basic Mechanisms of the Epilepsies" (H. H. Jasper, A. A. Ward, and A. Pope, eds.), pp. 481-505, Little, Brown, Boston, Massachusetts.

Purpura, D. P. (1970). *In* "The Neurosciences" (F. O. Schmitt, ed.), Rockefeller Univ. Press, New York (in press).

Purpura, D. P., Carmichael, M. W., and Housepian, E. M. (1960). *Exp. Neurol. 2,* 324.

Purpura, D. P., and Housepian, E. M. (1961). *Exp. Neurol. 4,* 377.

Purpura, D. P., and Pappas, G. D. (1968). *Exp. Neurol. 22,* 379.

Purpura, D. P., Shofer, R. J., Housepian, E. M., and Noback, C. R. (1964) *Progr. Brain Res.* 187-221.

Purpura, D. P., Shofer, R. J., and Scarff, T. (1965). *J. Neurophysiol. 28,* 925.

Purpura, D. P., Prelevic, S., and Santini, M. (1968). *Exp. Neurol. 22,* 408.

Rall, W., Smith, T. G., Frank K., Burke, R. E., and Nelson, P. G. (1967). *J. Neurophysiol. 30,* 1169.

Schwartz, I. R., Pappas, G. D., and Purpura, D. P. (1968). *Exp. Neurol 22,* 394.

Shofer, R. J. (1970). Unpublished observations.

Shofer, R. J., Pappas, G. D., and Purpura, D. P. (1964). *In* "Response of the Nervous System to Ionizing Radiations" (T. J. Haley and R. S. Snider, eds.), pp. 476-508, Little, Brown, Boston, Massachusetts.

Shofer, R. J., Sax, D. S., and Strom, M. G. (1969). *In* "Neurobiology of Cerebellar Evolution and Development" (R. Llinas, ed.), pp. 703-717, Am. Med. Assoc., Chicago Illinois.

Voeller, K., Pappas, G. D., and Purpura, D. P. (1963). *Exp. Neurol. 7,* 107.

CHAPTER 3 Problems in Assessing Biochemical Ontogeny

Arthur Yuwiler

By definition, ontogeny extends from conception to death and spans the scientific distance between embryology and geriatrics. In operation, it is a chronological slice through the heart of biology, and its goal of describing and explaining the sequential, coordinated, processes of growth, differentiation, and interaction, touches upon most of the fundamental questions of biology. No single volume could hope to fully detail so vast and fecund an area of scientific inquiry, and it would be absurd to attempt it in an introductory chapter. Instead, this must be a Cook's tour of some of the more interesting sights, pressing problems, and current views to serve as a framework for the more detailed sections to follow.[1]

The intricate journey from egg to birth is as amazing as it is familiar. Even before the first division of the fertilized egg, the process is marked by order, and the change from single cell to metazoan complexity is unmatched for precision in timing and events. The total process is one of continual control, and the biochemical questions are the fundamental ones of metabolic regulation and cellular differentiation.

However, birth is only a transition point in ontogeny and not its end. The journey from infant to adult is no less amazing than its antecedent, and, because it is less ordered, it is even more complex. A continuum of ordered internal influences become comingled with adjustments to more random external influences, and genetic possibility is bent to fit the mold of environmental certainty. The process here is one of continual adaptation and the questions are those of metabolic interaction and adjustment.

---

[1] Indeed, because this chapter attempts a broad overview of a vast literature, it seemed inappropriate to single our particular references, lest other equally important contributors be inadvertently slighted, and unwieldy to cite all of the authors whose work and ideas provide the content of this chapter, lest the remainder of the book become one vast bibliography. As a result of these considerations, specific references have not been included in this chapter, although they can be made available to any reader upon request.

The entire process from egg to adult is thus a continuous balance between the fixed and the plastic, occuring at all levels from the biological development of the single cell to the complex social interactions of the neonate. Generally, the direction is from decreasing to increasing cellular commitment coupled with increasing to decreasing biological rigidity. The fertilized cell is totipotent and can construct the entire organism. The neuron is committed and cannot even reproduce its own kind. However, the single fertilized cell is committed to a journey which, for all its complexity, is stringently and rigidly fixed. The adult, despite the full commitment of his component cells, is a relatively free agent, freely adapting to and selecting from a continually changing set of environmental circumstances.

Flexibility within the framework of order begins with the egg itself. The cytoplasmic material in the sea urchin egg is ordered and inhomogeneously distributed between a so-called vegetal pole and an animal pole. In the sea urchin or in the frog, this inhomogeneity is not essential for subsequent development, and normal larva or tadpoles develop even after radical redistribution of the cytoplasmic material in the egg by centrifugation. Similar treatment of a snail egg, however, scrambles the arrangement of tissues and organs. Thus, the apparent form of structural order differs between phyla. Structural order does exist for the sea urchin, however. The fertilized egg cleaves but the cleavage plane is not random. Rather, it divides along the animal-vegetal axis and the resulting two symmetrical cells become the right and left halves of the adult while their cleavage plane becomes the midline of the body. However, their destination is not immutable at this point for, if separated, each cell is still totipotent and can produce the entire organism. Artificially dividing the egg along the vegetal-animal axis will similarly lead to two normal larvae when the two separated halves are fertilized. But if the egg is artificially divided along a plane perpendicular to the vegetal-animal axis, the two halves develop differently; one becomes a permanent blastula with cilia but no endoderm, and the other a ciliated digestive tract. Thus, while the structural order of the snail egg involves cytoplasmic distribution and that of the sea urchin egg does not, both nonetheless evidence structural order.

Temporal order is even more central to ontogeny. Not only is ontogeny characterized by sequential changes, but also by periods marking the beginning or the ending of specific biological processes. In addition to the various "critical periods," "nonresponsive periods," "sensitivity periods," "imprinting periods," etc., which have been identified, there are the many more familiar turning points like birth and puberty. In each instance, the on and off signals are either unidentified or their actions are obscure. Consider even the humble phenomenon of tooth eruption in man. Sixteen or more years elapse between the emergence of the first baby incisor and the adult wisdom tooth. The interim consists of timed bursts of activity. The first permanent tooth erupts at 6 years of age. The last baby tooth falls out at 12. The baby molar is succeeded by an adult bicuspid. The canines await the prior resettlement of the incisors and molars before erupting between them. The manner of biological clock which continuously ticks over such a time span and strikes at such irregular intervals is yet to be defined, and tooth eruption is hardly the most complex example of temporal organization in ontogeny.

Discerning spatial organization is considerably simpler than discerning temporal organization. Spatial arrangements are directly perceived by the senses but chronological time is not necessarily the equivalent of developmental time. At the time of gastrulation the vertebrate embryo has several hundred times more cells than the equivalent invertebrate embryo. The vertebrate gastrula is also less susceptible to disruption by experimental intervention and is considered, therefore, more adaptive and less committed than the invertebrate embryo. Is this difference in adaptation a difference in embryonic kind, or a difference in cell number and developmental time? At birth, a marsupial is little more than a mouth and front legs. At birth, a rat is hairless and blind, with a brain but half developed. At birth, a guinea pig is a minature adult ready to go about the business of finding and eating food. Even within the same species, newborns in different litters may be of different sizes and different degrees of maturation depending in part upon differences in maternal nutrition and litter size, and such variance may contribute markedly to difficulties in defining developmental periods.

It is self-evident that any understanding of these complexities of spatial and temporal organization is attendant upon their recognition and description. Much of biochemical effort has thus gone into answering the biochemical equivalent of the reportorial who, what, where, and when. What compounds are present, how much of each, where are they located, how are they made, and how are they destroyed? The answers to these permit the subsequent question of how and why these changes occur and thereby permit consideration of their biological significance. The relevance of these answers, in turn, extends beyond ontogeny itself, for surely the same or similar answers must apply to other more general questions of metabolic control in biology. Ontogeny, then, has become a model for examining processes of biological control, and a tool for assessing biological relevance by temporal correlations between biological events.

Even the task of enumerating the changes occurring in ontogeny is not simple, for to be useful changes need be expressed in meaningful and commensurate units. In an organ as heterogeneous in cell types and regional function as the brain, this is particularly difficult. Cellular elements in the brain vary widely in size, volume and function. Development is accompanied by marked changes in many properties including local composition, as a result of myelinization, cellular classification as glia proliferate, and cellular distribution of neuronal cytoplasm, as neuronal volume changes from being primarily a respresentation of cell body volume to representing equally, dendridic and axonal volume. Thus, changes in enzymic activity or in composition expressed on a weight basis must be evaluated with regard to alterations in myelinization and consequent contribution of lipid to the total weight. DNA content is a useful and commonly used measure of cellular content (see also Chapter 14) but it must be recognized that some cells are polyploidal and that not all cells are equal in size, volume, metabolic activity, or function even if they are equal in DNA. The same factors complicate the use of protein as a basal measure. Indeed, expression of data in any single set of units provides only part of the potential information and expression of data in multiple forms can only clarify the significance of results. Indeed, a search for other dimensions for basal measures could fruitfully contribute to this whole field. For example, cholesterol deposition in brain is nearly linear during early development and may be useful as a basal measure to more clearly relate chronological and developmental time. Similarly, the S-100 protein, described by Moore as being unique to nervous tissue, has recently been shown to be of glial origin. In combination with other measures, such cellular markers permit rough quantitation of cellular types and thereby assessment of the contributions of these cellular types to the observed ontogenetic biochemical changes.

Regional developmental studies in brain are particularly important because of the brain's heterogeneity. Each brain region has its unique complement of cellular types. Local differences in permeability, diffusion distances, and cellular metabolism result in unique microenvironments as well. Developmental differences would be expected to occur between such unique cellular groups in the same manner that developmental differences occur between different peripheral tissues. Analysis of enzymic development in whole brain is, at best, only an approximation of the general developmental pattern and, at worst, it may provide a misleading picture of the relationship between metabolic and functional events. Indeed, it would not be too surprising to find major metabolic shifts occurring even within the microregion of a single neuron before and after development of its glial complement. Detailed examinations of such microenvironments have yet to be carried out.

Some pioneering work on microdetermination of enzymes and metabolites in brain nuclei and even in single cells has been carried out by Lowry, Giacobini, Hyden, Caspersson, and their colleagues. These important studies have found only limited application, however, both because they are technically tedious and, more importantly, because detailed procedures have been developed for only a relatively narrow range of materials. Some of these techniques, particularly those of Lowry, could theoretically be extended to a large number of systems and such extensions hold great promise for future work.

The bulk of ontogenetic data, however, is derived from developmental studies on whole brain or gross brain regions, and this information provides the basis for extrapolations both on relationships between temporally congruent biological and functional events and on the mechanisms involved in development. A number of phenomena are now recognized which could influence the results of such studies and some reexamination of portions of this rich body of information seems required.

Generally, animals are sacrificed and assays carried out during the normal workday. However, it is now clear that many compounds of ontogenetic interest and many of their biosynthetic enzymes are subject to circadian rhythms. For example, liver tyrôsine aminotransferase activity in preweanling rats shows a diurnal rhythm, which is inverted from that of the adult. Daily measurements of this enzyme during the course of development could produce a misleading picture of high preweanling levels and lower adult levels if circadian rhythms are not taken into account. Indeed, many mammalian enzymes are now known to have rhythms related to the feeding cycle which may reflect alterations in metabolite levels or may be indirectly related to attendant hormonal changes. In either event, some differences between adults and infants may be related more to differences in their feeding pattern than to development per se. Further, intraspecies comparisons of developmental changes must consider differences in feeding patterns of nocturnal and diurnal animals as well as differences in relative rates of maturation.

These considerations are not limited to enzymic activities alone. Brain monoamines undergo diurnal rhythms with species variations in amplitude and phase variations between brain regions. In the cat, for example, serotonin rhythms occur in the inferior colliculi and the red nucleus while norepinephrine rhythms occur in hypothalamus, pons, and substantia nigra. If these or other neurohumors are functionally involved in such rhythmic activities as sleep, eating and emotion, rhythmic alterations in specific brain regions should not be surprising. The existence of rhythms, however, suggests that a reexamination of some ontogenetic patterns may be warranted. A discussion of these implications with regard to functional states may be found in Chapter 11 of this volume. Such a reexamination may also resolve discontinuities in the patterns of some enzymes. For example, the serotonin-forming enzyme 5-hydroxytryptophan decarboxylase and the serotonin degrading enzyme monoamine oxidase increase in a fairly regular manner until shortly after birth when they show an abrupt increase and an even more abrupt decrease in activity, followed by another increase. Glutamic acid decarboxylase in rabbit cortex slowly increases over the first 10 days of life, more abruptly increases over the next 20 days, and then slowly falls to adult levels. In contrast, GABA levels rise over the first 20 days of life and then level off. These patterns are most likely representative of the actual developmental pattern, but they may also be more complex reflections of diurnal changes and developmental shifts in the phasing of such changes.

A second interesting discovery to enrich biological ontogeny is the demonstration of multiple forms of enzymes and developmental changes in protein structure. It has been clear for some time that adult and infant organisms may synthesize quite different proteins. The classical instance of this difference is that between adult and fetal hemoglobin. Hemoglobin consists of a heme group common to all hemoglobins and a globin portion usually consisting of two sets of proteins combined to give a tetramer. The normal adult hemoglobin is formed from 2α chains and 2β chains which combine to give a tetramer $\alpha_2^A\beta_2^A$. The fetus produces the same α chain but couples it to a γ chain to produce $\alpha_2^A\gamma_2^F$. This difference in the globulin moiety results in a globin tetramer with quite different physical properties than that of the adult. Most notably, it imparts a considerably higher affinity for oxygen to the associated heme group than that of the adult form. At full term, fetal hemoglobin comprises 80-90% of the total, and by the end of the first year it is less than 1% of the total.

Similarly, the enzyme lactic dehydrogenase exists as a tetramer of two fundamental polypeptides, H and M, taken alone or in combination. The lactic acid dehydrogenase of fetal heart is an M_4 tetramer and during the course of development it successively changes through HM_3, H_2M_2 and H_3M, finally becoming an H_4 tetramer in the adult.

Lactic dehydrogenase and hemoglobin not only illustrate the alterations in protein composition which can occur during development but they are examples of protein modifications which can occur from alterations in the composition or combinations of subunits. A number of related proteins or isozymes are now known which are frequently polymeric forms of fundamental units. They are of importance to ontogeny because different members of an isozymic family may predominate at different stages of development and such differences may be important to the developmental process. For example, the various forms of lactic acid dehydrogenase differ in cofactor affinity and in substrate interactions. The H_4 tetramer is more sensitive to pyruvate inhibition than is the M_4, and some rationale for the differential development of these forms can be made on the basis of the relative anoxic states of the fetus and the adult. Similarly, the higher affinity for oxygen of fetal hemoglobin permits a degree of oxygen transport in the fetus which could not be met by the lower oxygen affinity of adult hemoglobin.

The functional significance of developmental changes in isozymic composition may also be more subtle. Hexokinase, which converts glucose to glucose-6-phosphate, is a key enzyme in the metabolism of glucose by brain. Hexokinase exists in multiple forms differing in physical properties, like electrophoretic mobility, and in enzymic properties like the affinity of the enzymic site for substrate. The enzyme is largely particle bound in the adult although a portion does exist in the cytosol. During development the cytoplasmic level is essentially constant while the enzymic portion in the particles dramatically increases, so that the ratio of free to bound enzyme constantly changes. It has been suggested, though not demonstrated, that the free and bound forms have different isozymic components and that their cellular distribution is functionally related to differences in substrate availability. The isozymic patterns of this enzyme do differ between tissues, and the pattern in brain differs between species.

Monoamine oxidase also exists in isozymic forms which appear to change during development. This enzyme plays an important role in the metabolism of monoamines, and changes in amine binding, substrate specificity, or subcellular localization of isozymic components could affect both the development of monoamine levels in ontogeny and monoamine function. It has also been suggested that the key biosynthetic enzyme for monoamine formation may exist in isozymic forms of developmental importance. Tyrosine hydroxylase, the rate-limiting enzyme in catecholamine synthesis, is known to be inhibited by its end product, norepinephrine. Eiduson has suggested that serotonin may exert a similar effect on its regulatory enzyme, tryptophan hydroxylase. Since mono-amines accumulate during development despite such end product inhibition, it has been suggested that isozymic forms of these enzymes which are less sensitive to such feedback may exist in the neonate. Alternate explanations include ontogenetic changes in localization of enzyme and product within the develop-ing cell, complete development of the controlling enzyme prior to the onset of biosynthesis, etc.

Herbert Spencer pointed out that growth is an increase in amount, while development is an increase in organization. Growth and development are the key problems in ontogeny and both can be examined at many levels of observation. At the subcellular level they may be considered as problems in the regulation of protein synthesis and of the encoding of the organizational blueprint of the gene.

The model usually taken for this is some variant of that formulated by Jacob and Monod for regulation of protein synthesis in bacteria. Briefly, this assumes that protein synthesis is controlled by the action of three genetic units—a repressor gene, an operator gene, and a structural gene. The operator and structural genes are contiguous, forming an operon, and the operator gene controls transcription of the structural gene. Normally, the operator is held inactive, being repressed by a product of the regulator gene, termed, reasonably enough, a repressor. The repressor, however, can react with specific small molecules, called effectors, which remove the repressor from the operator gene and thereby permit transcription of the structural gene to take place. This transcription takes the form of the synthesis of a short-lived messenger RNA which is complementary in structure to the DNA base sequence on the structural gene. Once formed, this messenger RNA migrates from the nucleus to ribosomes in the cytoplasm where it acts as a template. Within the cytoplasm are a number of RNA molecules called transfer RNA, each of which is specific for an amino acid and is capable of combining with a triplet nucleotide sequence on the messenger RNA. A complete assembly of such transfer RNA's on the messenger RNA then reproduces, at one end, the RNA equivalent of the original base sequence of the DNA, and on the other end, a specific sequence of amino acids which, in a sense, represents the translation of the triplet bases of the gene into the amino acid sequence of a protein. The separate amino acids are then joined to form a polypeptide chain which folds and detaches from the ribosomal-messenger RNA complex. Depending upon its half-life, the messenger is then either reutilized or destroyed, and the process repreated from the beginning.

Growth is a function, then, of the activity of the active portions of the DNA; differentiation is a function of the repression and derepression of the gene. The law of universal gravitation arose when Newton asked, "Why doesn't the moon fall?" rather than "Why did the apple fall?" The laws of neurophysiology may well arise from the critical question of "Why doesn't a neuron fire?" rather than from the more obvious question of "Why does it fire?" The laws of biochemical ontogeny similarly may arise from the question of how selective repression is controlled.

The repressor is generally pictured to be some basic protein such as the histones, or some other positively charged macromolecule which is attracted to the operator region of the gene. The effector involved in its removal may either be some primary first messenger, like particular metabolites or hormones, or what has been termed by Sutherland and Rall, a second messenger, which is activated by the first messenger. Cyclic nucleotides, particularly cyclic 3'5'-AMP and possibly cyclic GMP and IMP, form one class of such second messengers. For example, thyroid-stimulating hormone, leutinizing hormone, adrenocorticotropic hormone, melanophore-stimulating hormone, parathyroid hormone, and vasopressin all stimulate, in specific tissues, the activity of adenyl cyclase, the enzyme-forming cyclic AMP, and increase intracellular levels of cyclic AMP. Other hormones such as insulin and melatonin decrease intracellular levels of cyclic AMP in specific tissues. Catcholamines and some prostaglandins increase cyclic AMP levels in some tissue and decrease levels in others. Finally, hormones like growth hormone, adrenalcorticoids, and thyroxine appear to have no direct effects on adenyl cyclase or cyclic AMP levels.

Hormones such as the ones in this last group, then, may function as first messengers directly interacting, in some unknown way, with specific repressor molecules to relieve genetic repression and permit transcription of protected portions of the code. Indeed, penetration of glucocorticoids into the nucleus of mammalian cells has been demonstrated. On the other hand, hormones such as those in the first group may require mediation via cyclic AMP, the second messenger, to carry their metabolic demands to the nuclear throne. The metabolic form of that message is thought to be the phosphorylation of the repressor protein by cyclic AMP and its consequent removal from the DNA.

Hormonal responses are tissue specific in adult animals and this specificity is partly related to differences in membrane receptors. Some of these appear to be contiguous with the enzymically active cyclase, so that the receptor-enzyme unit forms an adenyl cyclase system. Membranes of cells like the fat cell appear to have specific receptors for different hormones even though the hormones themselves all stimulate cyclic AMP formation. This suggests that there may be a family of adenyl cyclase systems.

In Chapter 17 we will see that infants and adults differ in response to hormones and in the tissue sensitivity of these responses. Whether these reflect differences in membrane receptors is unknown. They may also, however, reflect differences in hormonal metabolism or in the direct cellular effects of the hormone.

Although primary control of metabolism may be at the level of transcription from genetic code to messenger RNA, other levels of control are also operative in higher organisms. Indeed, the loose variation of the Jacob-Monod model decribed above is likely to be much oversimplified for its application to mammalian tissues. DNA is not wholly confined to the nucleus of the cell. A circular DNA associated with the mitochondria and probably involved in mitochondrial synthesis has been described, and evidence has appeared for the existence of an informational DNA that might serve part of the role pictured for messenger RNA.

Proteins are formed on messenger RNA-ribosomal complexes. The ribosomes themselves are complexities of protein and nucleic acid. Portions of the DNA code are set aside for formation of ribosomes and transfer RNA's, but neither the details of their synthesis nor their exact compositions are known. Whether adult and infant ribosomes function identically is uncertain, although, as mentioned, quite different proteins may be synthesized by them.

Other features of the cells of higher organisms also open possibilities for control that do not exist in the bacterial cell. Messenger RNA is labile, and the location of ribosomes within cytoplasm could influence the degree to which a message is translated into a metabolic action before it is destroyed. Many enzymes, once formed, are only active if cofactor is available. Levels and subcellular localization of cofactors during ontogeny are not generally known, but they may be critical in regulating enzymic activity. Indeed, cofactors may even play a role in stimulating formation of some enzymes, and cofactor levels may be important in protecting enzymes from degradation. Substrate levels, also, may be of critical importance and, again, knowledge of their concentrations and subcellular distribution during ontogeny is fragmentary. Indeed, although enzymic activity is often taken as a measure of *in vivo* metabolism, this may be wholly erroneous, and substrate availability for a particular reaction, rather than potential enzymic activity, may be the critical factor in controlling the rate of metabolic flow. Substrate limitations may be the general rule in development because the product of one slowly developing system is the substrate for the next metabolic step.

Products and substrates, however, are not only the passive material for biochemical transformation, they are also active participants in regulating the direction of metabolic flow. Metabolic flow is like a river with many branching tributaries, some of which loop back to the main stream or interconnect with other branches and loops, and some of which move along a single channel. At many, if not all, of these branch points there are regulatory enzymes whose activity, relative to enzymes at other branch points, diverts the flow of material into, or away from, particular channels. Products, substrates, and ions can act as "modifiers" or "effectors" altering such enzymic activities. These may facilitate transition of one enzymic form to another or they may bind to noncatalytic or "allosteric" sites on the enzyme surface to produce local conformational changes and thereby alter catalytic activity. Where enzymes are polymers of catalytically active subunits, "effectors" may facilitate cooperative interactions between such catalytic sites, altering their affinity for substrate in sequential steps or in a single step involving all the subunits. Whatever sets of mechanisms are involved, however, the important regulatory features are that these substances may be positive or negative effectors of several regulatory enzymes, and regulatory enzymes may be responsive to several positive or negative effectors. In a sense, then, this is the biochemical equivalent of a neurophysiological nerve net in which key neurons receive both inhibitory and stimulatory inputs and, in turn, stimulate and inhibit other neurons, and it is by the summation of these responses that integration of neural action is effectuated. So it is with biochemical integration. The simplest case is that of product inhibition along a simple metabolic tributary. Norepinephrine inhibits the activity of tyrosine hydroxylase, the first enzyme on the branch point of catecholamine biosynthesis and the rate-limiting step in that synthesis. When norepinephrine is lowered due to metabolic need, the inhibition is relieved and biosynthesis proceeds. When norepinephrine is excessive, biosynthesis is stopped and the metabolic stream diverted to a more useful channel. In tributaries with more complex interconnections, the controls are correspondingly more complex and the products more ubiquitous. The product of the breakdown of glucose is not only CO_2 and water, but ATP as well, and, indeed, it is to generate these energetic coins of the metabolic realm that the process is carried on. ADP and AMP are, successively, the products of ATP utilization and each serves as effectors in sets of reactions regulating the disposition of glucose into energy, fat, glycogen, or protein. When ATP is low, AMP is high and acts, as a positive effector, to convert glycogen to glucose, fructose-6-phosphate to fructose-1,6-diphosphate, and isocitrate to α-ketoglutarate, and as a negative effector, to prevent fructose-diphosphate from returning to fructose-6-phosphate. When ATP is high, it acts as a negative effector preventing acetyl CoA from entering the tricarboxylic acid cycle to generate more ATP, and, instead, with the positive effector help of citric acid, diverts the acetyl CoA to fatty acid synthesis. Such integrative actions are vital in the adult organism in creating order from the multitudes of metabolic reactions and demands, and may play an equally vital role in directing metabolic flow to meet the requirements of growth and differentiation in the developing organism.

Enzymic activities are not necessarily synonymous with enzymic concentration, so that, despite numerous studies on enzymic activities during development, little is known about enzyme concentrations during this process. Such studies are now possible using antigens to pure enzyme. This technique of antibody titration, however, is limited in its application to development both by the number of pure enzymes available and by the fact that the derived anti-bodies can only detect developmental or isozymic forms antigenically similar to the parent enzymes. To date, this technique has not been exploited even to the limits imposed by the number of pure enzymes now available.

Determinations of actual enzyme concentration are of more than heuristic value. An enzyme is a chemical entity and its instantaneous concentration is the resultant of its relative rates of synthesis and degradation. Although it might be expected that the appearance of an enzyme during development marks its increased synthesis, it could as easily reflect decreased degradation. In the adult, enzymes differ widely in their relative rates of degradation and synthesis. Some, like ornithine decarboxylase, are inactivated within minutes. Others, like tyrosine aminotransferase, are degraded within hours, and still others are stable *in vivo* for days or weeks. The mechanisms for such specific degradations of enzymes are not known, and the usual explanations of generalized degradation, lysosomal degradation, etc., raise as many questions as they answer. For example, if lysosomes are responsible for differential degradation, then a mech-anism seems required for marking the doomed enzymes and transporting them to their metabolic slaughterhouse. Substrates and cofactors appear to delay degradation of some enzymes and should, therefore, also be involved in the marking system. Similarly, if specific degradative enzymes are postulated, these, in turn, must also be degraded, and if specific enzymes are required for this, one arrives at an endless regression of an enzyme to degrade the degradative enzyme, which degrades the degradative enzyme, etc.

The developing organism must rapidly grow and differentiate, and it would seem economical to couple a low rate of synthesis with decreasing degradation. Without the stabilizing influence of substrate or cofactor, enzymes might be degraded as fast as they were formed and their constituents returned to the general metabolic pool for synthesis of enzymes for which substrates and cofactors were available. As the products of one enzyme become the substrates of another, protection would occur, degradation would be slowed, and enzyme would accumulate despite a low rate of synthesis. If degradation is further decreased, metabolite pools could be employed for the urgent work of con-structing the organism without the redundancy of constant turnover of already active enzyme. Although attractive, it is unlikely that this picture accurately represents reality. For example, in the analogous case of fasting in the adult, turnover of maintained enzymes does not appear to be significantly altered. Nonetheless, the rate of enzymic degradation during development is an impor-tant parameter in understanding metabolic regulation during development.

The control of the rate of synthesis of enzymes during development is the opposite and more familiar side of this metabolic coin. Here, too, however, the factors are obscure. If enzymic formation during development is due to repressors from the gene, then the question of how this is accomplished becomes a question of identifying the derepressor. To date, there is little real evidence, though much speculation, to implicate metabolities as derepressors. Further, there is reasonable evidence to suggest that agents, such as glucocorticoids, which induce specific enzymes in the adult, cannot do so in the immature organism, so that hormonal initiation of enzyme synthesis is not likely to be a general ontogenic mechanism. As pointed out by Schapiro, (Chapter 17), hormones may have quite different metabolic and physiologic effects at different stages of development and, indeed, these differences may be critical to development. However, there is the suggestion that one hormone, glucagon, may have a role in the developmental appearance of one enzyme, liver tyrosine aminotransferase. The question of what turns on the synthesis of glucagon is, of course, unanswered.

The molecular view of development is that of an enormous complexity of interacting and shifting metabolic controls at the heart of which lies the gene. The establishment of those controls by genetic expression and their modulation, and subsequent direction by the metabolic environment, are seen only vaguely. Yet, the form has a fragmentary outline, and clear delineation seems possible in the foreseeable future even if the details of the surface must await future eyes.

The cellular events in ontogeny are not only striking but are known with great precision. The mechanisms responsible for those events, however, are as obscure as the data is clear. Indeed, the biochemist faced with the grand migrations of neural elements, the lonely journeys of axons seeking end plates, and the formation of neural interconnections, asserts his belief that all this is a rightful consequence of the genetic code with some trepidation and with the inner knowledge that the assertion is an act of faith and not established fact.

At specific stages in embryonic development, waves of cells leave the neural crest and begin long migrations to specific loci, and these migrations have been elegantly studied by Cajal, Cowan, Levi-Montalcini, Edds, Weiss, and many others. Overtly, the movement seems as purposeful as the homeward-bound migration of people after work, as groups of neuroblasts move ahead, sometimes through crowds of neuroblasts moving in other directions, to their own adult homes. The distances traversed are often small, but the rate of movement is on the order of micra per hour and the migration may take days. The migrating neuroblast takes on a spindle shape, with a probing apical and a long tailing caudal filament, which generally becomes the axon of the migrating cell. The apical filament probes the way with constant elaboration of pseudopodia, some of which are extremely thin and narrow. The movement itself is amoeboid and is most likely similar to that described for amoeba by Allen. Essentially, this consists of a frontal thickening, contraction, and eversion of an endoplasmic plug of protoplasm which pulls the cell forward.

In most, if not all, instances, the neural route seems fixed, and the destination clearly, if mysteriously, marked. For example, three waves of neural emigrants leave the avian neural crest for the optic tectum. The first wave stops at a position that will become the deepest layer of that structure. The second wave migrates through the positions of the first to take up an intermediate location, and the third wave migrates through both of the preceding waves to stations nearest the tectal surface. Similarly, the neuroblasts destined to become Purkinje cells migrate as a swarm, but separate upon arrival at their new home, to line up in neat, spaced parallel columns.

These cellular migrations seem ordered in form and the final positions seem ordered in number. Once areas are filled with a specified number of immigrants, stragglers are no longer admitted, and having nowhere to go, appear to linger a bit and then die. Indeed, it has been estimated that in some instances as many as 60% of the potential neurons die in this manner during development.

Axonal migration is even more obviously directional. This has been demonstrated in numerous transplantation and nerve regeneration studies which cannot be recounted here, but which show remarkable specificity in the connection between terminal end plate and central projection area. One example of this can be taken from Sperry's beautiful studies on the amphibian eye. In an early stage of life, the entire retina may be wholly regenerated from the epithelial pigment layer, and the axons of the new neurons have been shown to thread their way tortuously through and around the degenerating stumps of their predecessors to specific connections in the optic tectum and to establish again a point-for-point representation of the optic field. From similar studies on motor and sensory neurons in muscle and skin has come the clear demonstration that the nature of the end plate somehow codes the functional use of the axon. The flexor muscles of limbs inserted into the embryonic salamander function as flexors, whether the limb is transplanted in the normal anterior-posterior relationship or whether it is reversed. Transplanted tadpole skin sends forth sensations coded for the original skin location and not the transplanted location, and motor responses are coordinated to the intended and not actual location.

The precision of these responses is highly dependent upon developmental age. Regenerating axons to the fingers of the adult human may not always reach their proper destination, and proper function may require a relearning of motoric manipulations. Spatial relationships may be maintained even after end plates are gone, and the phantom limb effect of attempted scratching of the absent toe of a missing limb is a bitterly tragic example of such retention.

As yet, there is no clear explanation for these incredible maneuvers and responses. A variety of field theories based on chemotaxis and electrotonic gradients have been proposed, but none have received unequivocal or uniformly supporting data.

Three axes are required to uniquely define a path through the three-dimensional space of brain. A combination of chemical, electrical, and gravitational

fields could serve as such axes, but field migration carries the corollary requirement that the moving particle must be uniquely sensitive to these forces to
follow a specific balance point in their intersection. The form for such coding and
the mechanism by which intracellular events could prompt its elaboration are so
unclear as to make this explanation even more mysterious than the phenomenon
it is intended to explain. None of this, of course, negates the likelihood that
agents such as nerve growth factor or forces such as gravity or electric fields may
help orient directed growth. It is the magnitude of such orienting influences and
their interactions which particularly need clarification. Indeed, the principle of
contact guidance, which has been so brilliantly elaborated by Weiss, and which
probably plays a large role in cellular and axonal migration, is essentially a
microchemical and perhaps electrical recognition operation reduced to an orienting response and manifested in directed movement. Continual cellular attractions
and repulsions, by localizing thrusts of the advancing protoplasmic foot of the
axon or cell, would constitute a series of continual microorientations of the
entire tissue along a specific route. That cellular recognition does occur is
evidenced by such diverse phenomena as acceptance and rejection of tissue grafts
and by the self-assembly of complex structures from cellular dispersions. Again,
the mechanism for these recognitions is unclear. Cellular guidance and recognition are also most likely involved in establishment of nerve fibers, for, as Weiss
points out, once one pioneering axon has established contact with its target,
related axons need only be attracted to the pioneering axon to follow its route
and establish a multiaxonal fiber.

The successive layering of developmental events, each the basis for subsequent events, creates a complex four-dimensional resultant designed to prepare
the organism for independent life. The sequence of developmental controls must
be tempered for adaptation to the exigencies of the moment while not pre-
cluding the requirements of the future. Henceforth the organism must live as a
metabolic teeter-totter constantly balancing about a homeostatic fulcrum which,
itself, shifts with time. In Chapters 15 and 17, respectively, Geller will deal with
the behavioral and biochemical consequences of early environment and Schapiro
will discuss the profound influence of hormones on brain chemistry, structure,
and development. Little can be added here to their accounts. Each will point to
as many unanswered questions as have been raised here and the multitude of
unrecognized problems remaining will exceed the total manifold. Several considerations mitigate against despair at this overwhelming intricacy. The very
complexity of the panoply of phenomena considered argues for the ultimate
simplicity of the fundamental controls. It is common experience in this techno-
logical age that there is a direct relationship between malfunction and control
complexity. The very uniformity of the developmental product despite the
diversity of ontogenetic changes can only mean that the basic driving mechanisms are few in number, simple in operation, and powerful in effect. The
bewildering appearance of the phenomena stems from viewing the successive

overlays of driven events and not from the complexity of the driving force. Science is essentially a coalescence of understanding and its great joy stems from the sudden surprising juxtaposition of disparate findings to generate a unified explanation. As stated at the beginning, ontogeny is a slice in time through the body of biology. The current burgeoning of biological understanding may already have furnished some of the missing pieces which only need to be cleverly united with those on hand to increase our understanding of ontogeny.

CHAPTER 4 Problems in Correlating Behavioral and Physiological Development

Austin H. Riesen

I. INTRODUCTION

A. Innovation, Correlation, and Prediction in Brain-Behavior Research

The causes of behavior are complex. Simple rules do not exist to guide the discovery of neuropsychological correlates of behavioral development. Scientific method, ingenuity, and common sense advance the technology and the theory of brain-behavior research.

Having first worked out the essential background conditions, often a formidable task since environmental and organismic supports demand careful attention through time, the behavioral investigator attempts to relate a specified change in behavior to a critical physiological event as measured, or as produced by an experimental procedure. The scientific innovator makes his greatest contribution by producing one-to-one correspondence between antecedent and consequence. Straightforward as this may sound, such correspondence may be trivial, of moderate import, or a scientific breakthrough, depending upon the degree to which the correspondence had previously been overlooked and unexpected, on the one hand, *or* precisely predicted by tightly organized theory, i.e., by the strong hypothesis, on the other hand.

Much has been written about prediction and test. Satisfying as this concept of scientific method is, its application has contributed a relatively small part to the history of scientific progress. With increasing maturity the biological and behavioral sciences will presumably produce more of the hypothetico-deductive, quantitative formulations. Computer technology will lend a hand. Description and measurement of antecedent-consequent events remain as the foundation stones of brain-behavior (and behavior-brain) research. Brain *function* is the subject of study, both as cause and as result of behavior.

Since the discovery of correspondence is the task of science in a nutshell, any general approach that will assist in such discovery becomes a technical subdiscipline within a field of scientific endeavor. Electrophysiology of the nervous system and, before that, neurosurgical ablation and brain reconstruction were subdisciplines of physiology and psychology. A newer specialty is that of neurochemistry. And finally in recent years we have made extensive use of *developmental* antecedent-consequence correspondences, with or without neurochemical, neurosurgical, or electrophysiological interventions.

B. Advantages and Problems in Developmental Neuropsychology

Developmental psychobiology, valuable in its own domain as an ontogenetic discipline, contributes a dimension of independent organismic variables to the scientific effort. Less artificial or "nonphysiological" than ablation, or even electrical or chemical stimulation techniques, growth of the organism provides alterations in brain that may be monitored and correlated with behavioral change. The advantages of natural growth sequences should be appealing to the biologically initiated, if not to all psychologists. Structural changes, such as myelin formation in sensory tracts, or neurochemical changes, such as the rapid appearance of sulfhydryl groups, in the developing nervous system, have been successfully related to concurrent behavioral changes and to differentiation of evoked electrophysiological responses. Electrophysiology provides measures that correlate suggestively with behavioral indicators of improved sensory resolving power (i.e., visual acuity) or of depth discriminations or auditory localization.

There are complications, too, that plague us when we attempt to interrelate brain development and behavior. A pervasive problem results from the vast number of developmental measures that show gradual change through time. We can readily show progressive change in many structures, physiological processes, and behavioral measures simultaneously. Which are the correlations having true cause-and-effect significance? This becomes an important, often difficult, and most challenging question, once a close correspondence is discovered (McCormick and Francis, 1958). Fortunately, some guidelines can help our pursuit of valid information.

II. DISCOVERING CAUSE AND EFFECT

A. Correlations: Statements of Questions

An initial correlation, no matter how close to unity, may be incidental. *Interpret with caution* is the rule, and state the new question: What events and conditions produced the correlation? Two or more variables that exhibit covariance may or may not have antecedent-consequence relationships. Growing organisms show changes, through time, of many relatively independent processes. Eruption of teeth or growth of long bones, for example, correlates with an increase in cortical dendritic branching, but independence is revealed through selective experimental manipulations.

B. Problems of Multiple Determination and Interaction

1. Necessary and Interchangeable Antecedents

Many antecedent conditions and events contribute to a given behavioral outcome. Many will be necessary but not sufficient. Still others may be interchangeable. In biological processes one sees alternative combinations of conditions that may bring about a given result. Our tendencies to think in terms of machine analogies are misleading in biology. Man has typically designed machines using a straightforward cause-effect principle to accomplish a given result. This leads to search for causal events that are at the same time necessary and *sufficient,* a rarity in life sciences, although some dramatic examples may be found in physiological chemistry. In the event of mechanical breakdown, direct cause and effect design permits rapid diagnosis and repair. Evolution has ensured against breakdown rather than placing reliance on repair. Thus, crucial behavioral functions are overdetermined. Physiological substrates for a given behavior may be interchangeable, as in limited mass action of of the cerebral cortex.

Neuroanatomical substrates for behaviors may shift during development from one system to another. Functions that are shared at one stage of development may become more focused. Is this what happens, for example, in ontogenetic encephalization of perceptual functions? In Section III, B, examples will be presented that show a shift of emphasis from midbrain to cortex in sensory discriminations that involve shared functional localization.

Among multiple causal conditions are a class of possible obstacle situations or events. Making sure that such negating conditions are absent may be a crucial experimental requirement. As stated by Wolf (1929), logician and philosopher of science, "... the complete cause will consist of negative as well as positive conditions" (p. 63).

If it were possible to know all causes and conditions down to their ultimate details, the logic of science would hold that there exists only one constellation of causes that will produce a given effect. The practicing scientist must content himself with the knowledge that he may strive toward the discovery of such perfection of understanding but can never fully achieve it. The physicist no longer claims such precision of control as to account for each unique physical event. Biological research must place reliance on qualitative descriptions and the quantitative specification of boundary conditions within which a given class of results is to be expected.

2. Feedback that Creates a Vicious Circle

Behavioral differences that appear to reside in temperament or other inherent developmental factors may result from unsuspected interactions through positive feedback from the environment. The more we attempt to establish "natural" environments for our animal rearing conditions the more likely these unsuspected interactions are to go undetected. The resulting error is a common one: that of assigning cause to one event when two or more are in operation. Among many examples of this pitfall is one involving the newborn human infant. Gunther (1955) studied 150 mother and infant pairs. She found a relation between small protractility of the breast and nursing problems. In some there was also breast softness, and in either case hospital nurses and mothers were inclined to try to increase lip stimulation by pushing the baby's head toward the breast. The resulting interference with breathing caused the infant to fret and to fight the breast increasingly at succeeding feeding times. This frustration to the mother served only to augment tensions, thereby compounding the problem. Explanations typically focussed on "colic" or a fretful temperament. Use of "super normal" buccal stimulation with an artificial nipple usually induced vigorous sucking, thereby breaking up the "vicious circle" of interfering events. Reliance on bottle feeding was the frequent outcome. The maternal responsiveness of animal mothers has not infrequently confounded physiological and behavioral observations of infant development. Differential (and preferential) treatment of offspring by mothers has been the subject of a review paper by Meier and Schutzman (1968). Recent studies conducted in a number of independent laboratories are being directed toward the investigation of this class of developmental variables.

3. Development vs. Arrest vs. Atrophy (or the Fallacy of Unidirectional Relationships)

The one-variable experiment may mislead us if we assume that a specific treatment (the independent variable) will produce only the change in the organism that such a single variable "causes directly." The fallacy is obvious when we apply it to a nutritional variable, if in so doing we make the assumption that manipulation of one required nutrient will arrest or hasten growth only in those structures that incorporate the component in question. A set of other nutritive constituents may fail also to be utilized, or be utilized in atypical combinations.

Even when a one-variable experiment gives us more complicated results than anticipated, or leads us initially into errors of interpretation, the outcome may be a highly useful contribution, provided a range of alternative interpretations is examined. When a behavioral outcome, for example, is more severe than expected, futher examination of the organism as well as further follow-up of the behavioral effects are required. Deprivation experiments have frequently resulted in the finding of long-lasting effects, some of which prove to be irreversible. The general lesson to be learned is that development can seldom be temporarily halted and then permitted to continue in normal fashion from the point of arrest. Growth simply cannot be held in abeyance without widespread effects.

To further illustrate briefly, our efforts to separate maturational and experiential effects in the development of vision through visual deprivation produced more widespread consequences than were expected (Chow *et al.*, 1957). What was intended to be a simple stoppage of behavioral development turned into a much more complicated set of problems (Riesen, 1958, pp. 430ff.). Manipulation of a single external variable, such as a nutritional or a sensory input, may set off a complex sequence of organismic processes. The result of visual deprivation applied only to one eye may initially arrest neurophysiological development and be followed by retrogressive and then by pathological changes in the structure and function of neural substrates. The behavioral results and certain of the neurophysiological and neuroanatomical correlates of visual deprivation are by now better known, if not yet fully understood (Wiesel and Hubel, 1963a; Riesen, 1966; Ganz *et al.*, 1968; Ganz and Fitch, 1968; Boas *et al.*, 1969).

4. Individual and Species Differences as Confounding Variables

Laboratory mammals have in the past been selected for convenience, and the results from one species often accepted as widely applicable to others and to man. This practice has often been biologically useful and sometimes valid. Such acceptance can also lead to assumptions that prove to be quite wrong. Another experience of the writer is a case in point.

When originally planning some experiments on the behavioral effects of dark-rearing in newborn chimpanzees, Henry W. Nissen and the writer accepted the observations of Goodman (1932) in rabbits to the effect that absence of function would not impair the development of the retina or higher centers and tracts of the visual nervous system. Even earlier Berger (1900) had reported that he could find no changes in the lateral geniculate bodies of kittens whose lids had been sutured from birth to 2½ months of age, although he did report some retardation of development in the visual cortex. We assumed that early exclusion of vision would, if anything, have only functional effects by interfering with the development of central neural integrations. But chimpanzees (Chow *et al.*, 1957) and monkeys (Winsberg and Riesen, 1966) respond to the long-term exclusion of light quite differently at retinal and lateral geniculate levels than do rabbits and kittens. Although RNA concentrations fall to 50% of normal or below in the sensory cells of the retina in all of these animal forms (Rasch *et al.,* 1961) only in the primates do the ganglion cells atrophy and disappear. Behavioral effects of prolonged dark-rearing may thus require quite different interpretations. Brief periods of patterned light deprivation (Wilson and Riesen, 1966), or exposure to flashes of light without opportunities for visual fixation (Orbach and Miller, 1969) are experimental manipulations that can tell us more about the *development* of central integrative systems than more drastic deprivations. A similar advantage was found in the selective restriction of visual-motor interactions (Held and Bauer, 1967).

III. SIMULTANEOUS APPEARANCE OF PHYSIOLOGICAL INDICATORS AND BEHAVIOR

A. Electrophysiological Maturation Coincident to Developing Sensory Capabilities

We are still groping for physiological measures that relate to changes in learning and other complex behavioral processes. Much of the problem lies in the involvement of widespread physiological activity. More promise and actual recent progress can be seen when we deal with the onset of simpler events such as first appearances of discrete sensory or sensorimotor responses. This point has been made elsewhere in relation to human sensory development (cf. Riesen, 1960).

In an earlier chapter of this volume Rose presents a clear case for simultaneous development of shorter latency visual evoked potentials and the appearance of visually guided behavior. A particular species shows a unique schedule of the appearance of characteristic components of the cortical evoked response, and within a species one sensory modality typically leads another. The different ages of appearance of visual and auditory evoked potentials correlate well with what is generally known regarding the differing ages of appearance of corresponding behavioral capabilities (Ellingson and Wilcott, 1960). A systematic study of sound-guided behavior in young kittens is needed, but touch and sound are effective at earlier ages than is vision, which only commences to serve the newborn after more than 14 days. Rose and Lindsley (1968) have discussed behavioral as well as their own physiological measures of visual function in kittens of 2 to 4 weeks of age, and are able to document the close correspondence in time of the periods of major advances.

A corresponding sensitive period of rapid change in the visual behavior and brain of sheep-dog puppies has been reported by Fox *et al.* (1968). These workers were able to show that the occlusion of the eyes by means of foam rubber pads produced changes in anatomical, biochemical, and electrophysiological retardation or qualitative variation only in the first 5 weeks, and not when occlusion was imposed between 5 weeks and 10 weeks or during a 5 weeks' period in adult dogs.

B. Neurochemical Maturation and Sensory Indicators

The concentrations of amino acids in the developing rabbit retina were studied by Davis *et al.* (1969). Glutamic acid, glutamine, GABA, aspartic acid, and alanine, all relatively high in concentration during the first days after birth, fell to lowest values at 11 days, the time of eyelid opening and beginning of clearing of the media. Thereafter the values increased. Similar changes were found in three or four of the amino acids in occipital cortex, and superior colliculi. By 30 days the values approximated those for the adult rabbit. Earlier studies from the same laboratories stress the development of the mature form of the cortical evoked potential through this same period of changing biochemical values. Behavioral measures corroborate these indicators of developmental advancement. Onset of optokinetic, visual placing, and visual cliff avoidance responses, and their rapid progress to adult levels of performance (Fig. 1) are

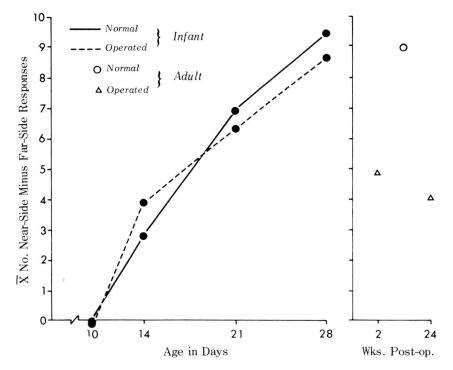

FIG. 1. The development of visual cliff avoidance behavior in infant Dutch-belted rabbits. Striate lesions disturbed this visually guided response in adults but not in 1-week old infants. (From Stewart and Riesen, 1970.)

seen to occur between 12 and 30 days of age in rabbits (Stewart and Zilbert, 1967; Stewart and Riesen, 1970). Neither in biochemical nor in electrophysiological measurement work have the variations among individuals of a given species been compared with possible correlated variations in the individual appearance of behavioral indicators. Although somewhat difficult technically, this type of study is necessary before we can be confident that the measures in brain physiology are directly responsible for the behavioral manifestations.

During the high variability, high amino acid concentration, and electro physiological immature phase of development, the pattern of structural growth retains plasticity, and the capacity for functional recovery is remarkably preserved. As the careful research of Stewart (Stewart and Riesen, 1970) has shown, complete removal of striate cortex (visual-I projection areas) at 1 week of age leaves the rabbit without significant losses in behavioral development, and subsequently permits visual-II occipital cortex to develop short latency-evoked responses such as are normally found only in visual-I. With behavior so little changed in these early operated animals, but so drastically impaired in adults following the same cortical lesions, we are faced with the unresolved issue: Is the behavior initially organized in the infant rabbit (and other mammals?) without functional participation of the geniculo-striate system? If so, in the intact brain does the visual-I projection system become incorporated during subsequent weeks by virtue of neural growth or by functional (environmental) requirements, or both? Much of the sensory deprivation literature *suggests* the latter, but we do not have the needed information from experiments in which the proper combinations of conditions (lesions or no, experience or no) have been conducted.

IV. UNRESOLVED QUESTIONS OF MECHANISM

A. Direct vs. Secondary Consequences of Stimulation

The question may be asked: Which appears first, structure or function? Again, there is obviously no simple answer. To make any headway in this area the scientist must become much more specific in phrasing questions for his data. While it seems clear that some neural structure must be present before it can function, once refinement and further growth of structure are observed, questions concerning role of function may be pointed toward clearly defined classes of structures and events. Exactly how are the increasing functional capacities of the growing organism interacting with developing structures, such as dendritic branchings, spines, synapses, and local molecular production? To review all of the recent work in this rapidly growing field of reasearch would be a formidable undertaking. Suffice it here to point toward some general problems and approaches toward their solution.

One of the basic problems in evaluating neural effects of environmental deprivations or enrichments concerns the discovery of mechanism. Is the effect direct or do intervening, and possible unsuspected processes, account for the change in a given neural or behavioral dependent variable? For example, in a recent experiment Edwards *et al.* (1969) were able to show in albino rats that 2 months of enriched environment begun at time of weaning produced a shortening of latencies in photic evoked potentials and a speeding up of learning of a brightness discrimination task. Although not inclined to commit themselves to "a specific model of brain functioning," the authors suggest that a difference in CNS arousal may underlie their results. Who is bold enough to suggest an alternative: more efficient processing of sensory input to the neocortex? Perhaps these are ways of designating two aspects of the same process.

When the question of direct *vs.* indirect effects is kept within the visual sensory system, it may become simply one of asking whether altered stimulation acts directly upon retinal mechanisms and secondarily on lateral geniculate and other visual centers. Retinal atrophy is known to mediate transneuronal degeneration of cells in the lateral geniculate. However, with much less damaging manipulations it is entirely possible that the altered levels of activation act directly on the higher visual centers as promptly and even more significantly in terms of altering functional capacities. This appears to be the better explanation for lateral geniculate losses after eyelid suturing in cats (Wiesel and Hubel, 1963a).

B. Delayed Effects and Their Explanation

When physiological factors bring about behavioral effects that are long delayed in appearance, the problem of correctly relating the two processes taxes the experimentalist's insight, ingenuity, and patience. Hormonal "priming" of the neonatal neuroendocrine system has become a classical example of this problem. Other behavioral examples include imprinting phenomena and a variety of early experience variables that result in long-lasting arousal, perceptual, and cognitive responses of organisms, some of which show great resistance to alteration even through the adult phase of growth and decline. In general, more is known about the behavioral than about the physiological mechanisms underlying these effects. This field is rich with promise, and in great need of vigorous research effort. In any long-term early experience research, much is to be gained by adding groups that may be interim tested, and possibly also one that is pretested, so as to provide information as to the time course of both physiological and behavioral changes. A recent behavioral study demonstrated some clear advantages of pretesting (Lessac and Solomon, 1969).

C. Multiple Determinants

Localization of function is a persistent problem of major proportions throughout the history of the study of interrelations of brain and behavior. The pendulum continues to swing, as it did during the lifelong work of Karl Lashley, from localization toward equipotentiality and back again. Many individual workers have become involved in smaller oscillations, and much progress continues, especially when the problems become more specific to meaningful behavioral categories. To say that the organism behaves as a whole may remind us that dissection can only go so far before we destroy what we seek, but it also accomplishes almost nothing by way of explaining the origins of behavior.

Another pendulum is that from neocortical to limbic structures (and below) and back again to the outer shell of the brain. The much greater acceptance of "systems" research in recent years yields reassurance that oversimplification in this area of intercorrelational endeavor has begun to yield to the evidence.

A recent proposal to separate visually guided behavior both developmentally and neuronatomically into two relatively independent functions is proving to be highly fruitful for directing experimental effort. For somewhat different empirical and theoretical reasons Held, Ingle, Schneider, and Trevarthen all argued in a symposium series that visual direction and visual identification are doubly dissociated by developmental (including dependence upon experience) and anatomical (cortex *vs.* midbrain in higher mammals) criteria. Normal vision employs both functions simultaneously or in such close interaction that separation is far from obvious, since that which is recognized is also fixated and either approached, avoided, or dealt with in some other directional manner. Behavioral analysis alone enabled Ingle (1967) to show that fish respond differently to orientation when the larger visual field is involved than when small objects are identified. By testing for interocular transfer he showed that right and left are maintained for small objects, but are reversed, and thus treated as nasal *vs.* temporal for larger visual areas. Orienting within and moving through the larger visual environment is a function that is completely (perhaps) retained by midbrain neural systems in newborn mammals. In this respect mammals may be said to have remained like the fish. Their cortex has evolved primarily as a feature-detecting organ (Wiesel and Hubel, 1963b).

Held (1968) has reviewed the evidence that mammals guide themselves through the enrivonment accurately only after the midbrain system has both matured and learned. Experience that combines motor and visual action (reafferent neural correlating activity) is required before cats, monkeys, or human infants may develop eye-limb coordinations for making appropriate visually guided responses. The problem of restricting this function to the superior colliculus and related midbrain structures arises from two sources. In monkeys it has long been known that eye orienting responses can be mapped from anterior occipital cortex, but the developmental history of these responses is not known.

The most convincing separation of identifying from orienting visual functions as related to cortex vs. midbrain is in the hamster (Schneider, 1967). Fortunately, Trevarthen (1968) has collected and skillfully evaluated the scattered but quite extensive evidence that primates share this separation of function, while at the same time enjoying the advantages of coordinating circuits to permit the cortical and subcortical systems to function together. His own work with split-brain monkeys shows that interhemispheric transfer of detail recognition (focal vision) is eliminated without a corresponding loss in the general orientation of the organism in (ambient) space. While this is a sketchy and simplified representation of what has been said by four contributors to a unified view of visually guided behavior, it is hopeful to see that from fish to man there is a continuity. Some major problems in the interpretation of behavior that has as many determinants as does visually guided behavior are showing promise of solution through a developmental comparative approach to the study of brain function.

V. Conclusions

The problems of correlating behavioral and physiological development are yielding gradually, not to studies that follow a straightforward set of rules of scientific method, but to the advances along several fronts in techniques of physiological analysis and recording, increasingly detailed knowledge of neuro-chemistry and neural morphology, and ingenious applications of behavioral methods. Behavior that approximates more closely the adjustments normally required of organisms is playing a major part in current investigations of neural and behavioral ontogeny and phylogeny.

REFERENCES

Berger, H. (1900). *Arch. Psychiat. 33,* 521-567.
Boas, J. A. R., Ramsey, R. L., Riesen, A. H., and Walker, J. P. (1969). *Psychon. Sci. 15,* 251-252.
Chow, K. L., Riesen, A. H., and Newell, R. W. (1957). *J. Comp. Neurol. 107,* 27-42.
Davis, J. M., Himwich, W. A. and Agrawal, H. C. (1969). *Develop. Psychobiol. 2,* 34-39.
Edwards, H. P., Barry, W. F., and Wyspianski, J. O. (1969). *Develop. Psychobiol. 2,* 133-138.
Ellingson, R. J., and Wilcott, R. C. (1960). *J. Neurophysiol. 23,* 363-375.
Fox, M., Inman, O., and Glisson, S. (1968). *Develop. Psychobiol. 1,* 48-54.
Ganz, L., and Fitch, M. (1968). *Exp. Neurol. 22,* 638-660.
Ganz, L., Fitch, M., and Satterberg, J. A. (1968). *Exp. Neurol. 22,* 614-637.
Goodman, L. (1932). *Amer. J. Physiol. 100,* 46-63.
Gunther, M. (1955). *Lancet I, 268,* 575-578.
Held, R. (1968). *Psychol. Forsch. 31,* 338-348.
Held, R., and Bauer, J. A., Jr. (1967). *Science 155,* 718-720.
Ingle, D. (1967). *Psychol. Forsch. 31,* 41-51.

Lessac, M. S., and Solomon, R. L. (1969) *Develop. Psychol. 1,* 14-25.

McCormick, T. C., and Francis, R. G. (1958). "Methods of Research in the Behavioral Sciences," pp. 4-8. Harper, New York.

Meier, G. W., and Schutzman, L. H. (1968). *Develop. Psychobiol. 1,* 141-145.

Orbach, J., and Miller, M. H. (1969). *Vision Res. 9,* 713-716.

Rasch, E., Swift, H., Riesen, A. H., and Chow, K. L. (1961). *Exp. Cell Res. 25,* 348-363.

Riesen, A. H. (1958). "Biological and Biochemical Bases of Behavior" H. F. Harlow and C. N. Woolsey, eds.), pp. 425-450. Univ. of Wisconsin Press, Madison, Wisconsin.

Riesen, A. H. (1960). *In* "Handbook of Research Methods in Child Development" (P. H. Mussen, ed.), pp. 284-307. Wiley, New York.

Riesen, A. H. (1966). *Progr. Physiol. Psychol. 1,* 117-147.

Rose, G. H., and Lindsley, D. B. (1968). *J. Neurophysiol. 31,* 607-623.

Schneider, G. E. (1967). *Psychol. Forsch. 31,* 52-62.

Stewart, D. L., and Riesen, A. H. (1970). *Advan. Psychobiol.* (in press).

Stewart, D. L., and Zilbert, D. E. (1967). *Proc. 75th Annu. Conv. Amer. Psychol. Asso. Vol. 2,* pp. 93-94.

Trevarthen, C. B. (1968). *Psychol. Forsch. 31,* 299-337.

Wiesel, T. N., and Hubel, D. H. (1963a). *J. Neurophysiol. 26,* 978-993.

Wiesel, T. N., and Hubel, D. H. (1963b). *J. Neurophysiol. 26,* 1003-1017.

Wilson, P. D., and Riesen, A. H. (1966). *J. Comp. Physiol. Psychol. 61,* 87-95.

Winsberg, G. R., and Riesen, A. H. (1966). *J. Histochem. Cytochem. 14,* 798-799.

Wolf, A. (1929). *In* "Encyclopedia Britannica," 14th ed. Vol. 5, pp. 61-63. London and New York.

PART II THE EMERGENCE OF STRUCTURE AND FUNCTION

CHAPTER 5 The Postnatal Development of Synaptic Contacts in the Cerebral Cortex

Anthony M. Adinolfi

I. INTRODUCTION

One of the more challenging problems in neuroanatomy today is to define the synaptic organization underlying specific activity in the mammalian cerebral cortex. Despite the laminar organization of cortical gray matter which affords a systematic approach to the study of synaptic patterns on neurons in the different laminae, recent studies suggest that the six-layered stratification is more of a histological convention than a reflection of the functional organization of the cerebral cortex.

The early descriptions of the qualitative histology of the cerebral cortex focused on the forms of individual neurons, their general organization in different cortical fields, or the distribution of the afferent fibers within the cortex (see review by Sholl, 1956). Neocortical neurons can be broadly defined as either pyramidal or stellate on the basis of dendritic or axonal configurations and are arranged in six layers tangential to the pial surface. Layer I, the molecular or plexiform layer, is relatively acellular and lies immediately under the pia. It consists of a dense tangential fiber plexus composed of the terminal dendritic ramifications of underlying pyramidal neurons and the ascending axons (recurrent collaterals) originating mainly from cells in layers V and VI (Szentagothai, 1964). Clusters of small and medium-sized pyramidal cells comprise layers II and III. These cells are vertically oriented with their apical dendrites projecting into the molecular layer and axons descending into the underlying white matter. Layer IV is the zone of stellate neurons and it is here that most of the thalamocortical projections terminate in relation to the apical dendritic shafts of layer V pyramidal neurons as they traverse layer IV (Globus and Scheibel, 1966). The long ascending dendrites of layer VI fusiform cells attain the molecular layer and give collateral branches into layer IV.

The cytoarchitecture of the cerebral cortex shows wide ranges of variation among animals of different species, among animals of the same species, and in successive sections of a single brain. Thus, the use of a simple model of organization becomes necessary for any study of cortical synaptology. If one examines a vertical strip of neocortex extending from the pial surface to the underlying white matter, all neuronal elements are represented and, theoretically, it should be possible to postulate the morphological bases for the transmission of impulses from the activation of vertically oriented elements by corticopetal projections, the tangential spread of activiation to successive units through a system of collateral fibers and stellate neurons, to the firing of corticofugal systems. The reader is referred to Figs. 71 and 74 of Lorente de No (1949) for the myriad possibilities of such cortical reflex arcs. Lorente de No (1949), assuming a relative constancy to the dendritic and axonal plexuses throughout the cortex, first suggested such an "elementary unit" of neocortical organization based on vertical chains of neurons linked by reflex arcs. The later work of Mountcastle (1957) and Hubel and Wiesel (1962) clearly demonstrated that a functional columnar organization existed within the cortex and these studies led Colonnier (1966) to reaffirm the concept that the basic structural units, as defined by dendritic and axonal patterns within the cortex, are most likely a series of radially repeating columns upon which all afferent fibres converge. The concept of elementary units has not gone unchallenged and this kind of over-simplification in an attempt to define the structural basis of cortical activity has been criticized (Sholl, 1956). However, the basic columnar unit, conceivably a simplistic view of cortical organization, does offer the neuroanatomist a practical means of analyzing the synaptic organization within the neocortex.

One approach to the evaluation of the basic cortical units lies in the study of the morphological characteristics of the newborn cerebral cortex and the observable changes during maturation and relating these structural changes with differences in cortical activity evoked from the maturing animal. Despite the value in a structure-function approach to neocortical ontogeny, the only significant contributions to date are those of Purpura et al. (1964) and Scheibel and Scheibel (1964) and the reader is referred to Chapters 1 and 2 of this volume.

II. THE POSTNATAL MATURATION OF NEOCORTICAL NEURONS

Our own studies on the ultrastructure of the developing cerebral cortex have been limited to observations on kittens. For purposes of general review and orientation, the following brief account, based on the more extensive descriptions of Golgi-impregnated kitten neocortex by Noback and Purpura (1961) and Scheibel and Scheibel (1963, 1964), deals primarily with the differential development of pyramidal and stellate neurons during postnatal maturation.

At birth all layers of the neocortex are identifiable and the pyramidal cells are radially oriented with apical dendrites extending to the molecular layer and axons directed toward the underlying presumptive white matter. In the immediate neonatal period (birth to 3 days), the apical dendrites in the molecular layer show some arborization and terminal branching. Many pyramidal neurons possess poorly developed and unbranched basilar dendrites. Others lack basilar dendrites at this stage. Apical dendrites send a few short collateral branches into layers II and IV but these lack spines. Both specific and nonspecific corticopetal projections are detectable as a relatively simple axonal plexus in layer IV in the vicinity of the apical dendrites of layer V pyramidal cells, but synaptic contacts could not be detected readily (Scheibel and Scheibel, 1964). By the eighth postnatal day, pyramidal cells have substantially differentiated and the terminal arborizations of apical dendrites in the molecular layer are virtually completed. Collateral branches are more prominent and spines are detectable on apical shafts. All cells have a full complement of basilar dendrites but these lack spines. Short axon collaterals are observed at this stage. Spines develop on all dendrites and collateral branches during the second postnatal week and by 21 days postnatally, the general morphology of pyramidal neurons closely resembles the adult.

Stellate neurons appear to differentiate later than the pyramidal cells and are more readily identified during the second postnatal week than in the immediate neonatal period. Scheibel and Scheibel (1964) noted that most of the stellate neurons of layers II and IV are in the neuroblast phase in the neonatal kitten cortex. The end of the first week marks the early stages of development of the stellate axonal plexuses and the appearance of developing dendrites. By the end of the third postnatal week, the maturation of stellate neurons is well advanced.

In summary, the postnatal maturation of neocortical neoronal elements involves three overlapping stages of pyramidal cell morphogenesis. The apical dendritic systems develop first, followed by the elaboration of the basilar dendrites, and finally the growth of axons and myelination. During the second maturational stage of the pyramidal neurons, the later developing stellate neurons begin to mature with the initial elaboration of axonal plexuses followed by the growth of the dendritic systems.

Thus, the basic columnar units of the newborn neocortex are represented by vertically oriented pyramidal neurons whose primary receptor surfaces are represented by the more superficially located apical dendritic systems. Differentiation of the oblique branches of apical dendrites and the basilar dendrites of pyramidal neurons and the maturation of the stellate neurons with short axons during the first postnatal month results in the elaboration of this elementary pattern by producing additional receptor surfaces laterally and basally and by establishing intracortical connectivity through a system of short-axoned intracortical neurons.

III. ELECTRON MICROSCOPIC STUDIES OF CORTICAL ORGANIZATION

Although a number of studies have dealt with the ultrastructure of neocortical synaptic contacts, relatively few have been concerned with the distribution of synaptic contacts along neocortical elements. Gray (1959) was the first to distinguish between axodendritic and axosomatic synaptic contacts in the cerebral cortex on the basis of the observable differences in the synaptic membrane thickenings, the size of the synaptic clefts, and the amount of extracellular material within the clefts. His type I synaptic contacts are found only on dendritic trunks and spines whereas type II contacts are restricted to the cell body surfaces and, occasionally, along dendritic trunks. Gray (1959) also verified the existence of the dendritic spine and described the spine apparatus. Similar observations were made in the cat by Pappas and Purpura (1961). Van der Loos (1963) included a description of the subsynaptic organelle and interlemmal elements in his study of the fine structure of synapses in the rabbit visual cortex. He later (1965) rejected Gray's classification of the types I and II synapses as two extremes of a single continuum and suggested, in addition, that the primary receptor site on neocortical pyramidal neurons was the dendritic spine. More recently, Colonnier (1968) examined the types and distribution of synaptic contacts in cat visual cortex and offered the first description of synaptic patterns associated with the different cell types within the neocortex. He confirmed the presence of two distinct synaptic types on the basis of membrane densities and described asymmetrical synapses, roughly analogous to Gray's type I contact, which contained spheroidal synaptic vesicles and symmetrical synapses, similar to Gray's type II contact but containing flattened or ellipsoidal synaptic vesicles. Most of the synaptic contacts on layer II pyramidal cells are asymmetrical and occur on dendritic spines. Comparatively fewer contacts are found on dendritic trunks and the cell bodies. Virtually all appeared to be of the symmetrical type. Stellate neurons in layers I and IV displayed both types of contacts on their somal and dendritic surfaces.

In our laboratories, the cytology of the mature pyramidal neurons in layer II and the stellate neurons in layers I and IV of the percruciate and orbitofrontal cortex has been studied by light and electron microscopy. The cerebral cortex of adult cats was fixed *in situ* by vascular perfusion and samples of tissue were oriented so that single sections extending from the pial surface to the underlying white matter could be obtained. Alternate thick (1.5 μ) and thin (500-750 Å) sections were examined.

A. The Fine Structure of Layer II Pyramidal Neurons

Small pyramidal neurons lie beneath the molecular layer and are readily identified in sections by their characteristic shape and apical dendrites coursing perpendicular to the pial surface into the molecular layer (Fig. 1). Cell bodies contain a basally situated and highly indented nucleus surrounded by a thin rim

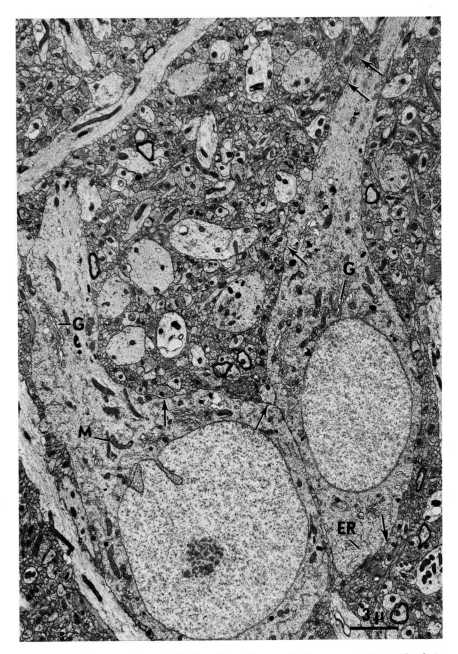

FIG. 1.   Two apposing cell bodies of small pyramidal neurons in layer II of the coronal gyrus from an adult cat. Cytoplasmic organelles are sparse. Single cisterns of the rough endoplasmic reticulum (ER) and mitochondria (M) are dispersed throughout the perikarya. Elements of the Golgi complex (G) are prominent in the apical cytoplasm and extend into the apical dendrites. Arrows indicate synaptic contacts.

of cytoplasm which is expanded at the apical end of the cell. Elements of the Golgi complex, mitochondria, ribosomes, and neurotubules are dispersed throughout the perinuclear cytoplasm and extend for varying distances into the proximal end of the apical dendrite. Profiles of apical dendrites within the molecular layer contain mainly parallel coursing neurotubules and mitochondria. Nissl bodies are sparse in the small pyramidal neurons and are represented by groups of three or four peripherally situated cisterns of rough endoplasmic reticulum. The axon hillock of these cells is small and gives rise to a thin straight initial segment directed from the base of the cell toward the underlying white matter. The fine structure of the initial segment (Fig. 2) does not differ significantly from the earlier descriptions of Sotelo and Palay (1968).

Observations on the synaptic contacts related to the layer II pyramidal neurons of the pericruciate and orbitofrontal cortex agree with Colonnier's description (1968) of the visual cortex. Two types of synaptic contacts are found. When the postsynaptic membrane is bordered on its cytoplasmic surface by a parallel density, variously named the subsynaptic web (DeRobertis *et al.*, 1961) and the sybsynaptic organelle (Van der Loss, 1963), the contact appears asymmetrical. Presynaptic terminals contain spheroidal synaptic vesicles. When the postsynaptic membrane is not bordered on its cytoplasmic surface by dense material, the apposing membranes appear more symmetrical and the presynaptic terminals contain spheroidal and ellipsoidal vesicular profiles. The total number of ellipsoidal profiles in each terminal appears to increase if the tissue is fixed initially in pure formalin rather than in a mixture of glutaraldehyde and paraformaldehyde.

Dendritic profiles in the molecular layer represent the arborizations of the apical dendrites of underlying pyramidal neurons. Synaptic contacts along surfaces of apical dendrites arising from layer II pyramidal neurons are symmetrical. Rarely, one finds an asymmetrical synaptic contact on large dendritic trunks in the molecular layer. However, the small dendritic profiles and dendritic spines display only asymmetrical contacts on their surfaces. If one assumes that the thinner dendrites represent the more distal branches of the dendritic arborization, then input to the more distal portions of pyramidal neurons is accomplished through asymmetrical synaptic contacts. More proximally, apical and basilar dendrites, cell bodies and initial segments of axons are contacted mainly by symmetrical synapses (Fig. 3). Synaptic contacts along proximal portions of the cell are few. No more than three to five contacts were observed in any single section of the cell bodies of layer II neurons.

B. The Fine Structure of Layer I and IV Stellate Neurons

The description of the fine structure of neuronal perikarya which are interpreted to be the stellate neurons of layer IV is based primarily on the observations made from sections of the pericruciate cortex. Deep to layers II and III lie

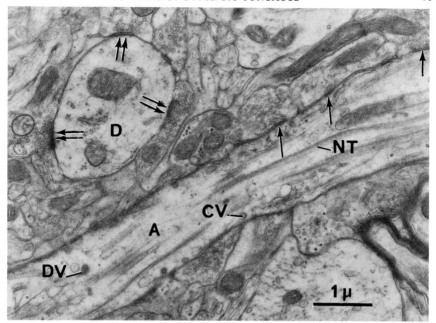

FIG. 2. The initial segment of the axon (A) of a pyramidal cell in layer II of the adult orbital gyrus contains fasicles of neurotubules (NT), free ribosomes, and occasional profiles of dense core (DV) and coated (CV) vesicles. Symmetrical synaptic contacts (single arrows) along the axon contain spheriodal and elliposoidal vesicles. Asymmetrical contacts (double arrows) on the dendritic profile (D) contain only spheroidal synaptic vesicles.

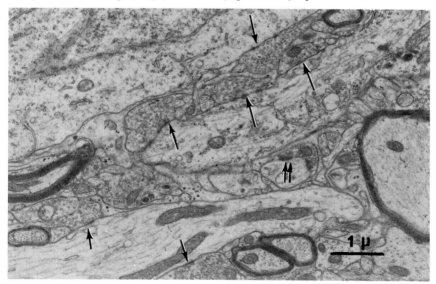

FIG. 3. Symmetrical synaptic contacts containing spheroidal and ellipsoidal vesicles (single arrows) occur on pyramidal cell bodies and basilar dendrites. Double arrows indicate an asymmetrical contact on a dendritic branchlet.

numerous oval and multipolar cell bodies surrounded by a neuropil rich in myelinated fibers and containing the traversing apical dendrites of the large pyramidal cells of layer V. In thin sections, the cytoplasm of most stellate cells resembles that of the more superficial pyramidal neurons (Fig. 4). Others appear

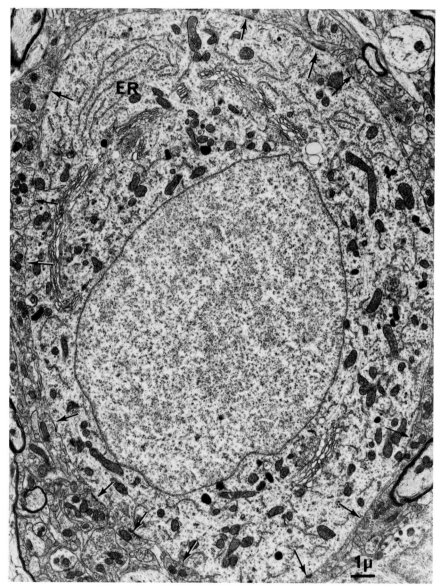

FIG. 4. In thin sections, the cell bodies of stellate neurons in layer IV of the pericruciate cortex are oval and display numerous axosomatic synaptic contacts (arrows). Cisterns of the rough endoplasmic reticulum (ER) occur singly or in parallel arrays in the peripheral cytoplasm.

darker because of the increased amounts of cytoplasmic organelles. Because of this variation in ultrastructural appearance, the interpretation that these profiles represent stellate neurons is based on their location deep to the superficial pyramidal cells, their shapes, and the larger numbers of synaptic contacts found on the cell bodies and proximal portions of the dendrites. Axosomatic synaptic contacts are either symmetrical or asymmetrical. The presynaptic ending is either a single terminal or, often, a "climbing" element coursing parallel to the postsynaptic membrane and forming numerous contacts. The dendritic shafts of layer IV stellate neurons are contacted by both asymmetrical and symmetrical synapses. Stellate neurons in the molecular layer differ only in the relative paucity of axosomatic synaptic contacts.

IV. THE ULTRASTRUCTURE OF LAYER II PYRAMIDAL NEURONS DURING POSTNATAL MATURATION

The following account of the postnatal maturation of the kitten neocortex will be limited to the discussion of the cytological features of developing pyramidal cells of layer II of the orbitofrontal and pericruciate cortex and the temporal changes in the synaptic organization related to these neurons during the first three postnatal weeks. The ultrastructure of pyramidal neurons in the newborn neocortex is quite variable. Cells in which the cytoplasmic organelles do not differ significantly from the fully mature small pyramidal neuron are found in all fields examined. In thin sections, the cell bodies are clustered immediately beneath the molecular layer and are readily identified by their triangular or bipolar contours and prominent apical dendrites directed toward the pial surface (Fig. 5). The basal nucleus is large and contains a prominent nucleolus. Unlike the mature cell, the nuclear envelope rarely exhibits deep indentations. The perikaryon, including the region of the apical dendrite, is filled with elements of the Golgi complex, ribosomes, mitochondria, and neurotubules. The Golgi complex often extends into the cytoplasm of the apical dendrite within the molecular layer. When present, Nissl bodies are small, peripherally situated, and often continuous with the smooth subsurface cisterns. The initial segment of the axon arises abruptly from the basal aspect of the cell body and contains fasicles of two or more parallel neurotubules, free ribosomes, and a very thin subsurface density. Cell bodies are contacted by one or more axon terminals. Axosomatic synaptic contacts in the newborn neocortex are always symmetrical and contain spheroidal synaptic vesicles (Fig. 6).

Many of the cells clustered beneath the molecular layer are less readily recognized. Radially oriented columns of oval and elongated or spindle-shaped perikarya, separated by a thin extracellular space or vertically coursing apical dendrites, comprise much of the superficial neocortex. Most of the cell body is occupied by the nucleus. The perinuclear cytoplasm contains free ribosomes and

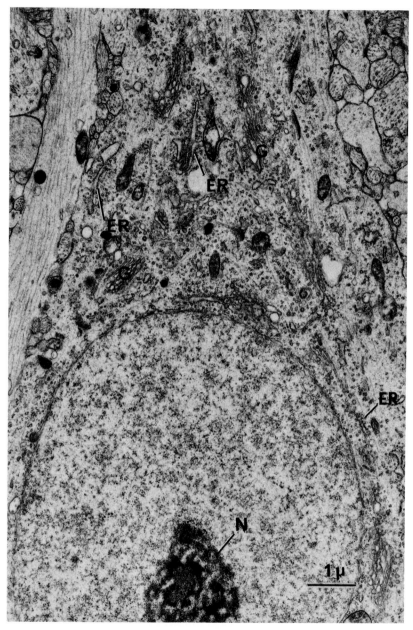

FIG. 5. A portion of the cell body of a layer II pyramidal neuron from the orbito-frontal cortex of a newborn kitten. The nucleus is rarely indented and contains a prominent nucleolus (N). The cytoplasm is filled with elements of the Golgi complex (G) and rough endoplasmic reticulum (ER), free ribosomes, mitochondria, and neurotubules. The cytology of this cell does not differ significantly from a fully mature small pyramidal neuron.

an occasional mitochondrion or dense body. The apical expansion contains vertical arrays of elements of the Golgi complex. Single cisterns of rough endoplasmic reticulum are present but Nissl bodies are absent. Axosomatic synaptic contacts are not found along these cells.

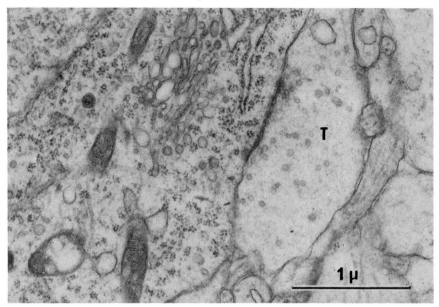

FIG. 6. Symmetrical synaptic contacts are found on the cell bodies of pyramidal neurons in the newborn neocortex. The axon terminal (T) is often expanded and contains scattered spheroidal vesicles.

Synaptic contacts on the pyramidal cells in the newborn neocortex occur mainly on apical dendrites and their branches within the molecular layer. Dendritic profiles in the molecular layer range in size from $0.1\ \mu$ to $2.5\ \mu$. Most of the synaptic contacts in the superficial neuropil are of the symmetrical variety. Few asymmetrical contacts are present and both varieties contain only spheroidal vesicles (Fig. 7). The number of vesicles varies from very few profiles in an expanded terminal to aggregates which entirely fill a terminal and are indistinguishable from the adult stage. Both terminal and *en passage* contacts occur with sufficient frequency to suggest that the more distal portions of the apical dendritic arborization represent the primary receptor sites in the newborn neocortex. Very few synaptic contacts are found on the cell bodies and the proximal portions of apical and basilar dendrites.

By the tenth postnatal day, a number of significant changes in the cytology of small pyramidal neurons and the synaptic organization of the superficial neocortex are observed. Many of the cells in layer II are still in close apposition but all are more easily identified by the characteristic shapes and prominent apical and basilar dendrites. The cytoplasmic volume has expanded and the cells

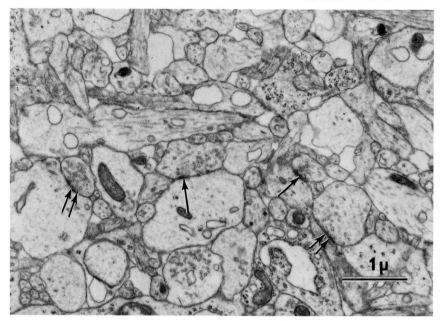

FIG. 7. Symmetrical (double arrows) and asymmetrical (single arrows) synaptic contacts occur on dendritic profiles in the molecular layer of the newborn neocortex. Only
spheroidal vesicles are observed in axon terminals at this stage.

closely resemble the mature pyramidal neurons. Axosomatic synaptic contacts
are encountered with more frequency and symmetrical contacts on the initial
segments of axons develop. Additionally, multiple synapses involving a single
axon terminal contacting a cell body and a dendrite in layer II (Fig. 8) or two
dendrites in layers I and II appear during the sixth to tenth days. During this
period, more of the dendritic profiles in the molecular layer measure less than
0.1 μ and small cuplike protuberances appear along dendritic surfaces. These
protuberances represent the developing dendritic spines, although the spine
apparatus could not be identified with certainty until the third postnatal week.
These spines are always contacted asymmetrically by an axon terminal (Fig. 9).
There are more asymmetrical axodendritic synaptic contacts in the neuropil of
the superficial neocortex than were present in the newborn. This observation
supports Mugnaini's recent hypothesis (1970) that the asymmetrical contacts
develop when the receptor neuron is at a more advanced stage of maturation.
Asymmetrical contacts in the newborn cortex probably occur on the dendrites
of those pyramidal cells which are more matured.

Synaptic vesicles in the 10-day neocortex are predominantly spheroidal and it
is not until the third week that ellipsoidal profiles appear in the symmetrical
contacts. By the third week, it is only the absence of myelinated fibers in the
superficial neocortex which allows one to distinguish between this stage and the
adult at the ultrastructural level. Synaptic organization at 21-days includes

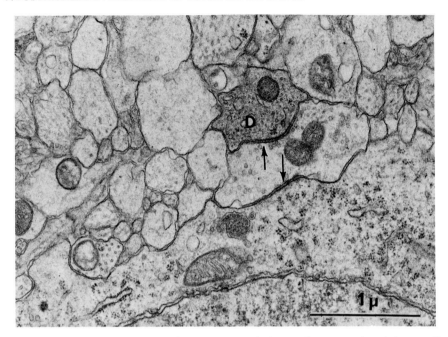

FIG. 8. A single axon terminal forming symmetrical synaptic contacts (arrows) on a cell body and dendrite (D) in layer II of the 10-day neocortex.

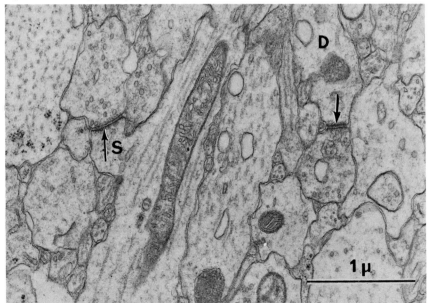

FIG. 9. A developing dendritic spine (S) in the molecular layer of the 10-day orbito-frontal cortex. Asymmetrical synaptic contacts (arrows) are found on developing spines and dendritic branchlets (D) by the tenth postnatal day.

symmetrical contacts on cell bodies and proximal dendrites, symmetrical contacts on the initial segments of axons, both types of contacts on dendritic shafts, and asymmetrical contacts on small dendritic branches and dendritic spines (Figs. 10 and 11).

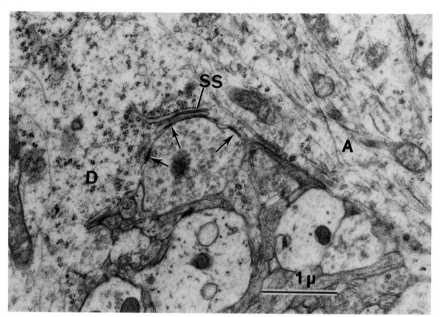

FIG. 10. A section of the basal end of a pyramidal neuron in layer II of the 21-day pericruciate cortex. A single axon terminal containing some flattened vesicles synapses symmetrically (arrows) on the cell body close to a subsurface cistern (SS) and the proximal portions of a basilar dendrite (D) and the axonal initial segment (A).

V. DISCUSSION

In Chapter 1 of this volume, Scheibel and Scheibel stressed the speculative nature of any correlation between histology and function during postnatal maturation of the neocortex. Temporal differences are not analyzed readily since the development of all cortical elements is progressive and many maturational changes are overlapping. At best, one can merely point out that the appearance of spontaneous cortical spindling is coincidental with the development of spines along apical dendritic shafts and that the reversal of polarity of evoked cortical potentials occurs at approximately the same time that one sees the development of basilar dendrites and related synaptic contacts or the development of stellate neurons in layer IV.

Electron microscopy, a latecomer to the study of neocortical ontogeny, has offered little more than confirmation of the appearance of dendritic spines and the development of submolecular axodendritic and axosomatic synaptic contacts during the second postnatal week. In order to establish a structural basis for the emergence of cortical activity during postnatal maturation, one must determine

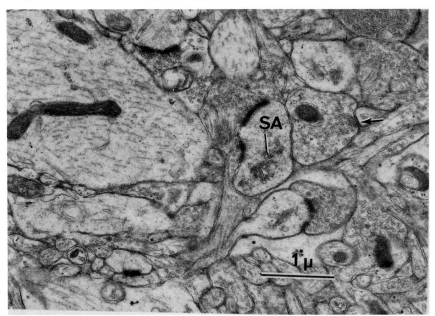

FIG. 11.   The spine apparatus (SA) is identified with certainty in the molecular layer of the 21-day neocortex. Dendritic spines are contacted asymmetrically and the terminals contain spheroidal vesicles. Rarely, one finds symmetrical synaptic contacts on dendritic spines or branchlets (arrow) and they contain both spheroidal and flattened vesicles in the terminals.

first the exact terminations of corticopetal projections on fully matured pyramidal and stellate neurons in a cortical field and the interconnections of these elements within that field. Such information would lend insight into the possible origins of developing synaptic contacts and, hence, developing connectivity. At present, relatively little is known concerning the specificity of receptor sites on neocortical neurons. A number of recent publications in which the loss of dendritic spines was used as an index of presynaptic terminal patterns (see Globus, Chapter 13) demonstrated that thalamic projections terminate on spines along the central one-third of apical dendrites of layer V pyramidal cells as they traversed layer IV, whereas callosal projections are restricted to the spines along oblique branches of apical dendrites. Thus, the rapid Golgi technique strongly suggests a specificity in the various axodendritic synaptic pathways related to pyramidal cells in the neocortex which, in part, is supported by electron microscopic observations. Several investigators (Colonnier, 1964; Jones, 1968; Szentagothai, 1965) have shown that axospinous synaptic contacts represent the terminations of corticopetal projections and that intracortical connectivity involves mainly the axonal branches of stellate neurons synapsing on pyramidal cell bodies. Inhibition of pyramidal cell activity may occur at these axosomatic synaptic contacts (Colonnier, 1968; Marin-Padilla, 1969; Szentagothai, 1965).

Ontogenetic studies can provide a systematic analysis of synaptic organization in the cerebral cortex. If the apical, oblique, and basilar dendrites, and cell bodies of pyramidal neurons represent specific receptor sites for corticopetal, intercortical, and intracortical projections, then the differential maturation of pyramidal dendritic systems and stellate neurons may reflect a differential development in neocortical connectivity. A definitive description of the structural maturation of these elements can be accomplished by the combined use of the rapid Golgi methods and electron microscopy. When changes in structural organization are coincident with the emergence of certain patterns of evoked activities, one can assume close structure-function correlations for the maturing neocortex.

In future studies, the cortical afferents might be destroyed prior to the critical periods for maturation of their receptor sites to determine, at the ultrastructural level, what effects such deprivation might have on the organization of the developing neocortex. For example, it is interesting to speculate that the loss of spines reported by Globus and Scheibel (1966) may reflect a situation in which the dendritic spines never developed because their axonal input was removed at birth. The question of spine plasticity in such experiments can best be answered by electron microscopy.

VI. CONCLUSION

It would be premature at this time to attempt to relate the basic cortical unit, as defined by Lorente de No (1949) and Colonnier (1966), to the immature neocortex. However, electron microscopic studies have shown that the development of the synaptic organization of the superficial neocortex progresses from predominantly axodendritic synaptic contacts along apical shafts in the molecular layer of the newborn neocortex to predominantly axospinous and axodendritic contacts on dendritic branchlets in the molecular layer of the 21-day neocortex. During this period, the appearance of axosomatic and axodendritic synaptic contacts along basilar dendrites suggests the progressive development of receptor sites deep to the molecular layer. The differential development of axodendritic and axosomatic synaptic contacts in the superficial neocortex of kittens was first reported by Voeller et al. (1963) and this study confirms those observations.

The maturation of synaptic contacts in the superficial neocortex appears to involve a shift from predominantly symmetrical synaptic membrane configurations in the newborn to largely asymmetrical synaptic membrane configurations by 21-days. Similar observations were made by Aghajanian and Bloom (1967) in a study of the development of synaptic contacts in the molecular layer of rat parietal cortex between the fourteenth and twenty-sixth postnatal days. They selectively stained the paramembraneous components of synaptic junctions with alcoholic phosphotungstic acid and demonstrated increasing asymmetry in the junctions caused in part by the increase in the postsynaptic paramembranous component. Observations on the late emergence of elliposoidal vesicular profiles in the symmetrical synaptic contacts are speculative and await a more extensive study of the effects of varying fixation procedures on the ultrastructure of synaptic contacts in the immature neocortex.

REFERENCES

Aghajanian, G. K., and Bloom, F. E. (1967). *Brain Res. 6,* 716.

Colonnier, M. (1964). *J. Anat. 98,* 47.

Colonnier, M. (1966). *In* "Brain and Conscious Experience" (J. C. Eccles, ed.), pp. 1-23. Springer, Berlin.

Colonnier, M. (1968). *Brain Res. 9,* 268.

DeRobertis, E. D. P., DeIraldi, A. P., DeLores Arnaiz, G. R., and Salganicoff, L. (1961). *Anta. Rec. 139,* 220.

Globus, A., and Scheibel, A. B. (1966). *Nature (London) 212,* 463.

Gray, E. G. (1959). *J. Anat. 93,* 420.

Hubel, D. H., and Wiesel, T. N. (1962). *J. Physiol. (London) 160,* 106.

Jones, E. G. (1968). *J. Anat. 103,* 600.

Lorente de Nó, R. (1949). *In* "Physiology of the Nervous System" (J. F. Fulton, ed.), pp. 288-330. Oxford Univ. Press, London and New York.

Marin-Padilla, M. (1969). *Brain Res. 14,* 633.

Mountcastle, V. B. (1957). *J. Neurophysiol. 20,* 408.

Mugnaini, E. (1970). *Brain Res. 17,* 1969.

Noback, C. R., and Purpura, D. P. (1961). *J. Comp. Neurol. 117,* 291.

Pappas, G. D., and Purpura, D. P. (1961). *Exp. Neurol 4,* 507.

Purpura, D. P., Shofer, R. J., Housepian, E. M. and Noback, C. R. (1964). *Progr. Brain Res 4,* 187.

Scheibel, M. E., and Scheibel, A. B. (1963). *Electroencephalogy. Clin. Neurophysiol.* Supply. 24, 235.

Scheibel, M. E., and Scheibel, A. B. (1964). *Progr. Brain Res. 9,* 6.

Sholl, D. A. (1956). "The Organization of the Cerebral Cortex." Wiley, New York.

Sotelo, C., and Palay, S. L. (1968). *J. Cell Biol 36,* 151.

Szentagothai, J. (1964). *Progr., Brain Res. 14,* 1.

Szentagothai, J. (1965). *Symp. Biol. Hung. 5,* 251.

Van der Loos, H. (1963). *Z. Zellforsch. Mikrosk. Anat. 60,* 815.

Van der Loos, H. (1965). *Neurosci. Res. Program, Bull. 3,* 22.

Voeller, K., Pappas, G. D., and Purpura, D. P. (1963). *Exp. Neurol. 7,* 107.

CHAPTER 6 Ultrastructure of the Developing Cerebral Cortex in the Rat

David W. Caley and David S. Maxwell

I. INTRODUCTION

The embryonic central nervous system develops from the neural tube which is made up of a layer of cells, the neuroepithelium. These cells display little specialization or complexity in the fetal brain. They multiply, migrate, and differentiate into the neurons and neuroglia of adult brain. The structural features of these cells as they develop include changes in the nucleus; in the cytoplasm and organelles; in the number, complexity, and contacts of the cellular processes; and in the shape of the cell. Most aspects of cortical cell maturation occur postnatally. [Details of differentiation of the neural and glial cell bodies have been reported elsewhere: Adinolfi (Chapter 5, this volume), Caley and Maxwell (1968a, b), Scheibel and Scheibel (Chapter 1, this volume), Stensaas and Stensaas (1968), Vaughn and Peters (1967), and Vaughn (1969).]

This discussion will focus on the development of the neuropil, the plexiform network of neural processes (terminal axons, dendrites, synapses) and glial fibers that form the major volume of the brain. The relations of the blood vessels and the extracellular spaces to the intertwined processes of the neuropil imparts to the brain unique structural properties found in no other tissue. All tissues are composed of cells and blood vessels surrounded by connective tissue fibers and extracellular spaces, but with a different organization for each tissue. By contrast, the brain lacks connective tissue fibers and prominent extracellular spaces. In their place is this complex entanglement of neural and glial processes, synapses, blood vessels, and extracellular spaces.

It is the development of these elements of cerebral cortex that we propose to examine in detail. The difficulties encountered in analysis of the complex adult neuropil are simplified by examining immature cortex. The neuropil is absent in the newborn rat and the sequence of development will be analyzed during the first three postnatal weeks.

Fetal, newborn, and rats up to 21 days postnatal age were studied. The animals were perfused with a buffered mixture of glutaraldehyde and formaldehyde. Slices of sensorimotor cortex were post-fixed in osmium and embedded in epoxy. Sections extending from the surface to the white matter were examined and photographed, using light and electron microscopes. Measurements of cortical thickness, cell number and size, and density of the blood vessels were made on light micrographs. Measurements of extracellular spaces were made on sample electron micrographs taken throughout the cortical depth. (See Caley and Maxwell, 1968a, for details.)

For purposes of clarity, this discussion of neuropil development will be separated according to the following scheme: the growth of the cortex as a whole; the development of the neuron; maturation of synapses; the development of blood vessels; and finally changes in volume and contents of the extracellular spaces.

II. THE DEVELOPMENT OF THE NEUROPIL

A. Growth of the Cortex as a Whole

Figure 1 is a composite of light micrographs of the cerebral cortex from 2-week fetal, newborn, 2, 5, 9, 15, and 21-day rats. The cortical surface is toward the top of the illustration and the cortical thickness is represented with the junction between the cortex and white matter at the bottom. The most superficial layer of the cortex, the molecular layer, is seen at all ages immediately under the pia-arachnoid membrane. The cells display a gradient of size and packing density from the surface toward the white matter. The smaller cells near the surface are more tightly packed together than deeper cells.

Figure 1 forms a growth curve of developing cortex. During the first postnatal week, the rate of cortical growth is highest, but growth is negligible during the second and third weeks. By 10 days, the cortex is almost equal to the thickness of the adult cortex. The thickness is 0.9 mm at birth, 1.8 mm at 5 days, and 2.1 mm at 21 days.

Between birth and 21 days most of the cells double in diameter from approximately 7 to 15 μ. The largest pyramidal neurons in layer 5 may develop to about 30 μ in diameter. The increase in cortical thickness during the first week cannot be explained by increase in the number or volume of cells but results from the growth of the neuropil, the structures between the cells. Cell packing density markedly decreases during this period. At birth about 3000 cells per mm^2 are found, all closely packed. The counts are 1500 at 2 days, 900 at 5 days, and 800 at 9 days. The numerical density of cells for the cortex was obtained by dividing the number of cell nuclei by the area of the section. Thus it

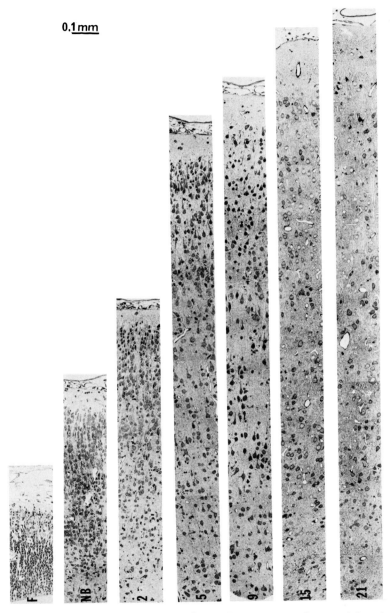

FIG. 1. Composite photomicrographs of sensorimotor cortex of rats aged 2 weeks fetal and newborn, 2, 5, 9, 15 and 21 days old. Each micrograph extends from the surface to the white matter. Comparison can be made of cortical thickness, cell packing density, and numbers of blood vessels. Maturation of the neuropil and neurons proceeds in a gradient beginning in the deepest layers.

can be seen that the major growth is not in cell size or number, but in the neuropil surrounding the cells. The dispersion of cells and rapid increase in cortical thickness is the result of the proliferation of the axons, dendrites, and extracellular spaces (Bass *et al.,* 1969; Caley and Maxwell, 1970; Scheibel and Scheibel, Chapter 1, this volume).

Electron microscopy verifies that it is the increasing numbers of neuronal processes and increased extracellular volume between the cell bodies that produce the increased cortical thickness and decreased cell density. Between the cell bodies is found a proliferation of microscopically small axons and dendrites that occupy the spaces between the dispersed cell bodies. This proliferation is largely a consequence of the growth of the elaborate dendritic tree of the pyramidal cells (Schade and Baxter, 1960). There is a large contribution to neuropil volume by the in-growth of axons, but it is difficult to assess their contribution because a clear distinction cannot be made between the smallest axons and dendrites except at synapses.

These maturational changes in the neuropil and dispersion of cells occur in a gradient from the depth to the surface. This gradient phenomenon can be easily visualized by examination of Fig. 1 (ages 1, 2, and 5). Cellular differentiation and dispersion are first found in the deepest layers of the cortex. With increasing age, more superficial layers are involved. By 5 days only the most superficial cortex possesses immature characteristics.

In the newborn and 2-day-old cortex, cells of the superficial layers are tightly packed together in vertical columns. No extracellular spaces are found between these cells. However, extracellular spaces are first found between the columns of cells where the neuropil and blood vessels are developing. This gradient may be a reflection of the way the cortex is formed during fetal life. During fetal development the first cells migrating into the cortex are found in the deepest layers of postnatal cortex. Cells migrating later take increasingly superficial positions (Langman, 1968). The deeper (older) cells and the surrounding neuropil, therefore, mature first with more superficial layers following.

Comparisons between the material presented here and that reported in a complete quantitative study by Sugita (1917, 1918) raise an interesting technical consideration. Sugita was aware of the shrinkage of his tissue after fixation in Bouin's fixative and paraffin embedment. He selected Bouin's fixative because it neither shrank nor swelled the brain, but the dehydration and paraffin embedding resulted in drastic shrinkage. All of his results, therefore, were published as measured on paraffin sections and also with a correction factor obtained by comparing cortical thickness of frozen brain sections with embedded sections. Sugita's corrected measurements of cortical thickness agree very closely with those of this study in which there appears to be negligible shrinkage after osmium fixation and plastic embedding. However, the measurements of cell diameters agree closely only if Sugita's uncorrected measurements are used. Apparently the shrinkage during paraffin embedment is differential, the neuropil undergoes greater shrinkage than the cell bodies.

B. Development of the Neurons

The differentiation of the neurons occurs in a gradient that parallels the growth of the neuropil. In the newborn rat, the pyramidal cells of the deepest layers display apical dendrites, axons, and differentiated nuclei and cytoplasm. In the more superficial layers the cells are round to oval, lacking cell processes, and possessing immature nuclei and undifferentiated cytoplasm.

The immature cells are characterized by their small size, a thin rim of cytoplasm containing few organelles, and a peripheral clumping of chromatin around the nuclear margins. As older or deeper cortex is studied, more mature cells are found. The nuclear chromatin becomes entirely dispersed or euchromatic and contains a prominent nucleolus. The cytoplasmic organelles increase in number as the cytoplasmic volume expands. In the 5 to 9-day rat, cortex is characterized by a phase of organelle swelling that is probably a result of the increased metabolic demand during the period of rapid neurite growth. The distension of the endoplasmic reticulum is so extensive that it can be seen with the light microscope. By 10-12 days, after this phase of organelle distension, the pyramidal neurons take on mature characteristics with a high concentration of cytoplasmic organelles that are not swollen. The cytoplasm and cell processes are indistinguishable from those of mature neurons. For detailed descriptions of these changes and illustrations of them, the reader is referred to Caley and Maxwell (1968a) and Caley (1970). The maturation of superficial pyramidal neurons in the feline neocortex was described by Adinolfi in Chapter 5.

C. Development of the Synapses

Structural changes in the formation of synapses parallel maturation of other elements of the neuropil in the developing cortex. Sequences in synaptic development are illustrated in Figs. 2 to 5 taken from 9, 12, and 21-day cortex. This report will be restricted to synapses found in the molecular layer (layer one) of sensorimotor cortex to avoid the problem of differential development in various areas and depths of cortex.

Numerous contacts between cellular processes presumably developing into synapses (Fig. 2) are found throughout the maturing neuropil during the first 10 postnatal days. These junctions are distinguished by an extracellular density between the opposed membranes. In some cases, subsurface thickenings are found inside the cell membranes at the site of the junction. It cannot be concluded in this study whether the extracellular or membrane densities appear first. However, it has been noted elsewhere (Adinolfi, Chapter 5) that synaptic contacts with asymmetrical membrane thickenings increase in number during the postnatal maturation of the superficial neocortex and these may represent a more "mature" form than symmetrical synaptic contacts. The contact areas differ in size; some are flattened and extensive while others are only touching of two rounded profiles. The large extracellular spaces characteristic of immature cortex are found around these presumptive synapses.

Figure 2 shows several immature synapses with different appearances. The area of contact is small, the intercellular substance is indistinct, and the immature synaptic cleft is contacted by extracellular spaces. A few presynaptic

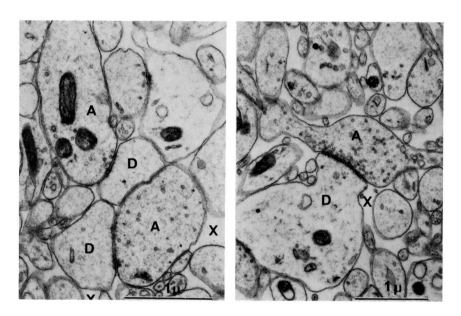

FIG. 2. Immature synapses from molecular layer of 9-day cortex illustrating small areas of contact with extracellular staining in the presumptive synaptic cleft, and a few presynaptic vesicles and subsurface thickenings are present. The large, unstained extracellular spaces have free access to these immature junctions. D, dendrite; A, axon; X, extracellular spaces.

FIG. 3. A more mature synapse from 9-day cortex showing extensive and uniform contact between the dendrite spine (D) and the axon (A). This intermediate stage is characterized by greater number of presynaptic vesicles, more uniform width and density of the synaptic cleft, and more prominent subsurface thickenings. The extracellular spaces (X) contact the synaptic cleft.

vesicles and some subsurface thickenings are noted inside the cellular profiles. A synapse displaying more mature features found in 9-day cortex is illustrated in Fig. 3 and possesses a more extensive and uniform contact between the immature dendritic spine and the axon. This intermediate stage is characterized by a greater number of vesicles, more distinct subsurface thickenings and a more uniform synaptic gap. The synaptic cleft is surrounded by extracellular spaces at this stage of development. It is not known whether these immature synapses are functional, but measurements of cortical activity suggest that they may be after 4 days of age (see Section III, A).

After 10 days, when the neuropil displays more mature characteristics, synapses are found which are indistinguishable from those found in adult cortex. Figure 4, from 12-day cortex, illustrates a cup-shaped synapse at the end of a dendritic spine. In the surrounding neuropil, the large extracellular spaces are gone. Only a small intercellular space of 150 to 200 Å separates the processes of the neuropil. The intra- and intercellular densities are moderately well developed. The synaptic cleft is more uniform in width, occupies a more extensive portion of the axon-dendrite interface, and is filled with dense-staining protein polysaccharide. By 21 days, most synapses appear to be mature (Fig. 5). The extracellular spaces surrounding the synaptic cleft are replaced by astrocytic

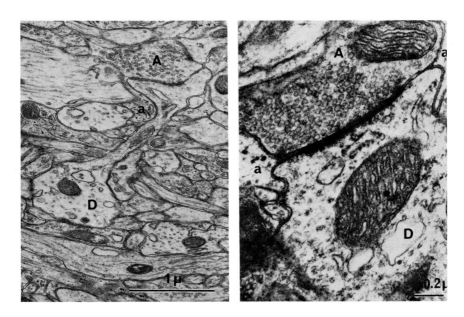

FIG. 4. Mature synapse from 12-day molecular layer. A dendrite (D) is cut in cross section and the synapse is on the end of spine (A). The extracellular spaces are reduced to a narrow cleft and the synapse is surrounded by astrocyte cytoplasm (a).

FIG. 5. Mature synapse from 21-day cortex with the dense and uniform contact between axon (A) and dendrite (D). The pre- and postsynaptic thickenings and large numbers of presynaptic vesicles are present. Astrocyte cytoplasm (a) appears to surround the synaptic cleft.

processes. The dendritic ctyoplasm is well developed, containing mitochondria, endoplasmic reticulum, ribosomes, and a dense proteinaceous background matrix. The development of the subsurface intracellular protein and the increased packing density of the presynaptic vesicles also contributes to the mature appearance of the synapses after 10 days. The extracellualar protein-polysaccharide in the synaptic cleft is very dense. [See Aghajanian and Bloom

(1967), Bass *et al.* (1969), Deza and Eidelberg (1967) for correlative studies of synaptic development.]

The elements of the neuropil do not develop in a rigid sequence. The various sequences of development overlap. It is difficult to find synapses with mature characteristics during the first week of development. During the second week a range of maturation could be found from immature contacts to well-developed synapses. By the third week, synapses could not be found that lacked the characteristics of mature synapses.

D. Development of the Blood Vessels

Light microscopy (Fig. 1) reveals few blood vessels in the rat cerebral cortex before 10 days. Most vessels present are thin-walled venules of large diameter. About 10 days, however, the mature density of blood vessels suddenly appears. Approximately 80 blood vessel profiles per mm^2 of tissue section are noted up to 10 days of age, but 250 to 300 profiles per mm^2 after the fourteenth day. These figures are averages of whole cortical sections obtained in the same way as the cell counts. Most vessels after this time are small capillaries. This seemingly sudden development of capillaries and appearance of the adult vascular pattern become understandable after analysis with the electron microscope.

During the period of rapid growth when few blood vessels are seen with the light microscope, many primitive unopened vessels are found in electron micrographs. Figure 6 is a cross section and Figure 7 a longitudinal section through these vessels. The wall is made up of endothelial cells joined together by typical junctional complexes. The outer surface is covered by a thin basal lamina. Most vessels during the first week are of this type, with an unopened lumen, although the tissue had been perfused at high pressures. The material in the lumen has neither the density nor other characteristics of blood plasma. However, at 10 days of age, most vessels possess a patent lumen (Fig. 8). This type of vessel would be filled with blood if the tissue had not been perfused. Before 10 days, the capillaries are present as a network of unopened vessels and their apparent sudden development comes about by opening of the lumen during a short interval of time. It is not known how the vessels open, whether it is an active process of the endothelial cells or if they are passively forced open by blood under pressure.

Neuronal and glial processes as well as extracellular spaces are in contact with the thin basal lamina during the first week (Figs. 6 and 7). During the second week, the vessel wall becomes progressively covered by astrocytic end feet. The basal lamina is found to be thicker and denser where the astrocyte end feet become applied to the vessel wall. Examples of the intermediate stage in development of the astrocytic sheath around the vessel are common in 9-day cortex. Figure 8 is an illustration of such a vessel displaying a patent lumen and an astrocytic investment that is incomplete with gaps between the astrocytic end feet. Figure 9 is a blood vessel from 12-day cortex to demonstrate the complete investment of a patent blood vessel by astrocytes with a junction between contiguous end feet and a thick, prominent basal lamina. The extracellular spaces decrease to adult dimensions as the astrocytes cover the blood vessel (Fig. 9). The opening of the lumen, the formation of the astrocytic sheath, and the loss of extracellular spaces occur uniformly throughout the tissue. A gradient in vessel and extracellular space maturation is not apparent. (For further discussion of this aspect of cortical development, see Caley and Maxwell, 1970.)

Based on the work of Craigie (1925), Strong (1961), and Klosovskii (1965) as well as our observations, it is reasonable to conclude that the vessels invade the developing brain as a cord of cells possessing only a primitive lumen. During the early postnatal development when the extracellular spaces are large, and before the neuropil is established, a network of presumptive, unopened vessels develops. The vessel lumen becomes patent and blood-filled in a matter of hours or perhaps days after the cortex achieves adult dimensions. The simultaneous

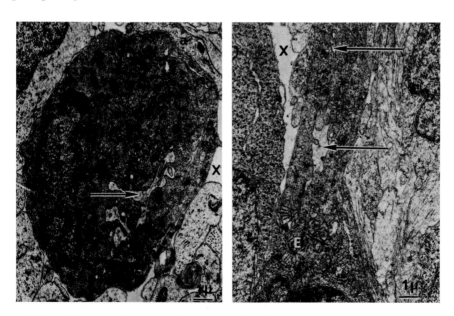

FIG. 6. Electron micrograph of a cross section through an immature unopened vessel from newborn rat cortex. The endothelial cell (E) surrounds a flocculent-filled primitive lumen (arrow). The thin basal lamina is in contact with astrocyte processes (a), extracellular spaces (X), and unidentified processes.

FIG. 7. Longitudinal section through vessel from newborn cortex whose unopened lumen (arrows) was followed for a considerable distance beyond this micrograph. As in Figs. 6 and 8, the endothelial cell (E) basal lamina is contacted by large extracellular spaces (X) as well as glial and neuronal cells.

maturation of the blood vessels and extracellular spaces suggests that before 10 days, the nutrition of developing cortex could be via the extracellular spaces. It is generally accepted that the blood vessels provide the primary network for distribution of metabolites in mature brain.

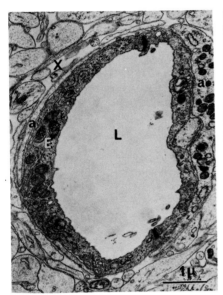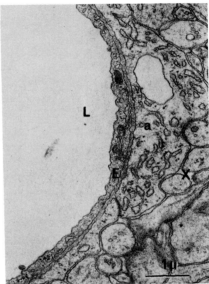

FIG. 8. Cross section through an opened vessel from 9-day cortex. The lumen would be filled with blood elements if the tissue had not been perfused. The extracellular spaces (X) are about 10–12% at this time. The astrocytic (a) investment is almost complete.

FIG. 9. Blood vessel from 12-day cortex to show the final maturation of the astrocyte end feet around the thick basal lamina of the endothelial cell (E). The vessel lumen (L) has been washed out by perfusion of the fixative. The astrocyte end feet (a) completely cover the blood vessel and are joined together. The extracellular spaces are greatly reduced, approaching the volume found in adult.

E. Changes in the Extracellular Spaces During Development

Extracellular volume as measured on electron micrographs by planigraphy is 10-12% of the tissue volume at birth and at 10 days of age. At 5 days, however, the extracellular volume rises transiently to 20%, only to return to the previous volume at 10 days. In 15 and 21-day cortex, the extracellular spaces are reduced to a narrow cleft between the tightly packed processes of the neuropil, as in the adult.

The absence of the large extracellular spaces after the second week of development may be an artifact and not represent the living state. Van Harreveld *et al.* (1965) produced convincing evidence that the lack of spaces in the mature brain is the result of conventional electron microscopic procedures such as were used in this study. It was suggested that some variable during fixation, perhaps oxygen lack, is responsible for a shift of extracellular ions and water into the cells, artificially reducing the extracellular volume. Anoxic conditions during fixation would then be responsible for the lack of prominent spaces in mature neuropil. The presence of the spaces in immature neuropil can be related to the fact that the immature brain is less sensitive to anoxia. A newborn rat can survive a nitrogen atmosphere for 50 min. Animals over 17 days old were dead after 1.5 min of oxygen lack (Fazekas *et al.*, 1941). Additionally, ischemia could not produce cerebral edema in rats less than 10 days of age (Spector, 1962). It is possible then that the spaces present in the developing brain are also present in the mature brain. The disappearance during the second week could be an artifact of fixation, reflecting the development of cortical sensitivity to anoxia. The problem is probably more complex than suggested here; nevertheless, there are better arguments for the presence of the spaces in mature neuropil than for their absence in immature neuropil. Further studies are necessary before we will be able to interpret fully the lack of extracellular spaces.

There have been a number of reports of histochemical studies of the extracellular compartment in brain (Bondareff, 1967; Caley, 1969; Hess, 1955; Meyers, 1969; Pease, 1966; Rambourg *et al.*, 1966; Rambourg and Leblond, 1967). Luft (1965) developed a technique using ruthenium red to stain extracellular acid polysaccharides, and it has been applied to brain with inconsistent results. Ruthenium red is a water-soluble dye added to the fixative. During fixation it penetrates the block of tissue and presumably becomes bound to the acid groups of polysaccharides. The osmium tetroxide used in postfixation renders the ruthenium red electron dense. In an effort to examine the contents of the extracellular spaces during development, we have studied newborn, 5, 10, and 100-day-old rat cortex after ruthenium red staining.

Ruthenium red penetrates into the tissue blocks only about 25 to 40 μ except in the case of 5-day rats in which the penetration was greater than 100 μ. Electron microscopy revealed that the tissue elements in most cases were unstained and pale. Where the ruthenium red penetrated, the cell surfaces as well as synaptic clefts and basal laminae were intensely stained. The details of the surface coat staining are illustrated in Fig. 13 and insert. The inner leaflet of the plasma membrane is visible as a separate dark line while the other leaflet is masked by the staining in the intercellular cleft.

In 5-day cortex, large gaps between cell processes were bridged by a three-dimensional latticework of ruthenium red positive material (Figs. 10–13). The electron-opaque images are best described as straight spicules or rodlets about 100 Å in diameter and about 1 μ in length, extending in all directions. Where the gaps between cells are greater than 1 μ, spicules are joined by 200 to 300 Å masses of electron-dense material. These spicules and connecting masses are continuous with the cell coating and have the same granular characteristics. In the cases of 1 and 10-day cortex, where the extracellular spaces are not as large as at 5 days, the staining is largely limited to the cell surfaces.

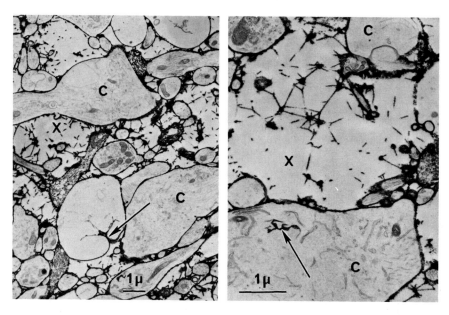

FIG. 10. Five-day cerebral cortex stained during fixation with ruthenium red. No counter stain other than osmium. The densely stained material is presumed protein polysaccharide coating cell surfaces as well as forming the spicules and spheres bridging the large extracellular spaces (X). When ruthenium red gains access to a cell via the cut surface of the block, the inside of the cell stains. Several unstained processes are labeled (C). Infolding of the plasma membrane is noted at the arrow.

FIG. 11. Micrograph of same tissue as Fig. 10. The large extracellular spaces (X) are unstained except where the complex of ruthenium-positive material forms a latticework. The cells or their processes (C) are also coated by polysaccharide. Intracisternal staining (arrow) may be continuous with the extracellular spaces as in Fig. 10. The subsurface cistern near arrow suggests that the lower cell (C) is neuronal.

The extracellular stain is rarely located in the 100-day cortex. The ruthenium red penetrates the narrow intercellular clefts in only a few places, and the staining was only found near the cut surface of the block. The synaptic clefts were prominently stained in contrast to the unstained neuropil but only within 25 μ of the surface of the block. This was the case even if no other staining took place. In contrast to the inconsistent staining of the extracellular spaces of the cortex, the spaces in subcortical white matter were bridged by spider weblike threads of stained material. The cell surfaces were covered by an electron-dense coating with the penetration of the ruthenium red into the myelin sheaths, staining the minor dense line.

The intracellular cytoplasm is also stained in some cases. Whenever a cell membrane is broken or cut (such as at the surface of the block), the ruthenium red gains access to the inside of the cell. The cytoplasm then becomes electron-dense, presumably due to the presence of acid protein groups. These profiles are easily recognized in the illustrations where the remaining cells and processes are pale and unstained. A second type of apparent intracellular staining is found occasionally when the interior of the cisterns of the smooth endoplasmic reticulum are stained (arrows Figs. 10-13). If these cisterns are sectioned in the appropriate plane, they are revealed to be continuous with the extracellular spaces. These apparent cisterns then are not intracellular but invaginations of the cell membrane (Fig. 10, arrow).

The unusual pattern of extracellular staining is present during the period of rapid neurite growth, when the extracellular spaces are the largest and the vascularity the least developed. Acid polysaccharides in the extracellular spaces may exert chemical or mechanical control over the direction of cell process

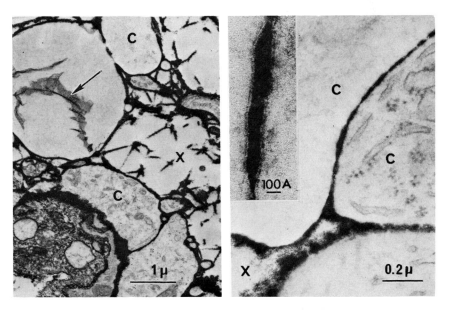

FIG. 12. Five-day cortex stained with ruthenium red and osmium to show the contacts between the surface coat, the spicules, and the connecting structures in the extracellular spaces. The cell in the lower left corner has been stained internally by rupture of its cell membranes. The process in the upper left displays the staining of intracellular cisterns.

FIG. 13. The granular nature of the ruthenium red positive material is demonstrated at high magnification where the extracellular spaces are large (X). The 100-250 Å cleft between two cells (C) is densely stained. A photographic enlargement (insert) of a portion of this contact demonstrates masking of the outer leaflet of the cell membrane by the extracellular staining. The inner leaflet of the unit membrane is visible as a separate dark line.

growth (Weiss, 1950). It may simply provide a supporting network for neurite growth. It may represent an active element in the extracellular spaces that opens them up, spreading the cells apart prior to the growth of the neuropil. The opening of the extracellular spaces may precede proliferation of the processes of the neuropil, providing a space and network into which the neurites grow. The shape of the material as visualized by this study could be an artifact of fixation or dehydration. The spaces might be filled with a homogeneous matrix. The spicules could be the result of precipitation of the polysaccharide by the dehydration procedures. The polysaccharides may form a matrix that permits rapid penetration of metabolites from distant vessels, during this growth period when vascularity is low.

The staining of the inside of the cisterns of intact cells with ruthenium red suggests that a canalicular system in developing cortical cells may be in continuity with the extracellular spaces. This is a new observation requiring further analysis to determine if it is an artifact of the method. In those cells which could be clearly identified, the cell membrane invaginations are present in neurons and neuroblasts and may simply represent transient cell invaginations (such as in phagocytosis) during growth.

III. CORRELATION BETWEEN ANATOMICAL, ELECTROPHYSIOLOGICAL, BEHAVIORAL, AND BIOCHEMICAL DEVELOPMENT

A. Electrophysiological Development

Cortical development is a continuous process of many simultaneous, parallel sequences that can be interrelated or independent. It is difficult to correlate the appearance of a given structure with the earliest recording of electrical activity (see Schiebel and Scheibel, Chapter 1, this volume). Nevertheless, Deza and Eidelberg (1967) have studied the development of electrical activity in great detail. Comparison of results may strengthen the conclusions reached here. Steady (DC) cortical and resting membrane potentials were present from birth. Action potential discharges not unlike those from adult cortex were present beginning on the fourth day and may represent the maturation of the neurons. The EEG activity becomes demonstrable from the sixth day, after the dendritic tree of the cortical neurons has developed. According to these authors, further maturation of the EEG to adult patterns reflects the relative closure of the extracellular spaces. When the extracellular spaces approach adult dimensions, at the end of the second week, spreading depression can first be elicited. These conclusions are in full agreement with this morphological study. A more detailed account of the development of EEG activity is presented by Rosen in Chapter 10.

B. Behavioral Development

The fetal rat displays only spasmodic twitching and general reflexes when stimulated. During the first postnatal week, the reflexes are essentially bulbospinal: breathing, crawling, sucking, righting, etc. During the second week the rats' behavior takes on more complex forms such as effective reactions to stimuli and play (Tilney, 1933). Between 7 and 10 days, the spinal reflexes become diminished. This is attributed to the development of cortical inhibition of the reflex arc via descending pathways (Flexner, 1955). While such crude behavioral methods tell us little about cortical development, at least the outward manifestations of cortical function are synchronized with anatomical maturation. More to the point would be the use of sensitive behavioral tests in the adult animal after manipulation of postnatal development. What behavioral deficits would arise by making lesions early in development? By raising and lowering thyroxine levels during development, examination of cerebral cortex would be compared with specific behavioral deficits. Of current interest would be a comparison between morphological and behavioral effects of postnatal malnutrition. The reader is referred to Chapters 17 and 19 in this volume for discussions of hormonal and nutritional influences on brain development.

C. Biochemical Development

The biochemical maturation of the cortex is only just being studied in detail sufficiently to allow comparison with structural studies (Bass *et al.,* 1969). Most studies consider the brain as a whole, without separate analysis for the cortex. For purposes of clarity, McIlwain (1966) has divided the development of the rat brain into four periods:

1. The fetal period when 97% of the cells appear, but the brain attains only 15% of its adult weight.
2. From birth to 10 days of age, when cell processes proliferate and the cortex attains almost mature size and weight.
3. Between 10 and 20 days of age, when myelination begins and the majority of the blood vessels develop.
4. From 20 days to puberty when the final stages of maturation and myelination are completed.

During McIlwain's first and second period of development the activity of most brain enzymes is only a fraction of that in the adult. The enzyme activities rise abruptly to mature levels during the third period (10-20 days). These changes in enzyme activities have been used as an index of brain maturation (McIlwain, 1966). If each enzyme is followed carefully in one structure, for example the cortex, instead of whole brain, there is not such an evident pattern of synchronous enzyme activation. Nevertheless, the parallel maturation changes from the chemical and anatomical approaches show promise for future study.

For example, counts of sectioned mitochondria in sample electron micrographs of cortex parallel the measured activity of cytochrome oxidase in cortex. Cytochrome oxidase is an oxidative enzyme associated with mitochondria. There are 25 mitochondria per 1000 μ^2 in rat cortex during the first week. There are 50 at 10 days, 76 at 15 days and 112 at 21 days (Caley, 1966). The levels of cytochrome oxidase enzyme activities in slices of cerebral cortex begin to rise at 10 days of age and attain adult level during the third period of development. This parallel increase in enzyme activity may not be simply a reflection of the development of the mitochondria. Nevertheless, the coincident rise in enzyme activity and the increase in numbers of mitochondria known to contain the enzyme may be significant. This rise in activity of an enzyme associated with oxidative metabolism corresponds to the same period in development when cortical sensitivity to anoxia develops. Perhaps this is due to the development of cortical dependency on oxygen that is more fundamental than extracellular spaces and blood supply, as discussed earlier.

IV. SUMMARY

It is useful to divide the maturation of postnatal rat cortical neuropil into three periods of 1 week each. The adult cortical thickness develops during the first week, due to the extensive proliferation of the dendritic tree of pyramidal neurons and the invasion of axons. At this time large extracellular spaces, few blood vessels, and presumptive synapses were found. The extracellular spaces contact the developing synapses and blood vessels. Ruthenium red positive material (presumed to be an acid polysaccharide) coats all cell surfaces and at 5 days bridges the extracellular spaces. The second week is a transition period. The blood vessel lamina open and the large extracellular spaces become reduced to 150-200 Å cleft. The astrocytic processes replace the extracellular spaces around the blood vessels and developing synapses. During the third week the changes lead to the establishment of the mature neuropil of tightly packed axons, dendrites, synapses, and glial processes.

ACKNOWLEDGMENT

The authors are indebted to Dr. Martin Netsky and Dr. Norman Bass for their critical review of this chapter and their helpful suggestions. Secretarial assistance of Mrs. Kathy Rubenstein and Mrs. Mary Loving is gratefully acknowledged. This work was supported in part by USPHS Grants NB 03604 and 07450.

REFERENCES

Aghajanian, G. K., and Bloom, F. E. (1967). *Brain Res. 6,* 716-727.
Bass, N. H., Netsky, M. G., and Young, E. (1969). *Neurology 19,* 258-267.
Bondareff, W. (1967). *Anat. Rec. 157,* 527-536.
Caley, D. W. (1966). Dissertation, University of California, Los Angeles, California.
Caley, D. W. (1969). *Anat. Rec. 163,* 163.
Caley, D. W. (1970). *In* "Cellular Aspects of Growth and Differentiation in Nervous Tissue" (D. C. Pease, ed.) U.C.L.A. Forum in Medical Sciences, University of California Press (in press).
Caley, D. W., and Maxwell, D. S. (1968a). *J. Comp. Neurol. 133,* 17-45.
Caley, D. W., and Maxwell, D. S. (1968b). *J. Comp. Neurol. 133,* 45-79.
Caley, D. W., and Maxwell, D. S. (1970). *J. Comp. Neurol. 138,* 31-48.
Craigie, E. H. (1925). *J. Comp. Neurol. 39,* 301-324.
Deza, L., and Eidelberg, E. (1967). *Exp. Neurol. 17,* 425-438.
Fazekas, J. F., Alexander, F. A. D., and Himwich, H. E. (1941). *Amer. J. Physiol. 134,* 281-287.
Flexner, L. B. (1955). *In* "Biochemistry of the Developing Nervous System" (H. Waelsch, ed.), pp. 281-294. Academic Press, New York.
Hess, A. (1955). *J. Comp. Neurol. 102,* 65-73.
Klosovski, B. N. (1965). "The Development of the Brain and its Disturbance by Harmful Factors." Pergamon Press, Oxford.
Langman, J. (1968). *In* "The Structure and Function of Nervous Tissue" (G. H. Bourne, ed.), Vol. 1, pp. 33-64. Academic Press, New York.
Luft, J. (1965). *J. Cell Biol. 27,* 61A.
McIlwain, H. (1966). *In* "Biochemistry and the Central Nervous System," pp. 270-299. Churchill, London.
Meyers, W. J. (1969). *Anat. Rec. 163,* 229.
Pease, D. C. (1966). *J. Ultrastruct. Res. 15,* 555-588.
Rambourg, A., and Leblond, C. P. (1967). *J. Cell Biol. 32,* 27-53.
Rambourg, A., Neutra, M., and Leblond, C. P. (1966). *Anat. Rec. 154,* 41-71.
Schade, J. P., and Baxter, C. F. (1960). *In* "Inhibition in the Nervous System and GABA" (E. Roberts, ed.), pp. 207-213. Pergamon Press, Oxford.
Spector, R. G. (1962). *Brit. J. Exp. Pathol. 43,* 472-479.
Stensaas, L. J., and Stensaas, S. S. (1968). *Zeitschrift für Zellforschung 91,* 341-364.
Strong, L. H. (1961). *Acta Anta. 44,* 80-108.
Sugita, N. (1917). *J. Comp. Neurol. 28,* 495-591.
Sugita, N. (1918). *J. Comp. Neurol. 29,* 1-278.
Tilney, F. (1933). *Bull. Neurol. Inst. New York 3,* 252-258.
Van Harreveld, A., Crowell, J., and Malhotra, S. K. (1965). *J. Cell Biol. 25,* 117-137.
Vaughn, J. E. (1969). *Z. f. Zellforsch. 94,* 293-324.
Vaughn, J. E., and Peters, A. (1967). *Amer. J. Anat. 121,* 131-151.
Weiss, P. (1950). "Problems of the Development, Growth, Regeneration of the Nervous System and its Functions." Univ. of Chicago Press, Chicago, Illinois.

CHAPTER 7   Postnatal Neurochemical Development of the Retina: A Prototype of Regional CNS Ontogeny

Richard N. Lolley

I. INTRODUCTION

An unformalized feeling that has for a number of years pervaded research in physiological psychology is now becoming of concern to neurochemistry. In a simplified form the premise can be stated as follows: Biochemical correlates of a definite neural function will be most clearly discernible in the anatomical regions of the nervous system which are actively participating in that pattern of neural response. This generalization applies equally to such diverse neural response patterns as the spinal reflex, on-off responses in the visual system, or sleep-arousal cycles in mammals. In each of these patterns of response, particular regions of the CNS are probably involved preferentially. One of the underlying results of this experimental philosophy, which is independent of the validity of the above premise, is the increasing interest in the functional and biochemical characteristics of anatomical regions within the CNS.

From a technical point of view, the strict localization of biochemical changes within discrete regions of the CNS is very difficult. Only the biochemistry of stable molecules has been possible by conventional techniques, since the *in vivo* content of labile compounds is dramatically affected while obtaining regional samples, i.e., by anesthesia, disruption of blood supply or surgical dissection. Special techniques, such as electron microscopic autoradiography and fluorescence microscopy, have made great advances in the study of protein synthesis and catecholamine metabolism in particular regions of the CNS. As special techniques have overcome traditional failings in biochemical studies, so also may the developmental patterns of specific regions of the CNS further the understanding of regional differences within the CNS.

The study of visual physiology is well advanced and the participation of the retina, lateral geniculate body, primary and secondary visual association centers in visual performance tasks have been discussed elsewhere in this book (Rose, Chapter 9). It is of general interest, however, that the involvement of the retina in the processing of visual information varies greatly between species. The degree of retinal participation seems to vary inversely with the level of development of the visual cortex; the retina of man is involved less in the processing of visual information than that of a frog or pigeon (Dowling, 1968).

While our knowledge of the biochemistry of the visual system is still rudimentary, much is known about the biochemistry of the retina. Indeed, our knowledge of the biochemistry of the retina exceeds that of any other region of the CNS. The metabolic and synthetic capacity of the retina has been explored by standard *in vitro* methodology and biochemical techniques. In addition, quantitative histochemical and fluorescent microscopic studies have mapped the distribution of numerous enzymes, substrates of metabolism, and synaptic transmitter agents within the structure of the adult retina. Concurrently, other investigators have demonstrated the electrical response of the individual neurons within the retina to flashing light (Werblin and Dowling, 1969), and others are identifying the neural circuitry within the retina by three-dimensional reconstruction from serial montages (Sjöstrand, 1961; Missotten, 1965; Dowling and Werblin, 1969). Soon, a complete picture of the anatomy, physiology, and neurochemistry of the retina may appear. Viewing the increasing volume of scientific literature which is related to the retina, the process seems to be autocatalytic since, as information accumulates, more investigators become interested in the retina, both as a prototype for study of regional biochemistry of the CNS and as a tissue with functional features of interest in itself.

II. MATURATION OF THE ELECTRORETINOGRAM (ERG)

This chapter shall concern itself exclusively with the events that occur after birth and with the changes that occur in the retina during the critical period of early postnatal life. Since the stage of maturity of the retina differs for different animal species, it is important to restrict the discussion to one animal species or to those that are very similar. The mouse retina has been studied with respect to its physiology, anatomy, and biochemistry and appears to offer the most comprehensive model for a discussion of the retina as a functioning tissue.

The retina of the mouse is functional when the animal opens his eyes at 11 to 12 postnatal days (Noell, 1965). This observation applies also to other animals (Hubel and Wiesel, 1963). Considering the electroretinogram (ERG) as an average measure of the electrical activity of the whole retina, gross electrical activity begins at about 9 postnatal days in the mouse (C57B1 mouse; Noell, 1965) and at 8 days in the rabbit (Noell, 1958).

A statement should be interjected at this point to clarify the reasoning behind the selection of the ERG as the physiological parameter for discussion. The alternative parameter would be the response of individual cell types to a particular visual stimulus. The selective response of the individual neurons of the adult retina to a flash of light has been investigated. In vertebrate retinas, the photoreceptor cells hyperpolarize, the horizontal and bipolar cells depolarize, and the amacrine and ganglion cells produce action potentials. The Muller cells appear to be the only glial element, and their electrophysiological response to light is yet unknown. The collective interaction of these cells to produce a gross response is still unclear. Even if it was known, however, it would be impossible to relate the electrophysiological activities of the individual neurons with biochemical data from the whole retina, or from the retinal layers. Eventually, biochemical methodology will become sufficiently sensitive and sophisticated so that the biochemistry of single cells may be related to the functional properties of that cell; but, at present, it seems necessary to relate the physiology and biochemistry from comparable levels of sophistication. In keeping with this philosophy, the physiological maturation of the retina will be discussed with reference to the ERG and the biochemistry of maturation with reference to representative samples of complete retina.

The maturation of the electrical response appears to follow similar patterns of development in most animal species. That of the rabbit has been studied in detail (Noell 1958). The level of visual adaptation appears to influence the mechanisms which generate the ERG because the pattern of development of the electrical response differs under photopic and scotopic conditions.

Under illuminated conditions, the photopic response of the rabbit retina is well developed before the eyes of the animal open. By 11 days, the retina responds to high intensity flicker stimulation. At 18 postnatal days, the flicker responses are essentially mature with no significant changes occurring after 30 to 90 days.

The above electrical response patterns also apply to single stimulus-evoked responses of the retina in a dark-adapted state. By 9 postnatal days, the whole pathway from photoreceptor to ganglion cell appears to be functional. Recordings from platinum electrodes indicate that the ganglion cells discharge in response to illumination of subliminal intensity for activation of the scotopic electrical response. At this early age, spontaneous ganglion cell activity as well as excitatory and inhibitory phenomena in response to illumination are evident.

The scotopic ERG of the rabbit retina makes its first appearance at about 8 postnatal days when miniature sensory receptors have developed in the central region. In contrast to the photopic response of the retina, the scotopic ERG develops to its mature form rather slowly. Its development has generally two aspects: (1) a general increase in amplitude and reaction rates, and (2) maturation of the adult relationship between a- and b-wave.

The early ERG consists mainly of a cornea-negative potential which resembles the isolated a-wave of the adult retina. A b-wave cannot be detected at this early age. The amplitude of the a-wave increases and the delay decreases until, by 18 days, the early portion of the ERG resembles that of the adult.

While the b-wave is not apparent in the very young retina, two distinct waves of cornea-positivity follow the a-wave. They are evident only with intense illumination. As maturation progresses, they merge with the rising phase of the developing b-wave. At 11 days, the b-wave has clearly developed but the a-wave is still the dominant feature of the ERG. By 18 days, the form of the ERG resembles that of an adult but it is still deficient in b-wave. By 80-90 days, the ERG is adult in all respects.

The electrophysiological data clearly indicate that the a-wave of the scotopic ERG appears some 3 to 4 days before the b-wave. The a-wave is thought to originate in the photoreceptors of the retina (Brown *et al.*, 1965) and the b-wave

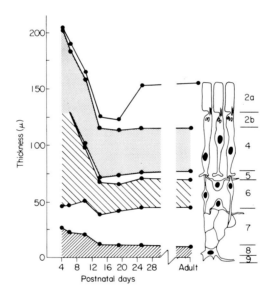

FIG. 1. Cytoarchitectural changes in developing retinas of DBA/1J mice. Eyes from immature and adult mice were rapidly excised, the sclera and lens were removed in gluteralde-hyde phosphate buffer, and the eye cups were cut into quadrants. Each sample was fixed in gluteraldehyde-phosphate (2 hr), postfixed in osmium (1 hr) and embedded in epon. Sections (1 μ), perpendicular to the tangent of the eye, where cut from the central portion of each quadrant (alignment being assessed by the shortest dimension across the retina), stained with toluidine blue and visualized by a Leitz microscope with micrometer attach-ment. The measured layers of the retina are illustrated schematically and labeled as follows: (layer 1, pigment epithelium was omitted); 2a, receptor outer segments; 2b, receptor inner segment; 4, receptor nuclei; 5, outer synaptic region; 6, bipolar layer containing horizontal and amacrine cells on the outer and inner boundaries, respectively; 7, inner synaptic region; 8, ganglion cell bodies; 9, nerve fibers.

at an inner retinal level (Dowling, 1967). In the next section, a morphological explanation for this sequence of electrical activity will be discussed.

III. MATURATION OF CELLULAR AND SYNAPTIC MORPHOLOGY

After birth, cellular division continues for some time (birth to 10 days). At this point, all the cellular types are differentiated and the cellular layers of the retina are established (Fig. 1). During the next several days, the retina grows to its adult dimensions through growth of the individual cell types (Table I).

TABLE I   DNA Content of Immature Mice Retinas[a]

	Complete retina			
Post-natal days	μg dry wt./retina	μg DNA/retina	10^6 Cells/retina	pg[b] dry wt./av. cell
5	410	41	6	68
10	436	44	6	72
30	584	41	6	97
	Retinal layers			
Post-natal days	Layer	μg DNA/μg dry wt.	10^3 Cells/μg dry wt.	pg[b] Dry wt./av. cell
10	Receptor	0.100	14	71
	Bipolar + ganglion	0.075	11	91
Adult	Receptor	0.061	9	111
	Bipolar + ganglion	0.065	9	111

[a]DNA and RNA were measured spectrophotometrically in extracts of PCA. Complete retinas were removed from freshly enucleated eyes in isotonic saline, lyophilized, weighed and extracted successively with chloroform-methanol, removing lipids; with cold PCA, removing RNA; and with hot PCA, removing DNA. Samples from specific layers of the retina were obtained by microdissection of frozen-dried sections, but otherwise treated similarly. In calculating the number of cells per unit of retina, the average cell was assumed to be diploid and to contain 7×10^{-12} gm DNA/cell.

[b]pg = 10^{-12} gm.

Even the most superficial inspection of a histological section from a 1 to 4-day-old mouse retina reveals numerous points of dissimilarity with the mature structure. The photoreceptor and bipolar layers are still unformed; the outer synaptic region is absent. Mitotic figures can be identified at the scleral border of the neural retina. Almost two-thirds of the retina appear to be undifferentiated. The one third which appears mature lies at the inner border of the retina and contains the ganglion cells and a clearly identifiable synaptic layer.

Light-microscopic studies have given support to the view that the retina matures morphologically in a centrifugal sequence from inner to outer layers with ganglion cells maturing before the photoreceptors. But the a-wave of the ERG which is believed to arise at the level of the photoreceptors can be observed several days before the b-wave, which is believed to arise at the level of the inner synaptic layer (see Section II). The electrophysiological data suggest that the retina matures in a centripetal sequence from outer to inner layers with photoreceptors maturing before the ganglion cells. This apparent contradiction probably reflects only our inability to compare the two experimental observations. Electron microscopic findings appear to confirm the sequence of maturation suggested by the electrophysiological data.

Assuming that the formation of synaptic junctions precedes any meaningful electrophysiological performance in the retina, Olney (1968a) has studied, by electron microscopy, the sequence of appearance of identifiable synaptic junctions within the layers of the developing mouse retina. His investigation indicates that a significant number of synaptic junctions are present in the primitive outer synaptic layer as early as the second postnatal day. The morphogenesis of the photoreceptor synaptic complex proceeds nearly to completion between the second and twelfth day.

Synaptic junctions in the inner plexiform layer were not present in early postnatal life, even though the gross morphology appears mature. A few typical bipolar terminals with synaptic vesicles, early forms of synaptic lamellae, and the dyad synaptic contacts began to form between the tenth and twelfth day. Development of the inner synaptic layer advanced rapidly after this age and, by the twentieth day, the synaptic junctions are adultlike in form. A similar sequence of development of synaptic junctions was observed in the retina of the rat. In addition to establishing a meaningful morphological basis for the electrophysiological findings, these experiments seem to signal that caution be employed in inferring definitive maturational sequences from light microscopic layering appearances in other regions of the CNS (Olney, 1968b).

By the time the retina has formed into layers, cellular division has terminated and it then begins a period of active growth (Table I). There is structural growth in the photoreceptor layer and in the cellular ramifications of the inner synaptic region. Much of the increase in the mass of the photoreceptor cell during development probably arises from the increasing size of the receptor organelle.

The photoreceptor is a biological transducer and its morphology is inseparable from its physiological role. So also is its chemistry, a continuum of its morphology. Figure 2 shows inner and outer segments of an immature mouse retina (DBA/1J mouse: 10 postnatal days). At this stage the synaptic contacts are already established but the inner and outer segments of the photoreceptor cell have only begun to mature. The length of the outer segment is one measure of its state of development. Another is the quantity of visual pigment (vitamin

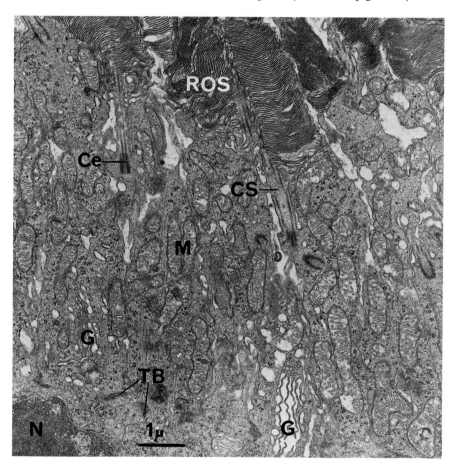

FIG. 2. Cytological features of photoreceptor cells in 10-day-old retina of DBA/1J mouse. Eyes were prepared, fixed, and embedded as described in Fig. 1. Sections of retina were stained with uranyl acetate and lead citrate and viewed with an Hitachi microscope (Model HS7S). The cellular components are labeled as follows: N, nucleus of photoreceptor cell; TB, terminal bars marking the outer limiting membrane; G, Golgi and M, mitochondria of the photoreceptor inner segment; Ce, centriole and CS, connecting stalk of the receptor outer segment (ROS). (Lolley and Erickson, 1970.)

A-opsin complex) that is present in the retina, for the visual pigments are an integral part of the structural matrix of only the photoreceptor organelle (Fig. 3). Both change during development with the same time index, reaching mature levels at about 30-40 postnatal days in mice and rats. Since visual pigment metabolism is unaltered when animals are reared in light or darkness (Dowling and Sidman, 1962), the biochemical changes, which are responsible for the activation and continuation of the synthesis of visual pigment, seem to be genetically programmed in the photoreceptor cell.

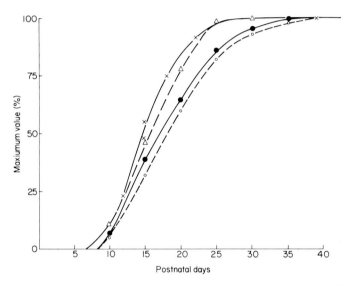

FIG. 3. Concurrent growth in length of photoreceptor outer segments and concentration of visual pigment, rhodopsin. Maximum values are as follows: length of rat ROS (X), 23.5 μ; concentration of rhodopsin per rat eye (0), 0.06 extinction[500]/eye/vol (Dowling and Sidman, 1962); concentration of rhodopsin per DBA/1J mouse eye (●), 16.7 extinction[500]/eye/vol or per milligram retina (△), 1.05 extinction[500]/wt of retinal/vol (Caravaggio and Bonting, 1963).

The visual system passes through a critical period of development (first 3 months of life in cat) in which an absence of visual stimuli results in blindness to the occluded eye (Hubel, 1967). Little is known about the biochemical mechanisms which are involved in producing this blindness or to what extent the visual environment, during early postnatal life, affects the metabolic potentials of the retina itself. The histology (light-microscopy of cat retina) indicates that the retina is less affected by light deprivation than other regions of the visual system. Still, it will be interesting to see from future experimentation whether the neurochemistry of a light-deprived retina might also exhibit a critical period of development which limits the functional potential of the retina of an adult animal.

IV. BIOCHEMICAL ASPECTS OF MATURATION

Having superficially explored the physiology and anatomy of the developing retina, using the mouse retina as the prototype whenever possible, the groundwork has been set from which to begin a more detailed discussion of the changes in biochemistry which occur during early postnatal development.

A. Protein Synthesis, Nucleic Acids, and the Hexose Monophosphate Shunt (HMS)

During early postnatal development, there are physical sings of growth which indicate that protein synthesis proceeds at an active pace (Table I). The protein content of the rat retina increases by 40% between 4 and 30 postnatal days (Hall, 1970). By contrast, when rat retinas of various ages are incubated with radioactive amino acids *in vitro,* the rate of incorporation of amino acids into proteins decreases with increasing age until a steady "turnover" rate is established (Fig. 4). As in the brain, the *in vitro* rate of protein synthesis is most rapid during the period of development in which cellular division occurs (birth to 10 days).

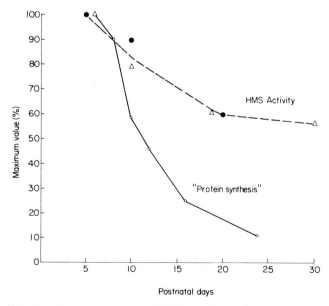

FIG. 4. Hexose monophosphate shunt (HMS) activity and *in vitro* "protein synthesis" in immature retinas. Maximum values are as follows: $1\text{-}^{14}CO_2$ released from glucose oxidation in retinas of DBA/1J mice (●), 4.5 mμmoles/retina/75 min (Noell, 1965); proportion of CO_2 released from shunt, glucose-1-^{14}C, compared to that from oxidative reactions, glucose-6-^{14}C in rat retinas (△), 2.9; glycine-^{14}C incorporated into protein during incubation of rat retinas (0), 16.7 mμmoles/mg protein (Reading, 1965).

A discussion of the biochemistry of protein synthesis requires some knowledge of the nucleic acids that support the synthetic process. Relatively little is known about DNA or RNA metabolism in the retina. However, autoradiographic studies indicate that both of these nucleic acids are synthesized within the developing retina and that the turnover rates of DNA and RNA differ during postnatal development; synthesis of DNA virtually terminating by 10 postnatal days, when cellular division ceases, metabolism of RNA continuing throughout life in a fashion that maintains a fixed RNA/DNA ratio (Table II).

TABLE II   RNA and Protein Content of the Developing Retina [a]

Postnatal days	μg RNA/μg dry wt.[b]	RNA/DNA[b]	μg protein/retina[c]
5	0.042	0.39	900
10	0.038	0.38	1200
20	0.028	0.34	1150
Adult	0.025	0.35	1300

[a]RNA values were determined spectrophotometrically as described in Table I.
[b]Mouse retina.
[c]Rat retina.

When cellular division ceases, the adult retina renews its cellular constituents by synthetic mechanisms. The protein "turnover" rate in adult brain is rapid, with the majority of proteins exhibiting a half-life of less than 20 days (Lajtha and Marks, 1969). A comparable figure for protein "turnover" in the retina has not been determined, but the half-life of opsin, the protein portion of the visual pigment, has been shown by electron microscopic autoradiography to be about 5-6 days in the retinas of adult mice or rats (Young, 1967). Major differences in "turnover" rate exist between species; the half-life of opsin in frogs is about 2.5-3.5 weeks.

In keeping with the historical tendency of scientists to seek quantitative descriptions of biochemical events, RNA and protein have been measured in retinas at various stages of development (Table II). Although the content of RNA or protein fails to indicate the relative proportion of the different classes of either RNA or protein that are being synthesized in the retina at any stage of development, the change in activity of particular enzymes during this period does offer a reasonably accurate portrayal of the activation and suppression of the synthesis of certain proteins during differentiation. During development, the concentration of some enzymes increases while that of others declines (Bonavita, 1965). Generally, only the enzymes associated with the hexose monophosphate shunt (HMS) decrease during development. The relative proportion of glucose which is degraded through the HMS is accordingly reduced (Fig. 4). As the activity of the HMS declines, the capacity for the production of ribulose-5-P diminishes. Therefore, by limiting the production of ribulose-5-P, the HMS influences indirectly the level of nucleic acid synthesis in the developing retina.

With recent advances in electron microscopic autoradiography, more dynamic illustrations of the complete sequence of protein synthesis are available, the synthesis of opsin being a pertinent example. It is informative to consider the different stages of protein metabolism (from RNA synthesis to protein degradation) as they proceed within the photoreceptor cell and to attempt to visualize these events as they might occur in other regions of the CNS.

In a recent series of experiments, Young and Bok have outlined the life history of the protein, opsin, following it from synthesis to utilization and ultimate degradation. The sequence of events is identical in the retinas of both immature and adult animals. The RNA and protein of the photoreceptor cell is in a continual state of renewal. Following an injection of radioactive cytidine, a precursor of RNA, the visual cells take up the nucleotide, concentrate it in the nucleus, and use it in the synthesis of RNA. A portion of the newly synthesized RNA passes through the nuclear membrane and migrates into the inner segment of the photoreceptor (see Fig. 2 for morphology). Some of the newly synthesized RNA remains within the nucleus, probably to participate in protein synthesis in that location. It is the migrating RNA, however, which contains the coded message for opsin synthesis. The labeled RNA ultimately settles in an area of the photoreceptor inner segment which is densely populated with ribosomes (Bok, 1968).

The assemblage of amino acids into protein occurs within the inner segment of the photoreceptor cells at precisely the site where the migration of RNA terminated. Subsequent to an injection of radioactive amino acids, the photoreceptor cell accumulates amino acids and assembles them into proteins. The protein molecules move from the ribosomes to the Golgi complex, perhaps there to receive an addition of carbohydrate. From the inner segment of the photoreceptor, newly synthesized proteins travel to their site of utilization (Young and Droz, 1968).

A small portion of protein remains in the inner segment of the photoreceptor cell. Possibly these proteins are associated with the general metabolism of the cell.

A second and major portion of newly synthesized protein migrates past the mitochondria of the inner segment, passes through the connecting cilium into the outer segment, and is there assembled into membranes at the base of the rod outer segment. This protein has been conclusively identified as opsin (Hall *et al.*,

1968). The protein is gradually displaced along the outer segments as a discrete band. When the moving band reaches the distal extremity of the outer segment, it is removed by the pigment epithelium of the retina (Young and Bok, 1969). The membranes of the outer segment can be recognized as "phagasomes" until they are degraded beyond recognition.

Cone photoreceptors renew the proteins of their outer segment in a strikingly different manner than that just described for rod cells. Newly synthesized protein crosses the inner segment and passes the connective cilium, as it does in neighboring rod cells, but thereafter a different process appears to operate for the outer segment membranes of cones. Membranes are renewed randomly within the structure of the cone by a process of "exchange" rather than *de novo* "reconstruction," as observed in the rod photoreceptor (Young, 1969).

A third portion of newly synthesized protein, intermediate in proportion to the two described above, filters past the nucleus and migrates to the synaptic body of the photoreceptor. The time course and pattern of protein migration are similar for both rods and cones.

If the migration of protein within the photoreceptor cell was unique to this cell, it would be of limited interest, but recent studies have shown that the intracellular transport of protein is common in nerve cells (Hyden, 1967). One need only cross to the opposite side of the retina for another example to illustrate this point. Two waves of protein move from the ganglion cells of the retina to the brain along the nerves of the optic tract following an injection of leucine-^{3}H. One moves rapidly at about 110-115 mm/day; the other quite slowly at 1-2 mm/day (Karlsson and Sjöstrand, 1968). Neither group of proteins has been specifically identified, but the accumulation of synaptic transmitters proximal to a nerve ligation suggests that the rapidly migrating fraction reflects the movement of synaptic vesicles along the axon (Dahlstrom and Haggendal, 1966). The slow wave of protein may be associated with the axon membrane if neurons renew the proteins of their axons by a process which is analogous to the renewal of rod photoreceptor membranes.

The process of protein synthesis has been expanded in this section to include the ancillary systems that support the actual synthetic process and the intracellular dispersal of some completed proteins. Our attention will now be directed from the chemical nature of a protein to some biochemical properties of protein molecules.

B. Glucose and Energy Metabolism

Numerous biochemical changes may be associated with the maturation of a fully functional retina. A variety of chemical systems arise during the course of differentiation. Furthermore, functional activity may provide further environmental cues for the induction of biochemical systems (Lolley, 1969) and for the maintenance of the differentiated state. Even though little information is at hand to allow a distinction between genetic and functional methods for enzyme induction, changes in the activity of the enzyme, hexokinase (Fig. 5), and in the rate of glycolysis during development (Graymore, 1958) strongly support the conclusion that the influence of differentiation is predominant during early postnatal life. These changes are precise and synchronized in the retina as compared to the brain, but even in the brain the sharp increase in metabolism during development seems to coincide with the critical phases of differentiation (Waelsch, 1955).

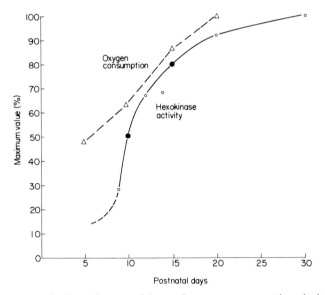

FIG. 5. Changes in hexokinase activity and oxygen consumption during postnatal development of retinas from DBA/1J mice. Maximum values are as follows: Oxygen uptake during incubation (Δ), 270 mμmoles/retina/75 min (Noell, 1965); hexokinase activity was measured fluorometrically after homogenization of freshly excised retinas. Animals were reared either in normal conditions of diurnal lighting (0) or in total darkness (●), 9.0 mmoles/g dry wt/hr.

The retina undergoes a maturational shift in metabolism from glycolysis to oxygen dependence but to a far lesser extent than brain. The capacity for converting glucose to lactic acid in the retina increases during development (Fig. 5), displaying the same pattern of change as aerobic respiration (Graymore *et al.,* 1959). Contrary to most tissues of the body, the production of lactic acid proceeds at a rapid rate both in the presence and absence of oxygen (anaerobic and aerobic glycolysis, respectively).

A teleological and a biochemical argument can be developed to account for this metabolic feature of the retina which is also found in embryonic tissues, tumor cells, and leukocytes.

The teleological argument attempts to explain through retrospection how the retina survived in an environment which was poorly supplied with oxygen. It questions whether the great capacity for glycolysis in the retina was an adaptation to its poorly developed blood supply or whether the distribution of blood vessels in the retina was an adaptation to its metabolic chemistry. Deductive reasoning from the following loosely related observations seems to favor the former alternative.

Even though the adult retinas of most living species have some degree of vascularity, the primitive retina was probably devoid of blood supply and, therefore, heavily dependent upon glycolysis for its maintenance. Today, only the adult retinas of rabbits and guinea pigs are completely avascular. Most other animal species have variable degrees of vascular penetration into the retina but even the retinas of these animals are avascular at birth. In mice retinas, the ingrowth of capillaries begins on about the second postnatal day at the vitreal border of the retina (Olney, 1968a). The arborization of the vascular tree enlarges until adulthood. Even then, the photoreceptor layer remains completely avascular.

The present degree of vascularity in the retina does not appear to control the distribution of glycolytic enzymes within the layers of the retina. A comparison of the distribution of the enzyme, hexokinase, in the avascular (rabbit) and vascular (monkey) retinas of adult animals indicates that the enzyme has a similar distribution pattern in the retinas of both species (Fig. 6). The distribution of hexokinase in monkey and rabbit retinas suggests similar expression of genetic information in both species. Therefore, it seems likely that a blood

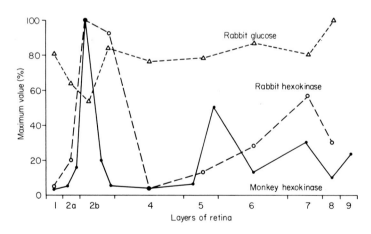

FIG. 6. Distribution of hexokinase and glucose within the layers of the retina. Values were obtained by standard histochemical techniques. Hexokinase activity of monkey retina (●), 27 mmoles/g of fat-free dry wt/hr; hexokinase activity of rabbit retina (0), 14.2 mmoles/g of fat-free dry wt/hr (Lowry, 1964); glucose content of rabbit retina (△), 14.6 μmoles/g dry wt (Matschinsky *et al.,* 1968).

supply to the retina from the vitreal border is a recent evolutionary event which has yet to influence the course of cellular differentiation within the retina.

The biochemical capacity of the retina to utilize glucose and to produce lactic acid or carbon dioxide by glycolysis or aerobic oxidation is established by the availability of specific enzyme systems within the retina. Comparing retina and brain, the enzymes which are associated with the glycolytic pathway or the citric acid cycle seem very similar in their physical and kinetic properties. Lactic dehydrogenase (LDH) appears to be the striking exception to this generalization since isoenzymes of LDH in the CNS promote aerobic respiration; the LDH of the retina and peripheral nerve facilitates glycolysis (Lowenthal *et al.*, 1964).

The biochemical argument explains the high level of aerobic glycolysis in the retina by the ability of its LDH to compete with respiration for the available pyruvate. LDH exists as a tetrameric combination of two distinct "M" and "H" subunits, designated by their predominance in muscle (4 M; M-LDH) and heart (4 H; H-LDH) tissues, respectively. The M subunits are characteristic of "anoxic" tissues and the H subunits are typically found in highly oxygenated tissues. M-LDH is the major and H-LDH is the minor isoenzyme of the immature retina. Their relative activities during development vary, but M-LDH remains dominant into adulthood (Graymore, 1963; Bonavita, 1965).

Subtle differences between the H and M forms of LDH are now becoming clear. They are distinctly different enzymes which display remarkably different kinetic properties. While both seem able to utilize either NADH or NADPH as the cofactor in the reduction of pyruvate, they respond differently to the substrate, pyruvate; the M form is unaffected by the level of substrate. The H form is inhibited by increasing concentrations of pyruvate (Graymore, 1966). This characteristic of the M enzyme facilitates the production of lactic acid during active glycolysis when levels of pyruvate may rise. For example, as the level of pyruvate rises, the relative activity of the M- and H-LDH increases and decreases, respectively. Therefore, the quantity of pyruvate which is converted to lactic acid depends upon the relative activity of the M- and H-LDH enzymes in the tissue. In retina, the remarkable ability of the M enzyme to compete successfully with aerobic oxidation for pyruvate is indicated by its high level of aerobic glycolysis.

The rates of oxygen consumption (Fig. 5) and carbon dioxide release by the retina illustrate the rapid onset of aerobic oxidation between 10 and 20 post-natal days (Noell, 1965). Correspondingly, the sharp fall in levels of tissue glucose suggest that glucose consumption has also accelerated (Fig. 7). These alterations in metabolism fit in exact temporal relationship with changes in the enzyme capacity to mobilize glucose, i.e., hexokinase (Fig. 5). The effects of the change in metabolic state are reflected throughout the pool of glucose metabolites, i.e., lactic acid and glycogen content (Fig. 7).

A relatively constant pool of glucose is supplied to the retina by the circulating blood. In mice, the concentration of glucose in the blood increases only slightly (9.35 to 9.95mmoles/liter) during maturation (Mayman, 1969), The transfer features and the time course of development of the blood-retinal barrier are still unclear, but it seems unlikely that the transfer of glucose restricts metabolism during this period.

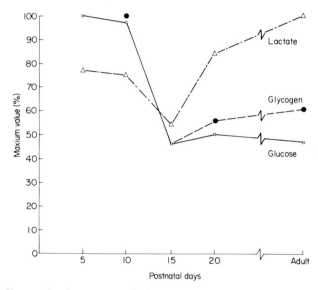

FIG. 7. Changes in the content of glucose and related metabolites during postnatal development of retinas from DBA/1J mice. Animals reared in normal conditions of lighting were frozen in isopentane (cooled with liquid nitrogen). Eyes were removed on Dry Ice, sectioned at $-20°C$ and lyophilized. Samples of retina were obtained by microdissection, weighed, and extracted with perchloric acid. The neutralized extracts were assayed by standard enzyme-linked fluorometric methods. Maximum values are as follows: glucose (0), 14.4 μmoles/g dry wt; glycogen (●), 13.9 μmoles/g dry wt; lactate (△), 30.5 μmoles/g dry wt.

Steady-state levels of glucose in the retina indicate only the relative balance between the reactions that synthesize and those which degrade it. In carbohydrate, lipid, or protein metabolism, the number of reactions that are involved in the synthesis or degradation of a particular compound are enumerable, e.g., metabolic pathways (Long, 1961). However, many reactions either utilize or yield biological energy in the form of ATP. This mechanism is so universally common that the reactions which synthesize or degrade ATP seem innumerable.

Collectively, ATP and P-creatine represent the pool of rapidly mobilizable energy, since they are tightly coupled by the enzyme, P-creatine transferase. The level of both ATP and P-creatine declines during postnatal development (Fig. 8), even though ATP is produced at a higher rate in the mature retina (assessed from O_2 consumption). Since the reactions which produce a balance between ATP synthesis and degradation are unknown, only a calculated guess can be made as to their identity.

The following sequence represents such a conjecture for the utilization of ATP: In the early stages of development, energy is used almost exclusively for the synthesis of cellular constituents. Later, the differentiated cells become functional, and, by maturity, the major share of cellular energy is degraded in the maintenance of ionic gradients and in the mechanisms of neural excitation.

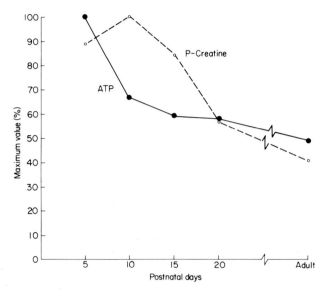

FIG. 8. Alterations in the high-energy phosphate pool during postnatal development of retinas from DBA/1J mice. Animals were reared normally. Freezing and processing of the eyes were performed in the same fashion as described in Fig. 7 but different enzyme-linked fluorometric assays were employed. Maximum values are as follows: ATP (●), 17.4 μmoles/g dry wt; P-creatine (0), 14.9 μmoles/g dry wt.

C. Excitation and Synaptic Transmission

It is unknown to what extent differentiation influences the metabolism of chemical transmitter agents. However, judging from the observation that morphologically identifiable synaptic junctions precede the appearance of functional activity in the retina (Section III), it is consistent to postulate that the biochemical mechanisms for synthesis, release, "re-uptake" and degradation of transmitter agents either precede or coincide with the formation of synaptic contacts. While a correlation between the genesis of synaptic junctions and of transmitter agents has not been established in the retina, it is known that the content of catecholamines in the retinas of the chick increases sharply in the first 4 days after hatching (Laties, 1969).

By adulthood, the functional characteristics of the retina are established and, as in other regions of the CNS, there appears to be an integrated balance between excitatory and inhibitory phenomena. Two synaptic regions within the retina and an unknown number of synaptic transmitter agents are involved in processing the electrical signal which is carried from the retina to the brain.

The outer synaptic region (see Fig. 1 for anatomy of the retina) contains axonal extensions of the photoreceptor cells and the dendritic branches of bipolar and horizontal cells (Sjöstrand, 1961; Missotten, 1965). Synaptic junctions are numerous in this region and the elaborate axonal terminal of the photoreceptor cell is richly supplied with synaptic vesicles. The presynaptic ending resembles an inverted chalice, the postsynaptic endings forming contacts within the cup and along the rim. The design of this synapse differs from all others in the retina, and its structure may be instrumental in preserving or accumulating transmitter agents within the region of the postsynaptic membranes.

Since the synaptic endings in the outer synaptic region contain numerous vesicles, a chemical form of transmission has been presumed. However, none of the transmitter agents which have been proposed for other parts of the CNS is localized within the outer synaptic region. Another feature of this region also appears exceptional. While excitable membranes are customarily enriched with a Na-K ATPase (pump mechanism), this region seems unusually deficient (Matschinsky, 1969). Therefore, the mode of synaptic transmission within the outer synaptic portion of the retina is still unresolved.

The inner synaptic region of the retina is anatomically quite complex. Bipolar, amacrine, and ganglion cell processes extend into this region and innumerable synaptic junctions occur between bipolar/amacrine, bipolar/ganglion, and amacrine/amacrine cells (Dowling, 1968). The relative proportion of individual combinations varies in the retinas of different species. For example, the relative number of amacrine/amacrine junctions decreases in frog, rabbit, and monkey retinas, respectively. A correlation has been suggested between the complexity of visual stimuli, which is required to initiate electrical activity in ganglion cells, and the relative abundance of amacrine/amacrine synaptic contacts (Dowling, 1968). The developmental aspects of this relationship (interneuron/interneuron junctions) have not been investigated.

In keeping with the synaptic complexity of the inner synaptic region, a number of potential synaptic transmitter agents have been identified within this region. Dopamine has been visualized by fluorescence microscopy within the soma and cellular extension of amacrine cells (Malmfors, 1963). GABA has been measured by quantitative histochemical techniques and found most concentrated within the inner aspect of the bipolar layer, probably in the amacrine cells (Graham *et al.,* 1970). Acetylcholinesterase, implying acetylocholine, has been shown histochemically to be localized in amacrine cells (Nichols and Koelle, 1968). Serotonin has been determined chemically, but has yet to be localized (Lolley, 1970). Thus, a variety of neurochemical transmitters are associated with the amacrine cells, but the chemical transmitter for the bipolar synaptic apparatus is still unknown.

The inner synaptic region is richly invested with the potential for active cation transport (Na-K ATPase) (Matschinsky, 1969). The capacity for ATP hydrolysis is low in immature rat retina but it develops, before 120 postnatal days, to the mature level (Bonavita *et al.,* 1966).

The inner synaptic region of the retina also contains a dopaminergic neural system. In its profile of neurotransmitter agents, this region resembles that of the telencephalon and is distinguished as the only such center outside the midbrain (Friede, 1966). It is, as yet, impossible to define the functional role of the dopamine-containing cells in the retina. They may be involved in inhibitory activity since the amacrine cells have been identified with "lateral inhibition" (Dowling, 1967).

Encoding of visual stimuli into a discharge pattern of ganglion cells of the retina is apparently achieved through numerous synaptic contacts which are serviced by a variety of excitatory and inhibitory transmitter agents. In this process, the retina utilizes transmitter agents which are common to other regions of the CNS, achieving modulation of the stimuli from a balance of excitation and inhibition. Attempts are currently being made to define the electrical responses, transmitter dependence, and the number and type of contacts within the synaptic layers of the retina, in order to formulate a hypothesis which may explain the encoding of visual stimuli in the retina. It is anticipated that such a hypothesis could conceptually explain information processing in other regions of the CNS.

ACKNOWLEDGMENTS

The author wishes to thank Drs. C. F. Baxter and D. G. Chase for their constructive criticisms, E. Racz and V. Valladares for their outstanding technical assistance, and Dr. J. O. Erickson for his collaboration. The work from the author's laboratory was supported by NIH Grant EY00395 and by funds from the Veterans Administration.

REFERENCES

Bok, D. (1968). Dissertation, University of California, Los Angeles, California.
Bonavita, V. (1965). *In* "Biochemistry of the Retina" (C. N. Graymore, ed.), pp. 5-13. Academic Press, New York.
Bonavita, V., Guarneri, R., and Ponte, F. (1966). *Experientia 22,* 720.
Brown, K. T., Watanabe, D., and Murakami, M. (1965). *Cold Spring Harbor Symp. Quant. Biol. 30,* 457.
Caravaggio, L. L., and Bonting, S. L. (1963). *Exp. Eye Res. 2,* 12.
Dahlstrom, A., and Haggendal, J. (1966). *Acta Physiol. Scand. 67,* 278.
Dowling, J. E. (1967). *Science 155,* 273.
Dowling, J. E. (1968). *Proc. Roy. Soc. Ser. B 170,* 205.
Dowling, J. E., and Sidman, R. L. (1962). *J. Cell. Biol. 14,* 73.
Dowling, J. E., and Werblin, F. (1969). *J. Neurophysiol. 32,* 315.
Friede, R. L. (1966). "Topographic Brain Chemistry." Academic Press, New York.
Graham, L. T., Jr., Baxter, C. F., and Lolley, R. N. (1970). *Brain Res. 20,* 379.
Graymore, C. N. (1958). *Biochem. J. 69,* 30P.

Graymore, C. N. (1963). *Exp. Eye Res. 3,* 5.
Graymore, C. N. (1966). *Exp. Eye Res. 5,* 325.
Graymore, C. N., Tansley, K., and Kerly, M. (1959). *Biochem. J. 72,* 459.
Hall, M. O. (1970). *Exp. Eye Res.* (submitted for publication).
Hall, M. O., Bok, D., and Bacharach, A. D. E. (1968). *Science 161,* 787.
Hubel, D. H. (1967). *Physiologist 10,* 17.
Hubel, D. H., and Wiesel, T. N. (1963). *J. Neurophysiol. 26,* 994.
Hydén, H. (1967). "The Neuron." Elsevier, Amsterdam.
Karlsson, J. O., and Sjöstrand, J. (1968). *Brain Res. 11,* 431.
Lajtha, A., and Marks, N. (1969). *Clin. Basic Sci. Correlations 30,* 36.
Laties, A. (1969). Personal communication.
Lolley, R. N. (1969). *J. Neurochem. 16,* 1469.
Lolley, R. N., (1970). Personal Observation.
Lolley, R.N., and Erickson, J. O. (1970). Unpublished data.
Long, C. (1961). "Biochemist's Handbook." Van Nostrand, Princeton, New Jersey.
Lowenthal, A., van Sande, M., Karcher, D., and Richard J. (1964). *In* "Comparative Neurochemistry" (D. Richter, ed.), pp. 139-148. Macmillan, New York.
Lowry, O. H. (1964). *In* "Morphology and Biochemical Correlates of Neural Activity" (M. M. Cohen and R. S. Snider, eds.), pp. 178-191. Harper, New York.
Malmfors, T. (1963). *Acta Physiol. Scand. 58,* 99.
Matschinsky, F. M. (1969). Personal communication.
Matschinsky, F. M., Passonneau, J. V., and Lowry, O. H. (1968). *J. Histochem. Cytochem. 16,* 29.
Mayman, C. (1969). Personal communication.
Missotten, L. (1965). "The Ultrastructure of the Retina." Arscia Uitgaven N. V., Brussels.
Nichols, C. W., and Koelle, G. B. (1968). *J. Comp. Neurol. 133,* 1.
Noell, W. K. (1958). *AMA Arch. Ophthalmol. [N.S.] 60,* 702.
Noell, W. K. (1965). *In* "Biochemistry of the Retina" (C. N. Graymore, ed.), pp. 51-72. Academic Press, New York.
Olney, J. W. (1968a). *Invest. Ophthalmol. 7,* 250.
Olney, J. W. (1968b). *Nature (London) 218,* 281.
Reading, H. W. (1965). *In* "Biochemistry of the Retina" (C. N. Graymore, ed.), pp. 73-82. Academic Press, New York.
Sjöstrand, F. S. (1961). *In* "The Structure of the Eye" (G. K. Smelser, ed.), pp. 1-28. Academic Press, New York.
Waelsch, H., ed. (1955). "Biochemistry of the Developing Nervous System." Academic Press, New York.
Werblin, F., and Dowling, J. E. (1969). *J. Neurophysiol. 32,* 339.
Young, R. W. (1967). *J. Cell Biol. 33,* 61.
Young, R. W. (1969). *Invest. Ophthalmol. 8,* 222.
Young, R. W., and Bok, D. (1969). *J. Cell Biol. 42,* 392.
Young, R. W., and Droz, B. (1968). *J. Cell Biol. 39,* 169.

CHAPTER 8　Development of Supraspinal Modulation of Motor Activity During Sleep and Wakefulness

Yoshiaki Iwamura

I. INTRODUCTION

It has been empirically observed and experimentally confirmed that newborn infants spend most of their time sleeping. Questions concerning the functional interpretation of these early manifestations of "sleep" are dealt with in detail in Chapters 11 and 18. The issues discussed should be kept in mind in relation to the use of the term "sleep" in the present context. Studies on the postnatal development of sleep patterns in both humans (Roffwarg *et al.,* 1966) and animals (Valatx *et al.,* 1964; Shimizu and Himwich, 1968; also cf. Hernandez-Peon and Sterman, 1966; Jouvet, 1967) have shown that the so-called paradoxical sleep or rapid eye movement (REM) state assumes a high proportion of total time in the first days of life and that its amount and ratio diminish as maturation proceeds. Such findings led to the belief that the primary function of paradoxical sleep is to assist the process of development of the central nervous system (Roffwarg *et al.,* 1966). These studies have also noted peculiar motor activity in the infant, such as exaggerated jerks or phasic movements of body and extremities, during paradoxical sleep. These peculiarities could be ascribed to the immature state of the central nervous system.

This presentation will deal with the discovery and investigation of an augmentation of the hindlimb monosynaptic reflex during paradoxical sleep in the kitten (Iwamura *et al.,* 1968, 1971), which contrasts with the depression of the reflex observed in the adult cat during this same state.

II. A REVIEW OF STUDIES ON SUPRASPINAL MODULATION OF MOTOR ACTIVITY IN ADULT CATS.

The tonic depression in muscle activity which is associated with sleep, particularly with the onset of paradoxical sleep, suggests the presence of centrifugal depressive control of spinal motor activity. Giaquinto *et al.* (1964a) first described the tonic depression of heteronymous monosynaptic reflexes and polysynaptic reflexes in the hind limb of the cat during paradoxical sleep. This was subsequently confirmed by other groups of investigators (Gassel *et al.,* 1964b; Kubota *et al.,* 1965; Baldissera *et al.,* 1966a). Depression of the monosynaptic reflex is tonic and nonreciprocal and has been postulated to be due to an active inhibition of the reflex pathway rather than to a withdrawal of tonic facilitatory influences (Giaquinto *et al.,* 1964b; Bizzi *et al.,* 1964). This inhibition was believed to be postsynaptic, since relative hyperpolarization of the motoneuron membrane was suggested from studies of motoneuron excitability (Morrison and Pompeiano, 1965a; Kubota and Kidokoro, 1965), and no evidence has been obtained which would indicate the presence of tonic presynaptic inhibition in the monosynaptic reflex pathway (Morrison and Pompeiano, 1965b; Baldissera *et al.,* 1966b; Tokizane, 1966). The descending spinal pathway responsible for such inhibition of the reflex was determined to be mainly the ventral half of the lateral funiculi which supposedly originate in the lower brain stem (Giaquinto *et al.,* 1964b).

In addition to tonic inhibition of reflexes, there are also phasic inhibitory influences superimposed on the reflex pathways. During brisk bursts of rapid eye movements, monosynaptic and polysynaptic reflexes are further depressed phasically (Gassel *et al.,* 1964b), and the excitability of group I afferent fiber terminals is increased (Morrison and Pompeiano, 1965b; Baldissera *et al.,* 1966b). This implies that the phasic depression of the reflex can be attributed to presynaptic inhibition. Presynaptic inhibition at the moment of REM bursts was also found in other sensory relay nuclei (Carli *et al.,* 1967; Bizzi, 1966; Sakakura and Iwama, 1965).

Myoclonic twitches or jerks are one of the characteristic features of paradoxical sleep. These twitches, according to Gassel *et al.* (1964a), are sometimes strongly correlated with REM, tend to be more frequent in distal than proximal muscles, and more prominent in flexor than extensor muscles. Partial transection of the spinal cord indicates that the dorsolateral funiculi mediate intermittent descending volleys responsible for these myoclonic twitches. The twitches which are associated with REM bursts were correlated with the burstlike increases in the discharge rate of neurons in both medial and descending vestibular nuclei and were abolished after bilateral lesions were made in these nuclei (Morrison and Pompeiano, 1966). Since a phasic increase in neuronal discharge rate at the moment of REM was found in various structures in the brain (Huttenlocher,

1961; Evarts, 1962, 1964), it is possible that the associated myoclonic twitches are the result of excitatory impingements on motoneurons from various supraspinal structures, including the vestibular system (Gassel *et al.*, 1964a).

III. SUPRASPINAL MODULATION OF MOTOR ACTIVITIES DURING SLEEP AND WAKEFULNESS IN THE KITTEN

A. EEG Pattern and Behavior During Sleep and Wakefulness in the kitten

Three main critical periods of EEG and behavioral development have been described in the kitten by Valatx *et al.* (1964) and Shimizu and Himwich (1968). During the first week after birth, cortical activity shows no changes associated with the animal's behavior. The EEG always shows a "synchronized" pattern, so that only behavioral observation makes it possible to differentiate wakefulness from sleep (see also Chapter 11 for a comparison with human newborn). Behaviorally the sleep state can be divided into two stages: quiet sleep and sleep with jerks. During the quiet sleep stage, the recorded neck EMG becomes quite flat, whereas sleep with jerks is characterized by the total loss of neck EMG, rapid eye movements and jerks in body and extremities. Some EEG variations begin to appear during the second week.

Figure 1 shows a polygraphic record in an 11-day-old kitten. High voltage spindles are replaced by a more desynchronized pattern during sleep with jerks. During behavioral arousal only very brief periods of desynchronized EEG were seen. From the beginning of the third week, two sleep stages, slow wave sleep and paradoxical sleep, as well as wakefulness, could be differentiated polygraphically by the same criteria used for adult cats (Fig. 2).

In the kitten it has been noted that jerks occur more frequently and are larger in amplitude than in the adult cat (Valatx *et al.*, 1964). However, it is rather difficult to evaluate the extent of such differences between adult and infant since exaggerated jerks are seen in adult cats after sleep deprivation (Vimont *et al.*, 1966), and in each kitten the individual jerks vary enormously. Figure 2a shows a short REM episode with only a few jerks in the upper extremities, while during another episode in the same animal, shown in Fig. 2b, jerks are more frequent and larger. A period of tonic muscle activity was observed at the end of this episode. Huttenlocher (1967) found a striking correlation between cortical unit discharges and involuntary motor activity in the unrestrained, unanesthetized kitten. He found that, in the immature kitten, cortical unit discharges tend to occur in brief synchronous bursts, followed by prolonged periods of silence. He postulated that the muscle jerks observed in the immature animal during sleep were due to the involvement of motor pathways in such bursts of spontaneous neuronal activity occurring over large areas of the cerebral cortex.

During maturation, as the tendency toward synchrony of neuronal discharges decreases, spontaneous muscular jerks also decrease in frequency. An alternative explanation would be that in the young animal neural elements involved in the supraspinal inhibitory control of motor activity are immature and, consequently, not capable of suppressing such phasic activity during sleep.

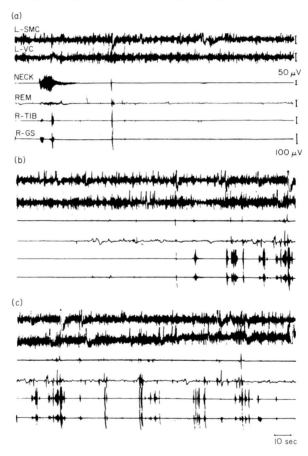

FIG. 1. Polygraph recording in an 11-day-old kitten. a, b, and c are a continuous record. L-SMC, EEG from the left somatosensory cortex; L-VC, EEG from the left visual cortex; NECK, neck muscle EMG; REM, rapid eye movements; R-TIB, EMG of right ankle flexor; R-GS, EMG of right ankle extensor (Iwamura, *et al.,* 1970).

B. Hindlimb Monosynaptic Reflex During Sleep and Wakefulness in the Kitten

Information concerning the development of supraspinal modulation of motor functions can be obtained through the study of changes in spinal reflex

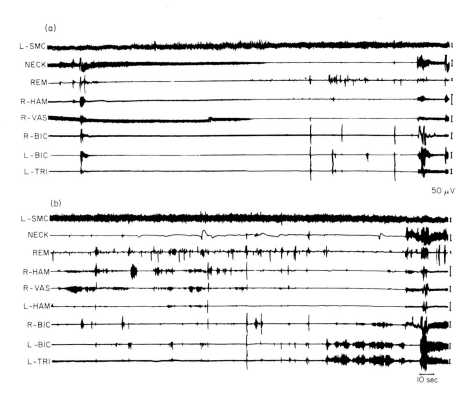

FIG. 2. Polygraphic recording in a 37-day-old kitten. a and b are records from different paradoxical sleep episodes in the same animal. Abbreviations: L-SMC, NECK, and REM are same as in Fig. 1. EMG records from right and left hamstring muscles (R-HAM, L-HAM), right m. quadriceps femoris (R-VAS), right and left m. biceps branchii (R-BIC, L-BIC) and left m. triceps brachii (L-TRI) (Iwamura *et al.,* 1970).

activity during various behavioral states as a function of age. We have utilized a single shock stimulation of the sciatic nerve to elicit the monosynaptic reflex (MSR) simultaneously in the common peroneal (ankle flexor) and tibial nerves (ankle extensor) in both adult cats and kittens (Fig. 3). These nerves must be ligated to interrupt their muscle innervation. The surgical and recording procedures as well as the electrodes were developed in studies on the adult cat (Kubota *et al.,* 1965) and the details are described elsewhere (Iwamura *et al.,* 1971). Recordings obtained from these nerves following stimulation are shown in the upper right portion of Fig. 3. The early potential occurring immediately after the shock is the directly excited nerve response. The late response is considered to be the monosynaptic reflex for the following reasons. (1) This late response is abolished by ligating the ipsilateral dorsal roots from L5 to S2. (2) The threshold for the late response is in the range of 1.1-1.5 times the threshold for direct excitation of the nerve. (3) The latency of the late response seems to depend upon the age of the animal. For example, the latency of the response in the tibial nerve is as long as 6.1 msec in a 15-day-old kitten and 5.5 msec in a 22-day-old kitten. It becomes progressively shorter up to the sixth week of age, and stabilizes at a value of 4.3 msec. This developmental change in latency is in quite good agreement with the results of previous acute experiments on the kitten (Skoglund, 1960b; Wilson, 1962) and it may be attributed to the increase in the conduction velocity of the peripheral nerves due to myelination.

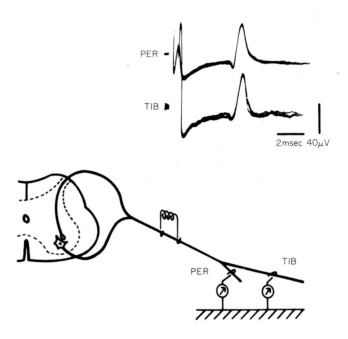

FIG. 3. Monosynaptic reflex in hindlimb of a kitten. The drawing illustrates stimulation of the sciatic nerve and recording the reflex from the common peroneal nerve (PER) and the tibial nerve (TIB) (Iwamura et al., 1970).

In our studies the MSR showed characteristic changes depending on the age and state of wakefulness of the animal. In kittens younger than 14 days of age, the MSR in both flexor and extensor nerves was very small during wakefulness, especially when the animal moved vigorously. As soon as the animal became quiet, the MSR size increased and was largest during sleep with jerks. In kittens between 14 and 40 days of age, the MSR was also smallest during wakefulness, larger during slow wave sleep and largest during paradoxical sleep, as is shown in superimposed records of such a reflex in Fig. 4a. This change in the reflex size was tonic and nonreciprocal.

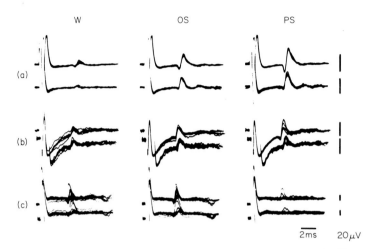

FIG. 4. Monosynaptic reflex curing sleep and wakefulness in kittens of different ages (a, 30 days old; b, 44 days old) and in an adult cat (c). W, wakefulness; OS, slow wave sleep; PS, paradoxical sleep. Superimposed records. (a modified from Iwamura *et al.*, 1968; b, Iwamura *et al.*, 1970; c, Kubota *et al.*, 1964.)

The adult type of reflex modulation, that is, the tonic depression of the MSR during paradoxical sleep, began in the period of 40-60 days after birth. In these kittens the increase in MSR size during sleep was reduced in magnitude and was less stable. During the transition from wakefulness to slow wave sleep, MSR size increased in a manner similar to that seen in younger kittens. However, as the REM phase started, the MSR did not show a further increase, as was characteristic in younger kittens. Instead, MSR size was variable, occasionally being larger than during slow wave sleep and sometimes being depressed to almost zero. Figure 4b illustrates such a record obtained from a 44-day-old-kitten. After total spinal cord transection this augmentation and depression of the MSR is abolished, indicating its supraspinal origin.

In kittens over 60 days of age, the MSR was tonically depressed during paradoxical sleep as compared with slow wave sleep, in a manner similar to that observed in the adult (Fig. 4c). Moreover, in kittens of this age the reflex size during wakefulness became more unpredictable. It could be larger during wakefulness than during slow wave sleep, or smaller, depending upon whether or not the animal moved or paid attention to a novel stimulus, as reported previously in adult cats (Gassel *et al.*, 1964b).

C. Postsynaptic Mechanisms: Excitability of Alpha Motoneurons During Sleep and Wakefulness in the Kitten

From the results mentioned above, one might conclude that supraspinal inhibitory influences on the monosynaptic reflex pathway during paradoxical

sleep are lacking in the kitten due to the immature state of development of the
central nervous system. However, other experiments show that this is not the
case. In the adult cat excitability of the motoneuron is tested by stimulating the
motoneuron pool directly with recording peripherally the response as either the
motor nerve compound action potential (Morrison and Pompeiano, 1965a) or
evoked muscle response (Kubota and Kidokoro, 1965). In the adult cat motoneuron excitability is depressed in parallel with the monosynaptic reflex during
sleep, particularly during the REM phase. Similar procedures were tried in
kittens younger than 40 days of age, where the monosynaptic reflex is augmented during sleep. We recorded the motor nerve compound action potentials
from either the tibial nerve or the peroneal nerve while stimulating the L7
ventral horn through an implanted tungsten wire electrode. Dorsal roots were
cut bilaterally from L5 to S2.

The experimental procedure is illustrated in Fig. 5. The traces at the left
indicate motor nerve action potentials recorded from the tibial nerve during
wakefulness and sleep. The amplitude of the response was considered to be a
measure of the number of motoneurons excited (Morrison and Pompeiano,
1965a). The potential followed high frequency stimulation up to 20 cycle/sec
without reduction in amplitude and its latency was as short as 1.5-1.8 msec.
Thus, its transsynaptic origin was unlikely. The compound action potential was

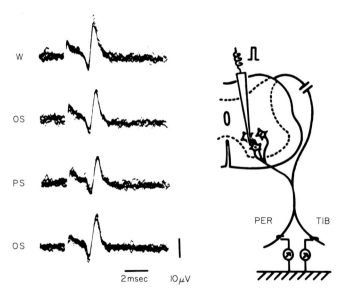

FIG. 5. Excitability test of alpha motoneurons in a 30-day-old kitten. The drawing
illustrates stimulation of the spinal cord and recording of motor nerve action potential on
either the tibial nerve (TIB) or the common peroneal nerve (PER). Four records were
obtained during a series of wakefulness (W), slow wave (OS), paradoxical sleep (PS), and
slow wave sleep (OS). Five traces were superimposed in each record (Iwamura et al., 1970).

largest during wakefulness (W) and became smaller during slow wave sleep (OS) and smallest during paradoxical sleep (PS). These results indicate that the excitability of the motoneuron is reduced during sleep in the kitten, as it is in adult cats. This conclusion is supported by additional observations: As shown in Figs. 3 and 4, the resting muscle activity in the extremities was very low during paradoxical sleep in most kittens. The polysynaptic reflex (flexion reflex) in the same spinal segments, evoked by stimulating the tibial nerve and recorded from the ankle flexor muscles, is also depressed during sleep, particularly during paradoxical sleep in kittens of all ages (Iwamura et al., 1968, 1971). Thus the augmentation of the monosynaptic reflex during paradoxical sleep must be explained on the basis of some neuronal mechanism other than changes in the excitability of the motoneuron soma.

D. Presynaptic Mechanisms

Frank (1959) postulated two types of remote inhibition of the monosynaptic EPSP in motoneurons which produced no recordable change in the motoneuron cell bodies. The inhibition of the EPSP could be due either to a diminished excitatory action of the group Ia presynaptic impulses such as by "presynaptic inhibition" (J. C. Eccles, 1964), or to an action exerted so far out on the dendrites of the motoneuron that no trace of the inhibitory influence itself could be detected by a microelectrode in the motoneuron soma.

During wakefulness such "remote inhibition" would act selectively on the monosynaptic reflex pathway to overcome the increased excitability of the motoneuron. During sleep the reflex pathway would be released from such remote interference and the size of the reflex would increase even though the excitability of the motoneuron was depressed. The following experiments were designed to measure the effect of presynaptic inhibition upon the MSR during sleep and wakefulness. For obvious technical reasons the effect of remote synaptic input on the dendrites could not be measured.

There is a wealth of evidence establishing that depolarization of presynaptic terminals (primary afferent depolarization: PAD) can produce diminution of the EPSP and a consequent inhibition of reflex discharge *(presynaptic inhibition)*. Depolarization of group Ia afferents in the monosynaptic reflex pathway can be elicited by activation of group I afferents, mainly from flexor nerves (J. C. Eccles et al., 1962). On the other hand, stimulation of brain stem structures also has a depolarizing effect on primary afferents in the spinal cord and thus a presynaptic inhibitory action (Carpenter et al., 1966). It is possible that such depolarizing influences are in continuous operation under certain physiological conditions, and that they control arriving afferent impulses by shifting the membrane potential of the presynaptic terminals in either a depolarizing or hyperpolarizing direction.

1. The Cord Dorsum Potential During Sleep in the Kitten

The tonic shift of membrane potential level of the presynaptic terminal can be detected by measuring the size of the phasic PAD which is evoked in the same terminals by stimulation of afferent nerves. The phasic PAD is measured indirectly by recording a slow positive potential called the P wave from the dorsal surface of the spinal cord in chronic animals (Baldissera *et al.*, 1966b; Tokizane, 1966). Thus, the amplitude of the P wave evoked by stimulation of group I afferents in the ankle flexor nerve and recorded from the cord dorsum at the L7 level was compared during sleep and wakefulness in a group of kittens younger than 40 days of age.

The P wave was smaller during wakefulness than during slow wave sleep, and occasionally was totally depressed. During paradoxical sleep, it became larger than during slow wave sleep. Such changes in the size of the P wave are quite similar to the changes in the monosynaptic reflex. Thus, the data suggest that presynaptic mechanisms may be involved in the previously described augmentation of the MSR in the kitten during paradoxical sleep.

2. Excitability of Group I Afferent Terminals During Sleep in the Kitten

It has been established in adult cats that if there is an afferent terminal depolarization which leads to presynaptic inhibition, the excitability of the afferent terminals should increase (J. C. Eccles, 1964).

A more direct way to detect the depolarization of the primary afferent terminals involves testing the excitability of the terminals by comparing the size of antidromic potentials on the tibial nerve, evoked by stimulation of the ventral horn, after cutting ventral roots from L5 to S2 (Wall, 1958; J. C. Eccles *et al.*, 1962). We stimulated the ventral horn of the lumbar spinal cord (L7 level) monopolarly, through a tungsten wire electrode and recorded the quickest response obtained (Fig. 6). The procedures were similar to those in experiments on adult cats (Morrison and Pompeiano, 1965b; Baldissera *et al.*, 1966b; Tokizane, 1966). The short latency responses observed (1.7-1.9 msec) and their low threshold indicated a group I afferent origin. The amplitude of the antidromic potential was considered to be a measure of the number of afferent terminals excited and was compared during wakefulness (Fig. 6A), slow wave sleep (Fig 6B), and paradoxical sleep (Fig. 6C). No significant difference in the size of the potential was detected throughout sleep and wakefulness. The only positive finding in regard to the potential size was its phasic facilitation at the moment of brisk REM, suggesting the presence of phasic presynaptic inhibition of the monosynaptic reflex pathway at that moment, as described in adult cats by Morrison and Pompeiano (1965b) and Baldissera *et al.*, (1966b). When stimulation of the spinal cord was preceded by brief repetitive stimulation of the peroneal nerve at the intensity of less than twice the threshold for nerve excitation (group I range), the antidromic potential was facilitated (Fig. 6D). The facilitation was maximal at 15-20 msec conditioning-test intervals and ended at about 100 msec. This conditioning effect is comparable with the results previously described in both adult cat (J. C. Eccles *et al.*, 1962) and kitten (R. M. Eccles and Willis, 1963), indicating the validity of this potential for testing excitability in this context. Thus, we could not detect a tonic change in the excitability of primary afferent terminals during sleep and wakefulness in the kitten. One explanation for such negative results is that membrane potential changes in the group I afferent terminals are asynchronous and are too subtle to be detected by the test used, but great enough to produce changes in the MSR and P wave amplitude. The P wave may be modulated by some other influence involving interference of the interneuronal activity within the P wave pathway.

The development of the supraspinal control of reflex activities in the kitten has been traced in relation to the unique augmentation of the monosynaptic

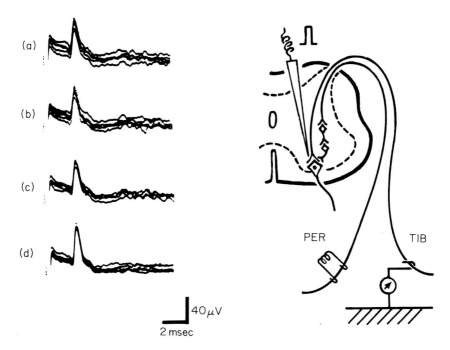

FIG. 6. Excitability test of group I afferent terminals in a 36-day-old kitten. The illustration shows stimulation of the spinal cord and recording of antidromic nerve action potentials on the tibial nerve (TIB). The common peroneal nerve (PER) was stimulated to provide a conditioning effect on the antidromic potential (see text). Superimposed records of the antidromic potential were obtained during a series including periods of wakefulness (a) slow wave sleep (b), and paradoxical sleep (c). The record shown in d was preceded by a conditioning stimulation of the common peroneal nerve with an interval of 15 msec, obtained during slow wave sleep (Iwamura *et al.*, 1970).

reflex in the hindlimb during paradoxical sleep. Experiments have suggested that certain presynaptic interactions on the monosynaptic reflex pathway could be responsible for such augumentation of the reflex, although the incomplete results preclude definite conclusions on its mechanism. The problem of specifying which developmental changes in the central and peripheral nervous system are responsible for the observed reflex modulation during sleep remains unsolved. However, it may be worthwhile to discuss the present findings in relation to both morphological and functional aspects of postnatal development in the nervous system of the kitten.

IV. DEVELOPMENT OF THE MOTOR SYSTEM

A. Behavioral aspects

The development of motor abilities in the kitten has been described most often in relation to other aspects of maturation (Langworthy, 1929; Tilney and Kubie, 1931; Skoglund, 1960a; also cf. Fox, 1966; Himwich, 1962; Skoglund, 1969). According to these authors, kittens at birth are not able to walk or stand, but have righting reflexes. They move around through crawling movements of the forelimbs. After 2 weeks they start to assume an upright position with the abdomen raised during locomotion. One may notice that at the end of the second week, which is thus a "critical period" in the development of motor ability, is also important in the development of motor activity during sleep: after this period, neck muscle tone is sustained during slow wave sleep and the paradoxical sleep stage is initiated by its total loss. These features seem to be based on the development of both central and peripheral mechanism for posture (Skoglund, 1960a, c). At approximately 25-30 days, kittens take a few running steps. By the end of the sixth week only slight differences in motor ability are observed in comparison with the adult. This may be correlated with the elaboration of mechanisms for voluntary motor performance, such as maturation of motor cortex and myelination of the pyramidal tract (Purpura *et al.,* 1964). It is perhaps more than an interesting coincidence that the monosynaptic reflex starts to be depressed during paradoxical sleep at this same time.

B. Morphological Aspects

The postnatal development of the nervous system has attracted considerable attention and many attempts have been made to correlate function with various morphological signs of maturity, particularly myelination. However, it is obvious that mere correlation sometimes may have no functional implication. Langworthy (1929) systematically studied the correlation between the development of motor performance and myelination within the spinal cord in the kitten. He found that when compared to the corticospinal tract and voluntary behavior, brain stem systems such as medial longitudinal fasciculus, reticulospinal, vestibulospinal, and tectospinal tracts are myelinated earlier, corresponding to behavioral signs such as the righting reflex etc., which appear earlier than performance. Since the inhibition of motoneurons during paradoxical sleep is thought to be dependent upon descending influences along the reticulospinal tracts (Giaquinto et al., 1964b), our conclusion that the supraspinal inhibitory influence exerted on motoneurons during paradoxical sleep starts relatively early in life seems reasonable.

Langworthy also found that the dorsal roots are more slowly myelinated than the ventral roots. It appears quite likely that many of the reported differences between the newborn and adult in properties of hindlimb reflexes are due to the properties of peripheral fibers, particularly afferent fibers and their intraspinal collaterals (Skoglund, 1960b; Wilson, 1962). Observations, including intracellular studies, provide further evidence that the unique reflex behavior in kittens is due more to the immature properties of fibers than to the motoneuron somata themselves (Naka, 1964; Wilson, 1962; R. M. Eccles et al., 1963; R. M. Eccles and Willis, 1963). It is thus likely that augmentation of the MSR during paradoxical sleep in the kitten is due to functional speciality in the presynaptic component of the reflex pathway, and may result from the immaturity of very fine terminals.

C. Maturation of Supraspinal Structures

As suggested above, the observed augmentation of the MSR in young kittens may be due to variation in the functional properties of group I afferent fibers during paradoxical sleep. However, it is possible also that the immaturity of higher brain structures results in a different hierarchal arrangement of supraspinal motor modulation in these young kittens, as mentioned earlier. Thus certain centrifugal influences on the spinal cord may be temporarily exaggerated in the kitten. In this regard, it is interesting to note that adult cats with the neuraxis transected at midbrain level show an augmentation of spinal reflexes during paradoxical sleep similar to that observed in young kittens (Iwamura et al., 1969).

ACKNOWLEDGMENTS

For permission to refer to published and unpublished results, the author is indebted to Drs. Kubota, Kudo, Niimi, and Tsuda. The author wishes to thank Mrs. E. Gardner for assisting with this manuscript, and Miss K. Hilten for help in preparing figures.

Bibliographic assistance was received from the UCLA Brain Information Service which is part of the Neurological Information Network of NINDS and is supported under Contract # DHEW PH-43-66-59.

REFERENCES

Baldissera, F., Broggi, G., and Mancia, M. (1966a). *Arch. Ital. Biol. 104,* 112.

Baldissera, F., Ceba-Bianchi, M. G., and Mancia, M. (1966b). *J. Neurophysiol. 29,* 871.

Bizzi, E. (1966). *J. Neurophysiol. 29,* 861.

Bizzi, E., Pompeiano, O., and Somogyi, I. (1964). *Arch. Ital. Biol. 102,* 308.

Carli, G., Diete-Spiff, K., and Pompeiano, O. (1967). *Arch. Ital. Biol. 105,* 52.

Carpenter, D., Engberg, I., and Lundberg, A. (1966). *Arch. Ital. Biol. 104,* 73.

Eccles, J. C. (1964). "The Physiology of Synapses." Springer, Berlin.

Eccles, J. C., Magni, F., and Willis, W. D. (1962). *J. Physiol. (London) 160,* 62.

Eccles, R. M., and Willis, W. D. (1963). *J. Physiol. (London) 165,* 403.

Eccles, R. M., Shealy, C. N., and Willis, W. D. (1963). *J. Physiol. (London) 165,* 392.

Evarts, E. V. (1962). *J. Neurophysiol. 25,* 812.

Evarts, E. V. (1964). *J. Neurophysiol. 27,* 152.

Fox, M. (1966). *Brain Res. 2,* 3.

Frank, K. (1959). *IRE Trans. Med. Electron 6,* 85.

Gassel, M. M., Marchiafava, P. L., and Pompeiano, O. (1964a). *Arch. Ital. Biol. 102,* 449.

Gassel, M. M., Marchiafava, P. L., and Pompeiano, O. (1964b). *Arch. Ital. Biol. 102,* 471.

Giaquinto, S., Pompeiano, O., and Somogyi, I. (1964a). *Arch. Ital. Biol. 102,* 245.

Giaquinto, S., Pompeiano, O., and Somogyi, I. (1964b). *Arch. Ital. Biol. 102,* 282.

Hernández-Peón, R., and Sterman, M. B. (1966). *Annu. Rev. Psychol. 17,* 363.

Himwich, W. A. (1962). *Int. Rev. Neurobiol. 4,* 117.

Huttenlocher, P. R. (1961). *J. Neurophysiol. 24,* 451.

Huttenlocher, P. R. (1967). *Exp. Neurol. 17,* 247.

Iwamura, Y., Tsuda, K., Kudo, N., and Kohama, K. (1968). *Brain Res. 11,* 456.

Iwamura, Y., Sterman, M. B., and McGinty, D. J. (1969). *Physiologist 12,* 260.

Iwamura, Y., Kudo, K., and Tsuda, N. (1970). Unpublished data.

Iwamura, Y., Kudo, K., and Tsuda, N. (1971). In preparation.

Jouvet, M. (1967). *Physiol. Rev. 47,* 117.

Kubota, K., Iwamura, Y., and Niimi, Y. (1964). Unpublished data.

Kubota, K., Iwamura, Y., and Niimi, Y. (1965). *J. Neurophysiol. 28,* 125.

Kubota, K., and Kidokoro, Y. (1965). *Jap. J. Physiol. 16,* 217.

Langworthy, D. R. (1929). *Carnegie Inst. Wash. Contrib. Embryol. 20,* 127.

Morrison, A. R., and Pompeiano, O. (1965a). *Arch. Ital. Biol. 103,* 497.

Morrison, A. R., and Pompeiano, O. (1965b). *Arch. Ital. Biol. 103,* 517.

Morrison, A. R., and Pompeiano, O. (1966). *Arch. Ital. Biol. 104,* 214.

Naka, K. (1964). *J. Gen. Physiol. 47,* 1003.

Purpura, D. P., Shofer, R. J., Housepian, E. M., and Noback, C. R. (1964). *Progr. Brain Res. 4,* 187.

Roffwarg, H. P., Muzio, J. N., and Dement, W. C. (1966). *Science 152,* 604.

Sakakura, H., and Iwama, K. (1965). *Tohoku J. Exp. Med. 87,* 40.

Shimizu, A., and Himwich, H. E. (1968). *Electroencephalogr. Clin. Neurophysiol. 24,* 307.

Skoglund, S. (1960a). *Acta Physiol. Scand. 49,* 299.

Skoglund, S. (1960b). *Acta Physiol. Scand. 49,* 318.

Skoglund, S. (1960c). *Acta Physiol. Scand. 50,* 203.

Skoglund, S. (1969). *Annu. Rev. Physiol. 31,* 19.

Tilney, F., and Kubie, L. S. (1931). *Bull. Neurol. Inst. New York 1,* 231.

Tokizane, T (1966). *Progr. Brain Res. 21B,* 230.

Valatx, J. L., Jouvet, D., and Jouvet, M. (1964). *Electroencephalogr. Clin. Neurophysiol.* *17,* 218.

Vimont, P., Jouvet, D., and Delorme, J. F. (1966). *Electroencephalogr. Clin. Neurophysiol.* *20,* 439.

Wall, P. D. (1958). *J. Physiol. (London) 142,* 1.

Wilson, V. (1962). *J. Neurophysiol. 25,* 263.

CHAPTER 9   **Relationship of Electrophysiological and Behavioral Indices of Visual Development in Mammals***

Guenter H. Rose

I. INTRODUCTION

Until recently, most developmental electrophysiological studies were limited to the reporting of *normative* changes of spontaneous and evoked electrical activity as a function of age, an essential but limited endeavor. However, a recent and increasing emphasis in electrophysiology is in the utilization of such normative data as an initial step for the separation, during development, of evoked response components which may be obscure in adult records, and which may give cues as to the evolvement and involvement of various cortical and subcortical structures and their roles in behavior. In addition, recent strategy reorientations have emphasized the combined manipulation of external stimulus parameters or environments, and the internal anatomical and physiological systems as dependent and independent variables. These newer strategies to elucidate the mechanisms responsible for the electrophysiological, neurochemical, and behavioral changes seen during maturation have caused a rapid resurgence of interest in developmental psychobiology.

This chapter will focus on the electrophysiological properties of the immature nervous system with major emphasis on the visual system. Since a comprehensive review is not intended, the specialized reader is referred to recent reviews on the maturation of spontaneous (Ellingson and Rose, 1970) and evoked electrophysiological activity (Rose and Ellingson, 1970; see also Himwich (1962) and

*Research reported herein was supported in part by Grants No. NB-06816 and HD-00370 from the National Institute of Neurological Diseases and the National Institute of Child Health and Human Development, respectively. I wish to acknowledge the considerable assistance of Mrs. Shirley Thornton in preparation of the manuscript.

145

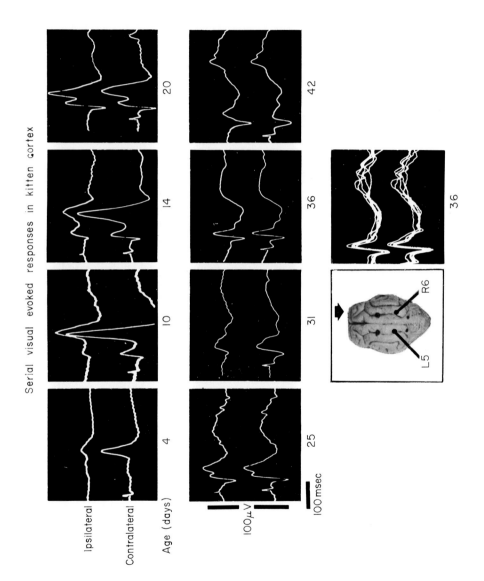

Himwich, 1970). Specifically, this report will: (1) delineate the normative sequence of changes in the parameters of visual evoked responses (VERs) in several species under various conditions; (2) review attempts to differentiate mechanisms contributing to such wave form changes in line with new scientific stratagems, and (3) emphasize multidisciplinary approaches in the subsequent analysis of the ontogeny of brain-behavior relationships. While considerable space is devoted to normative data, such information becomes more meaningful when related to the subsequent topics.

II. DEVELOPMENT OF VISUAL ELECTROCORTICAL RESPONSES

The ontogenesis of the visual evoked response (VER) to flash stimulation has been studied in the rat (Callison and Spencer, 1968; Klingberg and Schwartze, 1966; Mourek *et al.*, 1967; Rose, 1968a; Sublett, 1969; Wilson *et al.*, 1966), rabbit (Hunt and Goldring, 1951; Marty, 1962), cat (Ellingson and Wilcott, 1960; Marty *et al.*, 1959; Marty, 1962; Rose, 1968b; Rose and Lindsley, 1965, 1968), dog (M. Fox, 1968; Myslivecek, 1968), and monkey (Ordy *et al.*, 1965). Although disagreement exists as to the subsequent developmental sequence, the initial wave form in every instance is a single or double negative wave of long latency first occurring at the age of 8-10 days in rats, 7-10 days in rabbits, 2-3 days in kittens, 1-3 days in dogs, and at or near birth in the monkey. This section will concentrate on VER developmental studies undertaken in our laboratories on kittens and rats.

A. Anesthetized Preparations

The *longitudinal* sequence of VER changes as a function of age in the *same* kitten, lightly anesthetized for each recording session, is shown in Fig. 1. The earliest responses in the younger animals are very fatigable, necessitating long intertrial intervals (up to 30 sec in the youngest animals). Prior to 9-12 days of age the eyelids were closed, but could be gently pulled apart and held open with an eye speculum.

FIG. 1. Development of cortical potentials evoked by 15 μsec light flash in same kitten studied at successive age levels (days of age); monocular stimulation by collimated light beam brought to a focus near cornea of animal's right eye; pupil dilated with homatropine. Monopolar recordings from ipsilateral (R6) and contralateral (L5) visual cortex. Arrow indicates eye stimulated. Initial upward deflection indicates light flash. Superimposed tracings at day 36 show consistency of response (flash at onset of trace). In this and subsequent figures upward deflection indicates negativity at the active electrode. Calibration: 100 msec.; 100 μv. (Adapted from Rose and Lindsley, 1965, 1968.)

148   GUENTER H. ROSE

The first responses were obtained at 3-4 days of age in this animal consisting of a long latency negative wave (N2), of widespread cortical distribution, and peak latency of approximately 170 msec. The contralateral response matures earlier, has a greater amplitude, and a slightly shorter latency (2-5 msec) than the ipsilateral response. By 10 days of age the amplitude of this negative response is increased and the latency is reduced to 140 msec. In addition, a shorter latency positive-negative response, confined to the primary visual cortex, has appeared. The development of the shorter latency negative (N1) wave usually precedes that of the short positive wave (P1). With increasing age both the short latency

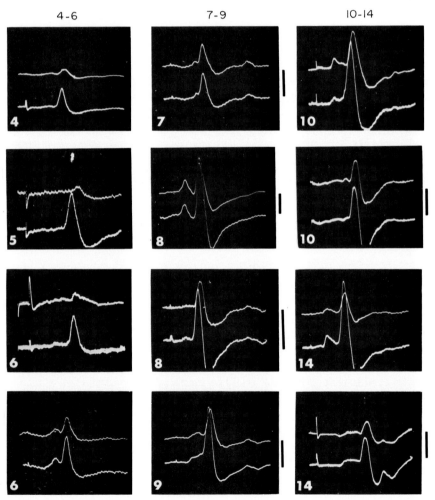

FIG. 2. Serial visual evoked responses in kitten cortex. Visually evoked potentials in kittens of different ages ranging from 4 to 36 days of age. Right eye stimulation. Top tracing, R6, bottom tracing, L5, from right and left visual cortex, respectively. Age of each kitten in

positive and negative components increase in amplitude. They decrease only slightly in latency, however, both in the same proportion. Concurrently the initial long latency negative wave continues to decrease markedly in latency and amplitude until at approximately 30 days the two negative waves appear to coalesce. By 30-40 days the visually evoked potential is similar to that of the adult cat. A similar sequence has been obtained by Marty (1962) in response to direct optic nerve stimulation.

Figure 2 presents the responses recorded in 24 *individual* animals at various age levels. These cross-sectional samplings show results similar to those exhibited

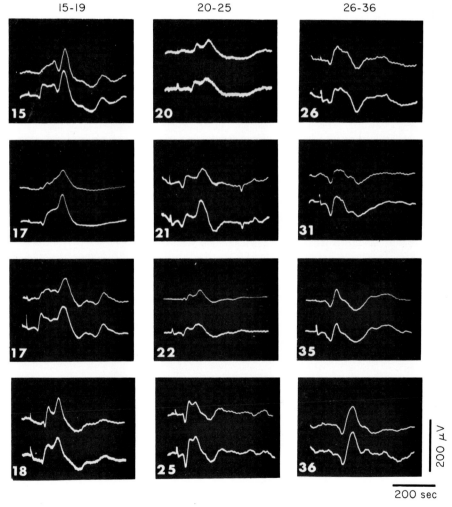

columnar group shown by white number. All vertical calibrations: 200 μv. (Rose and Lindsley, 1968.)

in the animals studied longitudinally and also illustrate slight variations in the initial appearance of the various components. Thus, between age 4 and 9 days the principal VER response is a long latency negative wave, although in two or three of the animals a short-latency negative wave is beginning to appear. Between 10 and 19 days of age in all cases except one, both the short and long latency negative waves are present, including in most instances the short latency positive response. Between ages 20 and 25 days, the full complement of waves is present, and the long-latency negative response is beginning to merge with the shorter latency negative response. Between 26 and 36 days all animals show a positive-negative response similar to that of the adult.

A similar cross-sectional study of the development of visually evoked responses in *rats* was undertaken to ascertain whether a comparable developmental sequence could be found. Surprisingly similar results were obtained as illustrated in Fig. 3, which compares the rat data shown at the top, with the previously illustrated kitten data at the bottom. As is evident, a similar VER sequence develops beginning with a long latency negative wave at 11 days of age, which is preceded, a day later in development, by a shorter latency positive-negative complex. At approximately 15 days the negative waves appear to coalesce, eventuating in a positive-negative complex at about 16 days of age similar to that obtainable in the adult rat.

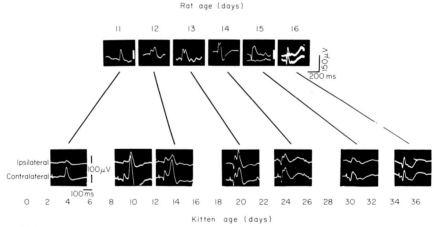

FIG. 3. Comparison of visually evoked cortical potential sequence in rat (upper tracings, contralateral responses) and kitten (lower tracings). Monocular stimulation, monopolar recordings. Lower tracings in 15 and 16-day-old rats are ipsilateral response, and with different reference, respectively.

It is uncertain whether the progressive diminution in amplitude and latency of the original negative wave (N2) to a point of apparent coalescence with the shorter latency negative wave at approximately 20-30 days means that it merely remains coincident with the shorter latency negative response or disappears completely. When the N2 wave is not evident in 20-30 day kittens it can be made distinguishable again by reducing the intensity of the light flash as shown in Fig. 4. This figure presents changes in latency and amplitude of the wave components as a function of decreasing stimulus intensity in a 31-day kitten from which a single negative wave was recorded at the standard intensity. With a reduction of flash intensity by one-half log unit or 50% transmission, both negative components are again clearly distinguishable. This is also evident at an intensity reduction of one log or 10% of the standard intensity. In fact at a two log intensity reduction the shorter latency negative wave is nearly eliminated and the longer latency wave shows a slight amplitude increase. With decreasing intensity steps there is a concomitant increase in the *latency* of all components as expected.

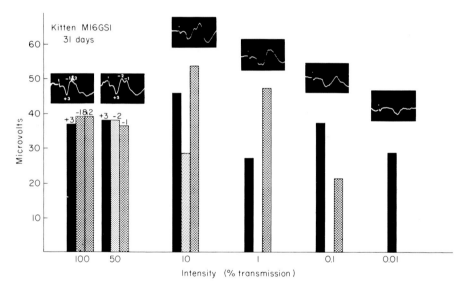

FIG. 4. Bar graph of mean amplitudes of evoked potential components in 31-day-old lightly anesthetized kitten, plotted as a function of decreasing light intensity (% transmission) sample oscilloscope tracings of evoked potentials shown for each intensity level (Rose, 1965).

These results, however, fail to distinguish whether a "hidden" N2 wave, due to temporal overlapping, becomes evident at lower light intensities as a function of unequal conduction rates, or a reduced N2 wave under high flash intensity is more evident at lower flash intensities due to release of inhibitory factors as postulated in adult cat preparations (Auerbach *et al.*, 1961). The disappearance, rather than the coalescence, of the N2 wave is suggested by Marty's observation

(1962) that with increasing age the N2 wave gradually disappears under pento-barbital in both the primary and extraprimary visual areas but can be made to manifest itself under chloralose throughout development. Data presented below on unanesthetized kittens also support this viewpoint.

It is evident, as shown, that similarities exist in the maturation of VER to light flash in the lightly anesthetized cat and rat. It is likewise clear that differences exist. Rats show very little ipsilateral response, and all components of the contralateral response appear relatively restricted topographically. Fur-thermore, the onset of the first VER occurs at 11 days of age in the rat in contrast to 2-4 days of age in the kitten. In spite of the later appearance of the electrocortical response in the rat, the mature wave form is attained vary rapidly, at approximately 15 to 16 days of age in contrast to 30 days of age in the cat. That is, a mature wave form is attained within 5 days after onset in the rat in contrast to a 4-week delay in the kitten.

Such comparisons between species in terms of absolute time can be deceiving. It is more meaningful to make comparisons in terms of a developmentally equivalent epoch, such as the percent of age to puberty. The onset of ovulation, used as a criteria of puberty, occurs on the average at 40 days in the rat and 8 months in the cat. For comparison, the species can be age-linked in terms of the proportion of this developmental period attained. By such a method the onset of the first response occurs at 25% of puberty age in the rat and 1% of puberty age in the cat. However, in *both* species it subsequently takes approximately 13-14% of puberty age to attain a mature wave form.

Similar comparisons can be made with regard to latency. The percent attain-ment of adult latency of the initial positive wave has been compared in terms of percent of age to puberty for humans, cats, and rats (Rose, 1968b). In the human and the cat near adult latency values are rapidly attained at 2% and 7% of puberty age respectively. The onset of the positive wave in the rat is not evident until 11 days or approximately 30% of puberty age. In fact, at 20 days or 50% of puberty age, the latency of the positive wave in the rat is still twice the adult value.

B. Unanesthetized Preparations

The data presented thus far were obtained from animals under light pentobar-bital anesthesia. The possibility that this barbituate could alter the sequence made an analysis of these changes in the *unanesthetized* animal imperative, especially when attempting to relate these changes to behavioral development.

Studies of the development of the VER in the unanesthetized animal were undertaken on 20 kittens prepared with indwelling cortical electrodes, including both cross-sectional and longitudinal age samples. Figure 5 illustrates the elec-trode implantation technique (Rose, 1966) whereby connector sockets are placed on either side of the midline to avoid the unfused sagittal suture in these young animals. This permits the skull to grow and expand laterally without breaking the slackened wire connected to recording screws. Kittens have been prepared in this manner as early as 3 days of age with subsequent recordings taken up to 60 days. The kittens were gently restrained, oriented toward a stroboscopic unit placed approximately 1 m away, and given single light flashes to both eyes. A second study on 40 unanesthetized but paralyzed animals (Flaxedil) was undertaken to duplicate the controlled stimulus presentation used in the original studies on anesthetized animals.

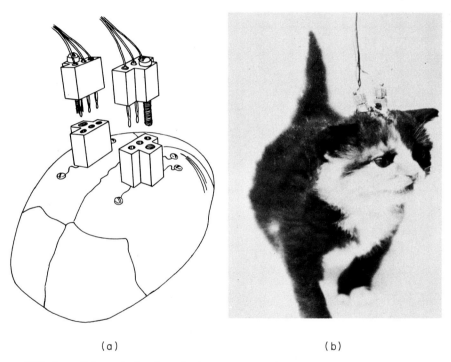

(a)   (b)

FIG. 5. a. Schematic drawing of strip connector sockets mounted on the skull on either side of the sagittal suture. The connector plugs with screw guide pins are shown above each socket. b. Photo of 4-week-old kitten with plug, socket, and recording leads in place (Rose, 1966).

The similarity of developmental VER changes obtained from the chronic and flaxedilized preparations is illustrated in Figs. 6 and 7. The occurrence of a recognizable sequence is maximized by using controlled focused monocular stimulation as originally used in the pentobarbital preparations and subsequently in the flaxedilized subjects. It can be seen that in the first 2 weeks of life the sequence that develops is very comparable to that obtained from the lightly

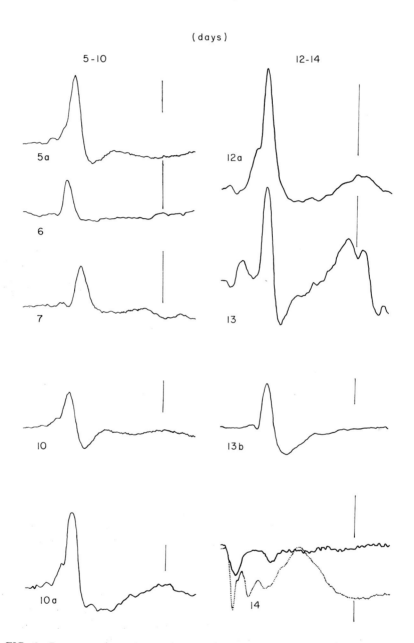

FIG. 6. Computer-averaged visually evoked potentials from awake unanesthetized kittens with implanted cortical electrodes. Stimulation (binocular) occurs at onset of trace. Monopolar recordings; neck reference. Numbers indicate age in days; letters indicate

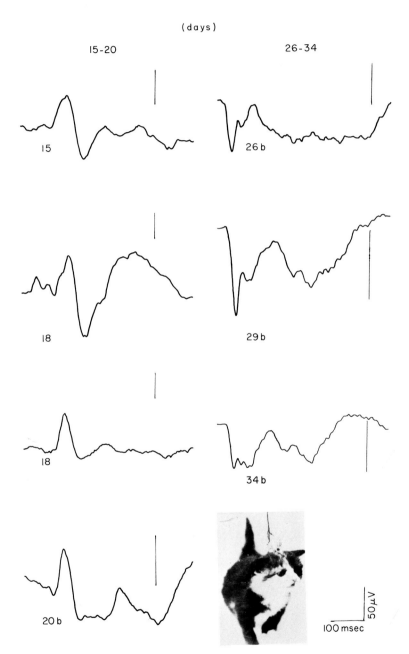

recordings from same animal (longitudinal series). Traces are algebraic summation of 25 successive responses to single flashes. 16-day-old kitten, see Fig. 12, A. (Rose and Gruenau, 1970a.)

anesthesized animals. Beginning at 2 weeks of age, responses from the unanesthetized preparations differed from those obtained under pentobarbital. A slight
negative (NA) deflection appeared between the original N1 and N2 negative
waves together with an increase in positivity (P2) preceding the original long
latency negative wave. These differences can be seen at 17 and 18 days of age
and become particularly obvious at 19 days of age (Fig. 7). *Subsequent* changes
consisted of the enhancement of both positive waves resulting, at about 30 days,
in a clearly definable double positive wave similar to that recorded in the adult.

Why this divergence in the sequence between anesthetized and unanesthetized
preparations beginning at 2 weeks of age? It is known that in the adult preparations states of wakefulness and sleep can alter the wave form of the evoked
response. These states develop gradually during maturation, as described by
Sterman and Hoppenbrouwers in Chapter 11 of this text.

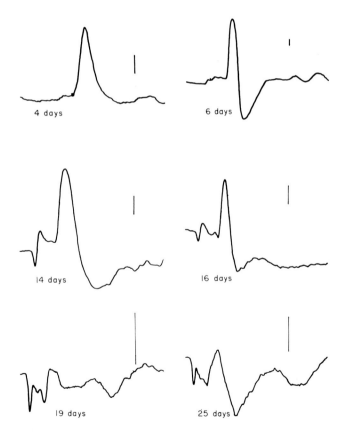

FIG. 7. Computer-averaged visually evoked potentials from contralateral cortex of
unanesthetized (flaxedilized) kittens at ages indicated. Focused monocular stimulation

Figure 8 illustrates EEG activity following a single light flash obtained from both a chronic (C) and flaxedilized (F) preparation. In immature animals, up to approximately 10 days of age, a single light flash is not followed by desynchronization, but rather by high amplitude spindlelike activity which can be quite synchronous. This activity is gradually replaced by a desynchronized pattern indicative of arousal in most animals by 2 weeks of age. This pattern of arousal is known to be mediated primarily by the reticular formation and blocked by barbituates.

Figure 9 illustrates the effect on VER's recorded from paralyzed preparations at two age levels of subsequent administration of pentobarbital. At 11 days of age, responses recorded under Flaxedil and under Flaxedil plus Nembutal are virtually identical, as shown in the superimposed tracings at c. This contrasts with the differences seen at 34 days between unanesthetized (A) and anesthe-

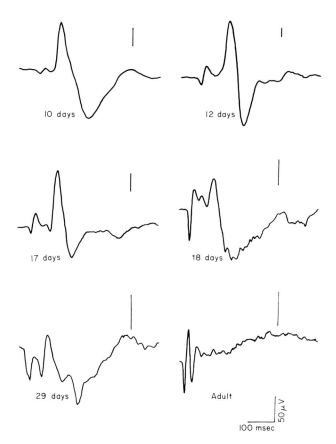

occurs at onset of trace. Monopolar recordings; neck reference (with ear reference check). Traces are algebraic summation of 25 responses.

tized (b) conditions in the same preparation. At c, the two responses are shown together, demonstrating that with barbituates the initial positive component increases in amplitude dramatically while the second positive component is essentially eliminated.

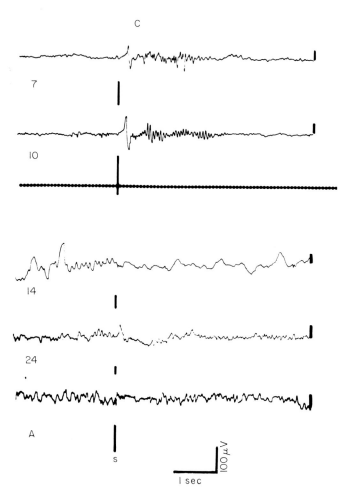

FIG. 8. EEG changes to light flash as a function of age (numbers indicate days) in unanesthetized kittens. Chronic preparations with implanted electrodes in row headed "C";

To complete the analysis of sequential VER changes with maturation, future studies will need to clarify in more detail the effects of functional state on the VER components. This necessitates devising a procedure for presenting controlled visual input, perhaps as suggested by several authors (Berlucchi *et al.*,

1966; Zattoni, 1968), to an unanesthetized chronic preparation in which behavioral and physiological states are constantly monitored. It should be added that questionable changes which have been reported in the literature as a function of development cannot be attributed solely to the emergence of consolidated

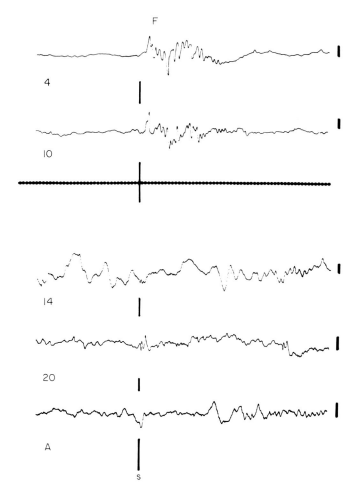

flaxedilized preparations in row headed "F." Letter S indicates light flash presentation. Monopolar recordings from marginal gyrus (L5). (Rose, Gruenau, and Spencer, 1970.)

behavioral states in older animals. Various experimental variables can also influence and drastically change the ontogenesis of the wave form, if precautions are not taken. Such factors as the use of unfocused stimulation, averaging procedures, variable interstimulus intervals and frontal reference electrodes in monopolar recordings can, in our own experience, produce misleading results (see Fig. 10).

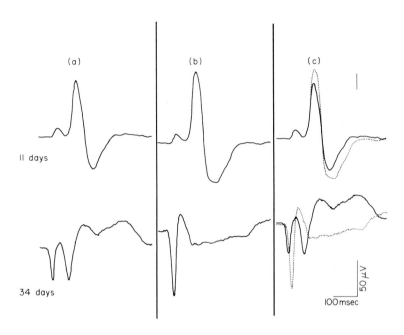

FIG. 9. Effect of pentobarbital anesthesia on visual electrocortical response recorded in unanesthetized (flaxedilized) preparation at two different age levels. a. Flaxedil, b. Flaxedil plus pentobarbital (Nembutal), c. Superimposition of a and b. Tracings are algebraic summation of 25 responses.

III. DIFFERENTIATION OF VER COMPONENTS

The immature visual system, as reflected in the gradual evolvement of VER components, provides a preparation in which anatomical substrata, as well as variations due to stimulus input during development, can be investigated. These components are distinguishable in terms of age of onset, latency, amplitude, and polarity. In our studies this has been accomplished in lightly anesthetized preparations, by (1) a study of the topography of the response components, (2) manipulation of internal states and stimulus parameters, and (3) observing the effects of selective subcortical lesions.

A. Topography

The early-appearing long-latency negative response can be recorded not only over primary or specific visual cortex, but also over clearly nonvisual cortical areas. For this reason it was labeled the nonspecific or diffuse component by Rose and Lindsley (1965, 1968), and is equivalent, therefore, to the *extra-primary response* or *component* A of Marty (1962). In contrast, the short latency positive-negative complex which usually develops between 10-20 days is found only over the primary visual area and was considered to be a *specific* response by Rose and Lindsley (1965, 1968) and called *component* B or *primary response* by Marty (1962).

Figure 11 shows the difference in distribution of these potentials over the cortical surface in a 13-day-old kitten. Tracings L5 and R6 from the primary visual cortex show both the long latency positive-negative complex identified as the specific visual response and the higher amplitude long-latency negative response of early origin identified as the nonspecific response. Other sites show only the long latency negative response. This differentiation between response components, which is also obtained in longitudinal studies, supports the original, more extensive analysis of Marty (1962). In cross-sectional recordings at increasing ages, he obtained data which suggest that the nonspecific or extraprimary response is the precursor of so-called association and/or polysensory region responses. The evolution of the extraprimary response in contrast to the primary response is shown in Fig. 12. As previously mentioned, the former response in older animals (i.e., beyond 2 weeks) is evident only under chloralose.

B. Stimulus Parameters

It has also been established that VER components can be further differentiated by the manipulation of external stimulus parameters. In the dark adapted state, between approximately 10 and 25 days of age, a single light flash produces the positive-negative-negative wave form previously outlined. If the kitten, however, is light adapted for 5 min and then presented with single flashes superimposed on the adapting light, there is a maximal reduction of the longer latency negative wave over both visual (R6) and nonvisual (R8) areas with minimal involvement of the shorter latency positive-negative complex.

C. Subcortical Lesions

The most definitive data indicating that the components of the immature VER reflect activity in different sensory pathways have been obtained in studies involving selective subcortical lesions. Rose and Lindsley (1965, 1968) postulated that the long latency negative component of *widespread cortical distribution* is dependent upon input to a nonspecific sensory system, probably via tectal and/or pretectal pathways involving the brachium of the superior colliculus (and possibly involving the reticular formation). In contrast, the positive-negative complex, restricted to the primary visual cortex, was felt to depend upon specific sensory input via the lateral geniculate. It was predicted that lesions of the lateral geniculate would interfere exclusively with the "specific" positive-negative complex projected upon the primary visual cortex. On the

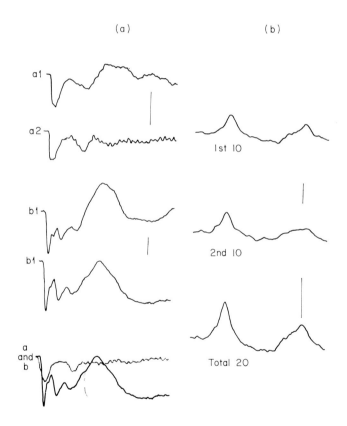

FIG. 10. Effect of experimental variables on visually evoked response configuration. Column a, 14-day-old kitten: a_1 and a_2 summated responses obtained from cortical electrodes in unanesthetized chronic preparation to nonfocused binocular stimulation; b_1 and b_2, same animal, same animal site but under Flaxedil and focused monocular stimulation; a and b = superimposition of chronic (dotted line) and Flaxedil (solid line) responses. Algebraic summation of 25 responses. Column b. 13-day-old unanesthetized (chronic) kitten showing algebraic summation of first 10, second 10, and total 20 responses. A clearly

other hand, lesions of the superior collicular-pretectal region should block the "nonspecific" long latency negative component.

Figure 13 illustrates the effect of a lesion of the right superior collicular-pretectal region in a 9-day-old kitten, whose cortical response to a single light flash consists only of the long latency negative response. Such lesions, in animals in which the shorter latency positive-negative complex has emerged, caused selective abolition of the long latency negative wave over the posterior primary visual areas as well as over ipsilateral mid-ectosylvian or nonspecific visual areas. In these cases there was no involvement of the lateral geniculate body, nor were

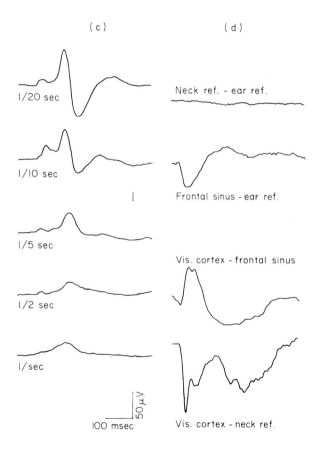

shorter latency positive-negative wave is seen only in the second 10 responses with minimal detection in the total 20 responses. This is a function, in part, of latency variance. Column c. 5-day-old unanesthetized (Flaxedil) kitten showing wave form distortion as a function of flash frequency. Column d. 29-day-old Flaxedilized kitten demonstrating wave form alterations as a function of reference utilized. Columns c and d. Algebraic summation of 25 responses. (Rose, Gruenau, and Spencer, 1970.)

the shorter latency PN_2 waves affected (Rose and Lindsley, 1968). In contrast, if a lesion was placed in the specific visual relay nucleus, the lateral genticulate, the short latency positive-negative complex was abolished, leaving the negative

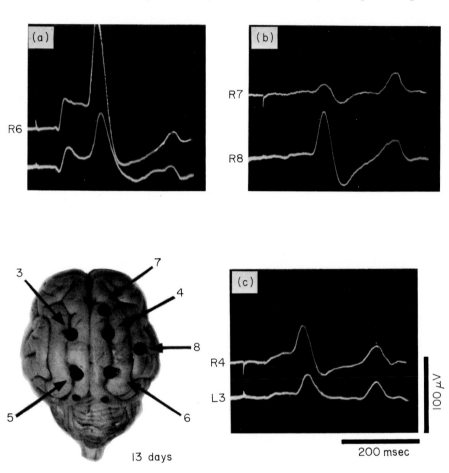

Kitten M 43 R2

FIG. 11. Topographical distribution of specific and nonspecific visually evoked response components in 13-day-old kitten under light pentobarbital anesthesia. Arrow: left eye stimulation. a. Records from posterior visual area showing short-latency positive-negative complex (specific response) and long latency (150 msec to peak), high amplitude, negative wave (nonspecific response). b. Records from nonvisual area electrode sites, R7, posterior sigmoid gyrus, R8, midectosylvian gyrus, showing only long-latency (150 msec to peak) negative wave (nonspecific response). c. Records from anterior margin of visual area II, well forward on marginal gyrus, showing mainly long-latency (150 msec to peak), negative wave (nonspecific response). Light flash at first sharp deflection of trace. (Rose and Lindsley, 1968.)

response relatively unaffected, as shown in Fig. 14. Note that the so-called secondary response, described by Brazier (1957), can be seen in a, and was also abolished after a lesion of the lateral geniculate nucleus. This, along with other evidence we have accumulated (Rose, 1968c), indicates its independence from the pathways mediating the long latency negative wave of interest here.

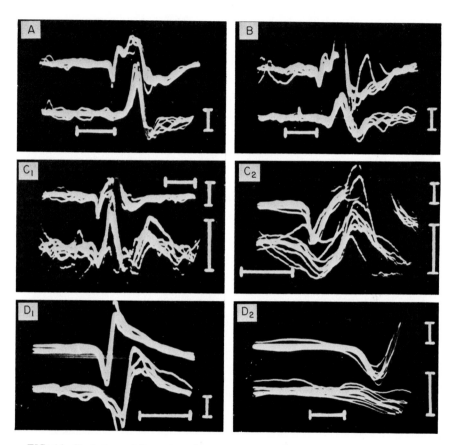

FIG. 12. Evolution of the extra-primary response to light stimulation in the chloralose cat. Cat ages: 16 day (A), 17 days (B), 24 days (C_1 and C_2) and 30 days (D_1 and D_2). Recordings from the posterior part of the lateral gyrus (all upper traces) and over the middle suprasylvian sulcus (all lower traces). Concerning the lower traces, note the progressive transformation of the long latency negative wave (A and B) to an "associative" type response (C and D). Time: 100 msec (A, B, C), 50 msec (C_2, D) and 10 msec (D_2). Amplitude 200 μV (A, B, C_1, C_2) and 500 μV (D_1, D_2). (Translated from Marty, 1962).

These results on acute preparations have been confirmed and extended by Kovar (1969) who did follow-up recordings at various intervals after specific or nonspecific subcortical lesions early in infancy.

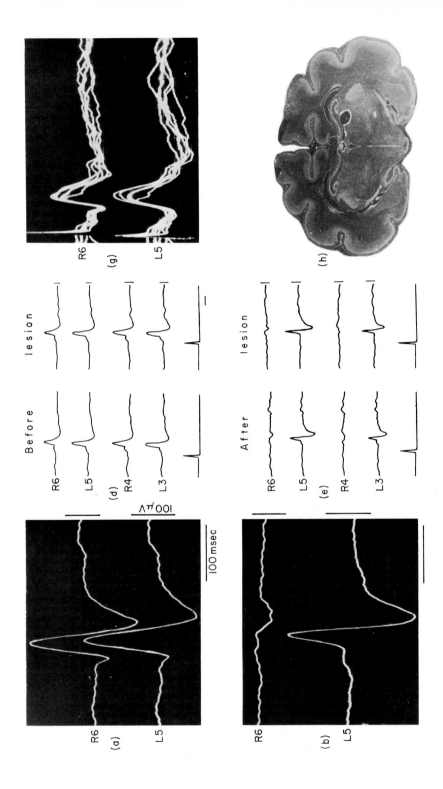

R6
L5
(g)

(h)

lesion
Before
R6
L5
(d)
R4
L3

100 μV

lesion
After
R6
L5
(e)
R4
L3

100 msec

R6
(a)
L5

R6
(b)
L5

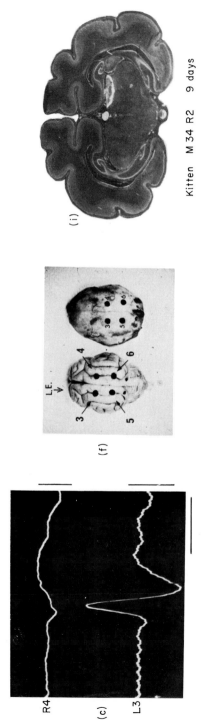

Kitten   M 34 R2   9 days

FIG. 13. Effect of electrolytic lesion of light superior colliculus and pretectal region on nonspecific, long-latency, negative component. Left eye stimulated. a and d. Before lesion; long-latency negative wave present in both posterior (R6 and L5) and anterior (R4 and L3) visual areas; positive-negative complex of short latency mainly absent at this age. g. Before lesion, electrical stimulation at electrodes in lesion site produces same type of wave in R6 and L5 as does light flash stimulation (a). b, c, and e. After lesion; long-latency negative wave abolished only in R6 and R4 on side of lesion. f. Locus of electrodes shown on skull, and diagramed over brain. i. Lesion of right superior colliculus and pretectal region. h. Small rostral extension of electrolytic lesion into thalamus, including portions of pulvinar and posterolateral nucleus, but without invasion of lateral geniculate body or optic pathways. (Rose and Linsley, 1968.)

It will be necessary to continue these studies to other subcortical structures in anesthetized and especially unanesthetized preparations. It would be desirable, also, to record gross VERs from subcortical structures and to achieve further analysis by intra and extracellular recordings. Such studies will not only extend our information with regard to the immature animal but will likewise provide data for the analysis of adult VER electrogenesis.

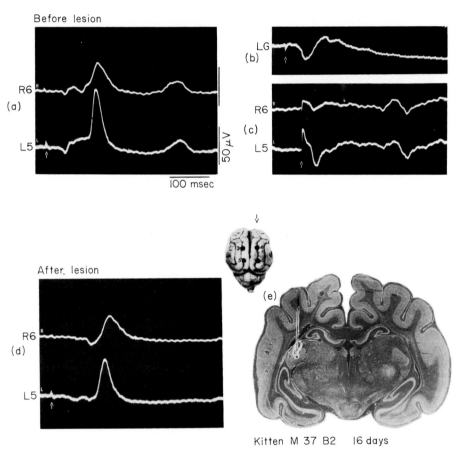

FIG. 14. Effect of lesion of left lateral geniculate nucleus upon specific short-latency response. Right eye stimulated. a. Before lesion, showing specific short-latency, positive-negative complex and nonspecific long-latency negative wave and followed by a lower amplitude, longer latency (340 msec) negative wave. d. After lesion of left lateral geniculate nucleus (area of necrosis outlined in white in e), showing removal of specific short-latency positive-negative complex in both right (R6 and left (L5) visual areas. b and c. Before lesion; b, lateral geniculate response to light flash (arrow), c, visual cortex response to electrical stimulation (arrow) of left lateral geniculate through electrodes with which lesion to be made. (Rose and Lindsley, 1968.)

IV. STRUCTURAL PHYSIOLOGICAL AND BEHAVIORAL RELATION-
   SHIPS

The specification of relationships between structural, physiological, and behavioral maturation, based on the developmental data acquired to date is difficult. Information at various age levels is derived either from conclusions drawn from independent studies undertaken in separate disciplines, or from experiments in which a combination of these approaches are utilized as independent and dependent variables in the same investigation. For the sake of discussion the former will be referred to as correlative and the latter as manipulative studies.

A. Correlative Studies

The expression of relationships between anatomical, physiological, and behavioral development, at this date, is hindered by (a) lack of sufficient information from a large number of species and (b) a deficiency in multidisciplinary data from a particular species. Whereas considerable recent data have been obtained on the maturation of structural and physiological systems in the kitten, there is a great scarcity of behavioral data. With regard to the onset of behavioral responses per se, we have hardly advanced beyond the meager and often conflicting data presented in Cruikshank's review (1946). The onset of nonvisual blinking in the rabbit, for example, is said to occur either on day 2 (Kao, 1927) or day 14 (Mills, 1898); initial response to sound in the kitten either on day 8 (Mills, 1898) or day 1 (Windle, 1930). In many reports controlled experimentation is lacking and the data are based on casual observation usually in conjunction with the investigation of another facet of development.

Nevertheless, several initial schema have been presented such as that shown in Fig. 15 from M. Fox (1970) which, as the data accumulate, can be elaborated upon. Himwich (1962) and Rose and Ellingson (1970) have published similar figures, the latter with respect to the characteristic VER pattern within a narrow age range. Initial behavioral or anatomical correlations with regard to visual electrophysiological development in kittens have been attempted also (the reader is referred to Ellingson and Rose, 1970, for correlative EEG changes).

The appearance of the long latency negative wave appears to correlate with maturation of the superficial apical dendrites and axodendritic connections. During this period the kitten displays no behavorial change in response to light with the exception, based on our observations, of nonvisual blinking (3-5 sec latency); the eyes first open at 9-12 days of age. During the second week of life when the shorter latency positive-negative component develops, there exists a coincident maturation of the basilar dendrites and axosomatic connections, according to Purpura (1961). Scheibel, on the other hand, suggests a relationship between the later maturing positivity and the development of a new neuropil field consisting of the terminating presynaptic arbor of the specific thalamocortical relay, as well as the appearance of short Golgi type II cells. Further details of these considerations are presented in Chapters 1 and 2 of this volume. Behaviorally during this period the kitten manifests initial visual pursuit activity. Between 9 and 15 days electrocortical sensory arousal first appears. The onset of classical conditioning with light as the CS should also occur during this period (interpolated from dog data, Fuller *et al.*, 1950). By 20 days of age the kitten walks and is guided by visual stimulation. Thus the onset and development of visual behavior seems to correlate with the approximate onset of spontaneous rythmic electrical activity, with the onset of specific visual evoked response components, and the progressive consolidation of "nonspecific" component with the shorter latency primary visual response.

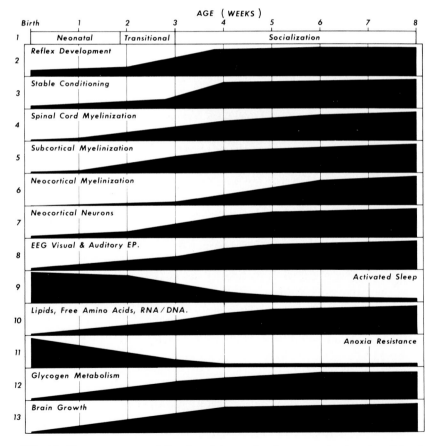

FIG. 15. Neuro-ontogeny of the dog. Schema showing approximate rates of development of various aspects of brain and behavior in the dog. (M. Fox, 1970.)

The involvement of the superior colliculus, pretectal and/or lateral thalamic regions (e.g., posterior-lateral nucleus), presumably relaying the diffuse N2 wave, in more cognitive type functions, aside from their "specific" role in visual reflex activity, is supported by lesion studies on adult animals. Their role in behavioral maturation will become clearer as developmental studies proceed.

At the cortical level, Thompson and Kramer (1965) have shown, for example, that lesions of the cortical regions from which nonspecific or polysensory evoked responses are recordable in adult cats prevented the subsequent development of sensory preconditioning involving paired light and tone. In addition visual as well as auditory and somatic electrocortical responses in these regions were significantly decreased during presentation of novel stimuli in any modality (Thompson and Shaw, 1965). The suggestion often made in these and similar studies is that the "nonspecific" cortical and subcortical regions have a primary role in attentional aspects of behavior, whereas the "specific" regions have the primary but not exclusive task of relaying modality specific information (Lindsley, 1958).

Until sufficient additional data are obtained on developmental electrogenesis in kittens, one can only offer initial speculations as to its relevance or role in behavioral maturation. Tentatively, therefore, the diffuse, polysensory nature of the earliest responses suggests general alerting or integrative functions as opposed to those systems which mature later and are concerned with specific afferent information of a particular modality. If arousal functions in immature animals are mediated independently of the classical visual functions, e.g., lateral geniculate, then bilateral destruction of this nucleus should drastically impair vision per se, but not behavioral and electrocortical arousal to light flash. No evidence is presently available on this point.

In summary, a greater sophistication in techniques to delineate the perceptual capacities of very young animals is a prerequisite to the assessment of these functions following specific or nonspecific lesions. The quantification of such activity, that is, measuring the animal's ability to perceive different objects at an age when a learning paradigm cannot be used, is extremely difficult. Techniques utilizing the visual cliff, optokinetic reflexes, and orientation reflexes such as used by Fantz (1965), Haith (1966), and Salapatek (1968) in the human infant will have to be devised.

B. Manipulative Data

Two types of studies may be found in the developmental field involving manipulations across disciplines: (1) those which evaluate the effects of early versus later experiential conditions on adult functions and (2) those concerned with direct studies *during* development involving several disciplines. Although considerable information exists concerning manipulations within a given discipline (i.e., the effect of early behavioral manipulations on adult behavior) this approach will not be considered in this section. Emphasis will be placed on multidisciplinary studies involving in particular the visual system.

1. Effect of Early Experimental Manipulations on Adult Functions

Studies of adult visual functions, in which the internal as opposed to the external milieu is altered in infancy, are few in number. The distinction between internal and external manipulations is for convenience only, of course, since external stimulation during development is often accompanied by anatomical and physiological changes.

   a. *Internal Milieu.* The most common early internal *manipulation* involves the ablation of brain tissue early in infancy versus similar lesions sustained in adulthood, with subsequent comparison of sparing or loss of function at later dates. A sparing of function following early lesions is the usual finding. Early versus late primary visual cortex lesions result in sparing of photic frequency and brightness discrimination in monkeys (Tucker *et al.,* 1968), pattern discrimination in cats (Wetzel *et al.,* 1965) and depth discrimination in rabbits (Stewart, 1968). In fact, early postnatal hemidecortication in kittens results in sparing of right–left spatial discriminations and the ability to orient quickly to a visual stimulus at various points within the visual field (Wenzel *et al.,* 1962). Lesions in adulthood severely affected most of the above functions.

   It must be stressed, however, that not all visual functions are spared. Thus, for example, both early and late lesioned monkeys failed to display visual tracking behavior and frequently bumped into objects while walking on the floor. Flicker and brightness discrimination was possible only in a controlled shuttle-box situation (Tucker *et al.,* 1968).

   Electrophysiological evidence for functional reorganization after infant lesions was obtained in two recent studies. Tucker *et al.* (1968) report a reduction of VERs outside the primary visual cortex in adult monkeys with early lesions as contrasted with late-lesioned and control animals, and Stewart (1968) reports that the latency of rabbit VERs recorded at posterior points, lateral to the lesioned striate cortex, are shorter for infant operates and controls than adult operates. The comparison of subcortical VERs of infant and adult operates and controls may also provide information as to the locale of relevant compensatory structures. The effects of some endocrine manipulations upon the development of cortical evoked responses are discussed by Schapiro in Chapter 17 of this text.

   b. *External Milieu.* The largest number of studies in this category are concerned with the later anatomical, physiological, and behavioral manifestations of early *deprivation.* Due to space limitations, visual electrophysiological data will be emphasized. For information regarding other modalities, the reader is referred to the excellent reviews by Riesen (1966) and M. Fox (1970).

Before proceeding, it may be useful to underscore several relevant points: (1) The effects obtained in the various disciplines (e.g., anatomy, physiology, behavior) due to light deprivation are inconsistent. This situation may be a function in part, of species differences, but is more likely due to variations in technique of assessment of the independent and dependent variables. Thus "visual deprivation" has included afferent denervation (enucleation), total or almost total dark rearing, unilateral or bilateral semideprivation by lid closure or occluders, with the procedures initiated anywhere from before birth to weaning, for varying lengths of time, and with and without adequate controls (see Fuller and Waller, 1962; King, 1958; Solomon and Lessac, 1968). (2) Visual deprivation may cause varying degrees of deficit in measures of some but not other disciplines (i.e., histological but not physiological, or in different measures or locales within a discipline such as histology (i.e., lateral geniculate but not cortex). (3) Unilateral deprivation may cause more severe defects than bilateral deprivation (see below). (4) The possible contaminating effects of social deprivation in addition to visual deprivation per se have usually been overlooked (e.g., Melzack and Burns, 1965).

To date, studies of the effects of early light deprivation on the electroretinogram (ERG) have been confined to the cat and monkey. The ERG is first seen between the sixth and tenth day of age in the cat (Zetterstrom, 1956; Hellstrom and Zetterstrom, 1956) and at or near birth in the monkey (Ordy et al., 1962, 1965). The onset of this response in the kitten can be delayed up to 3 weeks by dark rearing, although it is occasionally elicited with increased latency before this period. However, a normal ERG can be elicited from 4-week dark-reared cats as well as from younger animals after a period of light "priming." Baxter and Riesen (1961) reported no ERG abnormality in cats reared in darkness for 1 year in response to 1/min flashes but a selective diminution of the B wave to 1/10 sec flashes of high intensity. This effect was eliminated after exposing the animals to 48 hr of illumination. A similar effect on the B wave of the cat was obtained by Ganz et al. (1968) in animals with 1-6 months monocular deprivation. Cats reared for 12-18 months in total darkness showed an even greater reduction of the B wave, a diminished cortical flicker fusion (CFF), and deficient temporal resolution inferred from recovery functions of paired stimuli.

Comparable B wave reductions have been obtained also in the monkey exposed to continual darkness for 5 weeks. However, it should be noted that Cornwell et al. (1962), also report a reduction of the B wave recorded from the eye of an adult cat subjected to monocular deprivation for only 1 week. Of interest is the fact that whereas Baxter and Riesen report recovery after only 48 hr, a week recovery period appears necessary for adult cats (Cornwell et al., 1962).

The effects of light deprivation on spontaneous and evoked electrocortical activity have been studied in rabbits, cats, and monkeys. Scherrer and Fourment (1964) obtained EEG records from unanesthetized rabbits which had undergone 4-12 months of light deprivation. When obtaining records while the animals were in their rearing conditions (i.e., dark experimental chamber) the spontaneous EEGs were normal. However under such conditions EEG arousal to a novel stimulus (light, sound, electric shock) was longer than usual; when recordings were obtained in a dark but novel environment, an intense long-lasting (up to several hours) EEG arousal was manifest.

VERs in dark-reared animals differed from controls in their distribution, latency, wave form, and amplitude. Responses to electrical and sound stimulation increased in amplitude in all cortical areas, notably the occipital region, while responses to *flash* showed a considerable decrease in the positive but not the negative occipital component. Longer "extra-primary" responses to light flash in somesthetic and motor areas were noted also. Scherrer and Fourment (1964) point out the similarity of the latter responses to those of newborn animals as reported by Marty (1962) and by the author. A similar finding and conclusion is reported for the dog by M. Fox (1970). They further suggest that the change in VERs, as well as the excessive EEG arousal, are due to an induced hypersensitivity of nonspecific systems, supporting the concept of a duality of visual pathways.

Contrary to the above, Baxter (1966) reports no change in spontaneous EEGs recorded from unanesthetized cats dark-reared for one year beginning at 3 days of age. The experimental animals were able to follow from 1 to 50 flashes per second but with attenuated flicker-induced potentials (FIP). It is suggested that the FIP reduction is a consequence of "heightened arousal produced by the novel light environment." Wiesel and Hubel (1963a) report that VERs elicited from a previously occluded (2 months) eye are of longer latency with considerable reduction in the negative as opposed to the positive component. However, these results were obtained after monocular deprivation under a general anesthetic as opposed to the above studies obtained from unanesthetized preparations under binocular deprivation. Finally Riesen (1961) reported abnormal EEG "spiking" in dark-reared monkeys and Lindsley et al. (1964) reported an enhancement of ON-OFF responses and a reversal of EEG arousal effects (i.e., to darkness onset instead of light) in visually deprived monkeys.

In an important series of studies Wiesel and Hubel (1963a,b; 1965a,b) have delineated contrasting physiological and anatomical effects in cortical as well as subcortical structures as a function of binocular or monocular semi-light deprivation. Early visual deprivation by monocular eye lid closure or insertion of a translucent occluder causes marked atrophy of lateral geniculate layers receiving input from the deprived eye (Wiesel and Hubel, 1963b); however, electrophysiologically most geniculate cells responded almost normally. In contrast, no gross histological effects were seen at the striate cortex. (Subtle histological defects with regard to the dendritic spines have since been reported: Coleman and Riesen, 1968; Globus and Scheibel, 1967; Valverde, 1967). However, considerable physiological deficit was found. Most cortical cells can be driven from both eyes in normal cats, yet very few cells could be driven by the deprived eye. Opening of the deprived eye and allowing long (3-15 months) visual exposure produced minimal recovery, in contrast to the substantial recovery of gross VER's (Wiesel and Hubel, 1965a). Unexpectedly, however, binocular deprivation did not eliminate single cell responsiveness. A great number of responsive cells were recorded, half of them normal in spite of geniculate atrophy in all layers accompanied by severe visual deficits (Wiesel and Hubel, 1965b).

Ganz et al. (1968) confirm that binocular summation on single cortical cells is considerably reduced, and when present is abnormal. However, in contrast to Wiesel and Hubel's inability to drive cortical cells from the monocularly deprived eye (1965a,b), these authors report that as many cells could be activated via stimulation of the deprived (38.5%) as via the normal eye (36.1%). Wiesel and Hubel (1965b) and Ganz et al. (1968) suggest in part that the deficit seen in cortical cells stimulated by the monocularly deprived eye, but driven by both eyes, is a function of enhanced synaptic connections or efficiency of normal fibers at the expense of fibers from the deprived eye, resulting in a dominance of the former.

Wiesel and Hubel (1963a) in addition suggest that since the receptive fields of young inexperienced kittens are highly similar to those of the adult, connections which are intact at birth become defective through disuse in visually deprived animals, and not because early neural connections depend on visual experience.

It must be emphasized, however, that Wiesel and Hubel's youngest kittens were 8 days of age, which is the approximate age of onset of the specific VER, and that an early diffuse (negative) VER is first recordable between 2 and 4 days of age, at a time when single unit activity to light flash is also first recordable at the cortex (Huttenlocher, 1967). The earliest responses may or may not involve the geniculate relay. Furthermore, one must caution against the oversimplification of equating visual *system* with classical visual pathways since it is obvious that the latter path alone cannot subserve visual functioning, without correlating systems mediating attention, arousal, etc., some of which are phylogenetically older and ontogenetically mature earlier.

The data reported above have dealt with total or semideprivation with regard to the visual modality only, ignoring the possible additional effects of other sensory restriction and partial or total social isolation. Consideration of these variables is necessary since Melzack and Burns (1965) have shown that rearing dogs singly in restriction cages for 1½ to 2 years produces (1) excessive EEG arousal in the reticular formation and cortex upon visual exposure to a novel cage and (2) reduction in amplitude and alternation in wave form of responses evoked by click and flash in the reticular formation and cortex. The greatest effect was on the late rather than early evoked response components, those presumably traveling via multisynaptic pathways also involved in EEG arousal.

Several recent studies have further demonstrated histological and neurochemical changes as a function of early experiental manipulations as discussed in Chapters 14 and 15 of this volume.

In addition, there are studies in which selective stimulation or hyperstimulation of a limited nature or modality is given to the animal during development. It is known that early prenatal exposure to light can hasten the onset of VER development in chicks (Garcia-Austt and Patetta-Queirolo, 1961), and ducks (Paulson, 1965). Even without overt motor reflexes, the effect of early prenatal sensory stimulation (e.g., excessive light) can be evaluated later when motor connections are manifest (Gottlieb, 1968). These findings indicate that sensory systems can process "information" in the absence of reflex feedback. Finally Heron and Anchel (1964) report changes in VERs and spontaneous EEGs in adult rats who from birth to 3-6 months were constantly bombarded by 5/sec light flashes and synchronous clicks.

In our laboratories we have reared isolated mothers and their kittens under constant illumination for a period of 6-8 months. Although the experimental kittens, in contrast to controls (normal environment and dark-light cycle), were normal in terms of visual placing, attention to and ability to follow objects and visual cliff responses, they were deficient in blinking and pupillary responses. Contrary to expectations, the kittens' pupils remained dilated on exposure to light, in contrast to the response of the mother, as shown in Fig. 16. Recovery gradually occurred in the ensuing months. Electrophysiologically, no differences existed in the latency of VERs to single flashes, but there was a considerable increase in VER amplitude, as shown in Fig. 17. Although not controlled for, the effects do not appear to be due to isolation per se since isolation would be expected to reduce VER amplitude (Melzack and Burns, 1965); however, arousal effects due to the novel recording conditions cannot be excluded.

2. Direct Electrophysiological-Behavioral Manipulations

Assessment of brain-behavior relationships during ontogeny in terms of the traditional fields of psychology is almost nonexistent. There are virtually no neurophysiological studies concerned with the development of emotion, motivation, hunger or thirst mechanisms; the reinforcing properties of brain stimulation have not been assessed during development; the neurophysiological correlates of learning development are unknown, etc. Such developmental studies, of course, are beset with technical difficulties. As Campbell (1967) points out, some of the problems include: (a) equating motivation and reinforcement at various age levels, (b) assessing unlearned preferences (e.g., light) which may change with age, (c) controlling for early experiential effects and (d) choosing measures adequate for the age tested. We would emphasize the careful choice of independent as well as dependent variables; somesthetic but not visual stimulation may serve as a conditionable stimulus at a particular age level; likewise head turning but not leg flexion may be an appropriate age-related dependent variable.

FIG. 16. Effects of light rearing on pupillary constriction. Photographs taken in well-lighted room. LK, light-reared kittens; LA, light-reared adult (mother); NK, normal kitten; NA, normal adult. Note pupillary size in LK animals. Kittens are 8 months of age. (Rose and Gruenau, 1970b.)

Corner *et al.* (1966) have correlated changes in EEG activity in chicks between 1 and 13 days of age, with various behavioral changes in a test condition. As familiarization with a normal environment and approach behavior toward home (familiar) environment increased, the EEG changed from a predominately high frequency pattern to one consisting of continual 2-5/sec slow waves. The authors remind us that such slow and fast wave activity occurs in the chick in the absence of a neocortex. In what may be the only study utilizing the

EEG as a dependent variable in a developmental learning situation, Scheibel (1962) demonstrated electrophysiological changes when vocalization of a kitten's name (CS) was followed by milk reinforcement. Whereas initially no change was noted following the CS, in subsequent trials a decrease in amplitude and an increase in frequency was evident to the reinforced name, but not to unreinforced names nor other unconditioned stimuli. However, these important initial studies were performed in older kittens (10 weeks).

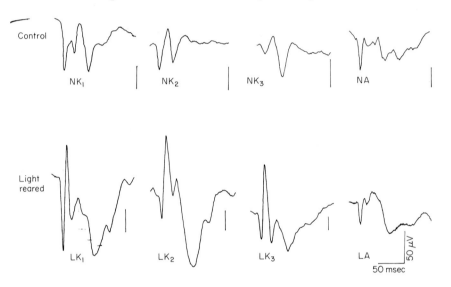

FIG. 17. Visual evoked potentials from light-reared and control animals. Tracings are monopolar recordings obtained from awake, unanesthetized animals with skull screws and represent the algebraic summation of 50 responses. LK, light-reared kittens; LA, light-reared adult (mother); NK, normal kittens; NA, normal adult. Kittens are 8 months of age. Vertical lines: 50 μV. (Rose and Gruenau, 1970b.)

In our own laboratories we have initiated a series of learning studies in younger kittens in which VERs are treated as dependent as well as independent variables. It is known, for example, in studies of adult animals that the amplitude of a conditionable stimulus, such as a click or a light flash, is greatly enhanced during subsequent conditioning trials when such a signal is followed by food (e.g., Hearst *et al.* 1960). The question arises as to whether the various VER components present at different age levels will be differentially affected, and whether the electrophysiological change may actually precede, maturationally, the motor response required in the conventional conditioning paradigm.

In the above situation, the behavioral conditions are preset by the investigator and variations in the VER noted. Interpretation of the evoked potential changes, however, is difficult. Without adequate controls one is uncertain as to whether the resultant changes are due to learning per se or to alteration in motivational, arousal, etc. states. Therefore, we have also begun studies in which changes in the components of the immature VER are treated as the independent variable or the contingency for reinforcement. In such a situation the components of the VER can be controlled and treated as a behavioral event. The immature animal's overt behavioral responses, coincident with VER modification, can then be assessed. This contrasts with the conventional conditioning paradigm in which the experimenter selects the behavioral criteria for reinforcement, which in fact the immature animal may be incapable of performing adequately. Recent elegant studies on adult animals and humans have shown that this procedure is feasible for autonomic responses such as heart rate, blood pressure, GSR, etc. (Miller, 1969) as well as for electrophysiological responses (S. S. Fox and Rudell, 1968).

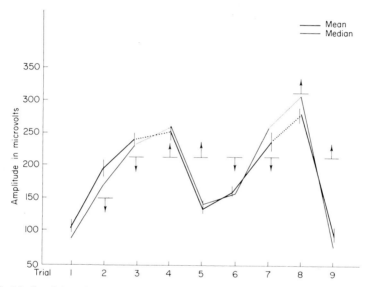

FIG. 18 Conditioned VER amplitude variations in a 10-day-old flaxedilized kitten. Each trial consists of 50 light flashes. Thick line: median amplitude; thin line: mean amplitude with standard deviations (vertical lines). Arrows point in direction of amplitude changes to be avoided, i.e., in downward direction, animal's task is to increase N2 wave amplitude. See text for details.

Pilot studies (Figs. 18 and 19) in our own laboratories have suggested that such techniques are possible even in very immature animals. Utilizing an avoidance conditioning paradigm in 10-day-old unanesthetized (flaxedilized) kittens, in which a prominent N2 wave is evoked by light flash, the immature animal could be made to either increase *or* decrease response amplitude to specified criteria to avoid shock.

Figure 18 presents data from one 10-day-old kitten in which N2 amplitude was made to decrease, then increase, decrease and finally increase over a series of 9 trials, involving 50 flash presentations per trial. The task for each succeeding trial (following a 10-min wait) was to either increase or decrease the median amplitude of the previous trial run. That is, the median N2 amplitude in trial 1 (initial standard run) became the criterion to be exceeded on trial 2, median N2 amplitude on trial 2 became the criterion to be exceeded on trial 3. The arrows indicate amplitude direction which was negatively reinforced (i.e., to be avoided, which in trials 2 and 3 was an amplitude decrease). In trial 4 the task was to avoid amplitude increase, i.e., to decrease N2 amplitude. This was not accomplished, i.e., the animal received mild shock, but amplitude reduction dramatically occurred in trial 5. Trials 6-9 are a repeat run.

The amplitude reductions in both trials 5 and 9 occurred after trials in which considerable negative reinforcement was given, raising the question whether some phenomenon akin to spreading depression, caused by shock, led to the subsequent amplitude decrease; hence a yoked shock control animal was imperative. Figure 19 presents percent amplitude changes with regard to the immediate previous trial for the experimental animal (E), a control animal (S) receiving identical negative reinforcement without regard to amplitude change, and an animal (L-control) receiving only light flashes to assess normal amplitude variations. As can be seen, not only are the percent variations considerably lower in

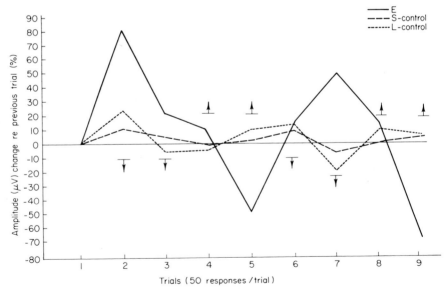

FIG. 19. Percent amplitude changes over trials (50 responses/trial) in experimental E—learning), shock control (S—control) and light control (L—control) animals during VER conditioning run with increase (+) or decrease (-) of mean amplitude with regard to the immediate previous trial indicated. See text for details.

the controls, but they are unrelated to the task conditions. After a considerable number of shock responses in trials 4 and 8, the shock control animals actually slightly increased their amplitudes on trials 5 and 9 reducing the possibility that the amplitude decreases in later trials in the experimental animal were a function of shock per se.

It is emphasized that these results are tentative, but they appear to indicate that responses previously labeled "automatic" are capable of active regulation, even in immature systems. Of greater importance perhaps is the fact that such procedures, in completely unanesthetized immature preparations, allow one to focus on the concomitant behavioral processes accompanying physiological changes (and vice versa) in immature preparations, with a very limited and hence more easily specified behavioral repertoire.

V. SUMMARY AND CONCLUSIONS

This chapter has been concerned with electrophysiological, and to a lesser extent, anatomical and behavioral indices of maturation of the visual system in animals. The number of such studies will increase as attempts to comprehend the complexities of the immature as well as the mature central nervous system continue. It is hoped that studies in animals concerned with the effects of early environmental conditions will become increasingly relevant in focusing attention on detrimental environmental and social conditions in humans which presumably cause similar effects.

REFERENCES

Auerbach, E., Beller, A. J., Henkes, H. E., and Goldfaber, G. (1961). *Vision Res. 1*, 166-182.
Baxter, B. (1966). *Exp. Neurol. 14*, 224-237.
Baxter, B., and Riesen, A. H. (1961). *Science 134*, 1626.
Berlucchi, G., Munson, J. B., and Rizzolatti, G. (1966). *Electroencephologr. Clin. Neurophysiol. 21*, 505-506.
Brazier, M. A. B. (1957). *Acta Physiol. Pharmacol. Neer. 6*, 692-714.
Callison, D. A. and Spencer, J. W. (1968). *Develop. Psychobiol. 1*, 196-205.
Campbell, B. A. (1967). *In* "Early Behavior: Comparative and Developmental Approaches" (H. W. Stevenson, E. W. Hess, and H. L. Rheingold, eds.), pp. 43-71. Wiley, New York.
Coleman, P. D., and Riesen, A. H. (1968). *J. Anat. 102*, 363-374.
Corner, M. A., Peters, J. J., and Van der Loeff, P. R. (1966). *Brain Res. 2*, 274-292.
Cornwell, A. C., Sharpless, S. K., and Kanor, S. (1962). *Fed. Amer. Soc. Exp. Biol. Proc. 21:2*, 357.
Cruikshank, R. M. (1946). *In* "Manual of Child Psychology" (L. Carmichael, ed.), pp. 167-189. Wiley, New York.
Ellingson, R. J., and Rose, G. H. (1970). *In* "Developmental Neurobiology" (W. A. Himwich, ed.), pp. 441-474. Thomas, Springfield, Illinois.
Ellingson, R. J., and Wilcott, R. C. (1960). *J. Neurophysiol. 23*, 363-375.

Fantz, R. L. (1965). *Ann. N. Y. Acad. Sci. 118,* 793.

Fox, M. (1968). *Electroencephalogr. Clin. Neurophysiol. 24,* 213-226.

Fox, M. (1970). integrative Development of the Brain and Behavior." Univ. of Chicago Press, Chicago, Illinois (in press).

Fox, S. S., and Rudell, A. P. (1968). *Science 162,* 1299-1302.

Fuller, J. L., and Waller, M. D. (1962). *In* "Roots of Behavior" (E. L. Bliss, ed.), pp. 235-245. Harper (Hoeber, New York).

Fuller, J. L., Easler, C. A., and Banks, E. M. (1950). *Amer. J. Physiol. 160,* 462-466.

Ganz, L., Fitch, M., and Satterberg, J. A. (1968). *Exp. Neurol. 22,* 614-637.

Garcia-Austt, E., and Patetta-Queirolo, M. A. (1961). *Acta Neurol. Latinoamer. 7,* 179-189.

Globus, A., and Scheibel, A. B. (1967). *Exp. Neurol. 19,* 331-345.

Gottlieb, G. (1968). *Quart. Rev. Biol. 43,* 148-174.

Haith, M. M. (1966). *J. Exp. Child Psychol. 3,* 289-295.

Hearst, E., Beer, B., Sheatz, G., and Galambos, R. (1960). *Electroencephalogr. Clin. Neurophysiol. 12,* 137-152.

Hellstrom, B., and Zetterstrom, B. (1956). *Exp. Cell Res. 10,* 248-251.

Heron, W., and Anchel, H. (1964). *Science 145, 946-947.*

Himwich, W. A. (1962). *Int. Rev. Neurobiol. 4,* 117-158.

Himwich, W. A. (1970). "Developmental Neurobiology" Thomas, Springfield, Illinois.

Hunt, W. E., and Goldring, S. (1951). *Electroencephalogr. Clin. Neurophysiol. 3,* 465-471.

Huttenlocher, P. R. (1967). *Exp. Neurol. 17,* 247-262.

Kao, H. (1927). Unpublished Master's Thesis, Stanford University.

King, J. A. (1958). *Psychol. Bull. 55,* 46-58.

Klingberg, F., and Schwartze, P. (1966). *Pfluegers Arch. Gesamte Physiol. Menchen Tiere 292,* 90-99.

Kovar, C. W. (1969). *Diss. Abstr. 29.* No. 10, 3943-B.

Lindsley, D. B. (1958). *In* "Reticular Formation of the Brain" (H. H. Jasper, ed.), pp. 513-534. Little, Brown, Boston, Massachusetts.

Lindsley, D. B., Wendt, R. H., Lindsley, D. F., Fox, S. S., Howell, J., and Adey, W. R. (1964). *Ann. N. Y. Acad. Sci. 117,* 564-587.

Marty, R. (1962). *Arch. Anat. Microsc. Morphol. Exp. 51,* 129-264.

Marty, R., Contamin, F., and Scherrer, J. (1959). *C. R. Soc. Biol. 153,* 198-201.

Melzack, R., and Burns, S. K. (1965). *Exp. Neurol. 13.* 163-175.

Miller, N. E. (1969). *Science 163,* 434-445.

Mills, W. (1898). "The Nature and Development of Animal Intelligence." Allen & Unwin, London.

Mourek, J., Himwich, W. A., Myslivecek, J., and Callison, D. A. (1967). *Brain Res. 6,* 241-251.

Myslivecek, J. (1968). *Brain Res. 10,* 418-430.

Ordy, J. M., Massopust, L. C., Jr., and Wolin, L. R. (1962). *Exp. Neurol. 5,* 364-382.

Ordy, J. M., Samaorajski, T., Collins, R. L., and Nagy, A. R. (1965). *AMA Arch. Ophthamol. [N.S.]73,* 674-686.

Paulson, G. W. (1965). *Exp. Neurol. 11,* 324-333.

Purpura, D. P. (1961). *In* "Brain and Behavior" (M. A. B. Brazier, ed.), pp. 95-138. Madison Print. Co., Madison, New Jersey.

Riesen, A. H. (1961). *In* "Sensory Deprivation" (P. Solomon, ed.), pp. 34-40. Harvard Univ. Press, Cambridge, Massachusetts.

Riesen, A. H. (1966). *Prog. Physiol. Psychol. 1,* 117-147.

Rose, G. H. (1965). Unpublished data.

Rose, G. H. (1966). *Electroencephalogr. Clin. Neurophysiol. 21,* 395-396.

Rose, G. H. (1968a). *Develop. Psychobiol. 31.* 35-40.

Rose, G. H. (1968b). *In* "Ontogenesis of the Brain" (L. Jilek and S. Trojan, eds.), pp. 347-358. Charles University, Prague.

Rose, G. H. (1968c). *Brain Res. 7,* 465-468.

Rose, G. H., and Ellingson, R. J. (1970). *In* "Developmental Neurobiology" (W. A. Himwich, ed.), pp. 393-440, Thomas, Springfield, Illinois.

Rose, G. H., and Gruenau, S. P. (1970a). Submitted for publication.

Rose, G. H. and Gruenau, S. P. (1970b). Submitted for publication.

Rose, G. H., Gruenau, S. P., and Spencer, J. W. (1970). Submitted for publication.

Rose, G. H., and Lindsley, D. B. (1965). *Science 148,* 1244-1246.

Rose, G. H., and Lindsley, D. B. (1968). *J. Neurophysiol. 31,* 607-623.

Salapatek, P. (1968). *J. Comp. Physiol. Pathol. 66,* 247-258.

Scheibel, A. B. (1962). *Recent Advan. Biol. Psychiat. 4,* 313-327.

Scherrer, J., and Fourment, A. (1964). *Prog. Brain Res. 9,* 103-112.

Solomon, R. L., and Lessac, M. S. (1968). *Psychol. Bull. 70,* 145-150.

Stewart, D. L. (1968). *Symp., Comp. Stud. Visual Develop. Effects Infant Brain Damage Rabbits, West. Psychol. Asso., 1968.*

Sublett, F. L. (1969). Unpublished Master's Thesis, University of Nebraska, Omaha, Nebraska.

Thompson, R. F., and Kramer, R. F. (1965). *J. Comp. Physiol. Psychol. 60,* 186-191.

Thompson, R. F., and Shaw, J. A. (1965). *J. Comp. Physiol. Psychol. 60,* 329-339.

Tucker, T. J., Kling, A., and Scharlock, D. P. (1968). *J. Neurophysiol. 31,* 818-832.

Valverde, F. (1967). *Exp. Brain Res. 3,* 337-352.

Wenzel, B., Tschirgi, R. D., and Taylor, J. L. (1962). *Exp. Neurol. 6,* 332-339.

Wetzel, A. B., Thompson, V. E., Horel, J. A., and Meyer, P. T. (1965). *Psychon. Sci. 3,* 381-382.

Wiesel, T. N., and Hubel, D. H. (1963a). *J. Neurophysiol. 26,* 1003-1017.

Wiesel, T. N., and Hubel, D. H. (1963b). *J. Neurophysiol. 26,* 978-993.

Wiesel, T. N., and Hubel, D. H. (1965a). *J. Neurophysiol. 28,* 1060-1072.

Wiesel, T. N., and Hubel, D. H. (1965b) *J. Neurophysiol. 28,* 1029-1040.

Wilson, E., Bogacz, J., and Garcia-Austt, E. (1966). *Acta Neurol. Latinoamer. 12,* 91-105.

Windle, W. F. (1930). *J. Comp. Neurol. 50,* 479-503.

Zattoni, J. (1968). *Physiol. Behav. 3,* 211-212.

Zetterstrom, B. (1956). *Acta Physiol. Scand. 35,* 272-279.

CHAPTER 10 Developmental Fetal EEG Studies in the Guinea Pig, with Comments on the Sheep and Human Fetus

Mortimer G. Rosen

I. INTRODUCTION

Fetal electroencephalographic (EEG) studies began almost 30 years ago (Lindsley, 1942). It is apparent from viewing the paucity of publications that such studies of the fetal brain have not established a broad interest among investigators. This review is being written with the hope that the techniques learned from investigations in the guinea pig, sheep, and most recently the human fetus will provoke more interest and more widespread study of the EEG of the developing brain *in utero*. For in the fetus, as in the adult, the EEG responds rapidly to environmental changes and these responses may be measured and studied.

The Laboratory for Fetal Brain Research began more than 5 years ago with human neonatal EEG studies. Although the neonatal brain wave had already been well studied in other laboratories (Dreyfus-Brisac *et al.,* 1962; Parmalee *et al.,* 1968; Torres, 1963), it was felt that familiarity with the patterns of the newborn infant EEG was a vital prelude to understanding the human fetal EEG.

Soon it became apparent that an analog to test some of our hypotheses (as to the usefulness of fetal EEG) was needed. Of particular importance at that time were questions relating to the brain wave responses to asphyxia and to brain wave changes which might occur with birth.

The fetal guinea pig studies provided both such a model as well as an opportunity to gain needed experience relating to the effects of many stresses on the EEG of the developing brain. Ultimately, limitations imposed both by the size as well as the maturity of the fetal guinea pig led to the study of the fetal sheep. For obstetricians the sheep was more appropriate, since already existing studies provided a large amount of cardiovascular fetal information to which could now be added fetal brain studies. In addition, both the size of the sheep fetus as well as the ability of the sheep uterus to withstand surgery without precipitating premature labor strongly supported this change of species.

Periodically we returned to human fetal studies. Innumerable attempts at maintaining an isolated electrode recording point on the fetal scalp during childbirth were made and failed (Rosen and Satran, 1965). After 5 years and based on our earlier experiences, we were able to solve problems previously found insurmountable and achieve continuous artifact free recordings during childbirth.

Still remaining as a challenge is the study of the human fetal brain *prior* to the onset of labor. Environment does not begin to affect the developing brain after birth. Theoretically, environmental effect must begin *in utero*. As an example, we may refer to sound as heard *in utero*. On one occasion in our laboratory, at hysterotomy a small sound transducer was placed *in utero* adjacent to the ear of the sheep fetus. Later we listened to the very evident sounds caused by the maternal heartbeat, intestinal peristalsis, and the "booming" noises produced by tapping the sheep abdomen with our fingers. This single instance was an example of the presence of an environment potentially capable of stimulating a developing organism.

In this report we will present only work performed in the Laboratory for Fetal Brain Research in the Department of Obstetrics-Gynecology of the University of Rochester School of Medicine and Dentistry. Several other centers have studied the fetal EEG and will be noted when appropriate. By presenting only material we are clearly familiar with, we hope to make evident to the reader the benefit of our technical errors, as well as our published successes, that he may extend his studies more easily beyond these preliminary levels.

II. FETAL GUINEA PIG STUDIES

A. General Statement

The fetal guinea pig has been one of the animals studied most frequently in the past because of its availability, ease in being obtained in a pregnant state, small size, docility. and above all its easily recognizable brain wave patterns. Perhaps this last fact was most attractive.

Some of these attributes also became handicaps. The maturity of the brain wave (and brain) and the maturity of this fetus at birth makes it most different from the human fetus and neonate. It is yet to be determined if some of the changes seen in the fetal guinea pig will occur in less mature species. In addition, while the animal is easily obtained in the pregnant state, little attention has been directed toward the use of colony animals of known gestational dates. Most of the "dating" of guinea pigs has been performed by weighing the fetuses or measuring their crown-rump lengths and comparing this to existing tables (Draper, 1920).

This gross estimate of fetal maturity may be adequate in a very general way, but when we followed this procedure, several facts became apparent. Initially we found that many of our animals at the mature end of their gestational periods were 20-30 gm heavier than those weights normally listed for a 65-day guinea pig gestation. Next we noted that if the mother was relatively young, her litter would be smaller in number of fetuses as well as size of each fetus for similarly dated gestations. It was also apparent that differences in animal strains resulted in different fetal sizes. Therefore, for maturational studies a colony was established with known dates of conception.

B. A Technique for Colony Dating

The method of Karsch and Poulton (1967) was used with success and will be quoted in detail. Virgin bred animals of the English Short Hair Hartley strain weighing 700 gm were isolated in groups of three. Males of known potency were used. To inhibit ovulation 6α-methyl-17 α-acetoxyprogesterone* was administered daily by oral syringe to each female guinea pig for 20 days. Although forced oral feeding seems somewhat crude, and at times not all the progesterone may be ingested, it works quite successfully. It can be performed easily and with experience it becomes a simple technique.

The animals were exposed to the males from the third to the eighth day after withdrawal from progesterone. This resulted in a fertilization rate near 75%. A shorter interval of exposure, ranging around the fifth day postwithdrawal is possible, but lower fertilization rates must be accepted. Vaginal smears signifying estrus may be utilized for more accurate dating; however, after our initial studies we did not feel that this was necessary. In Fig. 1 we have constructed a weight-date curve from the pregnancies which occurred in our colony. A secondary gain of developing our own colony was the availability of known healthy animals with less tendency to abortion or *in utero* fetal deaths which were an unnatural complication of buying and transporting pregnant guinea pigs as we had formerly done.

C. Electrode Construction

Electrodes made of number 23 gauge stainless steel needles were embedded in an epoxy cement base joining them to a spring steel head band (Fig. 2). The

---

*Provera-Upjohn

epoxy was used both to fix the needle point firmly as well as to isolate the needle shaft from the electrically conductive steel band. The size of the head band will vary with the distance between the recording needle points. Depending on fetal maturity, the average distance between recording points will be 1.5 cm. This size can be changed at the time of surgery by bending the curve of the spring steel coil head band. The needle electrode (6 mm long) is coated to its

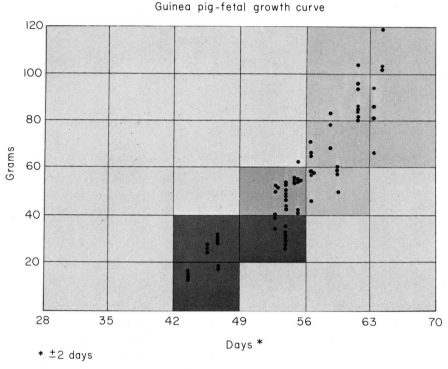

FIG. 1. Weight and dates at time of delivery of fetal guinea pigs of the Hartley strain. Each point is accurate to within 5 days of conception.

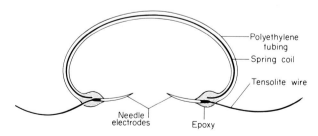

FIG. 2. Fetal guinea pig vertex electrode (as described in text). Distance between recording points can be varied by expanding spring coil at time of surgery.

recording tip with a nonconductive shellac. At the time of surgery the recording tip is scratched open to provide a conductive path. If the electrode is to be reused, the insulation must be reapplied and allowed to fix for 24 hr. If a recording portion of the needle is stripped of its insulation or exposed in any way to the surrounding tissue and amniotic fluid, the EEG potentials may be attenuated by the highly conductive amniotic fluid environment and further obscured by fetal heart complexes, which are of much greater amplitude and which will destroy the usefulness of the tracing.

D. Operative Procedure

The animals were fasted for 24 hr prior to surgery and deprived of water overnight. Local xylocaine (1/2%) was used to infiltrate the area of incision. A midline or a flank incision was made. A flank incision was placed over a palpable fetal skull and appeared to be somewhat more satisfactory than the midline abdominal incision. With the animal on its side, less respiratory problems were encountered.

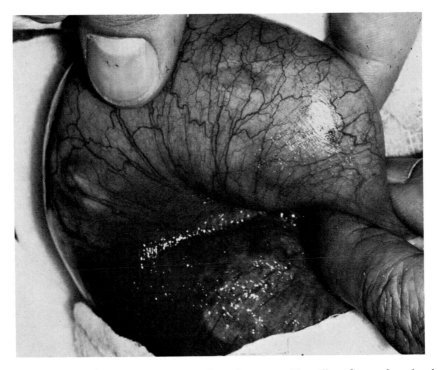

FIG. 3.   Guinea pig fetus *in utero* at time of surgery with outline of ear and eye barely visible, seen between upper thumb and forefinger.

Prior to opening the peritoneum, ether anesthesia (open system with face mask) was used to prevent the guinea pig from straining and forcing the abdominal contents onto the skin. Limiting the use of anesthesia, when possible, minimizes the trauma to the physiologic state of the animal studied. In addition, with only small amounts of gas anesthesia, potential aspiration of gastric contents was minimized.

Through the thin uterine wall the eyes and ears of the fetus (Fig. 3) were visible. The spring steel electrodes were extended under tension and pushed through the uterine wall and fetal skull. Tension produced by the steel band maintains the electrode in place. With the vertex close up against the myometrium, almost no amniotic fluid was lost (Fig. 4). Fetal heart patterns were

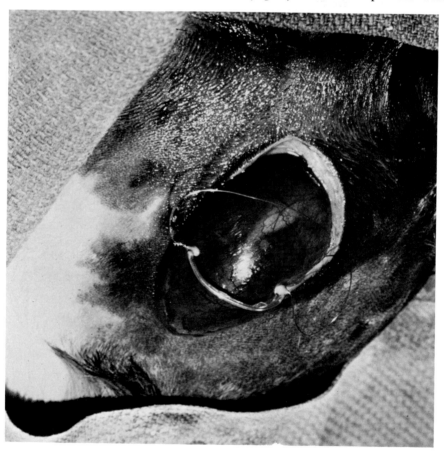

FIG. 4. Electrode in place over guinea pig fetal vertex and outside uterine wall as seen prior to repositioning uterus and closing abdominal wall. Despite the fact that the electrode needles perforate the uterus, the opening is sealed immediately by the pressure of the electrode.

obtained by suturing a stainless steel wire into the myometrium near the fetal back. Care was taken at all times to avoid traumatizing the placenta, which was easily seen.

The electrode wires were brought out through the abdominal wall and (for chronic experiments) inserted into female amphenol sockets. It was found more appropriate to bring these wires out through a separate stab wound incision, which was placed toward the maternal back for the chronic studies (Fig. 5). Ether anesthesia was discontinued when the peritoneum was closed. By the time surgery was complete, the maternal pig responded to pain and soon was alert, walking and drinking water.

FIG. 5. Schematic drawing for fetal studies after surgery has been completed. Note fetal head EEG electrodes at 1 and 2; EKG electrode at 3; ground electrode at 4; amphenol female jack at 5; and maternal EEG electrodes at 6 and 7.

E. Acute Stress

Initially our drug (Bleyer and Rosen, 1968; Rosen, 1967b; Rosen and Bleyer, 1968) and asphyxia (Rosen, 1967a) studies were carried out with the abdomen open and with moisture and heat maintained over the exposed uterus. While this may be adequate to document very gross changes such as drug transfer, it was often inappropriate to measure normal fetal responses and EEG patterns.

This was necessarily true for several reasons. First, the effects of the medications and the operative stress were apparent in the brain waves for several hours. In the very immature fetuses (15-40 gm) the low voltage activity may be suppressed almost entirely in the presence of drugs, falsely leading one to conclude that EEG is not yet present at that age (Fig. 6). Secondly, the fetal preparation was less stable physiologically with the abdomen open for long periods of time. For example, bradycardia occurred frequently and was indicative of such a compromised condition. In similar manner, cooling of the sponges overlying the uterus quickly depressed the fetal trace from a clearly visible one to a baseline pattern. Finally, in the presence of bradycardia, whether continuous or transient, or in the presence of gross visible fetal movements simulating "gasping" effects, one must consider the animal stressed and unacceptable for use in most studies.

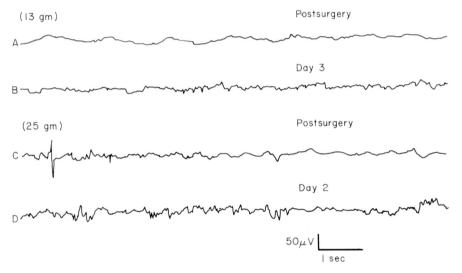

FIG. 6. A. Smallest guinea pig fetus (13 gm) at 41 days showing suppression of most activity immediately after surgery. B. Same fetus on day 3 following surgery. Increase in voltage is apparent. C. A 25-gm guinea pig fetus (44 days) at surgery showing voltage suppression. D. Same fetus on day 2. Activity is more continuous, higher in voltage and shows faster rhythms.

F. Maturation and EEG Activity

1. Selected References to Previous Work in This Field

In this section we will describe the maturation of the fetal EEG and the fetal acoustic evoked response (AER) in a colony of guinea pigs of known gestation. The earliest reports on guinea pig fetuses were made by Jasper *et al.* (1937), who reported on the rhythmical electrical potentials of the brain of the guinea pig. The fetal recordings were taken at surgery using an open technique with placement of the electrodes directly on the cortical surface. Some of the animals were dated, others had estimated dates of conception based on Draper's tables (1920). The results suggested that the 48-56 day period gave the earliest electrical activity. The initial activity observed was short EEG bursts based on a relatively flat background. The authors noted that at 60 days of gestation changes in the brain potential following stimulation became more apparent. An additional fact noted was an increase in the amplitude of the fetal EEG with age.

This work was confirmed by the later work of Flexner *et al.* (1950). These authors related the structure and the chemical changes temporally to the first evidence of cortical function in the brain of the guinea pig and correlated this with rhythmical electrical activity. This technique consisted of exteriorizing the fetus of a decerebrate maternal guinea pig preparation, placing it in Ringers' lactate solution, and exposing the brain. They could not find electrical activity in the group between 37 and 45 days. At that time the local application of strychnine was without result. Between the forty-sixth and forty-ninth days and continuing to birth rhythmic electrical activity was present and local application of strychnine produced electrical maturation of neuroblast to neuron between days 41-45 of the guinea pig cortex.

2. Technique for Maturation Study

All maternal animals were virgin bred and weighed between 500 and 700 gm. They were placed in cages and cycled 12 hr in light, 12 hr in darkness. Progesterone was used as described earlier. The surgical technique for these studies was similar to that described earlier. The EEG was recorded with a Beckman Dynograph. For maturation studies the EEG was repeated 2 hr later and again on the following day and each subsequent day the animal survived. For auditory evoked response (AER) studies the traces were recorded on a Precision Instrument magnetic tape recorder. A University Sound 1 D 20 watt driver unit (16 ohms) was used with a 3.5 msec impulse having a 15 V peak and repeated every 2.2 sec in the acute experiment. This produced a sound pressure level of 132 decibels (or otherwise recorded as 120 ♭ Newtons/meters^2) as recorded at the abdominal wall on a General Radio Sound Level Meter. The Beckman Dynograph was set with a time filter of 0.3 and a high frequency filter of 2. For the pentobarbital injection after the initial stimulus 5 mg/kg of barbiturate was used. The animals were placed in a sound enclosure and the speaker was placed 4½ inches away from the maternal abdomen. A 250 stimulus series was run along with a similar interval control period. In the acute studies barbiturate, as noted above, was added and the series was repeated. Barbiturate at this dose increases the amplitude of the AER (Scibetta and Rosen, 1969). In earlier studies needle electrodes were placed in the fetal skin, in the uterus overlying the fetal vertex, and at the maternal abdominal wall in order to confirm that the origin of the AER was from within the fetal head. The animal was then delivered and finally sacrificed after the stimulus was repeated in the neonatal state.

In the chronic maturation series the animals were stimulated almost every day until the experiment terminated due to delivery of the guinea pig or to deterioration of the EEG as seen visually. From previous experiences we found that animals survived as long as 16 days with electrodes in place. In general, they were maintained from 4 to 6 days without much difficulty for chronic continuous EEG studies. It became apparent if a preparation was deteriorating by noting the loss of voltage and slowing in the EEG trace.

3. Results Immediately After Surgery

(a) Following surgery in the guinea pig, drug effects can be seen, as noted by flattening of the EEG in the immature animal (Fig. 6), or an increase in fast activity of the more mature animal (Fig. 7) within the first 12 to 24 hr of the study.

Therefore, in addition to surgical stress, drug effects must be considered in acute study animal protocols. In our chronic studies (see below) EEG patterns in the undrugged animal can be seen at somewhat earlier times than previously reported (Flexner *et al.*, 1950; Jasper *et al.*, 1937) (Fig. 6).

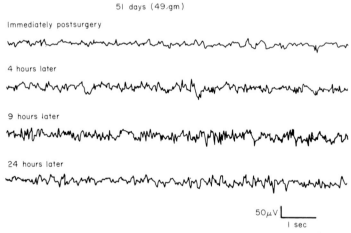

FIG. 7. In 51-day guinea pig immediately postsurgery, there is discontinuous activity, lower voltage and slower rhythms. Four hours later voltage increases. Nine hours later 15-25 sec 50 μV/cm rhythms are clearly seen. Twenty-four hours later patterns reached a stable state.

(b) Evoked responses were present in mature guinea pig fetuses prior to birth (Fig. 8). In the undated animals this period was found by estimating fetal head size and palpating the pubic symphysis, which began to separate and was easily detectable by digital palpation in the 48 hr prior to the onset of labor. The animals were studied at this time. Responses were increased in amplitude and very slightly delayed in latency with the small barbiturate injection (Scibetta and Rosen, 1969).

Tests after birth indicated an increase in AER amplitude. The AER disappeared when the animal was sacrificed. Controls for muscle movement and artifact were used in the early experiments. Electrodes were placed in the dorsum of the fetal guinea pig, in the uterus over the head of the guinea pig, and in the maternal abdomen directly beneath the skin. No evoked artifacts could be obtained in these areas.

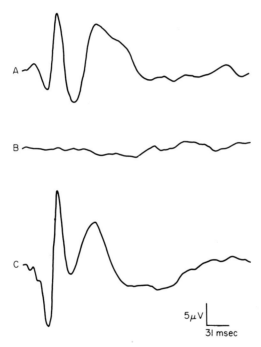

FIG. 8. *In utero* guinea pig. A. Evoked response to external sound stimulus. B. Control series. C. Extrauterine AER in same animal with electrodes in place.

4. Chronic Studies

In the chronic series of dated animals the earliest EEGs were found consistently from 42 days of gestation and later (Fig. 9, line A). At this time fetal weights ranged from a low of 13 gm to a high of 25 gm in the next 2 days (Fig. 9, line B). The EEG activity at this time was immature. This was defined as low voltage (less than 20 μV) wave forms spaced on long periods without apparent activity. In general, before the forty-fifth day the wave frequencies remained

slow (2-3 cycles/sec). About the forty-ninth day (Fig. 9, line D) almost continuous activity can be observed, with increases in both amplitude and frequency of
waves. In addition to wave changes, patterns appear. Patterns may be described
as containing alternate bursts and lower voltage activity similar to that termed as
"trace alternant" in the human neonate (Dreyfus-Brisac *et al.*, 1962). This is in
contrast to periods of continuous electrical activity without voltage suppression.
The guinea pig EEG began to show changes from slower waves with areas of 10
to 20 sec of flattening to those of continuous higher voltage fast activity running
from 15 to 25 cycles per second. At 52 days of gestation more mature EEG
activity patterns were observed in the undrugged nonstressed preparation (Fig. 9,
lines E and F). Astic and Jouvet have reported episodes of rapid eye movement

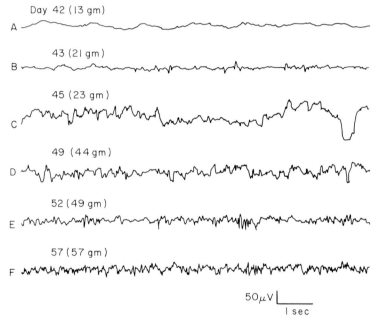

FIG. 9. Guinea pig. A. Forty-two day fetus immediately after surgery with low voltage,
slow 1 per second waves and discontinuous activity. B. Forty-three day fetus with increase
in voltage and presence of more activity. C. Forty-five day fetus with bursts of slow waves
and shorter periods of flattening. D. Forty-nine day fetus with almost continuous activity
and fast and slow frequencies. E and F. Fifty-two and 57 day fetuses with mature activity
and pattern formation.

sleep in the acute fetal guinea pig preparation (presentation at 1970 meetings of
the Association for Psychophysiological Study of Sleep).
    The evoked response appeared first in our series at 55 days (Fig. 10). In this
group of animals the latency of the first negative wave was 25 msec. This is in

reference to the first early deflection, whether positive or negative. Since this is bipolar recording, there is no reference point for positive or negative deflection but it may be assumed that these response components correspond to sensory evoked responses observed in other species at comparable stages of maturation, as described by Rose in Chapter 9 of this volume. A second component is present which is slower. Discussion of both EEG and AER must be general, since an insufficient number of animals were studied at each gestational weight to give

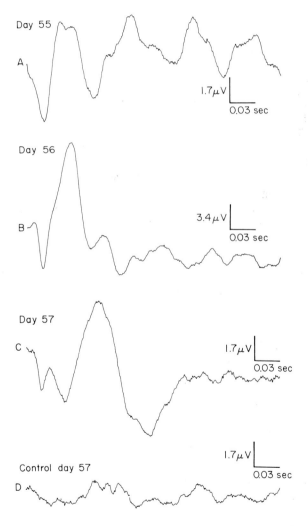

FIG. 10.   Guinea pig fetus. A. AER *in utero,* fetus age 55 days. B. AER same fetus, age 56 days. C. AER same fetus, age 57 days (animal died on following day). D. Control series (200 intervals without stimuli).

meaningful comparative data or to develop a curve for latency of response in relation to fetal maturity.

The fetal EEG terminated in the majority of implantations with the onset of labor and the delivery of the fetus. Early signs of labor were documented by the electrical patterns consistent with rhythmic muscle contractions. During this time the wave frequencies, previously present, slowed and voltages became depressed and finally inapparent. It must be noted here that the fixation of the fetal skull with the spring electrode made labor and its expulsive forces a traumatic procedure. This cannot be compared to electrical changes in the fetus with birth, since here birth was an abnormal (harmful) process. Recently (see notes on human technique) human fetal studies did not reveal any change in EEG patterns produced by the normal birth process.

Occasionally fetal death *in utero* preceded labor in the chronic fetal guinea pig studies. Sepsis or bowel incarceration in the wires or flank incision were documented. A technical cause for failure was electrode damage due to a break in the insulation of the wires or poor placement of the recording electrode points. If any portion of the electrode recording tip remained exterior to the fetal skull, fetal electrocardiographic patterns, several times the amplitude of the EEG, destroyed the usefulness of the brain wave recording.

Observations suggest that the fetus was able to grow and mature in spite of the implanted electrodes. At delivery the study fetus often weighed the same as its littermates who were undisturbed. The fetal weight and calvarium size were usually greater than estimates made at the time of surgery. Intracranial hemorrhage or necrosis was not evident on gross inspection of the brain. Electrodes have been located in the majority of cases in the superficial layers of the parietal cortex. Rarely was the tension of the electrode sufficient to produce visual distortion of the bony skull.

5. Summary of the Guinea Pig Studies

Continuous monitoring of the fetal brain wave provided numerous opportunities for studying the developing brain *in utero*. Reproducible variations in EEG and AER activity can be documented for periods longer than 24 hr thus allowing one to avoid some of the changes produced by anesthesia, surgical stress, and electrode implantation. Alterations in the fetal EEG may be correlated with changes both in the fetus and mother. The extent and duration of the drug altered EEG changes in both mother and fetus noted in acute studies may now be assessed over longer periods of time. Preliminary evoked response studies suggest that both at term and earlier the AER may be documented and studied with maturation. It is suggested that the guinea pig technique provides a simple model for fetal brain studies and analogs may be applied to other species.

III. BRIEF DESCRIPTIONS OF FETAL SHEEP STUDIES

Because of the guinea pig's small size and advanced fetal maturity, efforts were turned toward the fetal sheep as a desirable alternative. While not described in detail, several statements as to utility of this animal for future studies may be made.

The sheep lends itself (on a seasonal basis) to selective dated breeding. The ram is fitted with a marking device which after the female is mounted stains the dorsal aspect of the female sheep. Daily observations allow one to separate the exposed sheep with a dated pregnancy. We have performed experiments starting as early as 90 days of gestation.

Anesthetic techniques for studies of the sheep have been described by Dawes (1968). Epidural or spinal anesthesia was adequate. The sheep was shaved and placed in a lateral position exposing the flank over a palpable fetal head. The technique for surgery was similar to that for the guinea pig. The electrode construction was almost identical, with one major exception. Fetal cranial size at 70-90 days approaches that of the fetal guinea pig near term. From 90-150 days one must be prepared to affix an electrode of larger diameter.

The fetal vertex was held against the uterus, away from clearly visible placental cotyledons. The uterus and amniotic membranes were incised. The membranes and uterus were closed with a continuous suture along the margins to prevent myometrial bleeding during the electrode insertion.

During the procedure the fetal vertex was held firmly against the myometrium, preventing loss of amniotic fluid. The vertex may be manipulated to affix the electrode and other instruments as needed. We were able to suture a sound transducer as well as a light device against the vertex to test for sensory evoked responses.

All cables and wires were withdrawn outside the uterus. The uterus was closed with two layers of catgut sutures. The cables were twisted to form a single larger cable in order to prevent loops of bowel from herniating and then strangulating between individual wires. Following closure of the abdomen, maternal omentum seals off the single cable from the remainder of the abdomen. All connections were brought out through a separate stab wound-type abdominal incision and firmly sutured in place dorsally near the vertebrae. If the electrode was brought out near the lower abdominal incision, the muscle movement with respirations, etc., produced confusing slow wave artifacts. Examples of the tracings are presented in Fig. 11. Both maturational changes and drug effects were noted immediately following surgery, but were not present on subsequent days.

We have continued *in utero* EEG studies for 30 days without difficulty. The ability of the sheep to withstand the trauma of surgery without going into labor constitutes an additional advantage in the use of this animal for chronic studies.

IV. HUMAN FETAL ELECTROENCEPHALOGRAPHY

Unquestionably, the most desirable species for fetal EEG studies is man. It is only in man that techniques for supportive care have maintained the premature infant alive outside the uterus for long periods of time. In this respect a large volume of literature is available to the reader (see Chapter 11).

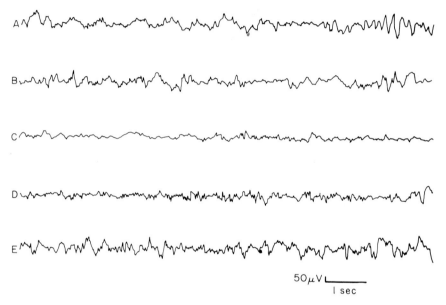

FIG. 11.   Fetal sheep EEG following surgery — same fetus throughout experiment. A. Day following surgery. B. Day 2. C. Day 5. D. Day 7. E. Day 10. (unpublished data Scibetta and Rosen)

We have developed a technique for the continuous monitoring of the human fetal brain prior to birth during the labor period (Rosen and Scibetta, 1969a). Fetuses of both mature and premature weights have been studied for as long as 12 hr. The earliest fetus we have studied was 1300 gm. In this fetus discontinuous activity varying from 20 to more than 100 μV/cm was seen. As maturity approaches and generally after the thirty-fourth week of a 40-week gestation, EEG patterning takes place, diminution of periods of flattening is noted, and there is a general increase in EEG frequencies (Fig. 12).

At this time it may be stated that in normal fetuses the EEG is present *in utero* prior to birth and is identical to the EEG seen after birth (Rosen and Scibetta, 1969b). In addition, evoked responses to sound prior to birth may be obtained and compared to responses in the neonate (Scibetta and Rosen, 1971).

Preliminary results are illustrated in Fig. 12. These are examples of the technical feasibility of such studies. Based upon the background of accomplished EEG studies in fetuses of subhuman primates, they introduce a new area for continuing study.

50 consecutive seconds of fetal EEG

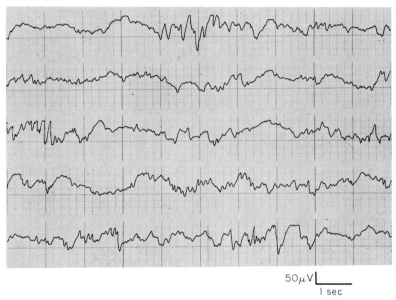

$50\mu V$ ⌞____

⌐ sec

FIG. 12. Lines represent 50 sec of continuous *in utero* human fetal EEG obtained during labor with membranes ruptured and cervix 6 cm dilated. Characteristic frequencies vary between 1 and 25 cps and about 50 μV/cm in amplitude. (Infant at 40 weeks gestation.)

V. CONCLUSIONS

It is possible to study fetal brain development in the uterine environment in a continuous fashion. Several species of animals tolerate this procedure, including the guinea pig and sheep fetuses. Such studies have been performed infrequently. That the fetus can respond to its environment is evident. The use of fetal EEG for normative studies of maturation and brain pathology is suggested.

ACKNOWLEDGMENTS

Appreciation is expressed to many people involved in this work over the years, including Doctors W. Bleyer, R. Tatelbaum, J. Scibetta, and L. Chik and also to Mrs. M. Steinbrecher, Miss P. Devroude, and Mr. L. Braun for their technical assistance. The project was supported by the John A. Hartford Foundation, Inc.

REFERENCES

Bleyer, W. A., and Rosen, M. G. (1968). *Electroencephalogr. Clin. Neurophysiol. 24,* 249.

Dawes, G. S. (1968). "Foetal and Neonatal Physiology." Year Book Publ., Chicago, Illinois.

Draper, R. L. (1920). *Anat. Rec. 18,* 369.

Dreyfus-Brisac, C., Flescher, J., and Plassart, E. (1962). *Biol. Neonatorum 4,* 154.

Flexner, L. B., Tyler, D. B., and Gallant, L. J. (1950). *J. Neurophysiol. 13,* 427.

Jasper, H. H., Bridgman, C. S., and Carmichael, L. (1937). *J. Exp. Psychol. 21,* 63.

Karsch, F. J., and Poulton, B. R. (1967). *J. Anim. Sci. 26,* 549.

Lindsley, D. B. (1942). *Amer. J. Psychol. 55,* 412.

Parmelee, A. H., Schulte, F. J., Akiyama, Y., Wenner, W. H. Schultz, M. A., and Stern, E. (1968). *Electroencephalogr. Clin. Neuropnysiol. 24,* 319.

Rosen, M. G. (1967a). *Obstet. Gynecol. 29,* 687.

Rosen, M. G. (1967b). *Obstet. Gynecol. 30* 560.

Rosen, M. G., and Bleyer, W. A. (1968). *Amer. J. Ostet. Gynecol. 101,* 918.

Rosen, M. G., and Scibetta, J. J. (1969a). *Amer. J. Obstet. Gynecol. 104,* 1057.

Rosen, M. G., and Scibetta, J. J. (1969b). *Neuropädiatrie 2,* 17.

Rosen, M. G. and Satran, R. (1965). *Obstet. Gynecol. 5,* 740.

Scibetta, J. J., and Rosen, M. G. (1969). *Obstet. Gynecol. 33,* 830.

Scibetta, J. J., and Rosen, M. G. (1971). *Amer. J. Obstet. Gynecol. 109,* 82.

Torres, F. (1963). *In* "Recent Advances in Degenerative Diseases of the Central Nervous System in Infants and Children" (G.M. Owen, ed.), report of the forty-second Ross Conference on Pediatric Research, p. 37., Ross Laboratories, Columbus, Ohio.

CHAPTER 11 The Development of Sleep-Waking and Rest - Activity Patterns from Fetus to Adult in Man

M. B. Sterman and Toke Hoppenbrouwers

I. INTRODUCTION

The elaboration in ontogeny of sleep and waking states constitutes a fundamental area for developmental investigation, for these states provide the framework within which all higher nervous functions will eventually develop. The emerging capacities for attention, integration and restoration all depend upon the maturing brain's consolidation of these processes into functional states which can serve effectively the growing infant. There is reason to believe that this developmental period in the elaboration of sleep and waking states is subject to the same interplay of nature and nurture which has such a meaningful impact upon the eventual expression of other nervous system functions.

The problems which usually are encountered in the study of functional systems in the brain, such as those responsible for sleep and wakefulness, are only magnified when one considers the developing organism. This is particularly true in the area of sleep, for a current resurgence of interest in this phenomenon has produced a wealth of new scientific information which has raised doubts about many time-honored concepts. It shall be our intention in this chapter to define some of the conceptual problems associated with the study of sleep in both the adult and the infant, and to utilize clues provided by developmental studies in an effort to resolve or redefine some of these problems. We shall present, also, some new data derived from fetal investigations which bear significantly upon these issues. Our primary subject shall be man himself.

Traditionally, sleep has been treated as a rather homogeneous process, initiated and maintained by specific and discrete changes within the central nervous system. Out of this frame of reference have emerged numerous theories attributing sleep variously to a suppression of wakefulness, a unitary brain process, a dual brain process and most recently, to mediation by specific neurochemical substances. The fact remains, however, that few of these theories can encompass the true complexity of adult sleep or bridge the obvious differences between sleep patterns in the infant and adult. Physiologically, sleep is far from a static condition, being characterized instead by a continuous flux of distinctive patterns. As we shall see later, these patterns are defined in the adult by *combinations* of events which tend to be organized into an orderly sequence, but within which there exists a significant allowance for variability (see, for example, the recently published manual for scoring of human sleep by Rechtschaffen and Kales, 1968).

Related to this question is the issue surrounding the peculiar stage of sleep manifest by abrupt physiological changes and including, in particular, rapid eye movements (REM's), motor atonia, phasic twitching and a desynchronized EEG. This pattern, which has been variously termed REM sleep, active sleep, and paradoxical sleep, was originally recognized by Aserinsky and Kleitman (1953) and subsequently associated with dreaming by Dement and Kleitman (1957). In his classic text, *Sleep and Wakefulness*, Kleitman (1963) suggested that the recurrent REM phase of sleep was the manifestation of a more fundamental physiological rhythm which continued to influence the functions of the central nervous system during wakefulness. He termed this the *basic rest-activity cycle*. This concept has been revived recently by a series of supporting observations, many of which will be discussed here. Its implication is that the REM cycle and the sleep-waking rhythm may reflect separate biological periodicities. This implication can be examined advantageously in the infant and could be a step in the direction of unraveling the intricate fabric of sleep.

II. SLEEP AND WAKEFULNESS

A. Adult Manifestations

Sleep and wakefulness have been defined both behaviorally and physiologically. Because of the complex nature of these states, neither definition is entirely unambiguous. However, under normal circumstances, polygraphic patterns in the adult human, and particularly the EEG, provide acceptable physiological criteria for their identification. Wakefulness is associated with a low-voltage fast EEG activity (desynchronized) alternating with an 8-12 cps high-voltage pattern (synchronized) termed the "alpha rhythm." Shifts between these patterns accompany adjustments in somatic, autonomic, and cognitive activities. Sleep onset is signaled by the gradual disappearance of the alpha rhythm and a sequence of EEG patterns involving in particular a characteristic spindle-burst phase which is progressively dominated and ultimately replaced by high-voltage slow waves. Autonomic activity is generally stabilized with many variables showing a progressive decrease, particularly during the early stages of sleep. At some point this sequence is reversed with the sudden reappearance of the spindle-burst phase, which gives way eventually to a mixed low-voltage pattern accompanied by phasic eye movements, irregular heart rate and respiration, gross body movements, and more local muscular twitching. This intriguing reversal of the general picture of physiological quiescence during sleep is the REM stage. The general sequence described above is seen to recur 4-6 times throughout the night, with a progressive disappearance of the large slow-wave pattern as morning approaches (Dement and Kleitman, 1957).

Some changes in endocrine function have been noted in relation to sleep, particularly those concerned with the pituitary modulation of growth hormone and adrenal steroid secretions. In the adult, a release of human growth hormone was found to occur specifically during the slow wave or synchronized sleep EEG patterns (Sassin et al., 1969), whereas plasma cortisol levels were found to follow a circadian distribution, being low at the beginning of a night's sleep and increasing irregularly over a period of several hours (Weitzman et al., 1966; Roffwarg et al., 1970). Behaviorally, the individual remains quiescent during sleep except for the episodic twitching of the REM phase and periodic postural adjustments. Throughout sleep he sustains a characteristic detachment from his physical environment which is reflected by increased thresholds for arousal in response to sensory stimulation.

Another parameter of the adult sleep-waking rhythm is its distribution in time. In fact, temporal modification of the sleep-waking rhythm (i.e., sleep deprivation) is usually accompanied by significant pattern alterations, a fact which suggests that the duration of these states is normally determined by specific physiological influences. In man, sleep is initiated at approximately the same hour each evening and is sustained for about the same duration of time, thus describing a circadian rhythm which approximates 24 hr. Whatever the basis for this universal rhythm, it is not ultimately dependent upon environmental cues, for a number of investigators have shown that subjects living without such cues in various isolated quarters continue to display a circadian or near-circadian sleep-wakefulness rhythm (Aschoff and Wever, 1962; Siffre, 1963; Mills, 1964). Thus, it has been suggested that the sleep-wakefulness rhythm reflects a "free-running" or "endogenous" cycling of two physiological processes (Halberg et al., 1959). Environmental factors such as light, temperature, and social patterns may serve specifically to set or adjust the phase of this intrinsic rhythm. The terms "synchronizer" and "zeitgeber" are frequently used in this regard (Halberg et al., 1959; Aschoff, 1965).

Much has been written in recent years about the physiological and psychological characteristics of sleep in the human adult. The interested reader can find additional information of a descriptive nature in Kleitman's revised *Sleep and Wakefulness* (1963) and in several more recent works (Clemente, 1967; Kales, 1969).

B. Infant Manifestations

While these general characteristics of sleep and wakefulness are well established and clearly demonstrable in the adult, there are many difficulties inherent
in attempts to define these states in the newborn. An infant lying quietly with
eyes closed appears behaviorally to be sleeping. Conversely, the alert, smiling,
writhing, or crying newborn would seem to be awake. Physiologically, however,
these states bear only superficial resemblance to their adult counterparts. The
immature status of sensory, motor, and other systems at this early stage of life
limits the behavioral repertoire of the organism primarily to reflexive activity
and produces manifestations which are unique to this early stage of development
(see for example, Chapters 1 and 2 in this text). Patterns which are cohesive and
sustained in the adult are absent, or at best fragmented, in the newborn. As
mentioned previously, this makes interpretation of functional state by adult
standards extremely tenuous. Kleitman (1963) acknowledged this problem by
reference to "primitive" sleep and waking states in the infant. Prechtl (1968) has
applied the concept of "state patterns" to the newborn through the use of
correlations between observable behaviors and extensive physiological data.
Before dealing further with the question of functional interpretation, let us
review briefly the behavioral patterns which characterize the newborn period
and relate them in more detail to the physiological criteria of sleep and waking
states in the adult.

1. Behavioral Quiescence

These periods in the newborn are usually associated with closed eyes, regular
respiration, and various irregular EEG patterns, particularly the so-called *trace
alternant* configuration described by Dreyfus-Brisac (1964). The undifferentiated, low-voltage nature of EEG patterns at this early age contrasts sharply
with the prominent spindle-burst activity and high amplitude slow waves seen
during quiescent (sleep) periods in older infants and in the adult (Fig. 1). Quiet
periods last usually 3-4 hr. (Parmelee *et al.*, 1964; Kleitman, 1963), and are
evenly distributed throughout the day and night (Hellbrügge, 1960; Rutenfranz,
1961). Several studies have indicated an increased tendency toward quiescence
in the day and activity at night in babies maintained on fixed feeding schedules
(Hellbrügge, 1960). This has been attributed to an increased activity during the
night when longer interfeeding intervals are imposed by the parents. When the
newborn is placed on a demand feeding schedule, this circadian difference is no
longer observed. Recent studies of growth hormone secretion and plasma cortisol levels in the newborn and in older infants gave no evidence of circadian
modulation or of changes related to the quiescent state, in contrast to the
sleep-related release of these hormones mentioned previously for the adult
(Anders *et al.*, 1970; Finkelstein *et al.*, 1970; Shaywitz *et al.*, 1970).

2. Behavioral Activity

In this state the newborn's eyes are either open or closed, respiration and heart rate are phasically irregular, and body movements can occur spontaneously or in relation to crying, and feeding. The EEG is usually but not always⁻

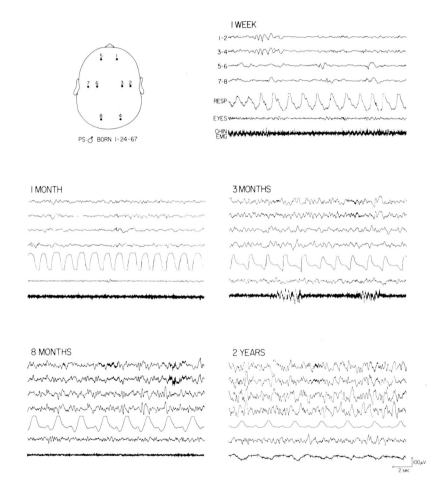

FIG. 1.   Ontogenesis of EEG and other physiological indices of the quiescent state in the same human infant from 1 week to 2 years of age. By 3 months the EEG, as well as other criteria mentioned in the text, begin to approximate the pattern defined as synchronized sleep in the adult. Differences in the configuration of the EMG and respiration leads are due primarily to electrode placement. Episodes of spontaneous sucking, which are common during this state in the infant, are reflected here in the EMG lead at 3 months. Eye movements are typically absent in this state and only spread of EEG slow waves can be seen from eye electrodes.

desynchronized. This state, therefore, has a number of possible configurations. Additionally, it is rarely sustained for more than several hours (Parmelee *et al.*, 1964; Kleitman, 1963) and is evenly distributed throughout the day and night. As mentioned previously, one of the primary features of adult sleep and wakefulness is its systematic distribution over a 24-hr period, resulting in a characteristic circadian rhythm. It is significant that this feature is absent in the newborn (see Table I, from Rutenfranz, 1961).

TABLE I   Day-Night Differences in Various Functions[a] (Based on experiments with 297 children during 1418 days)

	Age at which statistically significant differences are found	
	5% level of confidence	1% level of confidence
Electrical skin resistance		1 week
Sleep and wakefulness pattern		2-3 weeks
Body temperature		2-3 weeks
Urine excretion	2-3 weeks	4-20 weeks
Heart rate		4-20 weeks
Potassium excretion		4-20 weeks
Sodium excretion		4-20 weeks
Phosphate excretion		16-20 months
Creatine excretion		16-20 months
Creatinine excretion	16-22 months	
Chloride excretion	16-22 months	

[a]Used with permission of author: Rutenfranz (1961).

3. The REM State

Both quiescent and active periods are regularly interrupted by this unique third state. It is usually brief, lasting 10-30 min and characterized by rather dramatic physiological changes. Respiration becomes higher in rate and more irregular, gross body movements and phasic twitches occur sporadically, the eyes are seen to dart about within the orbit, and the EEG often shows a sustained low-voltage pattern. A variety of adultlike facial expressions, resembling various emotional states, frequently occur during these periods, often in association with bursts of phasic motor discharge. A distinguishing feature of the REM state in young infants is its rather systematic recurrence at intervals of approximately 40-60 min throughout the day and night. This aspect of newborn behavior will be examined in greater detail later in this discussion.

With increasing age, definitive patterns of sleep and wakefulness emerge in the human infant. The most dramatic aspects of this developmental change are the consolidation and maturation of behavioral and physiological criteria (Dreyfus-Brisac, 1964; Monod and Pajot, 1965; Parmelee *et al.*, 1967; Metcalf and Emde, 1969) and the ability to sustain long periods of sleep (Parmelee *et al.*, 1964). This transition is gradual and is usually completed in normal children by 3 months of age. Thus, Metcalf (1969, 1970), in a detailed study of the ontogenesis of EEG sleep spindles, has pointed out that rudimentary spindles are first seen in the EEG of the quiescent infant at about 4 weeks of age and are only

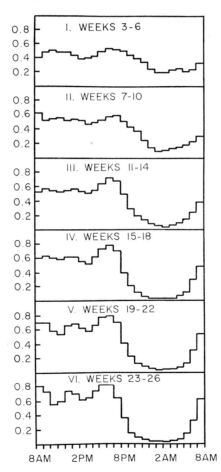

FIG. 2.   The mean sleep-wakefulness distribution in each of six successive 4-week periods of observation of a group of human infants is shown here from the study of Kleitman and Engelmann (1953). The ordinate in each period indicates the mean proportion of the hour (abscissa) during which the group was awake. Note the stable day-night dichotomy in sleep and wakefulness apparent from the 11 to 14-week period (3 months) on.

fully developed in all infants by 12 weeks (see Fig. 1 for example). Moreover, Emde and Metcalf (1970) found that REM periods which occur during sucking, fussing, or crying in the young infant disappear by 3 months. A reversal of pattern sequence, unique to the infant, has the onset of quiescent periods always preceded by a REM state. This pattern disappears also by 3 months of age. Parmelee *et al*. (1964) state furthermore that the most dramatic aspect of the development of infant sleep is the "rapid increase in ability to sustain a single long sleep period" between 8 and 16 weeks of life. During this period a circadian rhythm of sleep and wakefulness also appears, with wakefulness dominant in the daylight hours and, to the relief of the parents, sleep continuing throughout the night (Fig. 2).

It becomes clear that there are some significant differences in the state characteristics of the newborn versus the older infant and adult. Sleep may take several physiological forms for a number of functional needs of the organism. This would account for its variable configurations in the adult and the changes observed with development. The limited capacities and greater requirements of the rapidly developing newborn contrast with the physiologically stabilized adult and may be manifest by a more rudimentary configuration, not involving higher brain mechanisms to a great extent. This position implies that the maturation of sensory and cognitive functions produces both the need and capacity for a more integrative process. This process would be subjected to a greater cephalic control and prolonged in response to an extended waking life and certain environmental and social influences. The primitive neural substrates of a definitive sleep process may be present in the newborn, but are not functional until a certain level of integration is achieved via the influences of maturation and experience. The quiescent period in the newborn could then be considered as either a primitive manifestation of this process or as an unrelated but antecedent baseline state peculiar to this early stage of life. In this context one is reminded of the possible advantages of a delayed onset in certain physiological activities suggested by Purpura (Chapter 2) and Schapiro (Chapter 17) in this text. Such delays in the final elaboration of neural organization could assure a prolonged period of adaptive plasticity in the development of complex nervous systems.

It seems advisable at this point to exercise a degree of caution in the comparison of adult and infant behavioral states.

C. Fetal Manifestations

Two basic methods have been employed in attempts to assess the development of brain electrical activity and behavioral state in the pre-term infant. As reviewed by Rosen in the preceding chapter, methods are available for the direct recording of spontaneous and evoked fetal neuroelectric activity in lower mammals, and preliminary recordings have been obtained during birth from the scalp of the human fetus. The second approach has involved observation and physiological measurement of the premature infant. With regard to interpretations of sleep and wakefulness, both methods suffer from the same objections raised in relation to studies of the newborn. Moreover, the variables introduced by surgical intervention, the labor process, and the artificial environment of the incubator create further problems.

Intrauterine recording techniques offer a potentially useful approach to the study of normal and abnormal central nervous system maturation; however, only limited knowledge has been obtained about the development of the non-specific structures in the brain which mediate processes such as sleep and wakefulness. For example, the auditory evoked potentials recorded in the fetal guinea pig by Rosen indicate that the receptor apparatus and primary sensory pathways are functional at this early stage of development, but they in no way reflect upon the status of integrative mechanisms essential for the attribution of wakefulness or sleep. Primary sensory-evoked responses are obtained from both comatose and anesthetized subjects and it has been well established that the pathways mediating these responses are not directly involved in the brain mechanisms for sleep and wakefulness (Lindsley et al., 1950).

EEG patterns recorded during parturition in the human fetus (see Fig. 12, Chapter 10) provide some evidence that functional states of consciousness are absent at this time. While the conditions of delivery would most certainly be arousing from the point of view of the fetus, the EEG patterns obtained by Rosen showed relatively high-voltage slow waves and bursts similar to the patterns ascribed to sleep in premature and term infants. This, again, reflects upon the wisdom of adjudging functional states from the unique and irregular EEG configurations presented by these infants. Fortunately, everyone seems to agree that no such designations can be made on the basis of physiological and behavioral data collected from premature infants under 8 months of conceptual age (Dreyfus-Brisac, 1964, 1968; Parmelee et al., 1967).

III. THE BASIC REST-ACTIVITY CYCLE

A. Adult Manifestations

As mentioned previously, Kleitman noted in adults the cyclic alternation between REM and synchronized sleep patterns throughout the night and proposed that this cycling continued also during wakefulness. His original concept of the basic rest-activity cycle emerged from the study of infants, in whom this oscillation was not restricted to any particular behavioral state or time of day. The concept as applied to the adult was based entirely upon observations during sleep and was overshadowed by the implied correlation between the REM state and dreaming. Kleitman, however, made reference to numerous earlier studies which supported this idea. Of particular interest was an investigation by Wada (1922), who recorded gross body activity from normal adult human subjects kept in bed for long-term experimental recording sessions. Wada found that these subjects showed discrete periods of spontaneous activity every 90-120 min., *both during sleep and wakefulness*. More recently, several groups have documented the continuous alternation of two basic CNS states within the sleep-waking rhythm of man. Othmer, Hayden, and Segelbaum (1969) studied eye movements, muscle tone, and EEG patterns in adult female subjects for periods of 24 hr. The subjects slept in the laboratory during the night and remained in bed or in a chair during the succeeding day with lights either on or off. They found recurrent REM periods throughout the night and day. During the normal daylight hours, REM periods emerged usually from an EEG pattern of light sleep, but were noted occasionally during wakefulness with eyes closed. They concluded that the REM state occurs regularly throughout a 24-hr period and constitutes a general "encephalic cycle," rather than a sleep-dream cycle. Kripke and O'Donoghue (1968) asked subjects to remain awake continuously for periods of 24 hr. Physiological and behavioral measures indicated a functional periodicity resembling in its timing REM cycles recorded during preceding sleep periods. More recently, Kripke *et al*. (1970) described a variable REM cycle in the rhesus monkey with a mean period of 66 min. This rhythm corresponded to a periodicity in EMG activity recorded from the same animals during the prolonged waking portion of 24-hr observations. Globus and co-workers are carrying out an extensive series of studies directed toward this problem in adult human subjects. A fundamental question which they pursued is the time of onset of the REM state relative to sleep onset. These studies indicated that REM state onset was as closely related to "real clock" time as it was to the time sleep was initiated (Globus *et al*., 1969). That is, a tendency existed for REM epochs to be anchored at certain points in time regardless of variations in the time of sleep onset. Additionally, they have found evidence for a rhythm of 90-110 min in measurements of the errors registered in a continuous performance task; subjects showed sustained periods of improved performance at these intervals (Globus *et al*., 1970). Thus, it was hypothesized that the REM cycle, which is so easily detected during sleep, is only a reflection of an ultradian (less than 24-hr) rhythm which continues also during waking and which is of behavioral significance. In a related study which is currently under way, these authors have obtained data which link this performance cycle to the REM state during sleep. We have recently obtained similar data from sleep and performance studies in the cat (Sterman, 1970a). The 20-30 min REM cycle during sleep in the adult cat is identical to and continuous with a definitive cycle detected during instrumental performance in this animal.

These studies provide sufficient evidence to suggest the existence of an ultradian cycle which is not specifically related to sleep, but constitutes instead a basic physiological rhythmicity, coexistent with the sleep-waking rhythm. The term originally proposed for such a cycle by Kleitman was the "basic rest-activity cycle." While this label is convenient because of its historical precedence and familiarity, it is somewhat confusing when one conceives of the manifestations during wakefulness. Whereas the relatively static nature of intervening quiet periods during sleep is consistent with the concept of a resting phase of the cycle, the dynamic character of most aspects of wakefulness is not. Although waking performance may become less accurate or efficient, these changes are not necessarily indicative of rest. Moreover, in the infant the REM state is seen often to intrude directly upon ongoing active behaviors such as feeding and crying (Prechtl, 1968; Emde and Metcalf, 1970). As suggested earlier, this cycle appears to interact with other determinants of nervous system function such as the sleep-waking rhythm. Its overt characteristics may depend, therefore, upon this interaction. While a suitable terminology awaits further clarification of the physiological processes involved, we have chosen tentatively to retain the label provided by Kleitman, with no physiological interpretation implied.

The rest-activity cycle is most easily detected in sleep. During this state it has been ascribed a duration of 80-90 min (Kleitman, 1963; Roffwarg et al., 1966). There is much variability, however, in the individual cycles which make up these mean values. We have observed intervals ranging from 58 to 176 min in a sample of eight subjects over 30 recording nights, with a mean value of 89.7 ± 28.2 min. Globus (1970) has recently completed an extensive statistical evaluation of this cycle in ten subjects over 93 nights and reported a mean value of 101.5 (S.E. 2.7) min, with a range of 38-165 min. The reasons for this gross variability remain obscure. If this rhythm is considered to reflect the operation of some "biological clock" mechanism, it must be concluded that this clock is not very accurate.

B. Infant Manifestations

The rest-activity cycle is unquestionably present in the human infant. Prior to the emergence of a mature sleep-waking rhythm, this cycle is clearly detected continuously throughout the day and night. It was precisely this clarification of the process in the infant which led Kleitman to propose a 50 to 60-min rest-activity cycle in young infants. Incorporating additional observations, he later revised this to a 40 to 60-min range (Kleitman, 1967). According to Kleitman, the basic periodicity does not disappear with the emergence of "advanced" sleep and wakefulness, but increases its period with development to 60-70 min in preschool children and 80-90 min in the adult.

Several definitive studies of recurrent physiological states in the newborn have appeared in the more recent literature. Stern et al. (1969) obtained polygraphic and EEG recordings from full-term and premature infants, at term

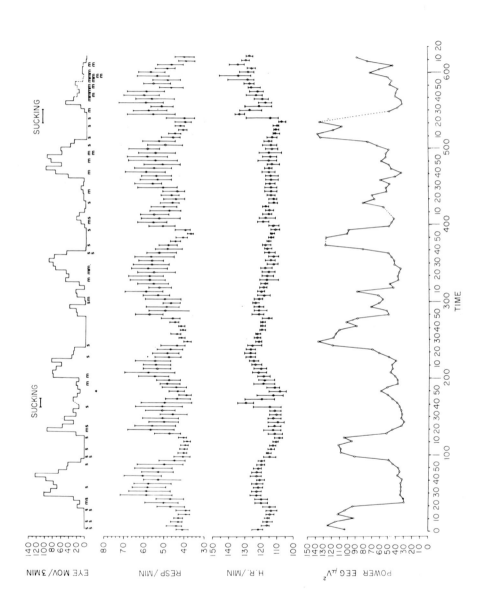

and 1, 3, and 8 months of age. Records ranging in length from 3 to 12 hr were classified into states of "wakefulness," "quiet sleep," "active sleep" and "transitional sleep." A cycle was defined as a continuous period of "sleep" beginning with an episode of active sleep followed by one episode of quiet sleep, and terminated at the beginning of the next active sleep state. Data from 3-hr recordings at term (one cycle) from 11 infants provided a mean cycle length of 47.0 min ± 10.4 min. However, lower values were obtained from a continuous 12-hr polygraphic recording and two 24-hr direct visual observations; these were 37.7, 39.6 and 42.9 min, respectively. Mean cycle values for infants 3 and 8 months of age were comparable for both long and short recordings. These age groups showed a combined cycle mean of 53.2 min, with the various subgroup means ranging from 49.7 to 57.3 min.

Prechtl (1968) has also reported polygraphic studies in newborn human infants. As mentioned previously, they have developed the concept of physiological "state patterns," which preclude the need for subjective labels. These investigators speak also of "state cycles," and their data provide some of the clearest evidence for the rest-activity cycle that we have encountered. Figure 3 presents a compiled polygram of an 8-day-old normal full-term infant, in which the cycling of the physiological state is manifest in recordings of eye and body movements, respiration, and EEG amplitude. From these data we have identified six cycles (utilizing increased rate and variability of respiration to specify the active-quiet-active period) with a mean duration of 53.9 minutes, and a range of 30.9 to 72.7 min. A similar polygram from a 2-day-old infant (Prechtl et al., 1969) provided a mean cycle duration of 51.4 min and a range of 33-77 min. Monod and Pajot (1965) utilized the *trace alternant* EEG pattern observed during the quiet state as their primary reference and determined state cycle values for three groups of infants: under 24 hr, 2-10 days, and 15 days in age. This procedure incorporated the transitional (quiet) period defined by Stern et al. (1969) into the active state. Nevertheless, they reported a mean cycle value of 46.5 min for the newborns and 60-70 min for older infants. A large variability of cycle lengths was observed also by these investigators.

The following conclusions may be drawn from these various findings. During the first weeks of life the human infant shows a rest-activity cycle which can be observed uniformly throughout a given 24-hr period. With the development of a sleep-waking rhythm, the observable manifestations of this cycle are increasingly associated with sleep, as the latter process becomes sustained and more readily distinguished from an emerging, dynamic wakefulness. The duration of this cycle

---

FIG. 3.   Compiled polygram from a computer analysis of a 6-hr record in epochs of 3 min. Normal infant, 8 days of age. Number of rapid eye movements per 3 min, medians and quartiles of respiration and heart rate and average power of the EEG in μV^2 are shown. M, gross body movements; S, startles. Bottle-feeding indicated by sucking. (From Prechtl, 1968.)

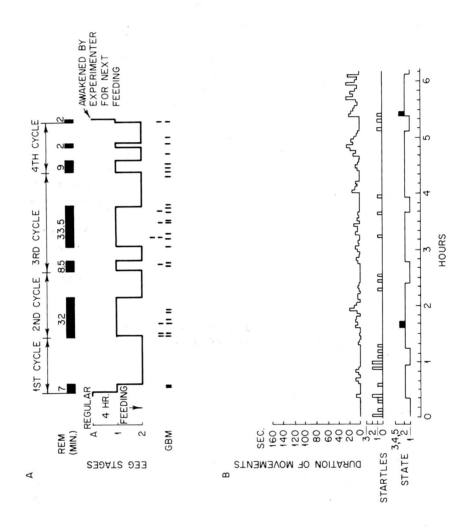

is variable at all ages, but is definitely shorter in the newborn. Most investigations report cycle means ranging from approximately 35-55 min at this age. Individual cycle values may be as low as 30 min, and as high as 70 min in duration. In older infants (1 week to 8 months) mean cycle values increase to a range of 50-70 min, while individual values as low as 30, and as high as 80 are obtained. A recent compilation of the scanty data available suggests a gradual maturation of this cycle, achieving adult values between 2 and 10 years of age in man (Sterman, 1970, 1971, in press).

Considering these data and the measures previously reviewed from adult studies, it is apparent that marked variability is a characteristic feature of the rest-activity cycle at all ages. This would seem to be a significant consideration since many tend to conceive of biological rhythms in terms of physical periodicities and to expect sine-wave regularity. According to Richter (1965), many biological periodicities lack such stability. He has pointed out that "homeostatic clocks" involving the operation of physiological feedback mechanisms are often inaccurate or variable, depending upon the physiological processes involved. Neurophysiological studies in the cat, which also shows a variable alternation of states comparable to those found in man, indicate that the physiological mediation of its basic rest-activity cycle is primitive in an evolutionary sense. Under a variety of laboratory conditions, the normal cat demonstrates a cycle time of approximately 25 ± 5 min, with a range of about 20-50 min (Sterman et al., 1965; Ursin, 1968). Several studies have indicated that this cycle is not significantly altered in brain-transected preparations in which the entire forebrain, and often also the midbrain, have been separated from the brain stem or entirely removed (Jouvet, 1965; McGinty and Sterman, 1970). It is apparent from these findings that the rest-activity cycle is a fundamental and intrinsically variable process.

C. Fetal Manifestations

The ontogenetic origin of the rest-activity cycle is also a matter of scientific interest and has been discussed rather extensively within the context of sleep states in the infant. It has been well established that the relative percentages of "REM sleep" are greatest in premature and newborn infants and decrease

---

FIG. 4.   Analyses of polygraphically defined states and their relationship to body motility in the human newborn are shown above from studies carried out in two different laboratories. A, from Roffwarg et al. (1966) indicates the correlation of gross body movements (GBM) with EEG stages and particularly with the REM state as defined by these investigators, in a 4-day-old newborn. B, from Prechtl et al. (1969) presents both the distribution and duration of body movements and startle responses in relation to polygraphically defined "state patterns" in an 8-day-old infant. State 1, quiescent; State 2, rapid eye movements, irregular respiration, etc. (see Fig. 3), States 3-5, feeding.

progressively with maturation (Roffwarg *et al.*, 1966; Parmelee *et al.*, 1967). There is some disagreement as to the age at which the adult level of 18-24% is reached (Kahn and Fisher, 1969). Whereas Parmelee *et al.* (1967) reported 23% at 3 months with computer analysis, and Petre-Quadens and Lambrechts (1965) found 22% by the second month, others have suggested that this level is not achieved until much later (Roffwarg *et al.*, 1966; Kohler, 1968). In spite of this disagreement, it is true that young infants show a greater percentage of the REM state during sleep. It is true also that they have a shorter rest-activity cycle than older infants, a fact which may be related to the increased percentages of REM, particularly since the mean duration of REM epochs does not appear to change reliably from term to 8 months of age (Stern *et al.*, 1969). Considering only the increased percentages in newborns, and particularly in premature infants, some have hypothesized a developmental "need" for this state which would be greatest in the fetus (Roffwarg *et al.*, 1966). We became interested in this and other problems related to the physiological origins of sleep states and undertook an extensive *in utero* study of behavior in the human fetus.

Among the several criteria utilized in identifying the rest-activity cycle in the newborn, perhaps the most reliable is muscular activity (Dreyfus-Brisac, 1967). In contrast to the relatively motionless nature of intervening periods, the active state is accompanied by almost continuous muscular contractions which take the form of gross body movements, prolonged episodes of tonic athetoid writhing of the body, and twitching of face and limb musculature. The close correspondence of body movements in the infant with REM's and other indices of this active state is shown in Fig. 4, from the studies of Roffwarg *et al.* (1966) and Prechtl *et al.* (1969). These data suggest that the periodic occurrence of this physiological state, and thus the rest-activity cycle itself, can be studied by reference to motility patterns in the fetus. This rationale provided a basis whereby the state characteristics of the human fetus could be assessed indirectly. An early report of the findings obtained utilizing this approach has been published elsewhere (Sterman, 1967). The data to be described below represent an extension of this study and will be directed primarily toward the context of the present discussion.

Fetal activity was recorded in eight normal pregnant women 21-28 years of age. These data were obtained during all-night recordings taken in the last two trimesters of pregnancy. After an initial night of adaptation to the sleep laboratory and recording procedures, each subject returned on 3-5 subsequent nights for experimental data collection. Recordings were obtained at approximately 30-day intervals until term. The subjects reported to the laboratory prior to their normal bedtime and were allowed to sleep until 8 A.M. the following morning.

Fetal activity was monitored by the application of three pressure-sensitive electrodes to the abdominal surface. After fetal position was estimated by Leopold maneuvers and maternal localization, the electrodes were taped to the abdomen over the fetal head, limbs, and buttocks (Fig. 5). A fourth electrode

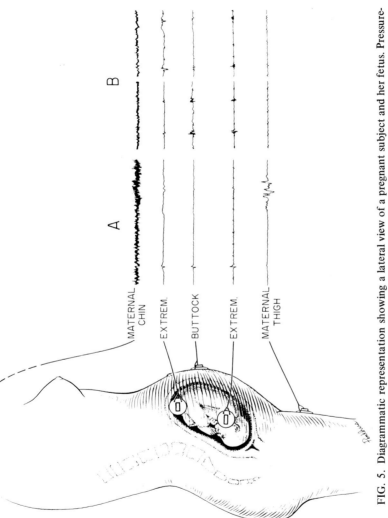

FIG. 5. Diagrammatic representation showing a lateral view of a pregnant subject and her fetus. Pressure-sensitive electrodes are indicated over various portions of the abdomen in relation to the fetus. Additionally, electrodes are shown over the dorsal surface of the thigh and originating from the maternal jaw muscles. Typical polygraphic recordings obtained from these electrodes are shown with appropriate reference in A and B. In A, a generalized fetal movement can be distinguished from maternal activity as indicated by increased muscle tone and thigh movement. In B, discrete foci of fetal activity are detectable through the differential patterns of recorded activity.

was fixed to the dorsal surface of the thigh to register maternal activity. The mother's sleep was monitored by standard polygraphic procedures which included the continuous recording of EEG, eye movements (EOG), and submental EMG. Pressure changes produced by fetal movements were amplifed and displayed together with the mother's physiological measures on a 10-channel polygraph. This technique for recording fetal activity proved to be quite sensitive and disclosed several different types of movement including abrupt kicks, squirming, and slow rotations. For the purpose of the present analysis these various types of activity were combined to determine overall motility. Distinct kicks were counted as single movements, and sustained activity was scored as one movement per two seconds (i.e., agitation lasting for 6 sec would be scored as three movements). Maternal sleep and waking patterns were measured according to the Sleep Scoring Manual of Rechtschaffen and Kales (1968).

Thirty all-night recordings of fetal activity were collected in this manner from eight subjects. A minimum of three recordings was obtained from each subject, ranging in duration from 5 to 9 hr. From the earliest recording age (21 weeks' gestation) to parturition the fetus demonstrated a surprising consistency of motor activity, similar in many ways to that seen in early premature infants

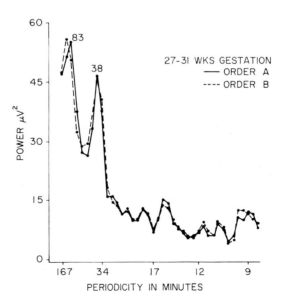

FIG. 6.   Two independent power spectral analyses of fetal activity are shown above for a group of four subjects whose data were combined to provide an adequate time series for evaluation of periodicity. The subject order was randomly altered in each instance in an effort to assess this variable. This control procedure indicated that the order of subject combination did not affect the periodicities detected by this analysis. In all orders tested, two separate peaks were invariably observed, indicating a slow and a faster activity cycle, as shown above.

(Parmelee *et al.*, 1967; Dreyfus-Brisac, 1968). There were no systematic gestational trends in the level of this activity, although the type of movements shifted progressively from abrupt jerks to more sustained agitation. Fetal activity was not uniformly distributed throughout the night, but showed an irregular alternation of peaks and troughs.

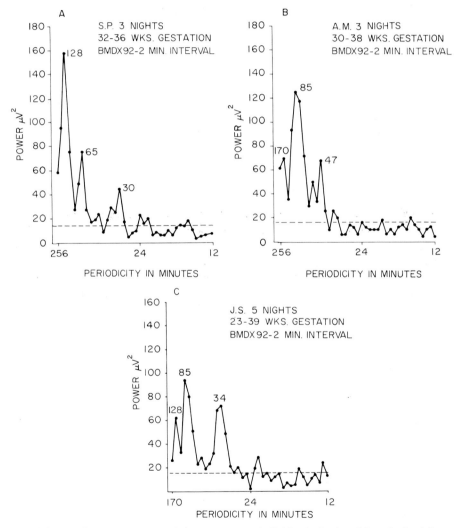

FIG. 7.   Power spectral analyses showing periodicities in fetal activity obtained from three subjects. In each instance, data were combined across gestation periods, as described in the text. These subjects slept normally throughout the periods of recording. Gestation ages and computer program utilized are shown at upper right. Note the presence of a relatively sharp fast cycle (peaks = 30, 34, and 47 min) and a more diffuse slower cycle with various peaks ranging from 65 to 170 min.

Quantitative analysis of these data was achieved by spectral analysis. Fetal movements were grouped in 1-, 2-, and 5-minute intervals and considered collectively for different subjects across a specific gestational period. To provide an adequate time series, records were knit together, with fetal activity values converted to standard scores and all linear trends removed. Spectral analyses were performed at the UCLA Health Sciences Computing Facility, utilizing program BMDX92 (Dixon, 1969). Analysis across subjects as a function of gestational periods disclosed two significant periodicities which were essentially the same at all gestational ages. One was relatively short, ranging from 30 to 50 min, and the second longer, ranging from 80 to 110 min. The data were recombined in different subject orders several times and submitted again to spectral analysis. The findings were essentially unchanged by this procedure (Fig. 6). The longest individual records were analyzed also without combination of data. The results were comparable, but interpretation of cycles exceeding 60 min was limited by the relatively short length of the recordings. Since no trends were noted as a function of gestational age, it was decided that the most valid combination of data was within subjects across sequential recordings. A combination of records from the same subject over three to five recording nights provided a desirable time series which, at the same time, minimized any distortions which might result from individual differences. The data obtained by this analysis in three representative subjects are shown in Fig. 7. Data from all subjects again disclosed two cycles, one with a mean of 39.6 ± 11.8 min, and a second with a mean of 96.4 ± 13.2 min (Table II). This was true whether or not the mothers slept soundly during the recording period (Fig. 8). Thus, regardless of the method of analysis, the data indicated the existence of *two* fetal activity cycles. It remained to determine the factors responsible for their occurrence.

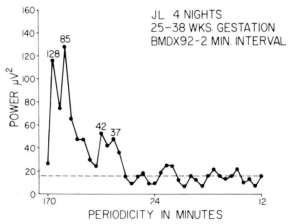

FIG. 8.   Power spectral analysis of fetal activity similar to those shown in Fig. 7. These data, however, were obtained from the fetus of a mother who showed little if any polygraphic evidence of sleep during the 4 nights of data collection. In spite of this, the same two basic periodicities, as seen in Fig. 7, were observed here.

TABLE II   Summary of Fetal Recordings and Mean Periodicities in Fetal Motility Obtained by Power-Spectral Analysis

Subject	Number of recording nights	Gestation period in weeks	1st cycle (minutes)	2nd cycle
E. L.[a]	2	21-23	20.0	96.0
P. S.	5	21-37	38.7	89.5
S. W.	5	21-39	57.0	105.0
J. S.	5	21-39	34.3	87.8
K. K.	3	25-35	50.3	121.3
H. L.	4	29-40	39.3	85.3
E. M.	3	31-37	47.0	81.2
S. P.	3	32-36	30.0	104.2
N = 8	N = 30	Range = 21-40 weeks	Mean = 39.6 S.D. = 11.8	Mean = 96.4 S.D. = 13.2

[a]Premature delivery at 32 weeks gestation.

In the present experiment maternal sleep parameters were recorded simultaneously with fetal activity. It therefore was possible to measure the mother's REM or rest-activity cycle during sleep and to compare this with the cycles detected in her fetus. Such a comparison is shown in Fig. 9. In this subject the slower fetal cycle was clearly apparent in graphic representation. Direct comparison of this cycle with the maternal activity cycle indicated a significant correspondence. Visual comparisons utilizing all of the data indicated that 65%

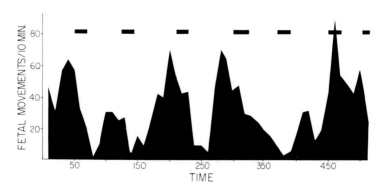

FIG. 9.   Comparison of maternal REM-cycle and fetal activity data. The maternal REM state is indicated by solid bars, superimposed upon the plot of fetal activity. Note the frequent correspondence between maternal REM state and peaks in the slow fetal cycle.

of the peaks in the slower fetal cycle occurred in direct relation to the maternal REM state. Thus, it is possible that this periodicity reflects the mother's own rest-activity cycle, communicated to her fetus by some undetermined systemic factor. This interpretation is supported further by the marked similarity between the slow fetal cycle (96.4 ± 13.2 min) and the previously stated mean normative values determined for the adult rest-activity cycle (101.5, Globus, 1970; 89.7, this study). Moreover, the fact that no behavioral periodicity in this range has been reported in the newborn suggests that it is unique to the uterine environment and of extrafetal origin.

Several of the infants monitored in this study were delivered subsequently at the UCLA hospital and studied by Parmelee and co-workers. These infants participated in the study by Stern et al. (1969) cited earlier. Therefore, it was possible to compare in these infants patterns of motility recorded in utero with state cycles measured directly in the laboratory. The fast cycle recorded in the fetus (39.6 ± 11.8 min) compared favorably with the short sample, mean rest-activity or "sleep" cycle at term reported by Stern et al. (47.0 ± 10.4 min). In one subject recorded for 12-hr as a newborn the mean cycle obtained of 37.7 min was almost identical to the fast fetal cycle of 38.7 min registered by this infant during gestation. We can assume, therefore, that the faster periodicity detected in the motility patterns of the fetus represents the earliest manifestation of the basic rest-activity cycle in man.

IV. SUMMARY AND CONCLUSIONS

We have attempted in this chapter to describe and compare the fundamental state patterns observed in man from fetus to adult. On the basis of an ever-increasing body of data, it appears that the sleep-waking rhythm must be distinguished from a second and perhaps more fundamental *rest-activity cycle*, expressed during sleep as the REM state cycle and during wakefulness as a similarly timed oscillation of central nervous system activity, influencing the efficiency of higher nervous functions.

Adult expressions of both sleep and wakefulness were found to be absent in the fetus and at best fragmented in the late premature and newborn infant. We have concluded that it is undesirable to speak of sleep and wakefulness in the fetus or newborn without consideration of these obvious differences from their adult manifestations. The findings of numerous investigators indicate, at least with regard to sleep, that the fragmented physiological and behavioral criteria of this state coalesce gradually throughout the first few months of life. Thus, a pattern which conforms to the definition developed for the adult can be identified at 3 months of age. Other evidence suggests that the temporal characteristics of sleep follow a similar course of development, achieving a sustained duration and nocturnal distribution at this time. We interpret the available evidence as indicating that the neural substrates of sleep and wakefulness are developed late in gestation but require additional maturation and post-$1 = 1$ natal learning to achieve the essential integration necessary for anything but the most primitive aspects of their function. Thus, the processes of sleep and wakefulness emerge gradually when the underlying neural mechanisms achieve a requisite level of development, in this case allowing the infant to act upon his environment and in turn to be influenced by that action. One outcome of this sequence, resulting probably from intrinsic factors which determine its duration, is a circadian or 24-hr distribution of sleep and wakefulness.

The basic rest-activity cycle was shown to be clearly present in the human fetus and similar in duration to that of the newborn infant. The physiological factors responsible for this fundamental cycle remain a mystery. However, its manifestation in the fetus, an organism which enjoys an unprecedented freedom from physiological need as well as social and other environmental influences, suggests that its pacemaker resides at a most basic level, perhaps involving metabolic regulation, as suggested by McGinty in Chapter 18 of this text. The functional significance of the cycle is also unclear at the present time. It has been suggested that it provides a framework for the development of other important physiological periodicities, such as sleep-waking and feeding (Kleitman, 1967). It is possible, furthermore, that this cycle provides a meaningful basis for the organization of cognitive functions during both wakefulness and sleep. The basic rest-activity cycle has not been considered in discussions of guiding influences in development or in considerations of the most efficient distribution of human effort. Hopefully, an increasing awareness of this phenomenon, together with continued investigation in basic and clinical laboratories, will yield a conceptual integration of this biological "missing link."

ACKNOWLEDGMENT

Studies reported here were supported by the Veterans Administration and by USPHS Grant # MH10083. Bibliographic assistance was received from the UCLA Brain Information Service which is part of the Neurological Information Network of NINDS and is supported under contract # DHEW PH-43-66-59. The authors also wish to express their appreciation for the comments and cooperation of Dr. A. H. Parmelee, Department of Pediatrics, UCLA. The assistance of Dr. R. Harper also was greatly appreciated.

REFERENCES

Anders, T., Sachar, E., Kream, J., Roffwarg. H. P., and Hellman, L. (1970). *Psychophysiology* 7, 311.
Aschoff, J. (1965). *In* "Circadian Clocks" (J. Aschoff, ed.), 95-111. North Holland Pub. Co., Amsterdam.
Aschoff, J., and Wever, R. (1962). *Naturwissenschaften 15,* 337.

Aserinsky, E., and Kleitman, N. (1953). *Science 118,* 273.

Clemente, C. D. (ed.) (1967). "Physiological Correlates of Dreaming." *Exp. Neurol.* Suppl. 4.

Dement, W. C., and Kleitman, N. (1957). *Electroencephalogr. Clin. Neurophysiol. 9,* 673.

Dixon, W. J. (1969). "BMD Biomedical Computer Programs, X-Series Supplement." Univ. of California Press, Los Angeles, California.

Dreyfus-Brisac, C. (1964). *In* "Neurological and Electroencephalographic Correlative Studies in Infancy" (P. Kellaway and J. Petersen, eds.), pp. 186-207. Grune & Stratton, New York.

Dreyfus-Brisac, C. (1967). *In* "Regional Development of the Brain in Early Life" (A. Minkowski, ed.), pp. 437-457. Davis, Philadelphia, Pennsylvania.

Dreyfus-Brisac, C. (1968). *Develop. Phychobiol. 1,* 162.

Emde, R. N., and Metcalf, D. R. (1970). *J. Nerv. Ment. Dis. 150,* 376.

Finkelstein, J., Anders, T., Sachar, E., Roffwarg, H. P., and Hellman, L. (1970). *Psychophysiology 7,* 312.

Globus, G. G. (1970). *Psychophysiology, 7,* 214.

Globus, G. G., Phoebus, E., and Moore, C. (1970). *Psychophysiology 7,* 215.

Globus, G. G., Gardner, R. and Williams, T. A. (1969). *Arch. Gen. Psychiat. 21,* 151.

Halberg, F., Halberg, E., Barnum, C. P., and Bittner, J. J. (1959). *In* "Photoperiodism," Publ. No. 55. pp. 803-878. Am. Assoc. Advance. Sci., Washington, D. C.

Hellbrügge, T. (1960). *Cold Spring Harbor Symp. Quant. Biol. 25,* 311.

Jouvet, M. (1965). *In* "Aspects anatomo-fonctionnels de la physiologie du sommeil," pp. 397-446. C.N.R.S., Paris.

Kahn, E., and Fisher, C. (1969). *J. Nerv. Ment. Dis. 148,* 477.

Kales, A., ed. (1969). "Sleep: Physiology and Pathology." Lippincott, Philadelphia, Pennsylvania.

Kleitman, N. (1963). "Sleep and Wakefulness." Univ. of Chicago Press, Chicago, Illinois.

Kleitman, N. (1967). *Res. Publ., Ass. Res. Nerv. Ment. Dis. 45,* 30.

Kleitman, N., and Engelmann, T. G. (1953). *J. Appl. Physiol. 6,* 269.

Kohler, W. L. (1968). *J. Pediat. 72,* 228.

Kripke, D. F., and O'Donoghue, J. P. (1968). *Psychophysiology 5,* 231.

Kripke, D. F., Halberg, F., Crowley, T. J., and Pegram, V. G. (1970). *Psychophysiology 7,* 216.

Lindsley, D. B., Schreiner, L. H., Knowles, W. B., and Magoun, H. W. (1950). *Electroencephalograph. Clin. Neurophysiol. 2,* 483.

McGinty, D. J., and Sterman, M. B. (1970). *Psychophysiology 7,* 189.

Metcalf, D. R. (1969). *Psychosom. Med. 31,* 393.

Metcalf, D. R. (1970). *Neuropädiatrie 1,* 428.

Metcalf, D. R., and Emde, R. N. (1969). *Psychophysiology 6,* 264.

Mills, J. N. (1964). *J. Physiol. (London) 174,* 217.

Monod, N., and Pajot, N. (1965). *Biol. Neonatorum 8,* 281.

Othmer, E., Hayden, M. P., and Segelbaum, R. (1969). *Science 164,* 447.

Parmelee, A. H., Wenner, W. H., and Schulz, H. R. (1964). *J. Pediat. 65,* 576.

Parmelee, A. H., Wenner, W. H., Akiyama, Y., Schulz, M., and Stern, E. (1967). *Develop. Med. Child. Neurol. 9,* 70.

Petre-Quadens, O., and Lambrechts, J. (1965). *Acta Neurol. Psychiat. Belg. 65,* 971.

Prechtl, H. F. R. (1968). *Clin. Develop. Med. 27,* 22.

Prechtl, H. F. R., Weinmann, H., and Akiyama, Y. (1969). *Neuropaediatrie 1,* 101.

Rechtschaffen, A., and Kales, A. (1968). "A Manual of Standardized Terminology, Techniques and Scoring System for Sleep Stages of Human Subjects." U.S., *Pub. Health Serv.,* Washington, D.C.

Richter, C. P. (1965). "Biological Clocks in Medicine and Psychiatry." Thomas, Springfield, Illinois.

Roffwarg, H. P., Muzio, J. N., and Dement, W. C. (1966). *Science 152,* 604.

Roffwarg, H. P., Sachar, E., Finkelstein, J., Curti, J., Ellman, S., Kream, J., Fishman, R., Gallagher, F. T., and Hellman, L. (1970). *Psychophysiology 7,* 312.

Rutenfranz, J. (1961). *In* "Circadian Systems" (S. J. Fomon, ed.), pp. 38-41. Ross Lab., Columbus, Ohio.

Sassin, J. F., Parker, D. C., Mace, J. W., Gotlin, R. W., Johnson, L. C., and Rossman, L. G. (1969). *Science 165,* 513.

Shaywitz, B. A., Finkelstein, J., Hellman, L., and Weitzman, E. D. (1970). *Psychophysiology 7,* 310.

Siffre, M. (1963). "Hors du Temps." Tulliard, Paris.

Sterman, M. B. (1967). *Exp. Neurol.* Suppl. 4, 98.

Sterman, M. B. (1970a). *Psychophysiology 7,* 215.

Sterman, M. B. (1970b). *In* "Maturation and Developmental Implications of Sleep; NICHD Symposium," in press.

Sterman, M. B., Knauss, T., Lehmann, D., and Clemente, C. D. (1965). *Electroencephalogr. Clin. Neurophysiol. 19,* 509.

Stern, E., Parmelee, A. H., Akiyama, Y., Schultz, M. A., and Wenner, W. H. (1969). *Pediatrics 43,* 65.

Ursin, R. (1968). *Brain Res. 11,* 347.

Wada, T. (1922). *Arch. Psychol. 57,* 1.

Weitzman, E. D., Schaumburg, H., and Fishbein, W. (1966). *J. Clin. Endocrinol. Metab. 26,* 121.

CHAPTER 12 Ludic Behavior in Young Mammals

Dietland Müller-Schwarze

I. INTRODUCTION

Children play. In common speech, all activities of a human child other than sleeping, eating, elimination or "work" are called "play." Whether a boy jumps over a creek, or wrestles with another boy or engages in a game of checkers with his sister, his activities are labeled "play." Even at first glance, quite diverse phenomena and possibly different functions and physiological processes are involved in these examples. If the term "play" is already vague when applied to human behavior, the confusion becomes complete when certain behavior patterns in other vertebrates directly or even remotely resembling the activities of children are labeled "play," too. Yet, the extension of the term "play" in its usual colloquial sense to animals may reflect an intuitively recognized similarity between children's play and that of, say, kittens and puppies. What similarities exist among the various "play" activities of young animals, when only subhuman species are considered? Our present knowledge will be summarized in this paper without attempting completeness. The large gaps of our knowledge will be pointed out. Perhaps new physiological and neurophysiological approaches will shed light on this puzzling behavior.

If we consult dictionaries for the conventional use of the term "play" we find the following: "to engage in a recreational activity; amuse or divert oneself; frolic, sport (children playing in the park ...)" " ...play, the most general, suggests an opposition to work " (Webster's Third New International Dictionary). The Encyclopedia Americana lists play only in the context with play therapy, while the Random House Dictionary of the English Language (1967) gives 74 meanings of "play."

When turning to scientific dictionaries we find definitions like this one: "Voluntary activity pursued without ulterior purpose, and, on the whole, with enjoyment or expectation of enjoyment (certain elements of play may not be enjoyed)" (English and English, 1958). A psychologist who has worked extensively on play defines this behavior as " . . .a wide variety of vigorous and spirited activities: those that move the organism or its part through space such as running, jumping, rolling and somersaulting, pouncing upon and chasing objects or other animals, wrestling, and vigorous manipulation of body parts or objects in a variety of ways. The goals and incentives of vigorous play consist of certain patterns of variable or changing stimulation of the sensory surfaces" (Welker, 1961). Although the goals and incentives are by no means clear, only definitions like the last one are useful as research tools for studies of nonhuman mammals. The definition is general and objective.

II. DESCRIPTION

Despite the confused terminology and the difficulties of new definitions for the various kinds of "play," there exists one distinct category of motor play. These are juvenile social and solitary behaviors which in context, sequence, and function differ clearly from other behaviors.

For example, Norway rats (*Rattus norvegicus*, strain BD IX) of the same litter, between 20 and 70 days of age typically move about sniffing their cage (in our studies 120 by 60 cm large) for 1 to 5 min after eating. During this slow olfactory exploring the rats occasionally run for 50 to 200 cm. This running often changes into an attack of one littermate by another. The attacks may result in an interaction in which one individual lies on the back, while the other is on top, facing the other and "boxing" it with its forelegs. Biting may also occur and the bitten individual squeaks. After the individuals have separated, they explore and run again, and sometimes chase each other. Such a bout of exploration and "mock-fighting" may last from 5 to 30 min (Müller-Schwarze, 1966). Here, motor patterns of the fighting behavior of the species are carried out. No immediate competitive situation can be detected by the observer.

Another example is the more complex motor play of ungulates (Figs. 1 and 2). As in other species, deer fawns engage in sudden outbursts of vigorous activity. In the blacktailed deer (*Odocoileus hemionus columbianus*) such a bout starts with head jerks and leaps, after which the animals butt each other. Then they run up to several hundred meters. Often the hindlegs thrust out and upward during running. The animals may intercept each other and strike one another with their forelegs. Occasionally, a fawn may paw the ground and lie down a few seconds before it resumes running. Individuals of either sex may also mount each other one or several times during a play bout (Müller-Schwarze, 1968).

There is usually a main play bout which lasts about 6 – 10 min. It is preceded by one or several smaller play bouts, separated by a few minutes of grazing, exploring or grooming. The total time from the first 20 m running (which may

FIG. 1. Typical play fight among two shoats (*Sus scrofa*). They strike each other at the shoulder with upward and sideward movements of the head. There is no recognizable competitive situation. Adult males fight with the same movements: the lower tusk hits the pachyderm side of the opponent.

FIG. 2. Social play in blacktailed deer. A male (right) and a female run in opposite circles and intercept each other. When they meet, they often strike each other with their forelegs.

occur during a small or the main bout) to the termination of the main bout we arbitrarily call "play period." The duration of a play period averages 30 min. The grazing immediately before a play bout appears fitful, indicating a change in the state of the animal.

In contrast to the rat, which has primarily motor patterns of fighting in play, the deer has a mixture of coordinations which belong to escape, fighting, sexual, and reclining behaviors of the species.

Carnivores show a rich and highly variable repertoire of play movements (Tembrock, 1958; Poole, 1966). Tembrock distinguishes 67 motor patterns of play in the red fox (*Vulpes vulpes*).

Finally, in young primates, play becomes more intricate by the extreme modifiability of the motor patterns, longer duration, and by the addition of facial expressions and vocalizations. For example, the slapping, wrestling, and pushing of chimpanzees is accompanied by half-closed eyes, a broad smile, and a panting laugh (Mason, 1967).

From these few examples it is already obvious that the significance an investigator attaches to this type of behavior and the conclusions he draws in terms of general behavior theory depend largely on the species studied. Thus, some of the differences of opinion can be traced to the taxonomic differences of the experimental animals used.

Basically, either sex carries out the movements of both sexes. Females, for instance, also mount in play. However, the frequencies of the movements are often sex-specific. In deer, for example, females mount less often than males. In rhesus monkeys males initiate play more often (Young *et al.*, 1964).

There are three classes of play movements in young mammals:

1. Some patterns occur in identical form in the adult. Subtle differences may be detected only in motion picture analysis. Examples are mounting and striking in deer.

2. Some patterns occur in different form, sequences, orientation, or completeness. Examples are circular running instead of straight escape of the adult or the absence of alert posture before and after running in deer.

3. Some patterns are not performed by the adult. In deer this would be butting in females and vertical leaping.

There are also behavior patterns of the adult mammal which do not occur in juvenile play. In the blacktailed deer these are the threat posture and vocalizations of threat and alarm, as well as lip smacking, performed by males when approaching females. The threat posture is complex, including ruffling of the fur, lowering the head, laying back the ears, spreading the tarsal hair tuft, pulsating the tarsal glands, and snorting twice while the head is thrown up and down once.

Furthermore, it is generally true that the simple, "consummatory" motor patterns of the end of a behavior sequence like mounting (sexual behavior), striking (aggressive behavior) and lying down (reclining behavior) occur in play.

The variable, complex preliminaries of sexual, aggressive, and other behaviors (commonly called appetitive behavior) rarely occur.

As to nomenclature we agree with Barnett and Evans (1965) that new words like "gene" are more useful for research than the results of semantic theft, such as "salt" or "force." Therefore it seems appropriate to replace the word "play" by the more technical term ludic behavior (from Latin *ludere* to play) as used by Piaget (1951) and Berlyne (1960).

As a working definition, motor play or ludic motor activity is the performance of a mixed sequence of mostly stereotyped behavior patterns by an immature animal. These patterns belong to different functional systems and do not serve their usual functions. The patterns occur often in a social situation, under moderate general arousal, but low specific motivation.

III. INTERRELATIONSHIPS

A. Ludic and Serious Behavior

In the scientific literature many different behavior phenomena have been called "play." "The term play covers a heterogeneous assortment of activities from the darts and gambols of young birds and mammals to the extremely ritualized games of adult humans" (Hutt, 1966). Typically, one or more of the following circumstances have led an observer to label a behavior "play." (1) Ontogenetic precursors or other incomplete behavior: The first attempts of carnivores to kill prey; or the mounting of a young mammal by another without intromission are called play. Groos (1930) listed a number of incomplete juvenile song and courtship patterns in birds under "play." (2) Satiation: A satiated animal or human child may still handle food, but not eat it any more. (3) Inadequate object: A gull drops a rock or rubber ball repeatedly as it usually does with shells in order to open them (Lohmann, 1967). (4) The object may be loose: When an ungulate pushes or rubs against a tree or post, nobody calls it play, but when the object that is pushed happens to be moveable (ball, bucket) the behavior has been termed "play with an object" (Inhelder, 1955a,b). (5) Repetition: Courtship or fighting movements are sometimes called "play" when they are repeated over and over again, for instance in gray whales (Sauer, 1963). (6) No observable releasing stimuli: An activity seems to occur spontaneously as, for example, with escape movements in captive ungulates. (7) Exploration: Often exploration of a novel object or the general environment by a young bird or a young mammal is called "play" (e.g., Lorenz, 1956). Because rigorous definitions have never been agreed upon, all authors have been free to use the term play for many different activities.

The above situations have in common only that the execution of a behavior pattern or sequence deviates somehow from the "normal" or complete functional performance of that same behavior. Therefore all the varieties of so-called play behavior can be delineated only in a negative way, as "nonserious behavior." Nonserious behavior does not serve the usual function, although it may serve a new function. Nonserious behavior then is a negatively defined *compositum mixtum,* as are, for instance, the "invertebrates" in taxonomy.

Because of the liberal use of the term play in the past it is necessary to define the behavior in question in every case. Exploration should be treated separately from ludic behavior as its own functional category (see Section III, C). Incomplete or repeated serious behavior in immature and adult animals is usually easy to recognize. Behavior patterns carried out with substitute objects may easily be ascribed to their specific behavior system.

After sorting out these variations of serious behavior there is left a category of behavior which we may call "ludic motor behavior" or "play *sensu stricto.*" These are the bouts of mixed motor coordinations described in Section II. This activity comprises patterns belonging to the agonistic (fighting), escape, sexual, preying and other behaviors which follow each other in a sequence atypical for "serious" behavior. The social play of puppies or the prey-catching and social play of kittens are typical examples. Table I contains the relationships between the so defined motor play and the "serious" behavior.

Although ludic behavior is usually well delineated from serious behavior by context and sequence and well understood as play by the participants, play may turn into serious behavior in some cases. Rensch and Dücker (1959) describe this for two species of mongoose (*Herpestes*): after a mongoose has crawled under a blanket or carpet during play, it will defend it by threatening and biting people (den defense). In human children playful fleeing sometimes "turns real" (Blurton Jones, 1967). "A child fleeing for a long time without chasing back, going faster and faster, may raise its eyebrows and stop smiling, and its laugh changes and becomes a more continuous vocalization, a tremulous scream" (Blurton Jones). Children frequently scream like this when encountering an insect running about the ground.

The sequences of motor patterns in ludic and serious contexts shall now be discussed. While we find ludic behavior typically in immature animals and its serious counterparts in adults, there are serious and play behaviors exhibited by the same young individuals. Therefore the mutual temporal relationships between the two behavior categories can be studied.

Because of its erratic appearance, play is often assumed to have lost the typical pattern sequences of the serious context (Meyer-Holzapfel, 1956; Marler and Hamilton, 1966; Loizos, 1966). When we investigated this question we found that in the blacktailed deer a period of play may last 30 min and consist of one main bout and several short bursts. These play bouts are separated by intervals of serious behavior, such as grazing, exploring, or licking themselves or

TABLE I   Comparison of Serious and Ludic Behavior in Young Mammals

	Serious	Ludic
Occurrence	Obligatory	Facultative; only after satiation of serious tendencies
Motor patterns	Species-specific, often composite movements	More general, simple movements
Sequence of single motor patterns	Typical sequence within one functional system	More variable; patterns of different functional systems are mixed
Position in hierarchy of functional systems	(at least temporarily) high	Always low
Releasing stimulus situation	Specific stimuli emanating from conspecific or environment	Unspecific stimuli, if any, not the usual stimuli (more spontaneous)
Overall organization	Sequences of appetitive and consummatory behaviors	No hierarchical organization
Motivation	Specific and independent for each functional system	Unspecific; motor play, exploration, or other locomotion are alternatives of overt behavior

other individuals. The serious behavior during these intervals maintains its typical pattern sequences, such as walking – grazing – alert posture, which we may call here motor pattern associations (MPA). Within the main bout of play, which may last from 6 to 10 min, certain MPA's exist also. For instance, running typically follows leaping, or striking another individual with the forelegs follows butting or running. All these MPA's of the play bout also belong together in the serious context: leaping and running are escape movements; butting and striking are parts of the fighting behavior; pawing and lying down follow each other when the animal reclines.

In a sequential analysis of 16,000 behavior pattern combinations in a male and a female deer fawn, the relative frequencies of the occurrences of two motor patterns one after another were determined. Their behavior was not different from 12 other observed individuals. The frequencies were ranked by means of Spearman's rank correlation coefficient. An array of 91 correlation coefficients for the various combinations of 14 behavior patterns was obtained for each serious and ludic context. The two correlation coefficients for each combination of two motor patterns in the two different contexts were compared. If ludic behavior were characterized by a general breakdown of typical sequence, the degree of correlation should decrease drastically from serious to ludic behavior. However, we found a high degree of stability. The correlation coefficients of serious behavior differed less between male and femate than the correlation coefficients of serious and ludic behavior. But in play the most frequent ludic motor patterns had a tendency to be correlated more with one another than they are in serious behavior. A more detailed and different statistical analysis of pattern sequence is presently being carried out and will be published elsewhere.

What makes the play bout appear so irregular is the alternation of sequences of ludic patterns and of serious sequences. But within each category a comparable degree of order prevails.

The transition from serious behavior patterns to ludic sequences is of particular interest. After eating, the deer fawns stand around and lick themselves or others occasionally. This behavior is followed by head jerks and leaps which start the play bout. The licking indicates a state of the animal in which no particular motivation is appreciably activated; the motivations are balanced at a very low level. This brings the beginning of a play bout close to the situations in which "displacement activities" occur. Grooming oneself is a common displacement activity in mammals. The difference consists in the activation of one or more functional systems when displacement activities occur, and in the absence of a specific activated system when play starts.

B. Ludic Behavior and General Activity Level

Wild mammals engage in social or solitary play only at certain times of their daily activity cycle. It is well known that the young of badgers, foxes, or deer play early in the morning or at dusk. These are usually the times of maximum activity of the species. The correlation between activity periods and play periods goes so far that, for instance confined blacktailed deer fawns during their first 10 days' of life play primarily around and before noon, which is the time of the maximum activity period at that age. With increasing age a small evening activity peak appears and the animals also play then (Müller-Schwarze and Müller-Schwarze, 1969; Fig. 3). In this species the longer the activity period, the more likely play occurs (Fig. 4). Usually there is no play in activity periods shorter than 15 min (Figs. 3 and 4).

In 1956 Meyer-Holzapfel hypothesized that motor play in young mammals is due to a general activity drive: "Play behaviour in all its various forms is assumed to spring from another motivation than does serious behaviour. Whereas the latter points in a certain direction frequent changes of direction are typical of play activity. This leads us to conclude that play behaviour arises from a general nonspecific activity drive, a readiness to be active in any manner whatsoever." In order to test this hypothesis, we deprived deer fawns of play and observed the effects. Short-term play deprivation, i.e., deprivation for 1 day, did not result in an increased readiness to play. This result would not be expected if an independent play motivation existed. Rather we observed longer activity periods, more locomotion and more exploration after the animals had been deprived of playing (Müller-Schwarze, 1968). Therefore the assumed "readiness to be active" has several options to express itself in overt behavior. Future research will have to determine the casual factors responsible for this readiness.

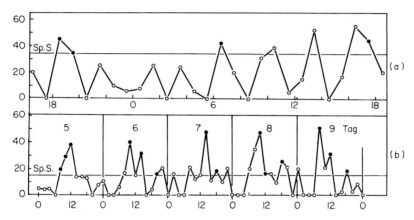

FIG. 3. Activity time per hour and occurrence of play in immature blacktailed deer.(a) 24-hr cycle of a 4-month-old female. Abscissa: hour of day; ordinate: activity time in min. 0-0, Nonludic activity periods; ●-●, activity periods with play. Sp.S.: play threshold.(b) Nonludic and ludic activity periods for a male from fifth to ninth day of life. [With kind permission of the editor, reprinted from *Bonner, Zool. Beitr. 20*, 282-289 (1969).]

C. Ludic Behavior and Exploration

In immature mammals, motor play and exploration of the physical and social environment occur in close temporal relationship. Wild-colored laboratory rats (strain BD IX) explore their enclosure before they engage in aggressive play (Fig. 5). The Egyptian mongoose (*Herpestes ichneumon*) and the Indian gray mongoose (*Herpestes edwardsii*) engage in olfactory and visual inspection of their home range during a play bout. This can be interpreted as the appetitive part of food-getting behavior (Rensch and Dücker, 1959). Because of this close temporal relationship, a common motivation has often been assumed for play and exploration. Many authors have used the two terms synonymously. (Thorpe, 1963; Lorenz, 1956). The latter speaks of "exploratory play" when describing the responses of a young raven to a new object. A number of authors however, have pointed out that exploration of the living and physical environment can be clearly separated from motor play.

Welker (1961) defines exploration as follows: "Exploration consists of gradually exposing the receptors (by biting, licking, sniffing, touching, looking, listening, and moving) to portions of the environment. The goals or incentives consist of sensory stimulation, and novel stimuli in any modality are especially important."

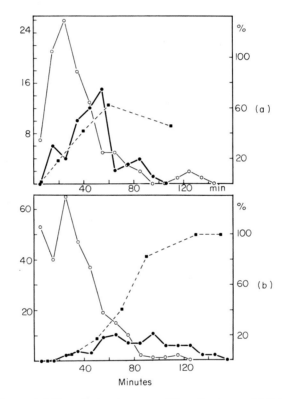

FIG. 4. The probability of play (squares with ordinate on right) in relation to the duration of activity periods (abscissa). Left ordinate: frequency of activity periods of different duration. 0-0, nonludic activity periods; ●-●, activity periods with play. (a) values for a male between the first and seventh week of life. (b) values for a male and a female between 3 and 5 months of age. [With kind permission of the editor, reprinted from *Bonner, Zool. Beitr. 20,* 282-289 (1969).]

According to Berlyne's classification (1960), specific exploration occurs in a novel situation and decreases with continued exposure to it, while diversive exploration occurs particularly in an impoverished environment as experienced by captive animals, particularly monkeys in small cages. Diversive exploration serves to vary or increase the sensory input. Hutt (1966) has pointed out that different types of exploration have to be distinguished for human children as well as for animals. Hutt suggests that only diversive exploration is closely related to motor play.

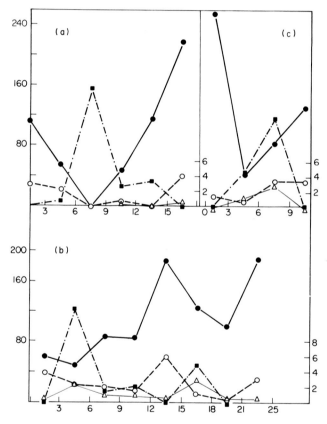

FIG. 5. Three ludic activity bouts of three different pairs of immature female rats, strain BD IX. Abscissa: time in 3-min intervals. With left ordinate: ●, exploration; ■, play fighting, both in seconds. With right ordinate: ○ running; △ attacking, both in seconds. (a) 21 days of age. (b) 25 days of age. (c) 27 days of age.

Blacktailed deer move about and sniff at various objects. In Berlyne's terminology this would be locomotor exploration. It would also be extrinsic exploration (Berlyne) because "the stimuli are sought only as cues for the guidance of some succeeding response with an independent source of biological value or reinforcement." The deer explore in all likelihood in search for potential food.

In blacktailed deer females explore more than males (Fig. 6). When captive deer were observed for 15 hr a day from dawn to dusk we found the intensity of extrinsic and diversive locomotor exploration to remain at the same level throughout the day (Fig. 6). The motor play periods in the morning and evening were not associated with any particular level of exploration (Fig. 6). Therefore the two daily peaks of motor play are independent from the exploratory behavior which occurs at the same rate in ludic and nonludic activity periods.

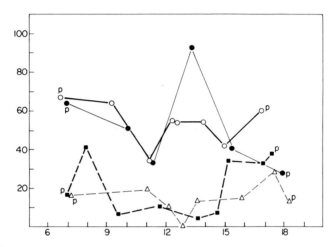

FIG. 6. Exploration in blacktailed deer. Abscissa: time of day. Ordinate: rate of exploration (= number of exploratory acts per 100 min). ○ ●, two daily cycles of a female on day 162 and day 175. ■ and △: two daily cycles of a male, 140 and 143 days old.

In female rats of the strain BD IX extrinsic and diversive locomotor exploration is negatively correlated with play fighting within one ludic activity period (Fig. 5). Slow moving about and sniffing objects vary directly with short quick solitary runs. Jumping at each other and wrestling increase and decrease together. The frequencies of exploring (including running) and play fighting usually show an inverse relationship (Fig. 5).

IV. FUNCTIONS

A. Short-term Functions

The amount of time and paper spent on speculations on possible functions of motor play in immature animals is in inverse proportion to the amount of facts available on this question.

There is no limit to hypotheses about potential adaptive values for the young animal itself. Stimulation of metabolism, training of sensory organs and the nervous and muscular systems, regulation of activity rhythm and synchronization with parents, shortening of activity periods as protection from predators, and socialization are a few (Müller-Schwarze and Müller-Schwarze, 1969).

Disadvantages for the organism have also been postulated: "Provided then, that the conditions of life are easy, play, however great in its practical value may be a means of learning about and so mastering the external world, is always in danger of becoming the main outlet for the animal's energies, and so dysgenic" (Thorpe, 1963).

Often young mammals do not play for days or weeks because of disease or bad weather. The effects of such natural play deprivation are not known.

B. Long-term Functions

It is often assumed that the main function of play is to practice specific motor patterns for life as an adult because the motor patterns of juvenile play are "borrowed" from adult behaviors. This is the basic theme of Groos' book on animal play (1930). Barnett (1963) ascribes to play the function of "deutero-learning" or learning to learn.

Recent experimental studies have shown that certain social and sexual patterns do not develop normally when the individual is deprived of playful contact with conspecifics at an early age. Harlow's well-known work on the rhesus monkey (Harlow and Zimmerman, 1959; Harlow and Harlow, 1962) showed that infant monkeys raised without their natural mother still developed normal adult sexual and aggressive responses if they had had daily contacts with other infants between the third and sixth months. During these contacts they engaged in social play and exploration, and manipulated objects. Isolated animals, however, later showed deficient sexual and defense behaviors. The effects of play deprivation are difficult to separate from other kinds of social deprivation, such as lack of general contact, mutual grooming, licking, competition, etc. In any event "the infant-mother affectional system is dispensable, whereas the infant-infant system is the *sine qua non* for later adjustment in all spheres of monkey life" (Harlow and Harlow, 1962).

Similar effects have been described for the polecat (*Putorius putorius*). Adult males sniff, and then seize a female in heat at her neck and carry her to the nearest cover before they mate. If a male has been raised in isolation from other young polecats, he sniffs the female, but grabs it at the root of her tail instead of the neck (Eibl-Eibesfeldt, 1963, 1967). As in the monkeys, the social play of the juveniles seems to be responsible for the proper orientation of the neck bite. Possibly other aspects of social deprivation may also contribute to the effect.

Gerall (1963) found that in guinea pigs (*Cavia porcellus*) mutual manipulation of the body and practice of mating responses are not essential for later normal sexual behavior. Guinea pigs developed normally after they were reared in isolation from other conspecifics, but separated by a wide wire screen through which they could smell the animals in the adjacent pen. Gerall argues that play behavior has to occur in the young animal in order to be "extinguished or superseded by sexual responses." If an animal is deprived of play in early life, the play behavior will later interfere with mating and other adult activities. This hypothesis is reconciled by Gerall with his experimental results by assuming that the presence of guinea pigs in the adjacent cage stimulated solitary play (leaping about, for instance) in the "isolated" individual. He also argues that the isolates have experienced stimuli which are essential for releasing later mounting and clasping behavior.

Also, general effects on the development of the neuro-muscular apparatus and the bone structure have to be expected.

The experimental evidence of long-term functions of juvenile play is so scant that any detailed discussion would be premature. Experimental methods of specific long-term play deprivation are particularly needed.

V. ONTOGENY

Thorough and quantitative descriptions of the ontogenetic development of ludic behavior are rare. The following two examples show the typical development of play in two species.

The first onset of play behavior in the blacktailed deer can be observed at the age of about 4 days. The animal suddenly jerks its head repeatedly, jumps five to ten times and runs over distances of 1 to 5 m. This happens typically between 7 and 12 o'clock, and then usually after drinking. With increasing age these play bouts become more intense. A 1-month-old male runs about 100 m and jumps about four times in one play bout. However, the figures for 5 months of age are 400 m and 16 leaps. More patterns are added with age: butting at 7 weeks, striking and mounting at 3 months. Neck craning and neck twisting start to occur at 4 months of age. In females the development is similar. The frequencies per bout of each of these patterns increase over the first 5-6 months, but the bouts become rarer as the animals grow older (Müller-Schwarze, 1968).

Rats (strain BD IX) start to engage in play activity at 3 weeks of age. A pair of 20-day-old females performed the following activities in the 5-hr observation period from 19:00 to 24:00 hr: 81 and 46 sec exploration, and 12.5 and 0 sec running. On day 21 we observed already 652 and 57 sec exploration, 146 and 1 sec running, 245 and 0 sec fighting, and 9.5 and 0 sec attacking each other. On day 30 when these rats are at the maximum of their play intensity, the figures were 612 and 1383 sec exploration, 12.4 and 7.4 sec running, 253 and 129 sec fighting, 3.6 and 3.6 sec attacking, and 8 and 11 sec chasing one another. From about 34 days of age on, the frequencies of the play fight patterns decrease steadily until play disappears at about 70 days (Müller-Schwarze, 1966). The rate of exploration, however, does not decrease.

Although species-specific patterns predominate in the play of most mammalian species, there are also "invented" plays. A badger often repeated skidding on ice after he had skidded once accidentally. The same individual once stood in the narrow space between a desk and a wall and tried to scratch his belly. He fell over forward, and repeated this movement, first in the space behind the desk, later "free" on the floor (Eibl-Eibesfeldt, 1950). River otters and apes have been observed to have developed such learned forms of play. Once invented, there is a tendency to repeat the same pattern regularly and at the same phase of the ludic bout. One of our male deer fawns used to terminate the intense running at the end of a play bout by stopping at the water trough and then striking and pawing the water with his forelegs. Often all the water was spilled when he finally tried to drink. A female kept with him always terminated the bout by running up eleven stairs on a landing where she would stay, pant, and look out (Müller-Schwarze, 1968).

It has often been stated that juvenile play differs from adult behavior in that is is "inhibited" at least as far as aggressive play forms are concerned. If one examines play fighting as it unfolds during ontogeny, the above statement is true for the earlier stages of development, but the play becomes more serious as the animal grows older. We observed in blacktailed deer that at the age of 3 - 5 months they strike each other very harshly. The attacked animal either fights back, or more often, steps aside and tries to avoid any further encounter with the individual who hit it. A similar development from "inhibited play" to serious fighting is reported for the polecat by Poole (1966). This development seems to be an important mechanism of social learning. Mounting in deer fawns is also gradually accompanied by more and more complete penile erection.

One striking peculiarity of ludic behavior is that the movements which occur at an early age belong to the end of a chain of responses in the adult animal. For instance, the young animal mounts but does not show any courtship patterns; it strikes but does not threaten. During maturation the various phases of appetitive behavior start to precede the original ludic components.

VI. CAUSAL FACTORS

A. Stimuli

Motor play appears to be spontaneous, i.e., the observer is at a loss to notice any releasing stimuli. Motor play seems to be governed more by internal states than by external stimuli, at least initially in ontogeny. In deer we observed spontaneous jumping during the first 5 months of age; but 6-month-old females sometimes jump away after sniffing some object on the ground, such as a piece of paper.

Once a play bout is under way, the animals themselves seem to provide stimuli eliciting further reactions. When deer fawns run and approach each other frontally, they are very likely to strike each other with their forelegs.

The spontaneity of ludic responses is also shown by the following observation: at the age of 11 weeks, optically isolated cats respond to a moving object with staring at it, lying in wait, jumping at it, seizing and grasping it. The more completely the cats are isolated the more likely they will attack tiny specks in the enclosure (Thomas and Schaller, 1954).

It should be emphasized again that play does not occur as a response to novel stimuli. On the contrary, one important condition for play is familiarity with the social and physical surroundings. Hutt (1966) formulated it this way: "In play the emphasis changes from the question 'What does this object do?' to 'What can *I* do with this object?'. While investigation is stimulus-referent, play is response-referent."

Some environmental stimuli facilitate play bouts in deer, such as barometric pressure drops or sudden rain. The same animals often start social motor play at a particular spot in the enclosure. Lions played when released into their familiar outdoor pen (Cooper, 1942).

B. Internal State

We know little about the internal, central nervous processes at the root of play behavior. So far play bouts have not been produced by brain stimulation in adult or immature mammals. Hediger (1956) remarked that a "play center" in the brain has not been found and that no animal possesses play organs, indicating that there is no specific play motivation. Meyer-Holzapfel (1956) suggested instead that "play behavior arises from a general non-specific activity drive, a readiness to be active in any manner whatsoever." Assumed this general activity exists, it has several possible ways of expressing itself as overt behavior. When deprived of rapid, intense motor play, deer fawns will move in a slow manner for the next 5 hr, will explore more, and will have extended activity periods for 10 hr after the deprivation (Müller-Schwarze, 1968).

Mason (1967) attempted to influence play with drugs. The level of play decreased after 1 mg amphetamine/kg body weight was administered to twelve chimpanzees, 2 to 4 years old. However the level of arousal and the clinging response increased. The failure to increase the frequency of play shows once more that the delicate internal state during play defies experimental manipulation.

Welker (1959) postulated "the maturation of a new set of functional connections within the central nervous system" as basis for the sudden appearance of motor play patterns in raccoons. The question remains of what causes certain motor patterns to occur during ontogenetic maturation while others do not appear until adulthood.

The study of correlations or even causal connections between neuroontogenetic events and the appearance and development of *specific* behavior patterns is still in its embryonic stage, to use a metaphor appropriate to this volume. Nevertheless, general rules have been formulated, as for instance, on the different development speeds of the myelination cycles (Yakovlev and Lecours, 1967). Fox (1964) found that in the dog the periods of neurological change precede the phases of behavior changes. W.A. Himwich and Dravid (1967), in turn, described a high level of accumulation of glutamic acid and its metabolic relatives prior to completion of neurological developments. For example, in various parts of the brain of the dog the concentrations of glutamic acid and related amino acids increase rapidly between days 15 and 35. Playful fighting starts at 15 days of age and increases during the "socialization period" between days 20 and 35 (Scott and Fuller, 1965). The latter period is characterized by particularly rapid development of reflexes, myelination of spinal cord and cerebrum, and development of the EEG (Fuller and Fox, 1969).

In the rat the glutamic acid concentration in the cortex increases sharply several times during ontogeny (Vernadakis and Woodbury, 1962). The adult level is reached at 25 days of age, the time when play intensity is highest. Also, the biogenic amines serotonin and norepinephrine increase in concentration in the young developing animal, but their role in the maturation of behavior remains unknown (H.E. Himwich *et al.,* 1967).

Sex differences in play have been shown, in the rhesus monkey (e.g., Young *et al.*, 1964). The authors showed that these differences are largely due to prenatal organizational effects of steroid hormones. They produced hermaphrodites by prenatal treatment with testicular androgens. These hermaphrodites initiated more play and engaged in more rough-and-tumble play than females did during the period from 1.5 to 5 months of age. For the rat the same authors found that the organizational phase in the male ends 10 days after birth. The organization of play behavior in the rat has not been studied.

Androgens not only organize but also activate male behavior traits during adulthood. In the immature laboratory rat there is a steep increase in the amount of total androgens and in the production of androgens between days 20 and 22 (Baptista, 1969). This is the same time when BD IX rats start to engage in play fights.

VII. PHYLOGENY

We are far from understanding phylogenetic relationships, because very little quantitative and experimental work as well as comparative studies have been carried out on motor play. Hall (1904), who studied children's play, suggested that children repeat the phylogeny of the human species in their games; e.g., cavedwelling, hunting, and fighting. If we look at lower mammals this hypothesis does not seem so far-fetched. Generally the motor patterns of juvenile ludic behavior are basic patterns, such as mounting, running, or striking, which are not species-specific, but rather common to a larger taxon. They are coordinations which in phylogeny must have preceded species-specific compound patterns such as the threat posture in the blacktailed deer.

Ludic behavior is particularly suited for comparative purposes, because its quality seems to be under less "functional pressure" than most other behaviors. On the basis of studies of play in foxes, Tembrock (1960) suggested that the rigid behavior patterns of play are particularly suited for comparative studies because they are phylogenetically conservative.

They have been useful for taxonomic purposes already. Rensch and Dücker (1959) found a close relationship between the motor play of the Herpestinae (mongooses) and the Mustelidae (weasels, etc.) which other taxonomists do not consider closely related. However, we would be on safer ground if more taxonomic units had been compared.

The ethological approach to the play of human children by Blurton Jones (1967) allows direct comparisons with other primates, a much-desired goal of comparative ethology and psychology. When a child is about to be chased by another, it gives the "open-mouth smile" with the teeth covered. This resembles the "play face" of monkeys, the chimpanzee, and the gorilla (Van Hooff, 1962). Blurton Jones describes many "fixed action patterns" in the play of human children 3 - 5 years old. In rough-and-tumble play nine patterns predominate, such as running, chasing, fleeing, or wrestling. That author stresses the fact that almost identical patterns occur in the rhesus monkey. Moreover, the ethological terminology permits comparisons beyond the primates; for instance we find running, chasing, fleeing, and wrestling in many mammals, e.g., deer and rats.

VIII. FUTURE RESEARCH

In 1945, Beach stated: "Present-day understanding of animal play is regrettably limited and current views on the subject are considerably confused." This could have been written today. Very little progress has been made during the past 25 years. The main difficulty for research is the spontaneity of play, which renders it largely inaccessible to immediate manipulation. Because one has to wait for the behavior to occur, play research is extremely time-consuming. As soon as play is staged — where possible at all — it is considerably altered in many ways. Another difficulty is a technical one: animals play only in large enclosures as they would in the wild. They must also be in excellent physical shape. On the other hand, we cannot be sure whether the smaller space in captivity facilitates motor play because of lack of opportunities for long-range locomotion. Therefore we urgently need quantitative data on wild species in their natural environment. It is known even to children that young badgers, foxes, etc. play in front of their den. But there is hardly any scientific information on the frequency or intensity of their play, even less on development and function. All quantitative data on play have been obtained from captive, domestic, or laboratory animals.

Experimental work will have to include the organizational and activating effects of hormones on play, as well as comparisons of drug effects on play and other behaviors, such as exploration, aggression, etc. The correlation of behavioral development with neural ontogeny must include ludic activities. The short-term and long-term functions of motor play can be elucidated only with the aid of specific play deprivation.

Birds as well as mammals show "irrelevant" juvenile activities. Grouse for instance mount each other as chicks and perform dodge flights *in vacuo* at the time of their activity maximum (Boback and Müller-Schwarze, 1968). The "subsong" of many passerines is a nonfunctional precursor of courtship displays.

Our goal of a truly comparative ethology is to work out a general theory of behavioral ontogeny of vertebrates based on comparisons between different classes. At the moment we are far from this stage.

If we want to experiment with play we first have to quantify ludic behavior in a variety of species. Only this will lead us to the understanding of the functions, causation, and evolutionary significance of motor play. We will have to focus on differences between various species as well as on the general features of this peculiar juvenile activity. At this time we can only assent to Marler and Hamilton's statement (1966): "More observation and experiment are necessary before we can begin to ask the proper questions let alone answer them."

REFERENCES

Baptista, M. H. (1969). Dissertation, Utah State University.

Barnett, S.A. (1963). "A Study in Behaviour." Methuen, London.

Barnett, S.A., and Evans, C.S. (1965). *Symp. Zool. Soc. London 14,* 233.

Beach, F.A. (1945). *Amer. Natur. 79,* 523.

Berlyne, D.E. (1960). "Conflict, Arousal, and Curiosity." McGraw-Hill, New York.

Blurton Jones, N.G. (1967). *In* "Primate Ethology" (D. Morris, ed.), pp. 347-368. Aldine, Publ., Chicago, Illinois.

Boback, A.W., and Müller-Schwarze, D. (1968). "Das Birkhuhn." Neue Brehm-Bücherei, Ziemsen Verlag Wittenberg-Lutherstadt.

Cooper, J.B. (1942). *Comp. Psychol. Monogr. 17*, 1.

Eibl-Eibesfeldt, I. (1950). *Z. Tierpsychol. 7*, 327.

Eibl-Eibesfeldt, I. (1963). *Z. Tierpsychol. 20*, 705.

Eibl-Eibesfeldt, I. (1967). *In* "Early Behavior" (H.W. Stevenson, E.H. Hess, and H.L. Rheingold, eds.), pp. 127-146. Wiley, New York.

English, H.B., and English, A.C. (1958). "A Comprehensive Dictionary of Psychological and Psychoanalytical Terms." David McKay Co., New York.

Fox, M.W. (1964). *Anim. Behav. 12*, 301-311.

Fuller, J.L., and Fox, M.W. (1969). *In* "The Behavior of Domestic Animals" (E.S.E. Hafez, ed.) pp. 438-481. Williams & Wilkins, Baltimore, Maryland.

Gerall, A.A. (1963). *Anim. Behav. 11*, 274.

Groos, K. (1930). "Die Spiele der Tiere," 3rd ed. Fischer, Jena (1st ed. 1898).

Hall, G.S. (1904). "Adolescence: Its Psychology and its Relation to Physiology, Anthropology, Sociology, Sex, Crime, Religion, and Education," Vol. I, p. 202. Appleton, New York.

Harlow, H.F., and Harlow, M.K. (1962). *Sci. Amer. 207*, 136.

Harlow, H.F., and Zimmerman, R. R. (1959). *Science 130*, 421.

Hediger, H. (1956). *In* "L'instinct dans le comportement des animaux et de l'homme" (P. P. Grassé, ed.), p. 640. Masson, Paris.

Himwich, H.E., Pscheidt, G.R., and Schweigerdt, A.K. (1967). *In* "Regional Development of the Brain in Early Life" (A. Minkowski, ed.), pp. 273-290. Davis, Philadelphia, Pennsylvania.

Himwich, W.A., and Dravid, A.R. (1967). *In* "Regional Development of the Brain in Early Life" (A. Minkowski, ed.), pp. 257-268. Davis, Philadelphia, Pennsylvania.

Hutt, C. (1966). *Symp. Zool. Soc. London 18*, 61.

Inhelder, E. (1955a). *Rev. Suisse Zool. 62*, 240.

Inhelder, E. (1955b). *Z. Tierpsychol. 12*, 88.

Lohmann, M. (1967). *J. Ornithol. 108*, 352.

Loizos, C. (1966). *Symp. Zool. Soc. London 18*, 1.

Lorenz, K. (1956). *In* "L'instinct dans le comportement des animaux et de l'homme" (P. P. Grassé, ed.), pp. 633-645. Masson, Paris.

Marler, P., and Hamilton, W.J., III. (1966). "Mechanisms of Animal Behavior." Wiley, New York.

Mason, W.A. (1967). *In* "Early Behavior" (H.W. Stevenson, E.H. Hess, and H.L. Rheingold, eds.), pp. 103-126. Wiley, New York.

Meyer-Holzapfel, M. (1956). *Z. Tierpsychol. 13*, 442.

Müller-Schwarze, D. (1966). *Naturwissenschaften 53*, 137.

Müller-Schwarze, D. (1968). *Behaviour 31*, 144.

Müller-Schwarze, D., and Müller-Schwarze, C. (1969). *Bonn. Zool. Beitr. 20*, 282.

Piaget, J. (1951). "Play, Dreams and Imitation in Childhood," Norton, New York (Engl. Transl., 1962).

Poole, T.B. (1966). *Symp. Zool. Soc. London 18*, 23.

Rensch, B., and Dücker, G. (1959). *Behaviour 14*, 183.

Sauer, E.G.F. (1963). *Psychol. Forsch. 26*, 399.

Scott, J.P., and Fuller, J.L. (1965). "Genetics and the Social Behavior of the Dog." Chicago Univ. Press, Chicago, Illinois.

Tembrock, G. (1958). *Zool. Beitr. (N.S.) 3*, 423.

Tembrock, G. (1960). *Z. Säugetierk. 25*, 1.

Thomas, E., and Schaller, F. (1954). *Naturwissenschaften 41*, 557.

Thorpe, W.H. (1963). "Learning and Instinct in Animals." Methuen, London.

Van Hooff, J.A.R.A.M. (1962). *Symp. Zool. Soc. London 8*, 97.

Vernadakis, A., and Woodbury, D.M. (1962). *Amer. J. Physiol. 203,* 748-752.

Welker, W.I. (1959). *Psychol. Rep. 5,* 764.

Welker, W.I. (1961). *In* "Functions of Varied Experience" (D.W. Fiske and S.R. Maddi, eds.), pp. 175-226. Dorsey Press, Homewood, Illinois.

Yakovlev, P.I., and Lecours, A.-R. (1967). *In* "Regional Development of the Brain in Early Life." (A. Minkowski, ed.), pp. 3-65, Davis, Philadelphia, Pennsylvania.

Young, W.C., Goy, R.W., and Phoenix, C.H. (1964). *Science 143,* 212.

PART III ENVIRONMENT AS THE SCULPTOR

CHAPTER 13 **Neuronal Ontogeny: Its use in Tracing Connectivity**

Albert Globus

I. INTRODUCTION

A neuron is not only dependent on its physiochemical microenvironment. Neuronal morphology also depends on the integrity of the neuron's synaptic connections. The normal function of the afferent axons to a neuron is more important than the morphological continuity of its own efferent axon. If an axon is severed, its soma undergoes chromatolysis and the satellite glia proliferate (Blinzinger and Kreutzberg, 1968). The form of the action potential remains unaltered and the neuron recovers. If, however, presynaptic axons to a neuron are severed, a microenvironmental upheaval occurs. Necrotizing presynaptic terminals are engulfed by microglia. Synaptic sites that are affixed to spines are incorporated within the dendrite or follow the rest of the synaptosome into the microglia (Colonnier, 1964). The exquisite balance of postsynaptic potentials swings from electrical silence to hypersensitivity (Burns, 1958; Cannon and Rosenblueth, 1949). If the interrupted afferent system is the principal occupier of the synaptic sites, transneuronal degeneration ensues (Hess, 1958). Interruption of afferents early in ontogeny accentuates these effects by stalling or altering maturation. Even afferent dysfunction without surgical intervention, early in life and before the relevant critical periods, produces measureable alteration of the postsynaptic neuron. These alterations may be used to measure neuronal connectivity and to provide a spotty foundation for an estimate of the functional significance of neuronal connections. The evaluation of these changes comprises the topic of this review.

II. EFFECTS ON THE MATURE NEURON OF SURGICAL INTERRUPTION OF AFFERENT SYSTEMS IN THE ADULT ANIMAL

Colonnier (1964) produced isolated slabs in the cerebral cortex of rats. This experimental method described by Burns (1958) severs afferent systems from adjacent cortical areas and subcortical nuclei. Using the electron microscope, Colonnier found that within 7 days several significant events occurred. Coincidental with the degeneration of the presynaptic terminals, the synaptic site, as well as the dentritic spines which surround it, underwent degenerative changes. Often the immediate pre- and postsynaptic structures, similar to the synaptosome, were seen undergoing degeneration within dendrites or adjacent microglia. This left the dendrite that bore the spine flat: a fact to be extensively utilized in later work with the Golgi technique (Globus and Scheibel, 1966; Illera, 1968; Valverde, 1967). It also attested to the physical affinity of the presynaptic terminal to the postsynaptic surface, which suggests a related codependence in maturation. The actual physicochemical nature of this codependence awaits, and would undoubtedly reward, extensive investigation. Later, Illera (1968), as well as Mathieu and Colonnier (1968), demonstrated denuded dendritic trees of Purkinje cells in the cerebellum following sectioning of the

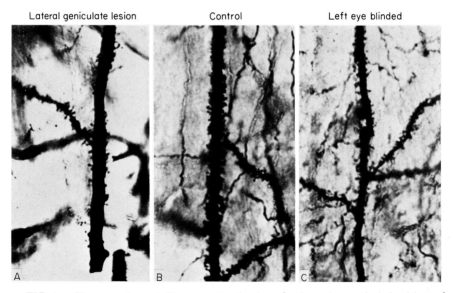

FIG. 1. The central panel illustrates the density of spines along apical dendrites of pyramids in the striate cortex found in a normal 30-day rabbit. The left panel shows the loss of spines as a result of a electrolytic lesion in the LGB before the second day of life. Enucleation at birth results in transneuronal degeneration of neurons of the LGB whose axons make up the optic radiation. The right panel shows that enucleation at birth results in a similar loss of spines as that seen in lesions of the LGB.

relevant parallel fibers. Spineless, and for the most part without synapses, many of the dendrites atrophied. Earlier, Globus and Scheibel (1966) showed degeneration of oblique dendrites of pyramids following interruption of callosal afferents at birth. Thus, complete degeneration of afferent systems to a dendrite results in irreversible, disuse atrophy of the relevant length of dendrite in addition to early degeneration of spines.

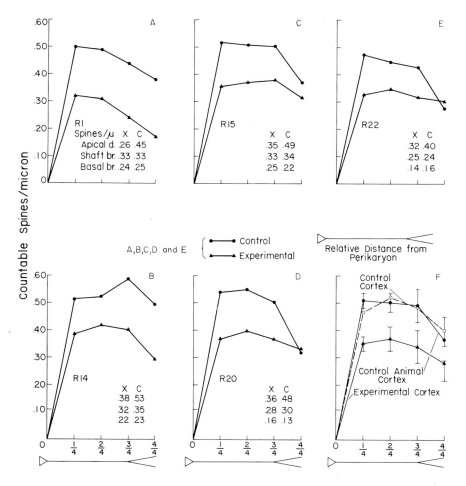

FIG. 2.   Effect of enucleation on the spine density on dendritic branches of pyramids in the contralateral area 17. A-E plots the reduction in number of spines along the central portion of the apical dendrite in experimental subjects (triangles) and controls (circles). The legend shows the averages for different parts of the dendritic complex. Graph F illustrates a comparison of averages of the control animal (dashed line); of the control cortices, ipsilateral to the enucleation (dark circles, solid line); and of the experimental cortices (dark triangles, solid lines).

III. EFFECTS ON THE DEVELOPING NEURON FOLLOWING SURGICAL INTERRUPTION OF AFFERENT SYSTEMS

In rabbits and mice the specific afferent radiation from the lateral geniculate body (LGB) terminates on the spines along the apical dendrite. Prior to 1966, these terminals were thought to synapse on the smooth and spineless dendritic surfaces of the short axon cell. The rapid Golgi studies of Lorente de Nó (1949), and Ramón y Cajal (1909, 1911) were the experimental foundation for this generally accepted statement. However, lesions of the LGB were followed by selective loss of spines along the apical dendrites of pyramids of area 17 (Fig. 1). There was no detectable shift in the percentage of the different cell types nor in the density of spines along other dendritic branches (Globus and Scheibel, 1966). For technical reasons, more reproducible results could be obtained by enucleation rather than LGB electrolytic lesions. Enucleation at birth produces complete transneuronal degeneration of the LGB— a complete severing of the specific afferent radiation to the striate cortex without opening the calvarium. In these preparations spine counts could be performed (Fig. 2). In rabbit, spines of the apical dendrites decreased 35% (Globus and Scheibel, 1967a), in mice, 22% (Valverde, 1968). In the rabbit there was no detectable reduction of spines along the other dendritic branches.

Two other experiments in rabbits illustrate the dependence of the spine development on the integrity of the afferent supply. Sectioning of the corpus callosum at birth leads to a 50% loss of spines on oblique dendrites in the parietal cortex and occasionally reduction in the overall length of these dendrites (Globus and Scheibel, 1967b). (Fig. 3). Cortical puncture wounds were used to study sites of axon collateral synapses. They produce a complex loss of spines. Extensive interruption of a variety of afferent systems occurs: specific afferents, callosal afferents, fibers of layer I, nonspecific afferents, and most importantly, axon collaterals. Since each pyramid gives rise to one axon and many arborizing axon collaterals (3-8) before it enters the white matter (Globus and Scheibel, 1967c), and as cortical efferents are three times as frequent as afferents (Sholl, 1956), the axon collateral may well be the numerically most important afferent system in any cortical area. A puncture wound to the medullary border destroys pyramids, and their axon collaterals as well as parts of the other afferent systems mentioned above. Taking into account the loss of spines due to degeneration of these other systems, one can infer the loss accounted for by interruption of the axon collaterals (Fig. 4). The loss of axon collaterals results in a massive reduction of spines along the basal and oblique dendrites.

A picture emerges of the postsynaptic surface of the pyramid, as an organized and segregated mosaic of afferent synaptic sites. These sites develop early in life. The maturation of the postsynaptic specialization called the spine (Gray, 1959) requires the anatomical integrity of its afferent supply.

IV. EFFECTS ON THE MATURING NEURON FOLLOWING FUNCTIONAL DISRUPTION

Additional support for the apical dendrite as at least one of the sites of specific afferent synapses came from the measurements of the effects of visual deprivation from birth. One group reported approximately 35% reduction in the

Apical dendrites and branches of pyramids in the
parietal cortex

Control animal   Corpus callosum sectioned animal

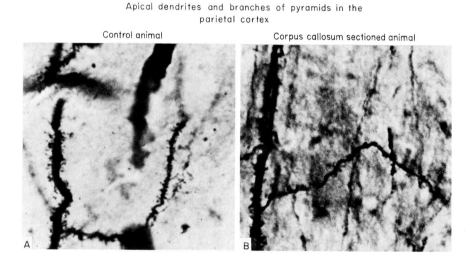

FIG. 3.   Photomicrograph of the effect of surgical interruption of the corpus callosum at birth on oblique branches of pyramids in the parietal cortex of 30-day rabbits. The density of spines is most markedly decreased toward the terminal portion of the oblique dendrite.

number of spines on the apical dendrites in the layer IV of the area striata of mice (Valverde, 1968); while Fifková (1968) showed a 25% reduction in spines in the apical dendrites of the visual cortex of rats. Similar experiments with rabbits showed increased deformity of the spine (Figs. 5 and 6) without a loss in total number (Globus and Scheibel, 1967d). The discrepancy in these findings may be due to counting under different magnifications or to different lengths of exposure to visual deprivation. In the same study it was shown that there was no change in length of basilar dendrites, in the number of neurons, in the relative frequency of neurons, or in the density of spines in other parts of the dendritic tree (Fig. 7).

While there is a consensus that the spines of apical dendrites undergo degeneration due to visual deprivation, conflicting reports relative to the dendrites of short axon cells have been published. Coleman and Riesen (1968) reported reduction in branching and overall length of the dendrites of short axon cells of layer IV of area 17 of kittens in two of three litter male pairs. Globus and Scheibel (1967d), with a less accurate method of measuring but a larger sample of subjects (rabbits) and a larger sample of neurons per subject, found no significant difference in either short axon cells of layer IV or throughout the

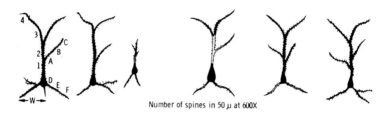

Number of spines in 50 μ at 600X

		Control	Lesion	→250 μ	→500 μ	→750 μ	→1,000 μ	→2,500 μ	→4,000 μ
Apical	1	17.7	5.1	8.8	9.5	8.6	15.0	17.6	18.7
Dendrite	2	19.7	6.4	8.3	11.5	8.5	11.7	15.4	16.4
	3	16.1	5.8	7.0	7.8	7.4	11.8	13.1	14.3
Terminal	4	9.3	3.1	1.9	4.0	2.9	6.3	7.1	7.1
Obliques	A	13.5	6.1	7.7	7.3	7.7	8.8	10.5	12.0
Above	B	11.2	5.9	7.4	6.3	6.6	8.9	9.3	11.5
	C	10.2	3.5	6.0	5.5	5.3	6.8	7.4	8.8
	A				8.0	3.4	6.5	12.0	13.2
Below	B				7.3	4.5	6.1	6.4	10.6
	C				4.6	2.0	3.5	7.3	5.3
Basal	D	0.4	0.1	0.1	0.0	0.0	0.0	0.0	0.1
	E	11.9	4.2	4.4	5.4	7.2	3.9	4.8	10.5
	F	7.9	2.8	3.8	3.6	4.0	2.3	4.3	8.4
Width		60.9	18.8		55.0	57.5	51.7	57.7	54.0

FIG. 4.   Effect of puncture wound produced at birth on the dendrites and their spines of pyramids situated at various distances from the periphery of the wound in 30-day rabbits. Pyramid in left upper quadrant shows the counting stations of 50 μ segments. Pyramids on the same level to the right indicate the effect. Dendrites with clear centers are areas thought to be significantly affected; also indicated by underlined tabulation of the actual counts in an individual animal as shown below. Each count is the average of ten counts within that concentric ring. Puncture wounds effect specific afferent terminals, resulting in reduction in spines along the apical dendrite to 750 μ; effect callosal terminals, resulting in reduction in spines along the oblique dendrite to 4000 μ, especially below, or lateral to the wound; effect the axon collaterals, resulting in reduction in spines along the basal, oblique, and terminal dendrites to 2500 μ. Changes in the width of the dendritic field and the dendritic length may be due to scarring and/or massive loss of afferent systems.

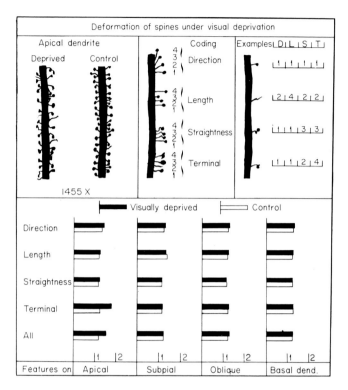

FIG. 5.   The effect of visual deprivation from birth on the dendritic spines of pyramids of the area striate of 30-day rabbits. The panel at the upper left is a drawing of a short segment of apical dendrite as seen under oil immersion. Note the increased frequency of deformity of the terminal portions of the dendritic spine in the experimental subject. The central upper panel shows the method of coding used to facilitate the quantification. The right upper panel shows some examples coded out. The bottom bar graph is the average of ten consecutive spines coded in the above fashion. The level labeled "ALL" is the total, averaged. Note that the differences are not significant except under the terminal classification on the apical dendrite.

cortical depth (Fig. 8). An as-yet unpublished study of Globus and Berger of short axon cells in 18-month-old pattern-deprived monkeys (from birth) failed to show a significant effect on number, branching, or overall length of dendrites of short axon cells. Fox *et al.* (1968) showed photo-micrographs of Golgi-Cox preparations of pyraminds in pups with reduced branching after visual deprivation. This finding is presented without quantification.

These findings following visual deprivation, the definite alteration in spines, and the less definite reduction in dendritic length of short axon cells and pyramids, must be contrasted with the well-proven reduction in cerebral cortical volume (Fifková, 1967; Gyllenstein *et al.* 1965, 1966; Globus and Scheibel, 1966). The known changes could not account for the volume changes reported by Fifková. As neuron type and number seem unchanged, glia changes should be investigated.

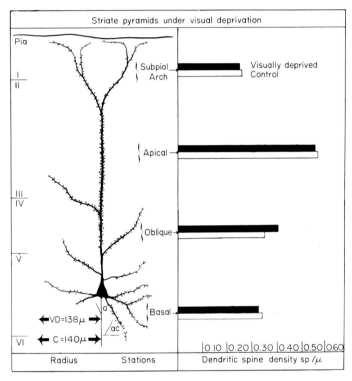

FIG. 6. The number of spines on pyramids of the striate cortex per 50 μ were counted in ten neurons from four visually deprived and four control animals. The density of spines was found to be similar. Under oil immersion, magnification was approximately 1000 X.

V. CONCLUSION

Neurons depend in several ways on the functional and morphological integrity of their relevant afferent systems. The dendrite's development, and perhaps maintainance, may depend on the morphological integrity of an afferent system. Oblique dentrites of pyramids degenerate following interruption of the corpus callosum at birth (Globus and Scheibel, 1967b) and dendrites of Purkinje cells atrophy following interruption of parallel fiber in the adult animal (Illera, 1968).

Dendrites of short axon cells may be stunted by visual deprivation and the spines of the apical dendrite are definitely affected adversely by visual deprivation. Interruption of afferent systems in the newborn leads to loss of spines. A pattern of experimental facts emerge which sketch the nature of the dependence of postsynaptic structures on the functional and morphological state of presynaptic structures. The mechanism of this dependence and its timetable may be filled out for other neuronal systems in the future. This search is motivated by the suspicion that the degree of maturational dependence may be an accurate index of the functional interrelation of neuronal systems in adult life.

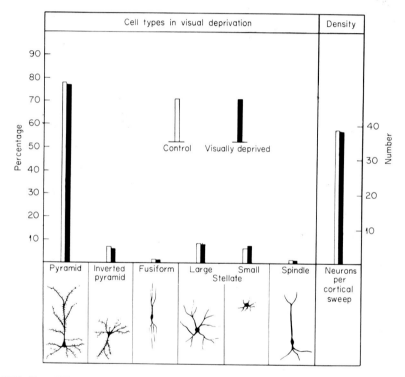

FIG. 7.   Effects of visual deprivation from birth to 30 days in neuronal types and numbers in rabbit. One thousand neurons were classified by major cell types in four control and four experimental animals. The bars represent the relative numbers, dark being the visually deprived and light being the controls. The number of neurons per sweep through the Golgi-Cox prepared cortex is illustrated in the far right.

The experimental method based on this dependence is capable of mapping the dendritic receptive surface. A comparison of this map with the intercellular events consequent on stimulation of presynaptic systems may yield important information relevant to dendritic conduction and the integration of afferent volleys of the same or different electrical signs. The method suffers from its statistical evaluation of the nature of the postsynaptic effect. The estimate of the effect of afferent interruption by surgical section or functional disruption is arrived at in one of two ways. Either spines on a group of neurons are estimated or the length of dendrites are measured, and then the average change is calculated. It may be very much to the scientific point that all neurons in an area receive equivalent numbers of synapses from a single afferent system, or that only a small group receive heavy afferent supply but all receive some, or that a few cells receive all the single afferent system while the rest receive their important input from other systems or through another cell of that area. Due to the grossness of the methods and the small samples from enormous populations

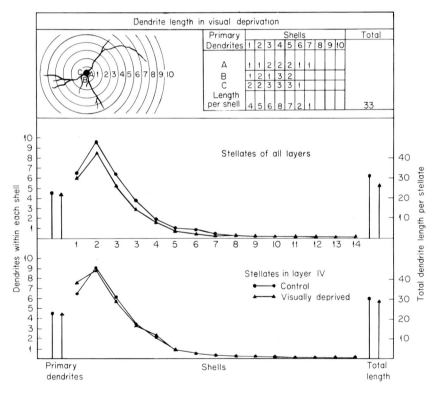

FIG. 8.   Effect of visual deprivation on the dendrite length of short axon cells of visual cortex of 30-day-old rabbits. Using Golgi-Cox preparations, a reticule of concentric rings was centered over the soma, as in left of the upper panel. The lengths of dendrites entering each ring were tabulated as in the right upper quadrant. The average of twenty stellates of all layers is plotted in the middle panel, the average of ten stellates of layer IV in bottom panel. Number of primary dendrites (A, B, C in left upper corner) are plotted in the left. Average of the total dendrite lengths are graphed on the right.

in these techniques, much important data may be overlooked. A more serious defect is the fact that the frequency of use of an input channel does not alter the effect of its interruption. An ideal method would yield information in individual neurons relative to four factors: (1) number of synapses, (2) location of synapses, (3) frequency of use of the relevant afferent system, (4) nature of the synapses (inhibitory, excitatory, type of transmitter). This paper deals with a technique which bears on factors 1 and 2 if the synapses are on spines. A method to elucidate factors 3 and 4 awaits development. Perhaps the intracellular iontophoresis of a labeled transmitter or its precursor with neurophysiological control of the activity of the labeled cells (Globus et al. 1968) may increase the amount of label at the synaptic sites, particularly in the synaptic cleft. There the postsynaptic neuron may incorporate the label in proportion to the frequency of use; that is, the amount of transmitter released. This suggestion is subject to autoradiographic validation.

REFERENCES

Blinzinger, K., and Kreutzberg, G. (1968). *Z. Zellforsch Mikrosk. Anat. 85,* 145.

Burns, B.D. (1958). "The Mammalian Cerebral Cortex." Arnold, London.

Cannon, W.B., and Rosenblueth, A. (1949). "The Supersensitivity of Denervated Structures." Macmillan, New York.

Coleman, P.D., and Riesen, A.H. (1968). *J. Anat. 102,* 363.

Colonnier, M. (1964). *J. Anat. 98,* 47.

Fifková, E. (1967). *Brain Res. 6,* 763.

Fifková, E. (1968). *Nature (London) 220,* 379.

Fox, M.W., Inman, O., and Glisson, S. (1968). *Develop. Psychobiol. l,* 48.

Globus, A., and Scheibel, A.B. (1966). *Nature (London) 212,* 463.

Globus, A., and Scheibel, A.B. (1967a). *Exp. Neurol. 18,* 116.

Globus, A., and Scheibel, A.B. (1967b). *Science 156,* 1127.

Globus, A., and Scheibel, A.B. (1967c). *J. Comp, Neurol. 131,* 155.

Globus, A., and Scheibel, A.B. (1967d). *Exp. Neurol. 19,* 331.

Globus, A., and Scheibel, A.B. (1966). Unpublished data.

Globus, A., Lux, H.D., and Schubert, P. (1968). *Brain Res. 11,* 440.

Gray, E.G. (1959). *J. Anat. 93,* 420.

Gyllensten, L., Malmfors, T., and Norrlin, M.L. (1965). *J. Comp. Neurol. 124,* 149.

Gyllensten, L., Malmfors, T., and Norrlin, M.L. (1966). *J. Comp. Neurol, 126,* 463.

Hess, A. (1958). *J. Comp. Neurol. 109,* 91.

Illera, A.J. (1968). *Anat. Rec. 160,* 369.

Lorente de Nó, R. (1949). *In* "Physiology of the Nervous System" (J.F. Fulton, ed.), *3rd ed.,* pp. 288-330. Oxford Univ. Press, London and New York.

Mathieu, A.M., and Colonnier, M. (1968). *Anat, Rec. 160,* 391.

Ramón y Cajal, S. (1909). "Histologie du systéme nerveux de l'homme et des vertébrés" (L. Azoulay, transl.), Vol. l. Maloine, Paris.

Ramón y Cajal, S. (1911). "Histologie du systéme nerveux de l'homme et des vertébrés," (L. Azoulay, transl.), Vol. 2. Maloine, Paris.

Sholl, D.A. (1956). "The Organization of the Cerebral Cortex." Methuen, London.

Valverde, F. (1967). *Exp. Brain Res. 3,* 337.

Valverde, F. (1968). *Exp. Brain Res. 5,* 274.

CHAPTER 14 Isolation-Induced Behavorial Modification: Some Neurochemical Correlates*

Walter B. Essman

I. INTRODUCTION

A considerable number of studies have indicated that rodents, housed in isolation, tend to show alterations in a variety of behavioral, physiological, pharmacological, and biochemical responses. Such changes appear to reside within those systems responsive to a number of parameters associated with conditions of differential housing.

In previous reports it has been indicated that isolation-housed animals develop a differential sensitivity to the emergence of gastric ulcers. Stress- or metabolically induced ulcerogenesis was marked by increased frequency and severity of gastric lesions in instances where these animals were isolation-housed (Frisone and Essman, 1965; Essman, 1966a,b; Essman and Frisone, 1966; Caputo *et al.,* 1968). Another behavior influenced by differential housing is the development of locomotor activity level. A higher level of locomotor activity has been shown to characterize isolation-housed animals, as compared with group-housed littermates (Essman, 1966c). More recently we have shown (Essman, 1968) that the development of increased locomotor activty levels in the isolated mouse is accompanied by alterations in the concentration and the metabolism of 5-hydroxytryptamine (serotonin) in the brain. Other behaviors in the mouse, such as competitive tube traversal and exploratory behavior, as influenced by isolation housing, also have been related to the metabolism of whole brain serotonin (Essman, 1969).

---

*The work summarized in this paper was supported in part by Grant HD-03493 from the National Institutes of Health.

II. Neurochemical Changes

The occurrence of alterations in serotonin concentration or its metabolism in the brain appear dependent upon a number of factors related to the onset and duration of isolation and the age at which biochemical determinations are made. In one instance where albino mice were isolated for 34 days, commencing immediately following weaning at 21 days of age, whole brain serotonin turnover rate was increased and turnover time was decreased with no associated significant difference in either serotonin (5-HT) or 5-hydroxyindoleacetic acid (5-HIAA) levels between the isolated and group-housed mice (Essman and Smith, 1967). Subsequent results from conditions where in albino mice of the same strain (CF-1) were isolated for 24 days, commencing immediately following weaning at 21 days of age, indicated an increase in the whole brain level of both 5-HT and 5-HIAA, and an increase in 5-HT turnoever rate of approximately 31% (Essman, 1968). It should be pointed out that whereas the age of weaning and the onset of isolation housing were identical for these experiments, the duration of isolation differed by 10 days as did the age of the animal at the time the biochemical measures were obtained. These findings contrast somewhat with other reports in the literature (Valzelli and Garattini, 1967), which have indicated that for several regions of the mouse brain there were no differences between isolated and group-housed animals in 5-HT level, whereas there was a decrease in 5-HIAA level, suggesting the possibility of an isolation-induced alteration in 5-HT metabolism. This result was further explored (Garattini et al., 1967) and it was shown that as a result of isolation there was a decreased 5-HT turnover rate and an increased 5-HT turnover time, suggesting that the synthesis and degradation of this biogenic amine in the brain was reduced as a consequence of isolation. In these experiments the duration of isolation was 4 weeks, but the onset of isolation appears to have taken place at some period following weaning.

In another study, where animals were housed under isolation conditions beginning at 23 days of age, or 2 days following weaning, for a period of 74 days, the results obtained were quite similar to those observed by Garattini and co-workers; there was no appreciable change in whole brain 5-HT, whereas in isolated mice 5-HIAA levels were changed, 5-HT turnover rate was decreased, and 5-HT turnover time was increased (Essman, 1969). Another essential variation for these findings is the fact that these mice were 97 days of age at the time the biochemical determinations were made for the brain tissue. It therefore appears that there are at least several variables which can influence the direction as well as the magnitude of changes in serotonin and its metabolism produced by isolation. It should also be emphasized that whole brain measures of biogenic amines probably represent a composite change and may, in many instances, actually mask alterations in metabolism or level which are accounted for by individual structures of the nervous system.

A regional analysis of the concentration of several biogenic amines in isolated and group-housed mice is shown in Table I, where several observations may be made. For those regions of the mouse brain sampled, norepinephrine concentration did not differ as a function of isolation. These data apply to CF-1 strain mice isolated or group-housed for 28 days, with the onset of differential housing initiated at 21 days of age. Under these same conditions of onset, with a duration of 34 days of differential housing, isolated animals showed a lower brain norepinephrine level than did group-housed animals, and norepinephrine level under these conditions was inversely related to locomotor activity performance in isolated mice (Essman and Smith, 1967). 5-Hydroxyindoleacetic acid concentration was significantly elevated as a result of isolation, as observed in Table I, and this finding is consistent with those previously reported. This change was specific for the cerebellum and for those structures comprising the diencephalon. Serotonin concentration, while extremely low in the cerebellum,

TABLE I   Mean ($\pm\sigma$) Regional Concentration (μg/gm) of Several Biogenic Amines in Isolated and Aggregated Mice

Condition	Brain region				
	Olfactory bulbs	Cerebellum	Mesen-cephalon	Dien-cephalon	Cerebral cortex
Isolation					
Serotonin	0.075	0.068^a	0.805	0.698^a	0.068
	(.007)	(.006)	(.179)	(.047)	(.046)
Norepinephrine	0.068	0.061	0.618	0.605	0.061
	(.021)	(.012)	(.124)	(.099)	(.010)
5-Hydroxyindoleacetic acid	0.036	0.028^b	0.252	0.307^b	0.031
	(.010)	(.009)	(.020)	(.004)	(.005)
Aggregated					
Serotonin	0.080	0.085	0.883	0.824	0.073
	(.069)	(.014)	(.010)	(.100)	(.014)
Norepinephrine	0.065	0.058	0.602	0.675	0.065
	(.014)	(.011)	(.121)	(.067)	(.010)
5-Hydroxyindoleacetic acid	0.029	0.025	0.239	0.264	0.024
	(.003)	(.016)	(.005)	(.020)	(.000)

[a] $P < 0.05$
[b] $P < 0.02$

nevertheless was lowered still further as a result of isolation. Again, these findings apply to 49-day-old mice where other studies have usually derived observations regarding biogenic amines from older animals. For animals of the same age, under the same experimental conditions, brain serotonin turnover for several regions of the nervous system are summarized in Table II. The consistent finding which emerges in these data is the lower brain serotonin turnover time in isolated animals, with a significantly lower time obtaining for olfactory bulbs, cerebellum, and cerebral cortex. Again, these findings are consistent with previous results (Essman and Smith, 1967) obtained for animals less than 60 days of age that were differentially housed at the time of weaning, but these findings contrast with others (Garattini et al., 1967; Essman, 1969) in which turnover time was increased as a result of isolation, where mice were isolated either postweaning and/or the data were obtained for animals after 60 days of age.

TABLE II   Brain Serotonin Turnover Rate and Turnover Time Estimated for Several Areas of Mouse Brain[a]

	Brain region				
Condition	Olfactory bulbs	Cerebellum	Mesen-cephalon	Dien-cephalon	Cerebral cortex
Isolation					
Rate (μg/gm/hr)	0.10	0.93	0.97	1.00	0.08
Time (min)	68	50	54	47	70

[a] $P < 0.05$.

The results discussed above suggest that the relationship between isolation-induced changes in brain biogenic amines and those behaviors which characterize isolation housing appear dependent on a number of factors that govern the emergence and/or direction of both. This raises several questions concerning possible differences in cellular ontogeny within those structures implicated in the morphogenesis of systems affect by, or altered with, isolation housing. Isolation produces a certain degree of sensory restriction and/or deprivation, particularly as it involves inputs to the somato-sensory system. Deprivation to the somato-sensory system or provision for a functional denervation through isolation housing may, in one respect, be expected to resolve itself in the development of altered thresholds within such a system; the well-known Cannon-Rosenbleuth principle of "denervation-supersensitivity" may be applicable in the sense that cellular sensitivity, both physiologically and metabolically, may be altered by isolation, and where such isolation interacts with cellular ontogeny, further differences may be expected to emerge.

III. CELL NUMBER

Several initial approaches to the question of cell number were made, based upon the suggestion that the DNA content per diploid cell remains constant and may, therefore, serve as a means of assessing cell numbers in structures within the central nervous system (Zamenhof et al., 1964). Recent suggestions have been made regarding the possibility that brain cells may be polyploid (Muller, 1962; Lapham, 1965); these data have been obtained from human brain tissue without any clear control. It has been pointed out that the assumption regarding diploid cells and their DNA content is generally valid for normal brain tissue (Friede, 1966) and there is no evidence to suggest otherwise for any area of the mouse brain. The validity of applying such a technique to the estimation of cell number was verified through calculations based upon available anatomical data and estimates of DNA content per diploid cell. The DNA content per diploid cell was estimated at approximately 6×10^{-6} g (Leslie, 1955; Hess et al., 1969). This value has been used to calculate the cell number estimates presented and anatomical data has been used to validate these chemically based estimates. In the latter regard, it has been shown that the rat cerebellum, weighing 0.275 gm, contains approximately 506,922 Purkinje cells, or 1014 cells per cubic millimeter of tissue (Inukai, 1928). This ratio, and the morphological characteristics of the Purkinje cell, would directly apply on an equipvalent basis to the mouse cerebellum (Pillari, 1959); it was therefore determined that a mouse cerebellum, weighing 0.0560 gm, should contain approximately 103,227 Purkinje cells. The number of neuroglia was estimated from ratios derived from the work of Friede (1963) relating neuroglia to Purkinje cell numbers; the result approximated 516,138. In accord with anatomical data derived from the work of Smolyaninov (1965), in which further cell estimates were based upon the number of estimated Purkinje cells, the total remaining cell numbers from the granular and molecular layers were estimated at 26,833,020. In the present case, the total cell number estimated for mouse cerebellum, derived entirely from anatomical data, reached 27,458,385 cells. For the same cerebellum, chemically based cell number estimates, based upon the DNA concentration of 3.90 mg/gm of cerebellar tissue, was determined as 2.7×10^7 cells. It appears therefore that chemically based estimates can correspond very closely to anatomically based estimates, especially in the present case for the cerebellum. As a further check on the reliability of the present method, average RNA content per single cell for the various regions of the mouse brain sampled were obtained by dividing the estimated cell number into the obtained tissue RNA values; for the present example, the RNA content per single cell was estimated at approximately 15 $\mu\mu$g. This estimate is in accord with single cell RNA estimates determined by UV absorption (Hydén, 1967).

In a series of replicated experiments where, for each, ten tissue samples were utilized, the eight estimates of cell number presented in Table III, were obtained; variations in the cell number estimates over the eight experiments are accounted for by variations in cerebellum weight from experiment to experiment; i.e., whereas for any given experiment all ten animals were matched littermates, the age at which these were obtained differed for each of the experimental series, therefore accounting for tissue weight differences. It should be further pointed out that these estimates correspond closely to anatomical estimates that would be derived as a function of tissue weight.

TABLE III   Estimated Mean Cerebellar Cell Number for Several Replicated Experiments (N/Exp = 10)

Experiment No.	Cell number ($\times 10^6$)
1	36.8
2	34.8
3	22.6
4	28.5
5	23.5
6	31.8
7	29.8
8	33.1

For groups of male mice subjected to differential housing initiated at 21 days of age, for a duration of 28 days, diploid cell number was estimated for several areas of the brain, based upon the techniques and assumptions described above; these data, summarized in Table IV, suggest that the diencephalon and cerebellum reflect the most marked influences of isolation housing. In both of these areas, the estimated diploid cell number was significantly reduced, where mice were housed in isolation between the ages of 21 and 49 days. The mesencephalon and cerebral cortex did not reflect differences in estimated diploid cell number produced by isolation initiated at 21 days of age.

The significance of the age factor in the onset of differential housing in contributing to differences in cell number, has already, to some extent, been

TABLE IV Mean($\pm\sigma$) Total DNA Content (μg) and Estimated Diploid Cell Number for Regional Areas of the Young Adult Mouse Brain

Housing conditions maintained for 28 days postweaning	Cerebral cortex		Mesencephalon[a]		Diencephalon[a]		Cerebellum[a]	
	DNA/ Brain	DP Cell No.	DNA/ Brain	DP Cell No.	DNA/ Brain	DP Cell No.	DNA/ Brain	DP Cell No.
Isolation	2.17 (0.16)	3.62×10^7	0.69 (0.09)	1.16×10^7	0.39 (0.19)	0.65×10^7	3.02 (0.02)	2.47×10^7
Aggregation	2.18 (0.18)	3.62×10^7	0.88 (0.08)	1.46×10^7	1.01 (0.00)	1.67×10^7	4.88 (0.08)	4.01×10^7

[a] $P < 0.001$.

indicated as a possibility in view of earlier findings regarding biogenic amines, where a difference between onset of isolation between 21 days of age (weaning) and 23 days of age (2 days postweaning) was indicated. In a further investigation of this variable, groups of male mice, matched across litters, were differentially housed (isolated or aggregated) at either 21 days of age (weaning), 23 days of age (2 days postweaning), or 32 days of age (11 days postweaning). Differential housing was maintained in each case for 28 days, at which time tissue samples were obtained from cerebellum, diencephalon, and cerebral cortex. Table V summarizes the percent differences in estimated diploid cell number between aggregation- and isolation-housed animals as a function of age of onset; it may be noted that with increasing age there was a decreased difference in cell numbers as a function of isolation for the cerebellum and diencephalon. However, cellular differences, as observed for the cerebral cortex, appeared more prominently when differential housing was initiated at a later age. This finding may bear some possible relationship to our earlier consideration of biogenic amines and how these are changed through differences in the onset and duration of differential housing; if isolation housing differentially affects specific structures more mark-edly at one age than at another, then perhaps delayed postweaning onset of isolation has greater significance for cholingergic structures in the brain than it does for those highly dependent upon the content of biogenic amines. In the same regard, if a delayed onset of isolation has more pronounced effects upon the cellular disposition of cerebral cortex, as compared with cerebellum and diencephalon, the latter probably represently key inputs to somatosensory activation, then one might predict that delayed onset of isolation might have a lesser effect upon those behaviors which normally characterize earlier isolation. To some extent, this hypothesis is supported by evidence indicating that the isolation of older animals is less likely to result in the development of aggressive behavior, hyperreactivity, and changes in locomotor activity levels (Essman, 1969).

The generality of limitations of the present data, particularly for cells of the cerebellum, which in the weanling mouse appear to be sensitive to a variety of biochemical and cellular changes resulting from differential housing, is the extent to which the observed phenomenon is strictly neuronal in nature, or whether it is more specifically concerned with glial cells, or whether it involves changes concerning both neurons as well as glia. A preliminary approach to this question was made through the application of a specific procedure for the isolation of glial cells from mouse cerebellum of animals differentially housed for 28 days with an onset at 23 days of age. The separation procedure essentially consisted of forcing weighed cerebellar tissue through cloth mesh, washing with 0.25 M sucrose and then following suction through 200 μ mesh, preparing a suspension in buffered 20% Ficoll. This suspension was filtered through 100 μ mesh and layered over a simple gradient consisting of 30% Ficoll and 1.3 M sucrose. Centrifugation was carried out (27 $\times$ 10^4 g min.) following which

TABLE V   Percent Difference in Estimated Diploid Cell Number (Aggregation-Isolation) as a Function of Age of Onset

Age of onset of differential housing (days)	Brain Region		
	Cerebellum	Diencephalon	Cerebral cortex
21	37^a	61^b	0
23	28^c	40^a	29^c
32	9	36^c	105^d

[a] $p < 0.02$
[b] $p < 0.01$
[c] $p < 0.05$
[d] $p < 0.001$

TABLE VI   RNA Concentration in Cerebellar Glia for Isolation- and Aggregation-Housed Mice Given Environmental Stimulation (ES) or no Stimulation (C)

Condition	Mean (±σ) cerebellar tissue weight (gm)	Mean (±σ) extract glial weight (gm)	Mean (±σ) glial RNA concentration (μg/mg)
Aggregation ES	0.1183 (0.03)	0.0023 (0.0005)	208 (16.0)
Isolation ES	0.1179 (0.08)	0.0029 (0.0013)	$48 (8.0)^a$
Aggregation C	0.1062 (0.05)	0.0010 (0.0015)	210 (10.0)
Isolation C	0.1029 (0.03)	0.0014 (0.0010)	$535 (11.0)^a$

[a] $p < 0.001$.

myelin and cellular debris were removed from the upper layers, red cells removed from the lowest layer, and a central band in the interfacial layer was resuspended in 10% Ficoll and recentrifuged (675×10^2 g min.) several times until a pelleted residue was obtained. This fraction was sampled by micropipet and prepared for microscopic examination by negative staining to reveal essential round cells with a cytoplasmic rimming, in addition to a small amount of granular debris and small axonal fragments. Glial elements of several types appeared to characterize the fraction obtained; there were obligodendroglia, identified as small, round cells, having a characteristic cytoplasmic rimming and round nuclei. Ovaloid bodies, with round nuclei (microglia), and elongated glial elements (fañanas elements), somewhat fragmented, were also associated with the resulting fraction. The fraction was further purified, washed, and following an ethanol rinse of the precipitated cells, the cellular mass was acidified and acid extracted with precipitation of RNA, which was estimated by its optical density.

The procedure described above was applied to an experiment in which 28 successive days of differential housing, with a 23-day of age onset, was carried out. Beginning at 52 days of age, one group of isolated and aggregated animals were given 14 days of environmental stimulation (ES), consisting of novelty stimulation, particularly for exploration of novelty environments, and presentation of intermittent sensory stimulation; also, these animals intermittently received tinker toy assemblies introduced into the home cage for 24-hour periods, and these assemblies were frequently interchanged. The other differentially housed animals, one set of isolated mice and one of aggregated animals, were nonstimulated (C), in that they were not exposed to any of the conditions presented over the 14-day period. On the fifteenth day, or at 66 days of age, all animals were killed by cervical dislocation and fresh cerebellar tissue was extracted, as previously described, for the isolation of glial cells and subsequent determination of RNA content.

The RNA concentrations for the cerebellar glial fractions isolated from tissue as described, in isolated and aggregated mice with (ES) or without (C) environmental stimulation, are summarized in Table VI, which also provides the cerebellar tissue weights and the weight of the extracted glial fractions. It is of interest to note that a comparison of the aggregation-housed animals, with and without environmental stimulation, shows essentially no difference; i.e., the glial RNA concentration was unchanged in group-housed animals by environmental stimulation. It is striking to observe that the concentration of RNA in the glial fraction from the cerebellum of isolated animals under control conditions was more than double that of the group-housed animals. This difference was highly significant statistically, supporting the suggestion that glial RNA metabolism in cerebellum may be operating at a much more highly active level in isolated animals. This may also provide some support for the general hypothesis that isolation, as functional denervation for specific cells of the cerebellum, leads to an increase in the activation of such cells, consistent with increased activation and cellular RNA increases provided through other means, such as electrical stimulation or pharmacological treatment. The susceptibility of isolation-housed animals to changes in the level of environmental stimulation, as has been indicated in previous behavioral work, is obviously apparent in the present data (see also Chapter 18). Isolation-housed mice, subjected to environmental stimulation, showed almost a five-fold decrease in the RNA concentration for the cerebellar glial fraction; this finding suggests that these cells may assume a markedly reduced metabolic role when somato sensory stimulation, which these animals were essentially deprived of previously, is environmentally provided. The difference between the RNA concentration under these conditions and those observed for the nonstimulated isolated animals, as well as for group-housed animals, was highly significant when tested statistically. This finding, again, may provide some support for the previously mentioned hypothesis regarding cellular excitability and somato sensory input; i.e., somato sensory stimulation does not appear to alter cellular excitability, as inferred from RNA changes in a glial fraction from mouse cerebellum, where functional denervation was not previously provided. Where functional denervation was provided through isolation, excitability, as measured by the same conditions described above, was increased, and with environmental stimulation superimposed, was markedly decreased. These findings, at least, provide some support for the hypothesis that isolation provides for differences in threshold excitability level in selected cells of the cerebellum, and such threshold differences clearly emerge when differential housing interacts with environmental stimulation, particularly to the somato-sensory system.

The present data are intended only as an indication of the direction in which our future research is proceeding. It is apparent, on the basis of the findings reported, that isolation housing represents one means of providing for reduced sensory input, particularly involving the somato-sensory system and those neural structures and connections which functionally represent that system. The interaction of functional denervation, as provided through isolation, with other critical variables, such as level of ontogeny, age of onset for isolation housing, postweaning period prior to isolation, duration of isolation, age of behavioral and biochemical determinations, etc., all appear to constitute important variables which govern possible cellular and metabolic changes in progress. Some new chemical effects of rearing rats in an enriched environment are described in Chapter 15. The constitution of a system within which sensory deprivation, as represented by the contrast between isolation and aggregation housing, can provide answers to important questions concerned with the integration of cellular, biochemical, and behavioral events modulated by specific loci and their interconnections within the developing nervous systems has been indicated.

REFERENCES

Caputo, D.V., Essman, W.B., Teitler, R., Loewe, G., and Frisone, J.D. (1968). *J. Psychosom, Res. 12,* 129-135.
Essman, W.B. (1966a). *Psychol. Rep. 19,* 173-174.
Essman, W.B. (1966b). *J. Psychosom. Res., 10,* 183-188.
Essman, W.B. (1966c). *Anim. Behav. 14,* 406-409.
Essman, W.B. (1968). *J. Comp. Physiol. Psychol., 66,* 244-246.
Essman, W.B. (1969). *In* (S. Garattini, and E.B. Sigg, eds.), "Aggressive Behaviour" p. 203-208. Excerpta Med. Found., Amsterdam.

Essman, W. B., and Frisone, J. D. (1966). *Psychosom. Res. 10*, 183-188.

Essman, W.B., and Smith, G.E. (1967). *Amer. Zool., 7,* 370.

Friede, R.L. (1963). *Proc. Nat. Acad. Sci., U.S. 49,* 187-193.

Friede, R.L. (1966). "Topographic Brain Chemistry," p. 329. Academic Press, New York.

Frisone, J.D., and Essman, W.B. (1965). *Psychol. Rep. 16,* 941-946.

Garattini, S., Giacalone, E., and Valzelli, L. (1967). J. *Pharm. Pharmacol., 19,* 338-339.

Hess, H., Embree, L.J., and Shein, H.M. (1969). *Proc. Ind. Int. Meet. Int. Soc. Neurochem., 1969* p. 42-43.

Hydén, H. (1967). *In* "The Neuron" (H. Hyden, ed.), p. 179-219. Elsevier, Amsterdam.

Inukai, T. (1928). *J. Comp. Neurol., 45,* 1-28.

Lapham, L.W. (1965). *J. Neuropathol. Exp. Neurol., 25,* 131-132.

Leslie, I. (1955). *In* "The Nucleic Acids" (E. Chargaff, and J.N. Davidson, eds.), Vol.   , p. 1-50. Academic Press, New York.

Muller, H.-A. (1962). *Naturwissenschaften, 49,* 243.

Pillari, G. (1959). *Acta Anat. 38,* Suppl., 1-122.

Smolyaninov, V.V. (1965). "Structural and Functional Models of Some Biological Systems." U.S.S.R. Press, Moscow.

Valzelli, L., and Garattini, S. (1968). *In:* Costa, E. & Sandler (Eds.). *Proceedings of the International Symposium on the Biological Role of Indolealkylanine derivatives.* N.Y.: Academic Press, 1967, p. 249.

Zamenhof, S., Bursztyn, H., and Rich, K., and Zamenhof, P.J. (1964). *J. Neurochem. 11,* 505-509.

CHAPTER 15 Some Observations on the Effects of Environmental Complexity and Isolation on Biochemical Ontogeny *

Edward Geller

I. INTRODUCTION

That the later behavior of animals can be altered by early experience is a widely held belief, forming the basis for many mystical notions of prenatal influence, some clearly erroneous, others less clearly so and still uninvestigated (Ferreira, 1965). Documentation does exist, however, to support the belief. Some of the data have recently been collected (Newton and Levine, 1968) and we now have considerable knowledge of some of the important systems involved, the ways in which different species are affected, and even some information on specific human responses. It is difficult to see why the concept of early experience as a modifier of brain chemistry should find such resistance except among the very few "fundamentalists" who can somehow, in their minds, dissociate behavior from a biological substrate. For most of us, however, it is axiomatic that associated with the behavioral repertoire are physiological and biochemical concomitants (if one chooses to avoid causality) inextricably involved in each unit of behavior. That such physiological and biochemical substrates are related in a feedback loop with the behavioral state of an animal, and therefore ultimately to the environmental determiners of behavioral response, is a reasonable hypothesis, susceptible to investigation. Some beginnings in this direction have been made.

*Supported in part by USPHS grant AM08775. Those results otherwise not reported in the literature, were obtained in collaboration with Drs. W. Greenough and A. Yuwiler.

II. BACKGROUND

The best known systematic investigations of the effects of varying environment during ontogeny on biochemical measures have been carried out by a
group at the University of California at Berkeley, initially composed of Krech,
Rosenzweig, and Bennett, and now being carried forward by Rosenzweig,
Bennett, Diamond, and a variety of collaborators and graduate students. Their
initial findings have been reviewed by Bennett et al. (1964), and more recently
by Rosenzweig et al. (1968b). The work has concentrated on certain differences
that can be observed between brains of littermate pairs of rats, one maintained
in a relatively impoverished environment, isolated from other rats (IC), and the
other kept in a more stimulating environment, enriched with a variety of objects
and the presence of other rats, and subjected to a program of training and testing
(ECT).* In some experiments they have also used as a third group animals
maintained under usual laboratory colony conditions. In most cases they have
introduced the environmental manipulations at approximately weaning age, but
they have also used mature animals in some studies. The results can be briefly
summarized. After a suitable period of time, usually 80 days, under the different
environmental conditions, ECT animals exhibited: (1) small (5%) but significantly increased weights of cerebral cortex; (2) greater activity of acetylcholinesterase in the total brain, but an apparent decrease in specific activity in
the cortex because enzyme activity does not increase as rapidly as weight; (3)
greater activity of pseudocholinesterase (nonspecific cholinesterase) in cortex,
the increase proportionally exceeding the increase in cortical weight; (4)
increased cortical depth. Using controls, handling and activity have been eliminated as important parameters responsible for the changes reported. More
recently Diamond et al. (1966) have reported increased glial proliferation in ECT
rats, confirming an earlier report by Altman and Das (1964), and Diamond
(1967) has also observed increased neuronal size in ECT animals.

Rosenzweig et al. (1969) have found that the changes detailed above are
significantly greater in occipital cortex than in other parts of the brain but are
not attributable solely to visual experience, for differences were found between
blinded ECT and IC rats or in rats in which the differential environments were
modified by the introduction of total darkness. Investigating the effects of
varying the daily exposure to ECT, Rosenzweig et al. (1968a) reported that
exposure to ECT for only 2-2½ hr per day for 1-2 months produced changes
similar to continuous exposure.

---

*ECT refers to environmental complexity and training. In our experiments, described
below, we have omitted the formal training component. Consequently, we refer to our
animals as EC's and to our environment as EC. Our IC animals are as described.

Some measures reported not to be affected by the environmental conditions are total protein, water content, hexokinase activity, and total brain serotonin (Bennett *et al.* 1964).

Isolation housing in mice also produces a number of biochemical and behavioral changes. This work is reviewed in Chapter 14. Many other investigators working with animals in relative isolation have emphasized its stressful nature (Hahn, 1965; Sigg *et al.*, 1966; Moore, 1968; B. L. Welch, 1965). These reports have focused on the pituitary-adrenal system as a measure of stress response and have generally reported pituitary-adrenal activation following isolation. Bennett *et al.* (1964), however, discount the importance of stress in their experiments.

Little work by other investigators designed to measure the effects of an enriched environment during early development on cellular aspects of brain chemistry exists, but some experiments with adult animals have demonstrated RNA changes (Dellweg *et al.*, 1968) and differences in aggregation of brain polysomes (Appel *et al.* 1967, see also Chapter 14).

A substantial literature exists on the biochemical effects of isolation and sensory deprivation — mainly visual deprivation. This literature is too voluminous to cover here; much of it will be reviewed in publications forthcoming shortly by Walker *et al.* (1971) on sensory deprivation and by Yuwiler (1971) on isolation and stress. Species-specificity enters strongly into results reported on sensory deprivation or isolation. In the rat, studies of the effects of dark rearing on components of the acetylcholine system have shown decreased levels of acetylcholinesterase in the lateral geniculate and superior colliculus (Maletta and Timiras, 1967) and a significantly decreased level of choline acetylase in the same areas (Maletta and Timiras, 1968). These studies did not reveal any differences in brain weights. Adrenal weights were higher in the visually deprived animals than in normal controls, suggesting, as other experiments have, the stressful effects of sensory deprivation. Some other effects of dark-rearing have been noted, such as RNA changes (DeBold *et al.*, 1967) and alteration in rate of protein synthesis (Rose, 1967). In the main, however, biochemical effects in the whole brain or the visual cortex following dark-rearing have been notably absent.

III. EXPERIMENTAL

We began our work in this area in possession of some of the basic findings of the group at Berkeley. We felt that the EC-IC conditions, already demonstrated to be sufficiently profound to alter brain weights and acetylcholinesterase activity, should be also sufficient to influence other biochemical systems in the brain. And, in light of the considerable knowledge of the stress effects of isolation, we felt that a more thorough examination of the possible role of stress should be made.

The experiments to be reported below were done over a period of several years. In many cases we have combined data from many different individual experiments. In other cases we have reported the individual experiment. This is necessary because not all measures were done in each experiment.

A. Methods

1. Subjects

Sprague-Dawley rats were used as subjects. Littermate pairs were matched closely for initial body weight, weaned at approximately 19 days of age (ranging from 16-21 days), and placed in the two living environments.

2. Differential Housing

Experimental animals (EC) of the same sex were housed substantially as described by Bennett et al. (1964) in groups of 9-12 in large social cages (25 × 25 × 17 inches) with hardware cloth sides, a sheet metal top and a sawdust-covered floor. Each cage contained a small wooden A-frame barrier (6 × 6 × 6 inches) which the rats used for nesting, two wooden ladders, a mirror and various plastic toys. Two metal food containers were placed on a wooden platform (25 × 6 × 1 inch) 9 inches above the floor. In addition, the rats, in groups of 9-12, were allowed 30 min each day for free exploration of a large open-field box (4 × 4 × 2 ft) with wooden sides and floor and an open top. Ten wooden barriers and ladders were randomly arranged daily in the open field to present a novel situation for exploration. No reward was present.

The littermate controls (IC) lived in individual isolation cages (8 × 11 × 9.5 inches) with the backs, sides, and tops constructed of sheet metal and with the fronts and floors of hardware cloth. The cage fronts faced a blank wall (somewhat reducing illumination) and the animals were maintained without contact or sight of other animals. Handling was restricted to weekly weighing and animals were given no opportunity for free exploration.

Both the experimental and control rats were housed in a temperature-regulated, partially soundproofed animal room and had free access to food and water. All animals were weighed once a week and on the day before they were killed.

Most animals were maintained in the differential housing conditions 29-31 days. Due to the large number of biochemical determinations performed on each animal, tissue from only 8-10 subjects (4-5 littermate pairs) could be analyzed every other day. Therefore, the chemical runs were divided into blocks consisting of four or five littermate pairs. EC animals remained in the social cages until they were sacrificed. The size of the EC group therefore, was decreased during the last few days of the treatment period.

In some experiments, animals were maintained in the environmental conditions for shorter periods of time. These animals were sacrificed after 2½, 6, 11, and 16 days of exposure. In other experiments, after 30 days of exposure, the EC and IC littermate pairs were placed in an ordinary laboratory cage and allowed to remain together for an additional 30 days before sacrifice.

3. Chemical Analysis

Littermates were sacrificed consecutively and tissues analyzed with the sequence randomized between the EC and IC member of each pair under code numbers that did not reveal their housing conditions.

The animals were sacrificed by decapitation and trunk blood was generally collected. The livers were rapidly removed, rinsed in saline, blotted free of extraneous moisture, weighed and, for most assays, homogenized in 5 vol of cold 0.15 M KCl. The homogenates were centrifuged at 30,000 g for 30 min at 4°C and the supernatant used for determining enzyme activities. For determination of tryptophan and phenylalanine hydroxylase activities, a portion of the liver was separately homogenized in 2 vol of 0.15 M KCl, 2.5 × 10^{-4} in NaOH, and treated as above. The protein content of each supernatant solution was estimated by measuring absorbancy at 260 and 280 mμ and applying the formula: mg protein/ml = 1.55 A_{280} − 0.76 A_{260} or by Lowry protein determinaton (Layne, 1957).

Tryptophan- and tyrosine α-ketoglutrate transaminase activities were determined at 37°C by the enol-borate-tautomerase method (Lin et al., 1958), both with and without the addition of 100 μg of pyridoxal phosphate. Tryptophan pyrrolase activity was measured by determining the kynurenine formed after 1 hr incubation at 37°C of supernatant with tryptophan (Knox and Auerbach, 1955). Tryptophan hydroxylase was determined by measuring 5-hydroxyindole fluorescence in 3 N HCl following incubation for 1 hr at 37°C of supernatant, tryptophan, NAD, and nicotinamide (Friedland et al., 1961).

Serum corticoids were measured fluorimetrically by the method of Guillemin et al. (1959), and adrenal corticoids and ascorbic acid were measured as described previously (Schapiro et al., 1962).

Brain serotonin was determined fluorimetrically (Bogdanski et al., 1956). 5-Hydroxytryptophan and glutamic acid decarboxylase activities were measured by counting the $^{14}CO_2$ liberated from 5-hydroxytryptophan-1-^{14}C and glutamic acid -1-^{14}C during incubation with enzyme in a specially designed reaction vessel (Slater et al., 1964).

For analysis of enzymes and catecholamines in specific areas of the brain, it was necessary to pool tissue from rats. For this purpose the animals were killed in groups of 4 EC's and 4 IC's. The animals were decapitated and the brain quickly removed and placed on a piece of saline-impregnated filter paper in a Petri dish placed over a bed of ice. The brains were separated into seven parts: cortex, cerebellum, pons-medulla, caudate nucleus, colliculi, hypothalamus, and remainder. Dissections were conservative; no attempt was made to isolate all of any particular area. Consequently, the remainder was consistently contaminated by varying amounts of the other areas isolated.

Pooled cortex, cerebellum, pons-medulla, and remainder were weighed on an analytic balance and homogenized in appropriate volumes of 0.4 N HClO$_4$ for norepinephrine and dopamine determinations or in 0.25 M sucrose for enzyme determinations. Caudate nucleus, hypothalamus, and colliculi were weighed in methyl cellulose capsules on a Cahn Electrobalance and then the entire capsule was homogenized. For the determination of norepinephrine and dopamine, the entire homogenate was used. Enzymes were determined in aliquots of the sucrose homogenate.

Norepinephrine was determined by the method of Bertler, Carlsson, and Rosengren (1958), and dopamine by the method of Carlsson and Waldeck (1958) as modified by Moore and Lariviere (1963).

Tyrosine hydroxylase was measured according to McGeer and McGeer (1967). Catechol-O-methyltransferase was determined using Axelrod's procedure (Axelrod, 1962) but with norepinephrine as substrate. Monoamine oxidase was measured by the method of Weissbach *et al.* (1960) using a Gilford Automatic Recording Spectrophotometer.

Choline acetylase was determined using the procedure of McCamen and Hunt (1965). Acetylcholinesterase was assayed according to the method of Ellman *et al.* (1961) and pseudocholinesterase by the same method but with butyryl-thiocholine as substrate. Carbonic anhydrase was measured by the colorimetric method described by Waygood (1955) but using a pH meter to determine the end point.

B. Results

1. Brain Weight

In Fig. 1 are shown the differences in brain weight between members of each of 68 EC-IC littermate pairs after 30 days' exposure to the differential environmental conditions. These 68 pairs comprise the animals from six different experiments over a period of 2 years. The mean brain weight difference is 63.82 mg and is highly significantly different from zero ($t=5.5$, $P<0.001$).

The difference observed here is of the same order of magnitude reported by Bennett *et al.* (1964) and Rosenzweig *et al.* (1968b), that is, a 63 mg difference in a brain of approximately 1 gm, or about 6%.

2. Brain Composition

Figure 2 shows some measures of tissue composition of whole brain after 30 days in eight pairs of EC-IC animals. Water content, nitrogen content, and

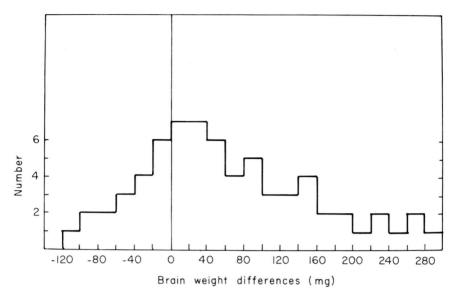

FIG. 1.   Differences in total brain weight between EC-IC littermate pairs. N = 68 pairs. Mean difference is 63.82 mg.

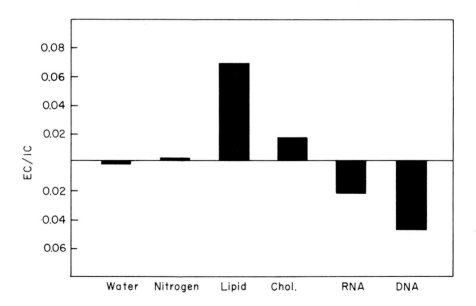

FIG. 2.   Difference in composition of EC and IC brain, expressed as $(\frac{EC}{IC}-1)$. N = 8 pairs of animals. Chol.-cholesterol.

cholesterol are equal in the two groups, but lipids are somewhat elevated in the EC group and RNA and DNA somewhat higher in the IC animals. These results are not what would be expected if the EC brain weight increase resulted from increased glial proliferation, as suggested by Diamond (1967). On the contrary, our results suggest a smaller number of cells with increased lipid content, a condition more likely to be found if neuronal cells are increasing in size and, perhaps, in degree of myelination.

3. Isolation as a Stress

In Table I are results from one of our earlier experiments designed to test the stressful effects of the IC condition. These results were obtained from 37 pairs of littermates. The adrenal weights of the IC animals were significantly higher than their EC littermates, suggesting a prolonged stress, contrary to the report of Bennett *et al.* (1964). However, neither the serum nor adrenal corticosterone concentrations were elevated, indicating that some time during the 30 days of the experiment the IC's had adapted to the condition and were no longer responding with adrenal activation. Table I also shows that both tyrosine and tryptophan transaminase activities were elevated in the IC group. This elevation was maintained after supplementation with pyridoxal phosphate, demonstrating an apoenzyme change in the IC group.

TABLE I   Effect of EC-IC on Adrenals and Stress-Responsive Enzymes

	EC mean±S.E.	IC mean±S.E.	P^a
Adrenal corticosteroids, µg/gm	16.27±2.93	13.14±2.23	N.S.
Serum corticosteroids, µg/100 ml	10.05±1.58	9.13±1.16	N.S.
Adrenal weight, mg	33.6±1.2	35.0±1.1	<0.05
Tyrosine transaminase[b]	1.138±0.192	1.821±0.254	<0.05
Tyrosine transaminase + pp[c]	6.977±0.641	9.228±0.789	<0.05
Tryptophan transaminase ($\times 10^2$)	7.198±0.493	11.138±0.542	<0.01
Tryptophan transaminase + pp ($\times 10^2$)	9.831±0.666	13.486±1.091	<0.01
Tryptophan pyrrolase µmoles/hr/gm protein	5.975±0.535	6.845±0.552	N.S.
Tryptophan hydroxylase µmoles/hr/gm protein	1.745±0.145	2.021±0.168	N.S.
Phenylalanine hydroxylase µmoles/hr/gm protein	67.9±4.3	75.9±4.6	N.S.

[a]P value derived from analysis of variance. N.S., not significant.
[b]Transaminases are substrate-a-oxoglutarate transaminase and are calculated as µmoles/min/gm protein.
[c]pp indicates addition of 100 µg pyridoxal phosphate to the assay medium.

Of particular interest is the observation that tryptophan pyrrolase activity was not different in the two groups. This result agrees with the findings that no adrenal activation was present at the time the animals were killed. Pyrrolase is the most responsive of the enzymes to adrenal corticoids and most closely follows the rise and fall of corticoids after stress. However, the results with the two transaminases support the suggestion of an earlier adrenal activation. Tryptophan pyrrolase activity is negligible in the livers of newborn rats but increases rapidly within days after birth and reaches adult activity in 2-3 weeks (Goldstein and Knox, 1963). Tyrosine transaminase activity, however, remains quite sensitive and does not stabilize at adult levels for about 8 weeks after birth (Knox et al., 1963). It is therefore entirely consistent with known facts to suggest that relatively early in the IC experience a stress-induced adrenal activation occurred. This stress lasted for a time sufficiently long to (1) induce small changes in adrenal weight, (2) increase transaminase activity, and (3) increase pyrrolase activity. Upon adaptation to the stress the adrenal activation subsided, and the increased pyrrolase activity subsided also. However, the adrenal weight change was not reversible and the transaminase activity remained at a higher basal level. This suggestion has been investigated and the results are given in a later section.

4. EC-IC Effects of Various Brain Constituents

Table II shows the results obtained upon analysis of the whole brain of EC-IC rats. Serotonin, norepinephrine, and dopamine assays were done on 19 of the 37 pairs of animals. The enzymes listed were assayed in the brains of the other 18 pairs.

TABLE II   Effects of EC-IC on Brain Constituents[a]

	EC mean±S.E.	IC mean±S.E.	P
5-HTP decarboxylase, μmoles/hr/gm protein	18.56±0.55	21.39±2.10	N.S.
GA decarboxylase, μmoles/hr/gm protein	16.37±3.63	16.12±1.37	N.S.
Acetylcholinesterase, μmoles/min/mg protein	0.148±0.005	0.139±0.005	N.S.
Acetylcholinesterase, μmoles/min/brain	25.69±0.91	23.07±0.89	<0.025
Serotonin, μg/gm	0.484±0.020	0.503±0.021	N.S.
Serotonin, μg/brain	0.764±0.029	0.771±0.032	N.S.
Norepinephrine, μg/gm	0.347±0.013	0.396±0.014	<0.01
Norepinephrine, μg/brain	0.556±0.021	0.661±0.020	<0.01
Dopamine, μg/g	0.491±0.037	0.520±0.044	N.S.
Dopamine, μg/brain	0.788±0.058	0.797±0.065	N.S.

[a]N.S., not significant; 5-HTP, 5-hydroxytryptophan; GA, glutamic acid.

We found no difference in 5-hydroxytryptophan decarboxylase activity, glutamic decarboxylase activity, or in the content and concentration of dopamine and serotonin. No change in serotonin had previously been found by Pryor (reported by Bennett *et al.*, 1964). Confirming the many reports of the Berkeley group, we found a significant elevation in total brain acetylcholinesterase activity in the EC animals.

We also found a highly significant difference in whole brain norepinephrine between the EC and IC animals — the IC's being about 14% higher.

5. Short Exposure to EC-IC Conditions

In a second series of experiments we placed 20 pairs of littermates in the differential environments and sacrificed five pairs at 2½ days, 6 days, 11 days, and 16 days after beginning of exposure. The results are given in Figs. 3 and 4. The body weights of the IC's were greater after 6 days and remained so; the liver weight followed the body weight, as did the adrenal weight for the later periods (11 and 16 days). The brain weight, however, followed a different pattern, the EC brain being heavier at 6 days and remaining so. Adrenal corticoids were higher in the IC's during the first part of the exposure but by 11 days no difference could be seen. Tyrosine transaminase activity in the liver of the IC's was markedly higher at 2½ and 6 days, and remained higher at 11 and 16 days (and also at 30, as reported above).

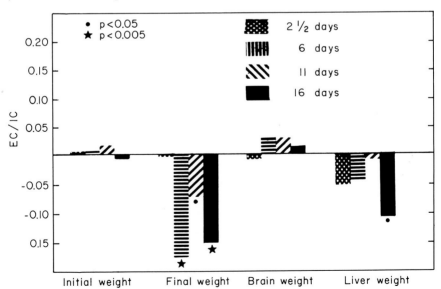

FIG. 3.   Some weight differences between EC and IC animals, expressed as $(\frac{EC}{IC}-1)$, as a function of time of exposure to the environmental conditions. N = 5 pairs at each time period.

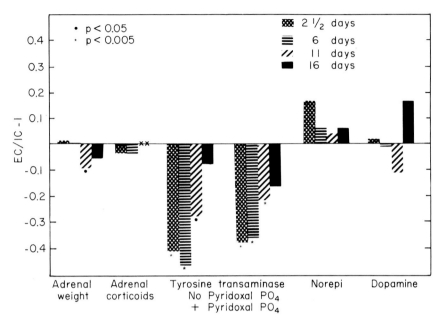

FIG. 4. Differences in some stress-responsive parameters in EC and IC animals, expressed as $(\frac{EC}{IC}-1)$, as a function of time of exposure to the environmental conditions. N = 5 pairs at each time period.

Norepinephrine in the brain followed an unexpected pattern, in that the EC brains were higher than the IC's for the 16 days of this short-term experiment, whereas, as we have seen above, at 30 days the IC's were higher.

These results are consistent with the speculation that early isolation produces a stress response in these animals.

6. Regional Effects of EC-IC on Norepinephrine

We were stimulated by the whole brain norepinephrine differences shown in Table II to look at different areas of the brain to see where the effect might be localized. The brains were separated into seven regions as detailed in Section III,A. Measurements of norepinephrine and dopamine in these areas are reported in Fig. 5, plotted as EC/IC ratios. A consistent and significantly (P<0.005) higher level of norepinephrine was seen in the caudate nucleus of the IC group. This difference was sufficient to almost account for the differences in whole brain norepinephrine noted above (Geller *et al.*, 1965).

The norepinephrine levels of the other areas did not show significant differences between the EC and IC groups. And in no area could a significant difference in dopamine be found.

7. Mechanism for Norepinephrine Difference

Several mechanisms could explain a high level of norepinephrine in the IC animals. Some of these are: (1) higher activity of synthetic enzymes – tyrosine

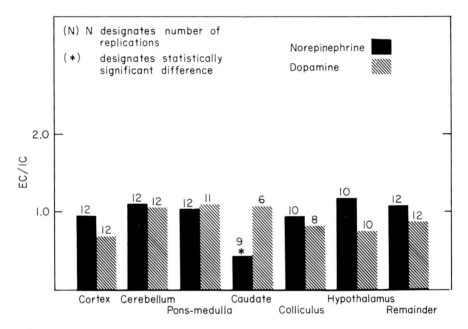

FIG. 5.   Differences in norepinephrine or dopamine in various areas of EC and IC brain, expressed as ($\frac{EC}{IC}$). (From Geller and Yuwiler, 1968.)

hydroxylase, dopa decarboxylase, and dopamine-β-oxidase – in the IC animals; (2) lower activity of degradative enzymes – monoamine oxidase and catechol-O-methyltransferase – in the IC animals; (3) a larger number of binding sites in the IC animals.

We have investigated these suggestions, but because of technical problems with the very small amounts of tissue used, it was not always possible to measure all the enzymes in all the tissues. Therefore, there are differences in the number of replications. In addition, we were not able to measure dopamine-β-oxidase. Figure 6 shows the data on the four enzymes we have studied. Some significant differences are seen. Tyrosine hydroxylase was higher in the cortex and colliculus of the IC animals and monoamine oxidase activity was significantly lower in these same tissues. This combination may explain the tendency toward higher values of norepinephrine and dopamine in these tissues in the IC animals. Differences in the caudate were minimal, however, and do not help in explaining the strikingly higher levels of norepinephrine in that area in the IC's. It is still possible that a greatly enhanced level of dopamine-β-oxidase will be found in this tissue.

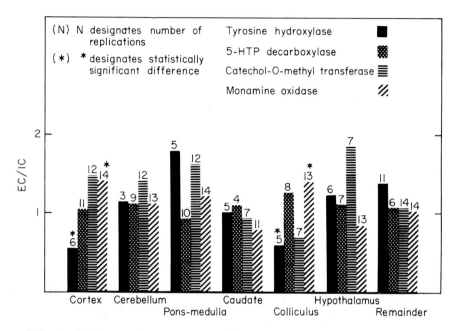

FIG. 6. Differences in some enzymes important in catecholamine metabolism in various areas of EC and IC brains, expressed as ($\frac{EC}{IC}$). (From Geller and Yuwiler, 1968.)

Differences in binding sites would seem to offer a reasonable explanation for differences in amine content, corresponding in chemical terms to the anatomical differences reflected by brain weight changes and glial number differences. A preliminary experiment we have done casts doubt on this hypothesis. Following administration of the MAO inhibitor Catron (JB 516), norepinephrine levels in whole brain rose to exactly the same level in the EC and IC groups, suggesting an equal number of binding sites in the brains of animals of both groups.

8. Activity of Some Other Brain Enzymes

We have also looked into the enzymes of the acetylcholine system — choline acetylase and acetylcholinesterase. In addition, because of the previous reports of increased glial proliferation (Diamond et al., 1966), we looked at two enzymes presumed to be located within glia (Koelle, 1955; Giacobini, 1962). These results are shown in Fig. 7.

No clear pattern of changes can be seen. Choline acetylase was higher in some areas of the brains of the IC animals while acetylcholinesterase was little changed. Whether the total activity within these areas was changed cannot be determined because our methods of dissection did not allow us to measure total tissue weight.

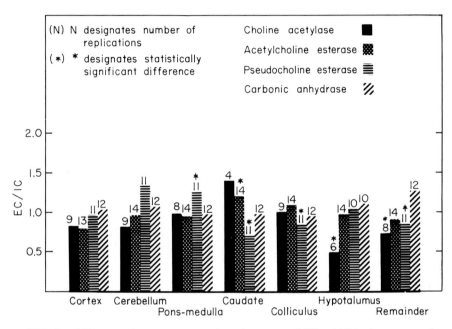

FIG. 7.   Differences in some enzymes in various areas of EC and IC brains, expressed as $(\frac{EC}{IC})$. (From Geller and Yuwiler, 1968.)

Some indications of increased activity of pseudocholinesterase and carbonic anhydrase in the EC animals are seen in Fig. 7. However, the pattern does not seem consistent enough to support the reports of Diamond *et al.* (1966) of increased amounts of glia in EC brains.

9. Effects of Rehousing EC-IC Animals

Table III shows the results obtained when EC-IC littermate pairs are rehoused together in ordinary laboratory cages and conditions for an additional 30 days after their initial 30-day exposure to the environmental conditions. Although some differences were still to be seen, they were smaller than the differences seen after the initial 30-day exposure. These results appear to show that the effects of the environment are reversible and tend to disappear.

TABLE III Values Obtained from Animals Maintained for 30 days in EC or IC Conditions, then Rehoused in Pairs for an Additional 30 days[a]

	EC mean±S.E.		IC mean±S.E.	P
Original body wt. (gm)	41.1±1.91		41.5±1.76	
Final body wt. (gm)	409.7±17.4	(14)	401.4±15.8	
Liver wt. (gm)	16.862±0.809	(15)	16.549±0.723	
Brain wt. (gm)	1.9607±0.0400	(15)	1.9613±0.0399	
Adrenal wt. (mg)	47.7±1.9	(13)	46.1±1.7	
ACS (μg/gm)	9.08±1.49	(6)	17.22±2.56	<0.001
SCS (μg/100 ml)	8.78±1.04	(10)	10.35±1.42	
AAA (mg/100 gm)	481.0±19.6	(10)	505.3±14.2	< 0.05
Serotonin (μg/gm)	0.682±0.046	(11)	0.705±0.085	
Serotonin (μg/brain)	1.315±0.079	(12)	1.352±0.124	
Dopamine (μgm)	0.683±0.066	(7)	0.960±0.154	< 0.05
Dopamine (μg/brain)	1.336±0.131	(6)	1.784±0.241	< 0.05
Norepinephrine (μg/gm)	0.585±0.078	(9)	0.602±0.092	< 0.05
Norepinephrine (μg/brain)	1.089±0.123	(10)	1.014±0.138	< 0.05
Acetylcholinesterase (μmoles/hr/gm Pr.)	0.136±0.004	(13)	0.131±0.004	
5-HTP decarboxylase (μmoles/hr/gm Pr.)	30.45±8.43	(11)	41.22±9.78	
Glutamic decarboxylase (μmoles/hr/gm Pr.)	21.83±2.59	(12)	23.99±4.11	
Transaminase (μmoles/min/gm Pr.)				
Tyrosine	1.677±0.273	(12)	1.858±0.362	
Tyrosine + pp	12.082±0.774	(13)	12.255±0.830	
Tryptophan x 10^2	11.426±1.034	(13)	11.735±1.030	
Tryptophan + pp x 10^2	14.042±0.947	(17)	13.631±0.940	< 0.05
Phenylalanine hydroxylase (μmoles/hr/gm Pr.)	62.53±3.20	(12)	63.57±3.72	
Tryptophan hydroxylase (μmoles/hr/gm Pr.)	3.511±0.579	(15)	3.251±0.393	
Pyrrolase (μmoles/hr/gm Pr.)	5.395±0.499	(11)	5.949±0.821	
Pyrrolase + hematin	16.455±1.808	(13)	15.548±1.431	

[a]Numbers in parentheses are number of pairs. The following abbreviations are used: ACS, adrenal corticosteroids; SCS, serum corticosteroids; AAA, adrenal ascorbic acid; 5HTP, 5-hydroxytryptophan; pp, pyridoxal phosphate.

IV. DISCUSSION

Two aspects of the results of our experiments merit special comment. One is the clear indication that isolation is stressful to these weanling animals, causing pituitary-adrenal activation and subsequent metabolic changes. The other is the changes in brain norepinephrine, particularly in the caudate nucleus, which are probably not the results of the stress but of some functional activity associated either with the EC or IC condition, or both.

The stressful component in isolation was first seen in our 30-day experiments in which both adrenal weight and hepatic transaminase activities were elevated in the IC group. Based on these observations, and the fact that neither adrenal nor serum corticoids were elevated in the 30-day group, we concluded that during the first days of the IC experience the animals were markedly stressed, and what we were seeing at 30 days was only that portion of the stress response that was sufficiently permanent to survive later adaptation to the stress. These speculations were reasonably well confirmed in the experiment designed to follow the course of the EC-IC effect over shorter periods of time. The general pattern of responses is what would be expected if isolation was a rather severe stress when first imposed but became less so with time.

It should be noted that many authors have reported isolation-induced aggressive behavior, this response being more consistently observed in mice, but seen in rats also (Bevan et al., 1951; Hatch et al., 1965; Stern et al., 1960; Sigg et al., 1966; Moore, 1968). However, we have not observed such aggressive behavior in our isolated rats, in agreement with Giacalone et al. (1968) and Krech et al. (1966). Our isolation, it is true, represents only a partial deprivation, but our isolated animals have no direct contact with others of their species except through smell and sound. This degree of isolation may not be sufficient to induce the aggressive behavior that would develop in total isolation. The age and duration of isolation also appear to be important variables (see Chapter 14).

Isolation does produce other behavioral changes in the rat, many associated with increased emotionality (Jewett and Norton, 1964; B.L. Welch, 1965; Hahn, 1965; Ader, 1969). Our rats do exhibit what we very generally call increased emotionality — they are more nervous, harder to handle, show increased defecation when handled — but we have made no systematic attempt to evaluate this condition. It is also particularly interesting that, when rehoused with its EC littermate, an IC rat invariably is the less dominant animal, and that, when groups of IC animals are housed together, they show clearly abnormal social adjustments. These behavioral abnormalities are obvious even to our untrained eyes.

The differences in brain norepinephrine in the IC animals are difficult to explain. Guarino et al. (1967) compared whole brain norepinephrine in 32-day isolated rats to norepinephrine in similar animals housed in pairs for the same period. They report no norepinephrine difference despite a considerable stress response in the isolated animals. However, their animals differed from ours in that they were 6 weeks old when placed in isolation. Giacalone *et al.* (1968) found no serotonin changes in isolated rats, but do not report values for norepinephrine. In mice the situation appears to be somewhat different. Serotonin changes during isolation have been reported (B.L. Welch and Welch, 1966; A.S. Welch and Welch, 1968b; Bliss and Ailion, 1969; Giacalone *et al.*, 1968), and some of these authors also have found changes in norepinephrine levels and norepinephrine turnover during isolation (A.S. Welch and Welch, 1968a; B.L. Welch and Welch, 1965). A correlation between aggressive behavior and brain serotonin levels in mice has been suggested (Giacalone *et al.*, 1968), but no correspondence to norepinephrine levels has been found. It is also unlikely that our norepinephrine changes are part of a generalized response to stress, for the majority of reports have indicated lowered brain norepinephrine levels following acute stress (Maynart and Levi, 1964; Barchas and Freedman, 1963; Freedman, 1963).

A difference in norepinephrine content without a concomitant difference in dopamine is somewhat unexpected. This could be the result of a spatial separation of dopamine and norepinephrine pools, or it may be that the rate-limiting step in those areas particularly affected by the EC-IC conditions is the conversion of dopamine to norepinephrine. The finding that the major locus of change in the IC brain is the caudate nucleus supports the latter argument. The caudate nucleus, part of the striatum, is particularly rich in dopamine but has relatively much less norepinephrine, suggesting that the conversion is normally limited. It would, therefore, be possible to increase the conversion of dopamine to norepinephrine by a small percentage without necessarily altering dopamine levels. Such a result would be reflected in increased dopamine turnover without increased concentration. We have no direct evidence to support or refute this possibility, but we have not found increased activity of the enzymes synthesizing dopamine we have measured. These enzymes may, however, be already in excess and so would not be a good measure of dopamine turnover. A direct study should answer this question.

One report has appeared showing a decreased monoamine oxidase activity in whole brain following stress (Ruckebusch and Brunet-Tallon, 1967). With such an alteration, norepinephrine levels would, perhaps, increase in the stressed IC animals. However, in that case, dopamine and serotonin should also increase, but do not. That fact, and the direct observation of no consistent changes in monoamine oxidase activity in our animals, argues against changes in that enzyme as the mechanism for the norepinephrine difference.

A lower rate of norepinephrine release from binding sites may also account for the observed differences. If such a mechanism exists, it represents a functional change, perhaps because of the reduced level of stimulation, and not a permanent alteration, because after their removal from isolation, the levels of norepinephrine in the IC animals approach the levels in the EC's. Why such a change is most apparent in the caudate is unanswered, for the relationship of the caudate nucleus to the behavior of the animal is as yet unclear. Buchwald *et al.* (1961) have reported that the caudate actively inhibits cortical activity. Perhaps the caudate is particularly inactive when the amount of stimulation requiring inhibition is greatly decreased. Divac *et al.* (1967) have suggested that the caudate may be equipotential with cortex and capable of assuming cortical functions. The lower level of cortical stimulation on the IC's then may be reflected by the caudate and magnified by the small size of the organ. Catecholamine metabolism is rapid in the striatum (Glowinski and Iverson, 1966 a,b), an area that includes the caudate, and evidence indicates that norepinephrine may accumulate in the dopamine-containing terminals found profusely in that area. Further experimentation will be needed to determine the relationship of these observations to the elevated norepinephrine in the caudate of the IC animals.

One further possibility that should not be dismissed is an alteration in circadian rhythm in either the EC or IC brain. Norepinephrine rhythms in the brain have been investigated thoroughly by Reis *et al.* (1968). They found extensive differences in rhythms in various areas of the brain but no rhythm at all in some areas, including the caudate nucleus. However, Friedman and Walker (1968) report a norepinephrine peak in the caudate during the dark phase of the illumination cycle. We cannot reconcile these contradictory reports, but if a cycle does indeed exist, it may be worth investigating EC-IC norepinephrine levels during different times of the light-dark cycle.

It is difficult to evaluate the importance of these EC-IC differences. The available information suggests that behavioral changes are relatively permanent in these animals. Our data indicate that some of the biochemical changes are less permanent, tending to disappear with time. However, we are only observing static concentrations of a very few substances. Whether other substances are more permanently affected, whether the dynamic state of metabolism has been changed, or whether the relative importance of alternate metabolic pathways has been influenced is unknown. Only with continued investigation can the importance of environmental conditions on biochemical ontogeny be assessed.

POSTSCRIPT: A CAUTIONARY NOTE

The studies reported here were completed some years ago. Interspersed with these were others in which we did not observe some or all of the effects noted. In those unreported attempts the EC and IC groups did not differ, but we never observed a reversal of the results given here. In some of our failures we have been able to point to extraneous outside influences that may have disturbed our experiments — construction in or near the laboratory, new animal caretakers not sufficiently warned or careful about the necessity of maintaining our isolated condition. In other cases, however, we were unable to find any specific interference. The very nature of these experiments makes such problems unavoidable except where laboratory facilities are designed for just such isolation conditions. These facilities we do not enjoy. It is for this reason that we have essentially stopped these studies. We are, however, reporting our positive findings in the belief that they are more important than our failures and represent the true effect of the differential environments. However, we may be wrong, and our findings may be artifacts of other, unsuspected variables. We hope, by this report, to stimulate those with more suitable facilities to repeat our experiments, and if they can be confirmed, to extend them.

REFERENCES

Ader, R. (1969). *Ann. N.Y. Acad. Sci. 159,* 791.
Altman, J., and Das, G.D. (1964). *Nature (London) 204,* 1161.
Appel, S.H., Davis, W., and Scott, S. (1967). *Science 157,* 836.
Axelrod, J. (1962). *"Methods, Enzymol."* 5, 748.
Barchas, J.D., and Freedman, D.X. (1963). *Biochem. Pharmacol. 12,* 1232.
Bennett, E.L., Diamond, M.C., Krech, D., and Rosenzweig, M.R. (1964). *Science 146,* 610.
Bertler, A., Carlsson, A., and Rosengren, E. (1958). *Acta Physiol. Scand. 44,* 273.
Bevan, W., Jr., Bloom, W.L., and Lewis, G.T. (1951). *Physiol. Zool. 24,* 231.
Bliss, E.L., and Ailion, J. (1969). *J. Pharmacol. Exp. Ther. 168,* 258.
Bogdanski, D.F., Pletscher, A., Brodie, B.B., and Udenfriend, S. (1956). *J. Pharmacol. Exp. Ther. 117,* 83.
Buchwald, N.A., Wyers, E.J., Lauprecht, C.W., and Heuser, G. (1961). *Electroencephalogr. Clin. Neurophysiol. 13,* 531 (1961).
Carlsson, A., and Waldeck, B. (1958). *Acta Physiol. Scand. 44,* 293.
DeBold, R.C., Firshein, W., Carrier, S.C., III, and Leaf, R.C. (1967). *Psychon. Sci. 1,* 379.
Dellweg, H., Gevner, R., and Wacker, A. (1968). *J. Neurochem. 15,* 1109.
Diamond, M.C. (with technical assistance by B. Lindner and A. Raymond). (1967). *J. Comp. Neurol. 131,* 357.
Diamond, M.C., Law, F., Rhodes, H., Lindner, B., Rosenzweig, M.R., Krech, D., and Bennett, E.L. (1966). *J. Comp. Neurol. 128,* 117.
Divac, I., Rosvold, H.E., and Szwarcbart, M.K. (1967). *J. Comp. Physiol. Psychol. 63,* 184.
Ellman, G.L., Courtney, D., Andres, V., Jr., and Featherstone, R.M. (1961). *Biochem. Pharmacol. 7,* 88.
Ferreira, A.J. (1965). *J. Nerv. Ment. Dis. 141,* 108.
Freedman, D.X. (1963). *Amer. J. Psychiat. 119,* 843.
Friedland, R.A., Wadzinski, F.M., and Waisman, H.A. (1961). *Biochem. Biophys. Res. Commun. 5,* 94.
Friedman, A.H., and Walker, C.A. (1968). *J. Physiol. (London) 197,* 77.
Geller, E., and Yuwiler, A. (1968). *In* "Ontogenesis of the Brain" (L. Jilek and S. Trojan, eds.), p. 277. Charles University, Prague.
Geller, E., Yuwiler, A., and Zolman, J.F. (1965). *J. Neurochem. 12,* 949.
Giacobini, E. (1962). *J. Neurochem. 13,* 655.
Giacalone, E., Tansella, M., Valzelli, L., and Garattini, S. (1968). *Biochem. Pharmacol. 17,* 1315.

Glowinski, J., and Iverson, L.L. (1966a). *J. Neurochem. 13,* 655.
Glowinski, J., and Iverson, L.L. (1966b). *J. Neurochem. 13,* 671.
Goldstein, L., and Knox, W.E. (1963). *Ann. N.Y. Acad. Sci. 111,* 233.
Guarino, A.M., Rosecrans, J.A., Mendillo, A.B., and DeFeo, J.J. (1967). *Biochem. Pharmacol. 16,* 227.
Guillemin, R., Clayton, G.W., Lipscomb, H.S., and Smith, J.D. (1959). *J. Lab. Clin. Med. 53,* 830.
Hahn, W.W. (1965). *J. Psychosom. Res. 8,* 455.
Hatch, A.M., Wiberg, G.S., Zwaidzka, Z., Cann, M., Airth, J.M., and Grice, H.C. (1965). *Toxicol. Appl. Pharmacol. 7,* 737.
Jewett, R.E., and Norton, S. (1964). *Psychopharmacologia 6,* 151.
Knox, W.E., and Auerbach, J.H. (1955). *J. Biol. Chem. 214,* 307.
Knox, W.E., Goswami, M. N.D., and Lynch, R.D. (1963). *Ann. N.Y. Acad. Sci. 111,* 212.
Koelle, G.B. (1955). *J. Neuropathol. 14,* 23.
Krech, D., Rosenzweig, M.R., and Bennett, E.L. (1966). *Physiol. Behav. 1,* 99.
Layne, E. (1957). *"Methods Enzymol." 2,* 454.
Lin, E.C.C., Pitt, B.M., Civen, M., and Knox, W.E. (1958). *J. Biol. Chem. 233,* 668.
McCamen, R.E., and Hunt, J.M. (1965). *J. Neurochem. 12,* 253.
McGeer, E.G., and McGeer, P.L. (1967). *Can. J. Biochem. 45,* 115.
Maletta, G., and Timiras, P.S. (1967). *Exp. Neurol. 17,* 513.
Maletta, G., and Timiras, P.S. (1968). *J. Neurochem. 15,* 787.
Maynart, E.W., and Levi, R. (1964). *J. Pharmacol. Exp. Ther. 143,* 90.
Moore, K.E. (1968). *Can. J. Physiol. Pharmacol. 46,* 553.
Moore, K.E., and Lariviere, E.W. (1963). *Biochem. Pharmacol. 12,* 1203.
Newton, G., and Levine, S., eds. (1968). "Early Experience and Behavior." Thomas, Springfield, Illinois.
Reis, D.J., Weinbren, M., and Corvelli, A. (1968). *J. Pharmacol. Exp. Ther. 164,* 135.
Rose, S.P.R. (1967). *Nature (London) 215,* 253.
Rosenzweig, M.R., Love, W., and Bennett, E.L. (1968a). *Physiol. Behav. 3,* 819.
Rosenzweig, M.R., Krech, D., Bennett, E.L., and Diamond, M.C. (1968b). *In* "Early Experience and Behavior" (G. Newton and S. Levine, eds.), pp. 258-298. Thomas, Springfield, Illinois.
Rosenzweig, M.R., Bennett, E.L., Diamond, M.C., Wu, S.-Y., Slagle, R.W., and Saffran, E. (1969). *Brain Res. 14,* 427.
Ruckebusch, M., and Brunet-Tallon, C. (1967). *C. R. Acad. Sci. 160,* 2131.
Schapiro, S., Geller, E., and Eiduson, S. (1962). *Proc. Soc. Exp. Biol. Med. 109,* 935.
Sigg, E.B., Day, C., and Colombo, C. (1966). *Endocrinology 78,* 679.
Slater, G.G., Geller, E., and Yuwiler, A. (1964). *Anal. Chem. 36,* 1888.
Stern, J.A., Winokur, G., Eisenstein, A., Taylor, R., and Sly, M. (1960). *J. Psychosom. Res. 4,* 185.
Walker, J.P., Boas, J.A.R., and Riesen, A.H. (1971). *In* "Sensory Deprivation" (A.H. Riesen, ed.). Academic Press, New York (in press).
Waygood, E.R. (1955). *Methods Enzymol. 2,* 836.
Weissbach, H., Smith, T.E., Daly, J.W., Witkop, B., and Udenfriend, S. (1960). *J. Biol. Chem. 235,* 1160.
Welch, A.S., and Welch, B.L. (1968a). *Proc. Nat. Acad. Sci. U.S. 60,* 478.
Welch, A.S., and Welch, B.L. (1968b). *Biochem, Pharmacol. 17,* 699.
Welch, B.L. (1965). "Symposium on Medical Aspects of Stress in Military Climate," Publ. 1965-778-714, p. 39. U.S. Govt. Printing Office, Washington, D.C.
Welch, B.L., and Welch, A.S. (1965). *Life Sci. 4,* 1011.
Welch, B.L. and Welch, A.S. (1966). *Fed. Proc. 25,* 623.
Yuwiler, A. (1971). *In* "Handbook of Neurochemistry" (A. Lajtha, ed.), Vol. VI. Plenum Press, New York (in press).

CHAPTER 16   Male-Female Differences in Sexual Behavior: A Continuing Problem*

Richard E. Whalen

Ten years ago, in 1959, Phoenix, Goy, Gerall, and Young reported that the female offspring of guinea pigs treated with testosterone propionate during pregnancy showed a reduced probability of female-type behavior and an enhanced probability of male-type behavior when treated with the appropriate hormones in adulthood. This most important observation has led to the concept of the "organizational" effects of gonadal hormones on those neural systems which control sexual behavior. Young (1965) expressed this idea in the following way: " . . .the evidence seems conclusive that when the developing female guinea pig is subjected to the influence of androgen the neural tissues mediating mating behavior are affected in such a way that there is a suppression of the capacity to display the feminine measures of sexual behavior, an intensification of the capacity to display the masculine components."

These observations and this theoretical structure has led to an intense research interest in the roles played by gonadal hormones in the *development* (rather than the expression or activation) of sexual responses. Our own interest in this problem followed the demonstration in 1962 by Harris and Levine that phenomena similar to those reported for the guinea pig could be produced in the rat by treating the female with testosterone propionate shortly after birth. The discussion will focus on our own research experiences in the rapidly expanding field.

Our first concern was with a complete description of the behavioral effects of neonatal hormone manipulation.† Some of the initial studies of the rat did not provide information on the effects of early treatment upon the probability of

---

*The experiments described were supported by grant HD-00893 to REW from the NICHD.

†Species differences in the effects of hormones on the developing organism do exist. Our discussion and conclusions may be relevant only to the rat.

297

each on the component responses which make up the male sexual pattern, namely, mounts without intromission, intromission-type responses, and ejacu- laton-type responses. In these germinal experiments all response types were con- sidered "masculine" and the data were tabulated in terms of overall masculine response frequencies. We felt that the next analytic step was an examination of early hormone influences on each of the component masculine-type responses. When we did examine these effects (Whalen and Edwards, 1967) we found that female rats administered 2.5 mg testosterone propionate on the day of birth showed an enhanced probability of intromission-type responses when adminis- tered androgen in adulthood, yet we also found that the early androgen treat- ment did *not* enhance the probability of mounts without intromission. Thus, these androgenized female rats did not attempt to initiate masculine-type mating behavior any more frequently than control females administered oil in infancy. *Both* androgenized and control females displayed mounting responses; only the androgenized females showed frequent intromission-type responses. These find- ings did not seem to us to be consistent with the hypothesis that early androgen treatment ' masculinizes" by its action on the brain. We felt that if early androgen stimulation had its effects by modifying the brain, it should have enhanced the probability of mounting behavior as well as the probability of intromission-type behavior.

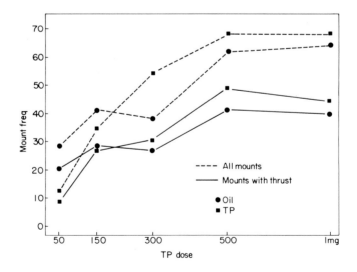

FIG. 1   Mean frequency of mounting responses in female rats treated with oil or with testosterone propionate (TP) prenatally and postnatally as a function of TP dose in adulthood. "All mounts" include mounts without thrusting as well as mounts with thrus- ting. Groups were not significantly different in mounting frequency. (From Whalen, *et al.,* 1969.)

Our inability to enhance the frequency of mounting responses by early androgen treatment could have several explanations. For example, we might have administered the wrong dose of androgen at the wrong time during the differentiation phase. In a series of studies we examined some of these parameters (Whalen *et al.*, 1969). We could find no evidence that perinatal androgen stimulation would enhance the likelihood that a female rat would attempt to mate with another female. Figure 1 presents data on this point from one of these studies. In this experiment pregnant female rats were administered either oil or 2.0 mg/day testosterone propionate on days 16-20 of gestation. Ninety-six hours after birth the female offspring of the androgen-treated mothers were administered 1.0 mg TP; control females received oil at the same time. When adult these females were again administered TP, the hormone dose being progressively increased each week during the 5-week test period, and they were tested for the display of masculine responses. At no dose level did the androgenized females exhibit significantly more mounting responses than the control females. We were forced to conclude that early androgen treatment neither enhances the potential to display mounting behavior nor reduces the behavioral threshold of reactivity to androgen stimulation. Again, these results did not seem consistent with the hypothesis that early androgen stimulation "masculinizes" the brain.

If androgen stimulation during the critical period does not masculinize the brain, what does it do to brain function to differentiate males from females? Our results, and those from several other laboratories, support the hypothesis that early androgen stimulation "defeminizes" the brain. Male rats which develop under endogenous androgenic stimulation and female rats stimulated with exogenous androgen (or estrogen) shortly after birth do not respond readily in adulthood to estrogen and progesterone stimulation with the display of those sexual responses characteristic of the female. Female rats which mature postnatally with or without ovaries, and male rats which mature without testes, on the other hand, all develop the potential to respond to estrogen-progesterone treatment in adulthood. These findings are illustrated in Fig. 2 which shows the probability of a lordosis response in male and female rats which developed under different conditions of hormonal stimulation. Our interpretation of these observations is that androgen stimulation during the critical period defeminizes the brain in the sense that it suppresses the development of a female-type reactivity to estrogen and progesterone at least in the rat.

It is important to point out that there is disagreement among the workers in this field about the interpretations presented here. Many workers feel that early androgen stimulation does in fact masculinize the brain. We do not yet accept this interpretation. All workers, however, seem to agree that early androgen stimulation lowers responsiveness to estrogen-progesterone stimulation. It is for this reason that we stress defeminization as the *primary* (although not necessarily exclusive) characteristic of hormone-induced sexual differentiation.

The brain masculinization hypothesis with which we disagree is supported by the observation mentioned above that early androgen treatment facilitates the potential for the display of intromission-type responses. In fact, our own observations of female rats treated both prenatally and postnatally with testosterone propionate indicates that treated females can show the complete masculine pattern including intromission-type responses and ejaculation-type responses and that the frequency and timing of these response patterns parallels those shown by the normal male (Whalen and Robertson, 1968). Figure 3 illustrates this finding and compares the frequency of intromission-type responses preceding the "ejaculatory reflex" in males and androgenized females as well as the duration of the "postejaculatory" intervals which follow ejaculations. For both males and females mating was allowed to proceed through several ejaculatory series until sexual satiation occurred. The similarity between the males and the androgenized females in the quantitative aspects of mating is indeed striking. Clearly, perinatal androgen stimulation does masculinize. One must ask, however, whether the data provide support for the hypothesis that early androgen treatment masculinizes the brain with respect to those systems which control behavior. We think not. We and others have shown that early androgenic

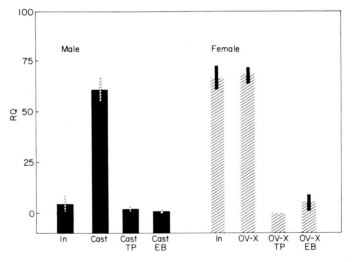

FIG. 2. Mean receptivity quotient (R.Q. = frequency of lordosis responses/ frequency of mounts with thrusting) of male and female rats hormonally manipulated at birth and administered estrogen and progesterone in adulthood. In incision control; animals gonadectomized in adulthood; Cast., males castrated within 12 hr of birth; Cast. TP, males castrated and treated with TP at birth; Cast EB males castrated and treated with estradiol benzoate at birth; Ov-X, females ovariectomized at birth; Ov-X TP, females ovariectomized and treated with TP at birth; Ov-X EB = females ovariectomized and treated with estradiol benzoate at birth. (From Whalen and Edwards, 1967.)

stimulation profoundly influences peripheral genital development. Females treated with androgen perinatally develop a peniform phallus which, as shown in Fig. 3, can serve as functional copulatory organ. We have argued earlier that this peripheral effect of androgen can account for the intromission-type and ejaculation-type responses which are observed in the androgenized female rats (Whalen, 1968). *Until definitive evidence for neural masculinization can be demonstrated, we prefer the rather conservative interpretation that early androgen stimulation in the rat differentiates males from females by masculinizing the genitalia, and by defeminizing the central nervous system.*

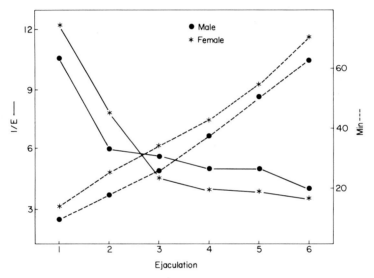

FIG. 3.   Masculine behavior in male rats and in female rats treated with testosterone propionate prenatally and postnatally. I/E, mean frequency of intromission-type responses preceding ejaculation-type responses during the course of sexual satiation. Min., mean minutes duration of interval following ejaculation-type responses before the onset of the subsequent copulatory series. (Female data from Whalen and Robertson, 1968; Male data from Beach and Jordan, 1956.)

NEURAL DIFFERENTIATION

Our interpretation of the effects of hormones on sexual differentiation stresses the inhibitory effect which early androgen treatment has upon adult reactivity to estrogen and progesterone (Fig. 2). Our next question must be: "What does this inhibitory effect represent in terms of altered brain function?" At present we have no answer to this question. One possibility, however, seemed worth pursuing. Michael (1961) and Eisenfeld and Axelrod (1965) demonstrated some years ago a rather selective uptake and retention of radioactive estrogen in brain areas presumably involved in the control of sexual behavior. We felt the possibility existed that such estradiol binding properties might be characteristic only of the female or that these properties might be characteristic of both male and female but to different degrees. We predicted further that perinatal androgenic stimulation of the female would alter the estradiol uptake and retention characteristics in the masculine direction.

To test our hypothesis we (Green *et al.*, 1969) administered estradiol^{-3}H to male, female, and neonatally androgenized female rats. All the animals were gonadectomized in adulthood prior to hormone administration to ensure that our measurements were uninfluenced by group differences in circulating endogenous steroids. Our results are illustrated in Figs. 4, 5, and 6. We found reliable

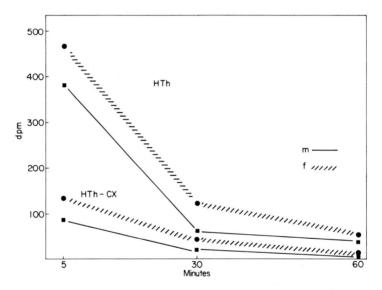

FIG. 4.   Mean radioactivity levels (disintegrations/min/mg) in adult male and female rats 5, 30, or 60 min after administration of tritiated estradiol. HTh, hypothalamic levels; HTh - CX hypothalamic minus cortex levels. (From Green, Luttge and Whalen, 1969.)

male-female differences in uptake and retention of radioactivity in hypothalamus, in the preoptic-diagonal-band region, and in whole pituitary. In each, radioactivity levels were lower in the males than in the females. In addition, neonatally androgenized females fell between the male and female groups and those females which had received 500 μg testosterone propionate 96 hr after birth were more similar to males than those which had received 100 μg TP neonatally. Thus, the data were found to be consistent with our predictions. Our

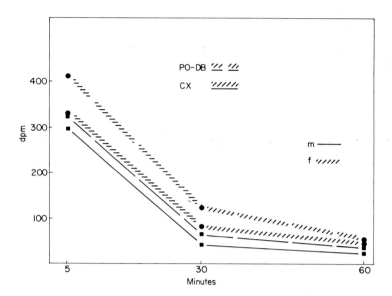

FIG. 5.   Mean radioactivity levels in adult male and female rats 5, 30, or 60 min after administration of tritiated estradiol. PO-DB, preoptic diagonal band tissue levels; CX, cortex levels. (From Green, *et al.,* 1969.)

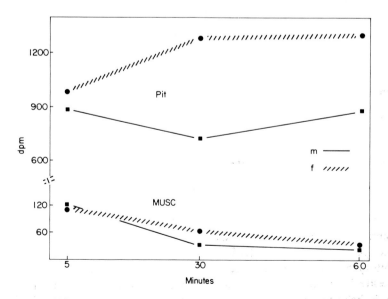

FIG. 6.   Mean radioactivity levels in adult male and female rats 5, 30, or 60 min after administration of tritiated estradiol PIT, whole pituitary levels; MUSC, muscle levels.

enthusiasm, however, was short-lived. While radioactivity levels were higher in females than in males or in androgenized females, these latter groups did show high absolute levels of radioactivity. It was impossible to conclude that androgenized animals are unable to incorporate estrogen. This conclusion is supported as well by autoradiographic demonstrations of radioactivity in the brain of male rats following treatment with tritiated estradiol (Pfaff, 1968; Stumpf, 1968). Furthermore, we soon realized that our groups differed on a dimension other than neonatal androgen stimulation; the groups differed on body weight, and in an order inverse to the degree of hormone uptake. We felt that it was entirely possible that the males (425 gm) had received a lower effective dose of tritiated estradiol than had females (324 gm). We therefore continued the study and compared the uptake of radiolabeled estradiol in male and female rats matched on body weight. The data are shown in Table I. Under these conditions males and females did not differ in the uptake of radioactivity. Subsequent work in our laboratory (Whalen and Luttge, 1970) has confirmed this basic observation. Males do not incorporate less estrogen than females.

TABLE I   Radioactivity Levels (Mean Disintegrations/min/mg±S.E.) in Brain and Peripheral Tissues of Male and Female Rats Matched for Body Weight 30 min After i.v. Administration of 6,7-^{3}H-estradiol-17β

Tissue	Male $\bar{X}$=337.8g	Female $\bar{X}$=336.0g
Cortex	51.2 ± 3.1	46.7 ± 1.4
Hypothalamus	76.6 ±3.8	74.1±4.0
Preoptic-diagonal-band	69.0±5.1	67.9±3.5
Pituitary	835.9 ±72.7	837.6± 92.5
Muscle	51.7 ±4.0	40.9± 2.4

Thus, we are able to demonstrate that androgen stimulation in the infant rat prevents the development of behavioral responsivity to estrogen and progesterone, yet we are unable to find a neural mechanism which can account for this inhibitory effect. Unfortunately, the next step toward gaining the information we desire is not at all clear. Possibly our understanding of male-female differences in behavior must await developments in the area of the molecular biology of hormone action.

REFERENCES

Beach, F. A., and Jordan, L. (1965). *Quart. J. Exp. Psychol. 8,* 121-133.

Eisenfeld, A. J., and Axelrod, J. (1965). *J. Pharmacol. Exp. Ther. 150,* 469-475.

Green, R., Luttge, W. G., and Whalen, R. E. (1969). *Endocrinology 85,* 373-378.

Harris, G. W., and Levine, S. (1962). *J. Physiol. (London) 163,* 42P-43P.

Michael, R. P. (1961). *In* "Regional Neurochemistry" S. S. Kety and J. Elkes, (eds.), Pergamon Press, Oxford.

Pfaff, D. W. (1968). *Science 161,* 1355-1356.

Phoenix, C. H., Goy, R. W., Gerall, A. A., and Young, W. C. (1959). *Endocrinology 65,* 369-382.

Stumpf, W. E. (1968). *Science 162,* 1001-1003.

Whalen, R. E. (1968). *In* "Perspectives in Reproduction and Sexual Behavior". (M. Diamond, ed.), 303-340. Indiana Univ. Press, Bloomington, Indiana.

Whalen, R. E., and Edwards. D. A. (1967). *Anat. Rec. 157,* 173-180.

Whalen, R. E., and Luttge, W. G. (1970). *Neuroendocrinology 6,* 255-263.

Whalen, R. E., and Robertson, R. T. (1968). *Psychon. Sci. 11,* 319-320.

Whalen, R. E., Edwards, D. A. Luttge, W. G., and Robertson, R. T. (1969). *Physiol. Behav. 4,* 33-40.

Young, W. C. (1965). *In* "Sex and Behavior" (F. A. Beach, ed.), p.89-107. Wiley, New York.

CHAPTER 17 Hormonal and Environmental Influences on Rat Brain Development and Behavior

Shawn Schapiro

I. INTRODUCTION

It is widely accepted that the behavioral repertoire of adult higher animals is some function of the interacting influences of both experience obtained during certain periods of CNS development and vague genetically preordained limitations of plasticity. Constitutional factors may in turn determine thresholds for effects of environmental influences. In order for these two interdependent influences to appropriately affect CNS development, a necessary biochemical climate bathing the developing neuron must also be present. Abundant evidence is accumulating that the internal biochemical environment may be a fundamental determinant of the impact that experience and genetic limitations exert on the plasticity of adult behavior.

The infant rat at birth, in contrast to the young of other species, i.e., guinea pig, horse, and cow, is a relatively primitive organism. Only slowly do its developmental potentialities unfold. Besides being blind and deaf during the first postnatal week, numerous adaptive mechanisms do not yet function effectively. These include ACTH secretion (see Schapiro, 1968a), vasomotor reflexes (Poczopko, 1961), temperature and osmotic regulation, cardiovascular, baroreceptor, and chemoreceptor reflex control (Adolph, 1965; Wekstein, 1965). As the primary responsibility of nature is to ensure survival of the newborn, it does not seem unreasonable to assume that absence of certain of these regulatory systems is in itself an adaptive device which contributes to survival of the neonate or perhaps lays the foundation for effective survival at later stages of the life cycle. Therefore, the particular ecological niche with which a species is historically identified and to which it is physiologically adapted should be associated with levels of neonatal development of specific adaptive systems vastly different from each other. Thus, at the risk of being unduly simplistic, the oppossum has well-developed grasping reflexes and is able to crawl effectively at birth after a gestation period of 12-13 days. This level of coordinated locomotor movement does not appear in the rat until about the third to fourth postnatal day following a gestation period of 21-22 days.

According to Anokhin's concept (1964) of systemogenesis, during prenatal life there is a selective maturational acceleration of specific neural functions which must be mature at the moment of birth in order for the newborn to survive. "They are evidently inborn ... and in fact, in the process of onto-genesis, they correspond demonstrably to the ecological factors of that species of animal." However, certain features of this process may provide for future adaptive success while temporarily appearing to compromise neonatal survival potential. For example, the human infant has the longest period of helplessness and maternal dependency of all animals. This prolonged temporal-experiential interval may provide for construction of a CNS into which is incorporated, largely as a function of environmental influences, a neuroanatomical foundation providing for great behavioral flexibility. Abundant clinical literature indicates that excess or deficiency of certain biochemical components in the internal environment will in some manner severely delimit the functional development of the CNS. Thus, too high a concentration of phenylalanine in the environment of the maturing neuron (as occurs in phenylketonuria) will severely delimit the later capacity of the CNS. Similarly, a deficiency of thyroxine during critical periods of the brain's growth will also impair effective CNS development. It is not inconceivable that mental abnormalities may represent some disturbance in the biochemical environment of the developing neuron that alters its responsive-ness to experience (afferent input). Failure of the brain to grow appropriately in complexity as a function of the afferent input it receives while developing will affect its later functional capability. During periods of brain growth this input normally aids in the development of a neuroanatomical framework upon which later temporary connections subserving behavior are constructed.

This chapter will be concerned with the influence of the neonatal hormonal environment on various aspects of development and behavior. It will also consider some effects of manipulating the external environment upon the development of fine dendritic structure and suggest a general theory of the mechanism whereby early experience influences later behavior.

II. NEONATAL HORMONAL MANIPULATION

In the neonatal rat immaturity of certain adaptive mechanisms may in itself be an adaptive device to aid survival during the perinatal period or provide for effective adaptation at later stages of the life cycle. Thus, it has been well established that if gonadal hormones were present in significant quantities during the first postnatal week, the serious consequences of sterility and/or inappropriate sexual responsiveness in both male and female would not become apparent until at least 5 weeks later. Evidence to date suggests that these hormones percolating through the brain [presumably the hypothalamus (Gorski, 1967)] during its period of rapid growth and development can in some way raise the adult threshold for neuroendocrine reproductive cyclicity and the elicitation of sexual behavior (Beach, 1970).

In our laboratory we have been concerned with mechanisms of adaptation during the early postnatal period. Mobilization of adrenal corticoids via ACTH stimulation occurs in the adult in response to an almost infinite array of real or imagined "stressful" stimuli. Operationally, increased secretion of adrenal cortical hormones has become the physiological criterion of stress. During the past 15 years numerous investigators (see Schapiro, 1968a) have observed that this basic adaptive mechanism functions at a very low level, if at all, during the first postnatal week. The small response that does occur in response to certain stresses, while statistically significant, is of dubious physiological or behavioral importance for the organism. The cortical hormones have profound biochemical effects in the adult, some of which, if they occurred in the infant (for example, protein catabolism), could compromise development. It seemed possible that immaturity of the ACTH secretion mechanism in the neonatal period might in some way aid survival or favorably affect adaptation. Similarly, during the first 10 days of life the rat is essentially poikilothermic, and within certain limits its body temperature assumes that of the environment (Adolph, 1957). During this time, however, levels of circulating thyroxine approximate that of the adult (Nataf and Sfez, 1961), and pituitary stores of TSH are not abnormal (Levey, 1962). Although goitrogens induce thyroid enlargement (Waterman, 1959; Mitskevich, 1959), indicating functional feedback is present, it is not yet known whether physiological activation due to temperature extremes alters thyroid secretion rate during the poikilothermic period. In this regard the steroid feedback mechanism is also functional before stress provokes ACTH secretion (Schapiro, 1962, 1965). In addition, we have observed (Schapiro, 1968b) that adrenal medullary activation in response to insulin hypoglycemia occurs within the first few days of life, long before autonomic control of heart rate and vasomotor reflexes become functional. These observations suggest that mechanisms responding to internal signals (metabolic or feedback effects) mature earlier than those responding to external signals (environmental change-stress, temperature).

The period of perinatal neuroendocrine quiescence may therefore be a device for protecting the animal against possible deleterious effects of changing hormone levels during a time of rapid growth and development of hormone-sensitive physiological systems. In order to test this assumption we administered thyroxine or cortisol to rats within the first few days of life and studied various developmental changes.

A. Growth and Development

Following a single subcutaneous injection of 200 μg cortisol acetate into the 1-day-old rat, a marked alteration in growth rate occurred. Similar observations have been described previously for mice (Schlesinger and Mark, 1964). In contrast to the mouse, however, which generally dies within a few weeks of an injection on days 1-5, the rat survives, but has an abnormal growth curve, is fertile, and has a normal pituitary adrenal response to stress (Schapiro, 1965). Neonatal cortisol administration to the hamster apparently fails to affect the growth pattern (Swanson and McKeag, 1969).

The cortisol-injected animals occasionally exhibit an abnormal pattern of tooth development. The front teeth are excessively large, curved, and if not clipped, may circle back to impinge upon the upper lip. The eyes of these "corticoid runts" open several days earlier than controls, although gross observations and neurophysiological studies (see Section D) suggest that functional vision is not precociously developed. One factor involved in growth retardation may be decreased growth hormone in the pituitary as well as almost complete absence of growth-hormone-releasing hormone in the hypothalamus-median eminence (Sawano et al., 1969).

The growth effect in rats is analogous to what has been observed in young children receiving large amounts of steroids for asthma and emphysema. However, in these children serum growth hormone is within normal limits, but growth is stunted and their tissues are apparently refractory to the anabolic effects of the hormone (Morris et al., 1968). We have not yet determined whether the corticoid runts respond normally to growth hormone.

The growth abnormality and physical appearance of the corticoid-treated rats strikingly resembles that occurring following neonatal thymectomy (Azar, 1964). Thymectomized animals, as adults, exhibit a deficient ability to produce antibodies in response to antigenic challenges (Osoba and Miller, 1963). Current thinking indicates that during early postnatal life the thymus, via a hormonal mechanism, lays the foundation for the later expression of immunological competence in the adult. As the thymus is a prime target for cortical hormone action, it seemed possible that a component at least of the "cortical runt syndrome" was related to effects upon the thymus. In support of this contention, it was subsequently observed that neonatal treatment with corticoid resulted in adult animals exhibiting an impaired ability to produce antibodies (Schapiro and Huppert, 1967) (Table I). Similar results were also obtained by Branceni and Arnason (1966) and Fachet (1966). It has been suggested that tissue transplantation grafts may also be less readily rejected in adult rats that received corticoids as infants (Fachet, 1966). Implications for clinical medicine are apparent; infants and young children are treated with corticoids for a wide range of afflictions and their immunological competence as adults has yet to be evaluated.

TABLE I Effects of a Single Injection of Cortisol on Postnatal Day 1 to 2 upon Immunological Capacity of the Adult Rat at 60 to 70 Days of Age

| Group | Body weight[a] (gm) | Immunological response[a] | | | |
| | | S. typhosa | | Sheep RBC | |
		Agglutinin titer[b]	Percent[c]	Hemolysin titer[b]	Percent[d]
Cortisol	144 (12)	0.42±.29 (12)	8 (1)	2.6±1.4 (8)	25 (2)
Control	190 (13)	3.4±.8 (13)	75 (9)	10.0± .7 (10)	100 (10)
Significance		t±3.5		t±4.3	

[a] Number of animals indicated in parentheses.

[b] Number of serial twofold serum dilutions (averages with S.E.) which gave a 3+ agglutinin response to *Salmonella typhosa* H antigen, or a 3+ hemolysin titer to sheep red blood cells.

[c] Percentage and number of animals giving 3+ agglutinin titer at three twofold serial serum dilutions or greater, or a 3+ hemolysin titer at seven twofold serial dilutions or greater.

[d] Data for thymus/body weight taken from previous publication.

Thus, an apparent permanent immunological defect results from a single injection of adrenal cortical hormone given to the infant rat at an age when immaturity of the ACTH secretion mechanism would severely limit endogenous mobilization of these hormones. It is not difficult to hypothesize that immaturity of this adaptive response during the perinatal period may provide for the later expression of adult immunological competence.

The effects of thyroxine administration (1 μg/gm) on postnatal days 2, 3, and 4 are quite different. The earliest detectable changes are in the thinning pinna of the ears. Within 3-4 days of hormone treatment the ordinarily thick rounded edge of the pinna becomes thinned and sharp borders appear. This is associated with enlargement and deepening of the convolutions and an earlier opening of the auditory meatus. In parallel with these changes, the eyes open earlier and the animals are considerably more active (Schapiro, 1968a). They tend to weigh less than untreated controls. In gross appearance they are more alert, active, and involved than controls or the cortisol-treated rats.

B. Behavioral Effects

Besides effects on growth, the most obvious difference between hormone-treated and control rats was on the development of certain behavioral and adaptive patterns.

1. Startle Reflex

This defensive reflex may proceed, developmentally, from the orientation reflex first described by Pavlov, which appears to be related to attention and learning mechanisms (see Lynn, 1966). The normal maturation of this reflex in the rat has been described by Eayrs (1964a,b). We studied the appearance of the startle reflex in normal and hormone-treated rats. Cortisol delayed the maturation of "startle" to a loud noise (toy cricket) as can be seen in Fig. 1; this correlated with effects of cortisol in delaying ear opening. Thyroxine administration, on the other hand, accelerated the appearance of the startle reflex in association with earlier age of ear-opening (Schapiro and Norman, 1967; Schapiro, 1968a,c). Thus, the ontogeny of this fundamental bioenvironmental behavioral response to external stimuli can be differentially manipulated by these hormones.

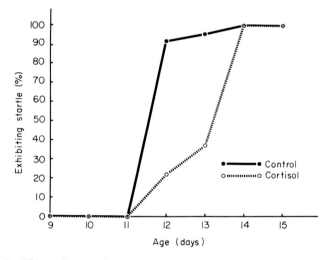

FIG. 1.   Effect of neonatal cortisol administration on maturation of startle reflex.

2. Adaptive Behavior

In searching for maturation of an organized behavioral response that is directly adaptive in nature, we accidently observed that during the first postnatal week, infant rats are unable to swim (Schapiro et al., 1970). We have found no reports in the literature on the maturation of swimming ability in the rat. Effective swimming is an adaptive response to a life-threatening situation that requires the integrated organization of a series of reflex responses, each of which is generally studied in isolation from any organized behavioral framework. These reflexes require the participation of coordinating centers at all levels of the neuraxis. Swimming ability thus may serve as a functional model with which to analyze the development of these neural elements and their plasticity. We determined that the development of swimming ability takes place progressively from aimless floundering during the first 7 days to organized contralateral reflex control and the maintaining of the head and nose above water by about day 12. Figure 2 shows representative pictures of the various stages of this development

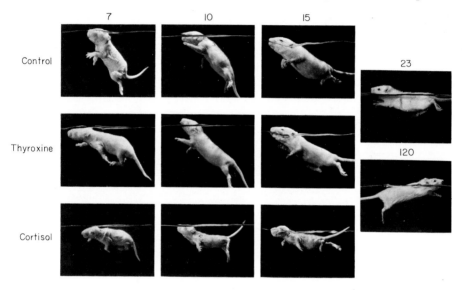

FIG. 2. Development of swimming patterns in normal and hormone-treated rats. Twenty-three and 120-day-old rats indicate the position of the front feet in parallel extension in the normal mature swimming pattern.

and demonstrates that the corticoid runt is retarded in the achievement of this vital response. Swimming ability as a function of age is shown graphically in Fig. 3. These data also indicate that the age at which swimming occurs can be altered as a function of neonatal hormone treatment, as can the rate of progression to a mature pattern.

An additional point worth commenting on is the unexpected inhibition of front feet activity that begins to occur in neonatal rats at about 15-16 days of age. From days 0-15, front feet are actively used in rapid, progressively coordinated, contralateral flexor-extensor movements during swimming. At day 15 this movement diminishes and by day 22 (7 days later), control animals swim with front legs held in inactive parallel extension as indicated in Figs. 2 and 3. Cortisol-treated rats were again delayed in the age and rate of development of this motor pattern, while thyroxine accelerated the progression of both these parameters. Neither thyroxine nor cortisol appeared to affect the sequence of

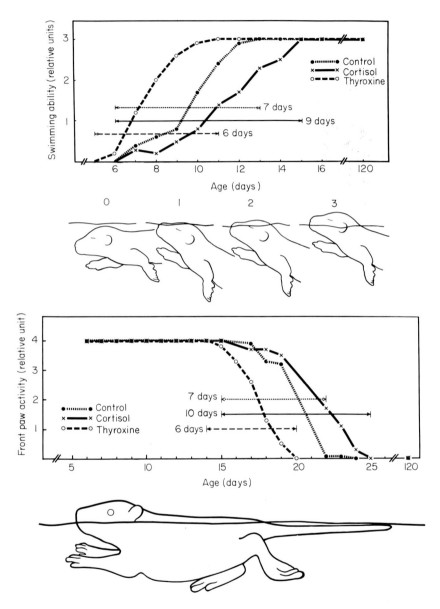

FIG. 3. Effects of neonatal hormone administration upon maturation of swimming behavior in the infant rat (a) Arbitrary scale (0-3) used to describe development of swimming activity. Horizontal lines through the graph indicate number of days encompassed in transition from units 0-3. (b) Progressive cessation of foreleg extensor-flexor movements during development of mature swimming pattern. A score of 0 corresponds to the drawing depicting relative extensor rigidity of the forefeet characteristic of the adult rat swimming position.

developmental changes. We have also observed that the pattern of front leg movement in the adult animal during free swimming depends to some extent on the species; the mouse and gerbil swim with front feet in parallel extension, while the rabbit, hamster, dog, and cat use their front feet actively in contralateral flexor-extensor movements. These species differences may reflect relative forelimb specializations as they equip different animals to function within their own historically determined ecological niches.

C. Learning

There have been few studies on the effects of perinatal administration of hormones on later learning capability. The dramatic effects of neonatal thyroxine or cortisol administration on gross development and behavior discussed above led to the obvious question as to what effects, if any, there might be on later learning ability. We compared the Lashley III Maze learning performance of 30-day-old rats that had received cortisol on postnatal day 1 with saline-treated controls. In this maze learning situation, the treated rats showed a consistent tendency toward improved performance. Similarly, improved performance on a Skinner box light discrimination task for food reward was observed. More difficult tasks may further discriminate between these two groups. Possibly related to these effects of neonatal cortisol are the observations of Money and Lewis (1966) that individuals with adrenogenital syndrome have higher I.Q.'s than matched controls; this clinical condition is associated with late fetal and/or early postnatal increased secretion of adrenal androgens.

More thorough testing was carried out on rats that received thyroxine on postnatal days 2, 3, and 4. At age 16 days the rate at which the treated rats acquired a conditioned avoidance response was assessed as described previously (Schapiro and Norman, 1967). The thyroid-treated rats learned more rapidly to avoid shock than vehicle-treated controls (Fig. 4). This difference was not solely due to their general increased locomotor activity (Schapiro, 1968c), as a preliminary passive avoidance task which required a sustained period of immobilization also produced evidence of more rapid learning. Additional passive avoidance studies will be needed to solidify confidence in these observations. The initial information-acquisition advantage demonstrated in the infant thyroxine-treated rats suggested that these animals might indicate a continued learning facility. We therefore tested hormone-treated rats when they were 35-45 days of age. For these tests we used the Lashley III Maze as before, and also an automated "Y" swimming maze, in which the alley with a safe platform was indicated by a light whose position was programmed randomly. Similar results were obtained on both tests (Schapiro, 1968c) and are shown in Table II. Much to our surprise, on both these tests the thyroid-treated animals did *not* perform as well as controls. Behavioral deficits were also referred to by Eayrs (1964a,b) in adult rats treated with thyroxine as infants. Thyroxine treatment in early postnatal life, therefore, accelerates the maturation of the CNS, judged by neonatal behavioral and learning criteria discussed above, but this appears to impair later learning ability.

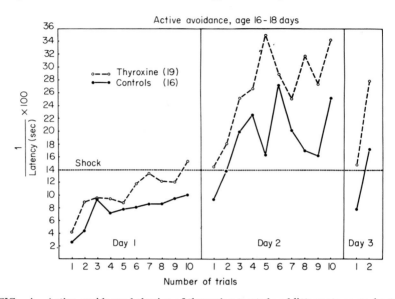

FIG. 4. Active avoidance behavior of thyroxine-treated and littermate control rats 16, 17, and 18 days old. Dotted line indicates application of shock 7 sec after placing infants on a charged grid (see text). Latency refers to time (seconds) before animals crawled to safe platform. An analysis of variance indicated that performance differences between groups on day 1 and 2 were significant at the 0.05 level and on day 3 at the 0.01 level. Number of animals indicated in parentheses.

TABLE II   Total Number of Errors Committed on Two Maze Learning Tasks by Two Different Groups of 35-45 day-old Rats that Received Thyroxine on Postnatal Days 2, 3, 4, and 5

Group	Swimming maze[a]			Lashley III maze[b]	
	Day 1	Day 2	Day 3	Day 1	Day 2
Control (10)	58	40	78	31.0	20.5
Thyroxine (10)	70	55	95	53.0	34.0

[a] Automated "Y" swimming maze: Subjects had to swim to safe platform in the correct alley indicated by a light. Alley choices recorded by photocells. A random program was used for the 14 trials conducted on each of two consecutive days. On day 3 the correct alley was one without a light cue.

[b] A standard Lashley III maze was used on the fourth day (day 1) and fifth day (day 2) after three pretraining days.

Thyroid deficiency in early postnatal life in the rat also leads to an impairment of later learning ability (Eayrs and Lishman, 1955). In this case, however, there is a retardation in appearance of developmental landmarks and of CNS ontogenesis. Thus, both accelerated CNS development and a retardation, as a function of excess or deficiency of thyroid hormone, results in a learning deficit

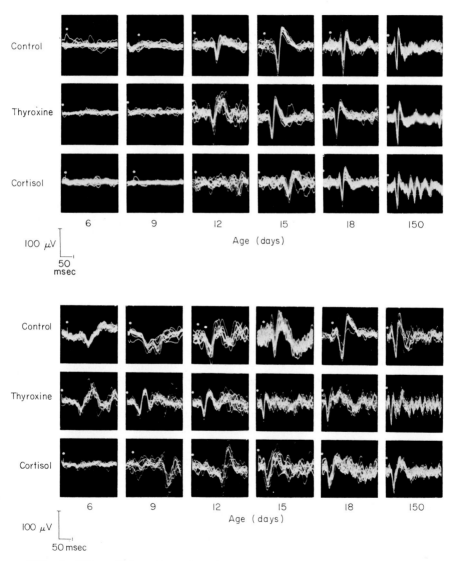

FIG. 5. Effect of thyroxine and cortisol upon the development of evoked potentials to light (visual cortex) and sciatic nerve stimulation (sensorimotor cortex). The white dot indicates onset of stimulation.

in later life. Paradoxially, neonatal cortisol administration will delay CNS development and this is associated with an apparent slight improvement in learning ability. Thus, there appears to be a certain optimum rate of progression of brain development. This may encompass a temporal-experiential interval during which dynamic organizational, biochemical, and morphological changes are taking place that provide an irreversible neuroanatomical foundation for later behavior. Too rapid a progression through these dynamic phases of brain development may prematurely limit later behavioral flexibility.

D. Effects on Neurophysiological Development

The maturation of the EEG in the normal rat has been described by many workers (see Deza, 1967). It is generally recognized that these surface potentials are not due to all-or-none action potentials, but summated waves of sub-threshold electrical excitation arising in the apical branches of large neurons (Purpura, 1960; see also Chapter 2 in this volume). In general, recognizable waves and frequencies do not appear until 8-10 days postnatally. In the adult rat "orienting" stimuli elicit an abrupt change in both EEG wave frequency and amplitude and this is considered to be one characteristic of the attention or arousal response. In addition, the development of sensory evoked responses during ontogenesis has been used as an indicator of brain maturation (see Chapter 9 in this volume for details). In normal and hormone-treated rats, we have recorded evoked potential responses to three modalities of sensory stimuli in animals of different ages. Details of the procedure have been presented elsewhere (Salas and Schapiro, 1970). Results were in general similar for each sensory modality. In control animals no cortical excitation occurred in response to light (Fig. 5) or sound stimulation before 12 days of age. Thyroxine advanced responsiveness by approximately 2-3 days and this parallels the earlier appearance of the startle response (Schapiro and Norman, 1967). The characteristics of the somatosensory response in thyroxine-treated animals also indicate a more mature pattern even at day 6, the earliest age studied (Fig. 5). In contrast to effects of thyroxine, cortisol substantially retarded the maturation of evoked responses to all three sensory modalities. Thus, the hormonal climate bathing the neonatal CNS materially alters the rate of development of the brain's responsiveness to sensory stimuli. It is generally accepted that the latency to the first component of the primary cortical response represents conduction time of the nerve impulse from the specific receptor through the sensory pathway to the cerebral cortex. Conduction time is markedly slowed in the cortisol-treated rats and this effect appears most noticeable in the visual cortex and may last into adulthood. Thyroxine, on the other hand, decreases the latency of the primary response (Fig. 6). These studies complement the classic observations of Eayrs (1961b) showing that thyroxine deficiency in early postnatal life delays develop-

ment of evoked potentials and prolongs their latency. Effects of cortisol on
neurophysiological parameters of brain function may be age dependent; thus,
before day 10, when myelinization has not yet progressed, cortisol does not
affect seizure thresholds, however, at days 11-15 the hormone increases brain
excitability (Vernadakis and Woodbury, 1963). It is of interest to note that both
cortisol and thyroxine-treated rats open their eyes 2-3 days earlier than controls.
However, in the case of cortisol, earlier eye opening is associated with *retarded*
development of the CNS and preliminary observations suggest, nonfunctional
vision. Thyroxine, on the other hand, *advances* eye opening as well as the above
behavioral and neurophysiological parameters of CNS development, and gross
observations indicate functional vision. Thus, age of eye opening is not a reliable
criterion of developmental acceleration or retardation following various experimental manipulations. Similarly, age of eye opening in the mouse may genetically bear no relationship to age of functional vision (Vestal and King, 1968).

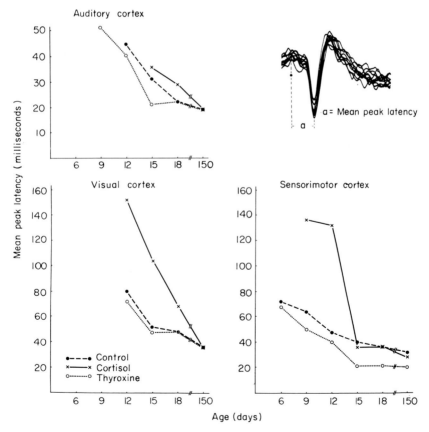

FIG. 6. Effect of neonatal hormone administration on the maturation of the mean
peak latency of the evoked response to auditory, visual, and sensory nerve stimulation.

Additional neurophysiological studies indicated that the maturation of the EEG and its response to novel stimuli were also advanced by neonatal thyroxine administration (Schapiro and Norman, 1967). The earlier appearance of the startle response, evoked potentials and EEG response to novel stimuli indicates an advanced age of bioenvironmental interaction which may contribute to the more rapid learning ability exhibited by these rats as infants. The more rapid acquisition of adult neurophysiological characteristics, as well as behavioral development, suggests an earlier consolidation of CNS organization. This accelerated neuroanatomical closure following a condensed temporal-experiential interval may contribute to the observed deficiencies of learning ability in later life.

E. Effects on Biochemistry

The effects of cortisol and thyroxine on growth, behavior, and neurophysiological parameters of CNS function suggest that certain biochemical events may also be involved and underlie these more grossly observed changes. It has been well documented that thyroxine deficiency in early life leads to profound consequences for later CNS functioning. The critical period for this to occur in the rat is within the first 10 postnatal days (Eayrs, 1961b). The infant rat has normal levels of circulating thyroxine (Nataf and Sfez, 1961) and pituitary stores of TSH are within normal limits (Levey, 1962). One of the main functions of the thyroid hormone in the adult rat is to regulate cellular metabolism and metabolic rate. As the infant rat is essentially poikilothermic, it seemed logical to assume that thyroxine did not have an important similar function during early postnatal life. In the rat, the period of poikilothermia corresponds to that period when thyroxine is necessary for the normal development of the CNS (Eayrs, 1961b). We have found that during this time (from day 1 to day 9) thyroxine is without an effect on systemic oxygen consumption or body temperature (Schapiro, 1966). In the pig, however, temperature regulation is present at birth and thyroxine exerts the expected metabolic effects (Kaciuba-Uscilko et al., 1970). Geloso et al. (1968) have reported that at days 10-12 thyroxine increased systemic metabolic rate in rats. This age corresponds to the animal's growing homeothermic capability. They did not test younger animals. Thus, this hormone and probably many others may serve a different function, at least in the rat, at different stages of development.

In the adult, the three tissues that do not exhibit an increased oxygen consumption in response to thyroxine are the testes, spleen, and brain (Barker and Klitgaard, 1952). In view of the importance of thyroxine for neonatal brain development, it is not surprising that this hormone *will* increase oxygen consumption of infant cerebral cortex and hypothalamus (Table III). Fazekas et al. (1951) had earlier reported increased oxygen consumption of whole infant rat brain in response to thyroxine. Hamburgh (1968) however, did not observe any increase in metabolic rate of the brains from 2-day-old rats treated with thyroxine *in utero*. His thorough studies indicate that developmental processes during intrauterine life are not "thyroid sensitive," whereas later developmental steps involving the nervous and skeletal system require the hormone. Furthermore, he suggests that growth hormone or elevated environmental temperature may partially compensate for this neonatal thyroxine requirement.

TABLE III   Effects of Thyroxine Administration on Whole Body, Brain, and Liver Oxygen Consumption of Infant and Adult Rats

	Age - 5 Days		Age - Adults	
	T_4	C	T_4	C
Rat[a]	21.2±.5(4)	22.5±.8(4)	27.2±.6(8)	21.5±.9(12)
Liver[b]	361±8(11)	336±39(11)	675(2)	472(2)
Cortex[b]	849±27(11)	538±20(11)	520(2)	560(2)
Hypothalamus[b]	840±100(4)	677±83(4)	763(2)	742(2)

[a] $ml = O_2/min/wt^2/3 \times 100$.

[b] $\mu l = O_2/hr/gm$ tissue.

The mechanism whereby thyroxine exerts its metabolic effect is unclear. It has been suggested (Bronk, 1963; Lee and Lardy, 1965) that the induction of α-glycerophosphate dehydrogenase (mitochondrial non-DPN dependent) may underlie the effects of the thyroid hormone on increasing tissue oxygen consumption. For this reason we studied its effects upon α-glycerophosphate dehydrogenase in liver and brain of animals at different ages (Schapiro and Percin, 1966). Thyroxine was an effective inducer of this enzyme in livers of animals at all ages and was without any effect on the brain enzyme (Fig. 7). Similar results for liver have also been reported by Geloso *et al.* (1968). Thus, in infant rats, when thyroxine does not exert a systemic metabolic effect, it still functions as a potent inducer of hepatic α-glycerophosphate dehydrogenase. Similarly, thyroxine increases metabolic rate of brain tissues in infant rats, but not that of adults, and is without effect on brain α-glycerophosphate dehydrogenase at any age. These results do not support the suggestion that α-glycerophosphate dehydrogenase induction underlies the metabolic effects of the thyroid hormone. The mechanism of action upon CNS development may be dependent upon, or related to, its calorigenic effects coupled to effects on central myelinization and/or protein metabolism. Hamburgh (1968) has reported that thyroxine accelerates myelinogenesis in tissue cultured cerebella from newborn rats. Using brain cholesterol as a crude measure of myelin effects, we have also observed that in the infant rat brain, but not in the adult, thyroxine increases cholesterol levels (Schapiro, 1966). In addition, the enzyme acetylcholinesterase is also increased. These data would suggest that thyroxine produces an accelerated progression of central myelinization.

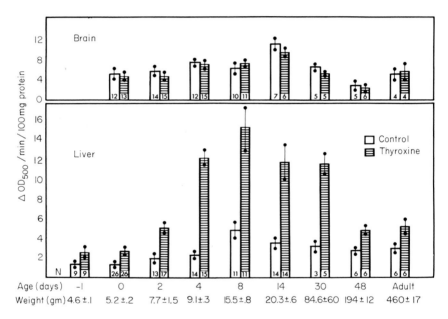

FIG. 7. Effect of thyroxine on activity of mitochondrial α-glycerophosphate dehydrogenase in livers and brains of rats at different ages. Values shown include standard error. Thyroxine (1 μg/gm body weight) injected on two consecutive days and tissue removed on the third day. Parturition is indicated by 0. Body weights were the same in both control and injected animals and the values shown represent the pooled averages with S.E.'s. Fetuses weighing 2-3 gm had no measurable activity. N indicates the number of determinations. Before 4 days of age each measurement was made on a pool of 2-3 livers or brains. After day 2 individual determinations were made.

Several studies indicate that thyroxine increases protein synthesis (amino acid incorporation) in infant rat brain. In the adult brain, thyroxine inhibits incorporation or has no effect (Gelber *et al.*, 1964). This differential effect on brain protein synthesis may be related to effects on oxygen consumption in the infant but not the adult brain (see Table III). Effects on brain development may also be coupled to these protein metabolic responses. The experiments of Gelber *et al.*

(1964) were carried out on 14-day-old rats. As the critical age for effects of thyroxine precede this, it would seem necessary to study younger animals and correlate changing amino acid incorporation sensitivity to thyroxine with the hormone's effects on the brain during its stages of thyroxine sensitivity.

Differential effects of thyroxine on infant and adult rat brain metabolism may be determined to some extent by availability of thyroxine to the brain. For example, Peterson et al. (1966) compared the brain's capacity to remove thyroid hormones from the blood in 1, 8, and 21-day-old rats. More of the hormone (as a function of the injected amount) entered the brain of the newborn and was bound to subcellular brain components than at the other ages. Decreased plasma binding in the youngest animals may have contributed to this, and also to the shorter metabolic half-life in the 1-day-old (28 min), than either the 8-day-old (56 min) or the 21-day-old (70 min) animals.

Adult rats and children raised on inadequate diets exhibit learning difficulties analogous to those obtained in neonatal thyroid deficiency (Barnes et al., 1966; Cabak and Najdanvic, 1965; see also Chapter 19 in this volume). Maturation of evoked potentials to light and sound are also delayed in nutrition-deprived infant rats (Mourek et al., 1967), further indicating that there may be a relationship between neonatal brain protein metabolism and thyroxine effects on CNS development and later functioning (see Eayrs, 1961a). These effects on protein synthesis, cholesterol, and acetylcholinesterase lend more basic support to our observations that thyroxine accelerates neurophysiological and behavioral organization of the CNS as a function of nonspecific influences on brain metabolism.

Effects of adrenal cortical hormones on biochemical aspects of brain development have been less systematically explored. The severe behavioral changes that occur would suggest marked alterations in biochemical substrates. In general the observations cited earlier indicate a delay in CNS organizational development and integrative function. Brain cholesterol in young animals receiving cortisol as infants was found to be decreased (Schapiro, 1965) and this may be presumed to represent a decreased rate of progression of myelinization. This conclusion is strengthened by an early suggestion that cortisol delays myelinization in young rats (Field, 1955). Additional studies by Howard (1965) have demonstrated that neonatal cortisol administration appears to interfere with the normal progressive increase in brain DNA that occurs in the mouse between ages 2-7 days. The hormone "completely prevented the increase in cell numbers that normally occurred . . . during this age period." The brain RNA increase with age was less affected. Effects of fasting, although in the same direction, were of considerably less magnitude. The pattern of normal whole brain DNA increase with age up to about day 14 in the rat has also been described (Winnick and Noble, 1965). In the cortisol-treated rat, whole brain DNA and RNA increase was blocked by cortisol (Fig. 8). However, recent work by Fish and Winnick (1969) indicates that protein, DNA, and RNA increase at different rates in different regions of the brain and it is likely that effects of cortisol on all brain areas are not the same. The cellular structures whose development is compromised by corticoid treatment and which contribute to the DNA/RNA changes observed are also unclear. Our work implicates the neuron as at least one target system and this is supported by histological studies which will be discussed in the next section. In the older literature (Sugita, 1918; Smith, 1934) it has been reported that cortical neurons may increase as much as 29% between postnatal days 2 and 7. As DNA levels remained stable in the corticoid-treated rats, it is possible that the hormone retards this neuron increase and some of the behavioral and electrical changes observed are reflections of this. It has been reported that cortisol both accelerates the rate of development of glial cells in tissue culture (Nadell and Vernadakis, 1970) and induces glyceral phosphate dehydrogenase in a cloned line of tissue-cultured glia from brain stem and cerebella of infant rats (de Vellis and Inglish, 1970). These findings, together with our observations, suggest that during development glia and neurons respond in opposite fashion to corticosteroids in the internal environment. This reciprocal metabolic relationship may even be a fundamental characteristic of CNS function; Hyden and Lange (1961) have shown, for example, that in response to vestibular stimuli the involved neurons exhibit increased metabolic and synthetic activity while surrounding glial elements are generally inhibited.

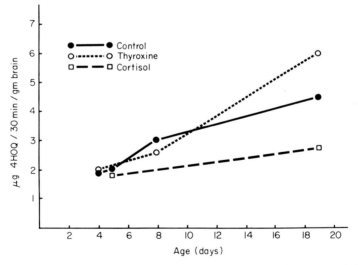

FIG. 8. Brain monoamine oxidase activity following the administration of thyroxine or cortisol to the infant rat. (From Kraml, 1965.)

As mentioned earlier, cortisol-treated animals as adults tend to be smaller and appear to be more irritable and nervous. In other ways, (e.g., retarded rate of development and locomotor activity) they seem to resemble rats thyroidectomized in early infancy. For this reason we assessed systemic metabolic rate, serum PBI and circulating thyroxine. Results shown in Table IV indicate that metabolic rates are significantly higher in the cortisol-treated rats, but that this is not due to any change in the other indices of thyroid function. We assume, therefore, that the increase in metabolism is not thyroidal in origin.

TABLE IV   Effects of Neonatal Cortisol Treatment on Weight, Metabolic Rate, and Thyroid Function of the Rat

	Weight (gm)		Metabolic rate[a]		PBI ($\mu g/100cm^3$)		T$_4$ ($\mu g/100cm^3$)	
	HC	C	HC	C	HC	C	HC	C
	46±3	76±4	23.3±.5	19.9±.4	4.9±.5	5.3±.3	5.2±.4	4.9±.4
N	42	40	42	40	5	5	5	5
Sig.	0.001		0.001		NS		NS	
	186±22	243±20	20.5±.7	18.4±.6	3.1±.3	3.8±.2	—	—
N	16	17	20	20	12	10		
Sig.	0.05		0.05		NS			

[a] Metabolic rate = $cm^3 O_2/min/wt^2/3 \times 100$.

Developmental curves for many enzymes involved in the metabolism of presumed neurotransmitters have been described (Karki *et al.,* 1962; Van den Berg *et al.,* 1965; Bennett and Giarman, 1965). One of these, monoamine oxidase, gradually increases in activity during the first two postnatal weeks. We have observed that cortisol treatment delays, while thyroxine accelerates the ontogeny of this enzyme (Fig. 9). The observations of Shih and Eiduson (1969) indicate that monoamine oxidase exists in several isozyme forms but whether all forms are equally affected is not clear. The effects on cholesterol deposition, monoamine oxidase activity, and brain DNA complement our behavioral and neurophysiological observations and indicate that delayed biochemical ontogeny underlies delayed functional development.

F. Effects on Neuron Development and Morphology

In previous sections it was pointed out that the neonatal hormonal climate can profoundly affect the development of the CNS. We are concerned here with how this may relate to the ontogeny of those functional units of the brain, the synapse, whose multitudinous interconnections represent the neuroanatomical substrate of behavior. We therefore decided to study the effect of hormone administration upon the maturation of the synaptic loci (dendritic spines) in the visual-auditory cortex. The growing body of knowledge about the dendritic spine, as a distinctive feature of the postsynaptic apparatus, has recently been

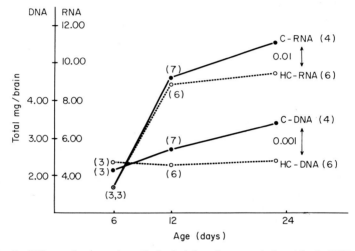

FIG. 9. Effects of neonatal cortisol administration on whole rat brain RNA and DNA at different ages. Figures in parentheses indicate number of animals.

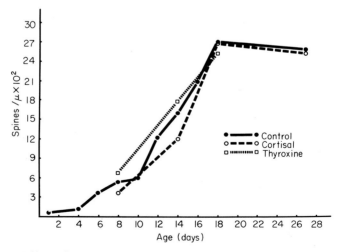

FIG. 10. Effect of neonatal hormone treatment upon the maturation of dendritic spines on the visual cortex pyramidal cell. Composite values represent averages from apical, basilar, terminal, and lateral branches of the dendrite tree.

reviewed by Scheibel and Scheibel (1968; and is discussed at length in Chapter 13 of this volume). These lateral extensions off the dendrite were first described by Cajal. Cortical dendrites of the neonatal kitten do not have spines (Scheibel and Scheibel, 1968) and in the rat they are also absent at birth and only obtain adult values at the time of weaning (Schapiro, 1968c). The spine density of the four different dendritic loci on pyramidal cells, described by Globus and Scheibel, (1967), were averaged in animals of various ages. Figure 10 indicates their normal developmental curve and the effects of cortisol and thyroxine (from work in progress in collaboration with Globus). Cortisol treatment delayed and thyroxine accelerated spine ontogeny, although the actual spine density finally obtained at day 18 does not appear to be different from untreated controls. It is tempting to suggest that the behavioral and neurophysiological retardation following cortisol administration is related to spine development. Similarly accelerated spine development with thyroxine may directly underlie precocial ontogeny of these parameters of CNS maturation. The mechanism whereby these hormones differentially affect neuron development is unclear.

Eayrs (1964a,b; Eayrs and Lishman, 1955) has shown that thyroxine deficiency decreases cerebral parenchymal circulation. This would affect the nutritional environment of the developing neuron, thus limiting its growth and organizational interconnections. In addition, neuron size, dendritic density, and areas of possible axodendritic interaction are also diminished. Increased local metabolic activity in response to thyroxine could cause regional vasodilation which would in turn shunt blood to their more metabolically active regions. This accelerated brain growth, however, may not necessarily be advantageous. As suggested previously, a compressed temporal-experiential interval may prematurely foreclose behavioral adaptability. In fact, an optimum interval may be necessary for brain development and experience consolidation. During this time afferent input is constructing a neuroanatomical foundation for later behavior. It is therefore not a coincidence that at the normal age of weaning, when the young must have acquired a behavioral repertoire to function independently, the spine complement has reached a developmental plateau, as have many other CNS biochemical and neurophysiological parameters (see Schapiro and Vukovich, 1970). The complexity of spine (synaptic) interconnections established during this time may represent that foundation. The behavioral patterns essential for independent survival are determined by the organization of these interconnections and they are therefore relatively difficult to redirect. As suggested by Scott (1962), the basic organizational process can be influenced only when it is occurring. As both neonatal thyroid deficiency and excess impair later learning, an optimal *stable* level of thyroid hormone may be necessary to ensure appropriate organizational development of the brain. Immaturity of the temperature-activated pituitary-thyroid axis provides for such a stable condition. As the infant rat is largely poikilothermic and effects of thyroxine on systemic metabolic rate and body temperature are negligible, one of the functions of thyroxine during this period could be to provide an optimal biochemical climate for the developing brain.

In the case of adrenal cortical hormones, immaturity of the stress-activated pituitary-adrenal axis also would provide a stable corticoid climate for the developing nervous system. Fluctuating levels of such hormones in response to an almost infinite variety of nonspecific stresses would all be expected to have the same effect on the developing nervous system and such a generalized response, as far as the organizing brain is concerned, would clearly not be adaptive in nature. In addition, effects on later immune capability might well be compromised. Preliminary results have indicated that the delayed CNS development following neonatal cortical hormone treatment may have improved learning ability slightly (see also Money and Lewis, 1966). The increased period of CNS growth and spine development, if not too severe, as in neonatal inanition (Barnes *et al.*, 1966; Rajalakshmi *et al.*, 1965; Cabak and Najdanvic, 1965) may facilitate consolidation of experience, and provide for a more flexible behavioral repertoire in later life.

III. ENVIRONMENTAL INFLUENCES ON BRAIN DEVELOPMENT

It is generally accepted that environmental influences during certain critical periods of early postnatal life have profound effects on later behavior. It was

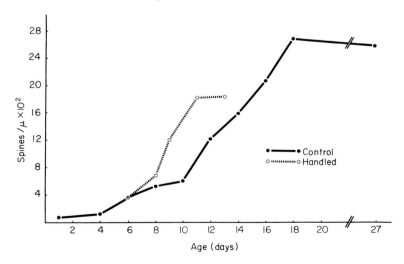

FIG. 11. Development of dendritic spines on pyramidal cells from the visual cortex of control rats and rats subject to multidimensional environmental stimulation (handled). Values shown are averages obtained from four different stations on the dendrite tree.

suggested in the previous section that a mechanism for this effect may involve influences of afferent input on the developing synaptic dendritic spine process so as to structure interconnections into organizational patterns which are relatively difficult to redirect. Numerous investigators have shown that marked differences in sensory experience after weaning (days 21-22) will produce slight biochemical and morphological changes in the CNS. The changes reported involve weight and acetylcholinesterase activity in cortical areas as well as regional changes in norepinephrine and dopamine (see Rosenzweig *et al.*, 1969; and Geller, this volume). The rat cortex by days 21-22 is essentially biochemically, morphologically, and neurophysiologically mature and the age of CNS plasticity is largely over. In addition, as discussed above, at weaning the neuroanatomical foundation underlying behavior is sufficiently organized to enable the young to function independently.

Qualitative studies in the cat (Scheibel and Scheibel, 1964) and quantitative studies in the mouse (Ruiz-Marcos and Valverde, 1969) and rat (Schapiro, 1968c) indicate that the major synaptic locus, the dendritic spine, appears slowly during development in association with increasingly complex behavioral and neurophysiological changes. Decreased visual stimulation (Valverde, 1967; Ruiz-Marcos and Valverde, 1969) or interruption of the visual pathway during periods of spine development decreases the number of spines in the visual cortex (Globus and Scheibel, 1967). It therefore seemed possible that afferent stimulation during the period of spine development could modify their ontogeny and the complexity of their interconnections. This in turn may be related to later behavior capability. Using this hypothesis as a model we subjected newly born litters of rats to a wide range of sensory stimuli, from the day of birth until they were killed at 8, 9, 11, and 13 days of age (Schapiro and Vukovich, 1970). Other litters were left undisturbed. Dendritic spine density in the stimulated animals at each of the ages studied was greater than in control animals (Fig. 11). Furthermore, the number of neurons visualized by the rapid Golgi technique was also increased in the manipulated animals (Table V). In association with advanced spine development, the activity of acetylcholinesterase and monoamine oxidase was also increased; in the stimulated animals there was no evidence of increased thyroid activity (Table VI).

IV. CONCLUSIONS: HORMONAL-ENVIRONMENTAL INTERACTIONS DURING EARLY POSTNATAL LIFE

In the preceding sections the marked effects upon the CNS of manipulating the internal (hormonal) and external environment (afferent input) have been emphasized. There are numerous examples of nonendocrine biochemical perturbations during early development which also affect the functional capability of the nervous system (Menckes, 1966). Hormones therefore, may be one of many factors in the perinatal internal environment that play an important role in the nonspecific development of the brain and later behavior of the organism. Within the framework of genetic limitations, it is the qualitative afferent inputs of early experience that differentially direct CNS organization into patterns which underlie the neuroanatomical foundation for later learning and behavior.

The biochemical-hormonal climate bathing the growing neuron at this time may provide an optimal internal environment for them to respond metabolically and organizationally to the afferent input associated with early experience. Thus, the internal environment may be a fundamental determinant of the impact that experience will have on the plasticity of the brain and its organizational complexity. In the absence of an appropriate internal environment, construction of this neuroanatomical foundation may be limited or abnormal.

TABLE V   Effect of sensory stimulation upon the number of cortical pyramidal cells visualizable by the rapid Golgi technique[a]

	Age in days	Treatment	Total number of sections	Total number of cells	Cells/Section
Series A	8	Control (3)	44	754	16.94
	8	Stimulated (3)	40	985	24.62
	11	Control (3)	59	1479	24.86
	11	Stimulated (3)	62	1996	31.94
	12	Control (3)	35	983	26.66
	12	Stimulated (2)	38	1199	31.56
	16	Control (3)	73	942	12.82
	16	Stimulated (3)	71	1055	15.10
Series B	9	Control (3)	72	1453	20.18 ± 2.92
	9	Stimulated (3)	67	2525	37.69 ± 4.82[b]
	11	Control (3)	74	1850	25.00 ± 2.19
	11	Stimulated (3)	75	2688	35.84 ± 3.92[c]
	13	Control (3)	55	706	12.84 ± 1.08
	13	Stimulated (4)	74	1439	19.45 ± 1.44[b]

[a] Number of animals in parentheses. In the first experiment, Series A, statistical analysis was not possible as individual slides were not tallied separately within each treatment group. In the second experiment, Series B, done several months later, the stained cells in each cortical section were tabulated individually. Data shown are with S.E. (Schapiro and Vukovich, 1970).

[b] Difference between stimulated and control significant at 0.001 level.

[c] Difference between stimulated and control significant at 0.01 level.

TABLE VI   Effects of Environmental Stimulation on Thyroid Function and Whole Brain Acetylcholinesterase and Monoamine Oxidase Activity of 16-day-old rats

	PBI (μg/100cm^3)	T$_4$	MAO[a,b]	Acetylcholinesterase[c,d]	
Stimulated (8)	5.14±.04	4.51±.25	5.75±0.7	1177±27(a)	7.11±.16(b)
Controls (8)	5.02±.07	4.98±.09	4.13±0.5	992±20(a)	6.06±.14(b)

[a] Significant at 0.05.

[b] Micrograms hydroxyquinoline formed/30 min/gm brain.

[c] Significant at 0.001.

[d] Micromoles acetylthiocholine hydrolyzed/min/mg protein (a), and /gm brain (b).

Since the early suggestion by Cajal (1895), it has been shown by many investigators (see Sokoloff, 1961), including the pioneering work of Serota and Gerard (1938), that certain parts of the adult brain receive an increased blood supply and have increased metabolic activity at moments of use. Interesting indirect studies supporting these observations on humans have also been reported (Chyatte et al., 1967). In a provocative book, Klosovski (1963) maintains that "each nerve cell develops under the influence of impulses reaching it from peripheral receptors." He suggested earlier (1961) that, "From the very period of development when the nerve fibers from the peripheric apparatus grow into the brain substrate, the nerve impulse . . . begins to play an ever increasing role in the construction of the brain." It is moreover, not unlikely that during development, afferent input causes regional changes in CNS metabolism and blood flow and these in turn play a fundamental role in directing the organization of the brain.

As a working hypothesis, therefore, we propose that:

1. The period of eary postnatal life, when experience has the greatest effect on organization, growth, development, and future capability of the CNS ("critical period") occurs prior to weaning, at the time when the most dynamic changes are taking place in the biochemical and morphological elements of the nervous system.

2. The rate at which these dynamic changes occur is subject, within genetic limits, to modification by both internal (biochemical-hormonal) and external environmental influences. A certain optimal biochemical climate and temporal-experiential interval is necessary for the establishment of the appropriate web of

neuroanatomical interconnections that provide the foundation for later behavior.

3. Afferent input during the "critical period" increases neuronal metabolism and increases blood flow to the neuron and the associated field involved in relaying and responding to the input. This increased activity in turn will affect the rate of maturation, characteristics of organization, and the synaptic interconnections established by that neuronal field.

4. The ability of the emerging neuronal field to appropriately respond to afferent input is determined in some measure by the biochemical climate in which the neuron is developing. Circulating hormone levels are one important component of the neuronal climate.

5. The relative immaturity of certain neuroendocrine mechanisms serves to maintain the circulating hormone levels bathing the developing CNS within relatively stable limits during "critical periods" of the brain's development.

6. Later behavioral flexibility (plasticity) is directly related to the complexities of the interconnections established between synaptic units during this early postnatal period when synaptic loci (dendritic spines) are developing.

7. This mechanism may thus provide the neuroanatomical framework underlying the complex of phenomena generally referred to as the influence of early experience on development and behavior.

REFERENCES

Adolph, A. F. (1957). *Quart. Rev. Biol. 32,* 89.
Adolph, A. F. (1965). *Amer. J. Physiol. 204,* 1095.
Anokhin, P. K. (1964). *Prog. Brain Res. 9,* 54.
Azar, H. A. (1964). *Proc. Soc. Exp. Biol. Med. 116,* 817.
Barker, S. B., and Klitgaard, H. M. (1952). *Amer. J. Physiol. 170,* 81.
Barnes, R. H., Cunnfold, S. R., Zimmerman, R. R., Simmons, R., MacLeod, B., and Krook, L. (1966). *J. Nutr. 89,* 399.
Beach, F. A. (1970). *In* "The Biopsychology of Development" (E. Tobach, L.R. Aronson, and E. Shaw, eds.). Academic Press, New York. (in press).
Bennett, D. S., and Giarman, N. J. (1965). *J. Neurochem. 12,* 911.
Branceni, D., and Arnason, B. G. (1966). *Immunology 10,* 35.
Bronk, J. R. (1963). *Science 141,* 816.
Cabak, V., and Najdanvic, R. (1965). *Arch. Dis. Childhood 40,* 532.
Chyatte, C., Mele, K. E., and Anderson, B. L. R. (1967). *Int. J. Neuropsychiat. 3,* 360.
de Vellis, J., Inglish, D., and Galey, F. *In* "Cellular Aspects of Growth and Differentiation in Nervous Tissue." (D. Pease, ed.), Univ. Calif. Press, Los Angeles (in press).
Deza, L. (1967). *Exp. Neurol. 17,* 425.
Eayrs, J. T. (1961a). *Growth 25,* 175.
Eayrs, J. T. (1961b). *J. Endocrinol. 22,* 409.
Eayrs, J. T. (1964a). *Arch. Biol. 75,* 529.
Eayrs, J. T. (1964b). *In* "Brain-Thyroid Relationships" (M. P. Cameron and M. O'Connor, eds.), p. 60. Churchill, London.
Eayrs, J. T., and Lishman, W. A. (1955). *Brit. J. Anim. Behav. 3,* 17.

Fachet, J. (1966). *Acta Morphol. Acad. Sci. Hung. 14,* 269.

Fazekas, J. F., Graves, F. B., and Alman, R. W. (1951). *Endocrinology 48,* 169.

Field, E. J. (1955). *J. Anat. 89,* 201.

Fish, I., and Winick, M. (1969). *Pediat. Res. 3,* 407.

Gelber, S., Campbell, P. L. Deibler, G. E., and Sokoloff, L. (1964). *J. Neurochem. 11,* 221.

Geloso, J. P., Hemon, P., LeGrand, J., LeGrand, C., and Jost, A. (1968). *Gen. Comp. Endocrinol. 10,* 191.

Globus, A., and Scheibel, A. B. (1967). *Exp. Neurol. 18,* 116.

Gorski, R. A. (1967). *Anat. Rec. 157,*63.

Hamburgh, M. (1968). *Gen. Comp. Endocrinol. 10,* 198.

Howard, E. (1965). *J. Neurochem. 12,* 181.

Hyden, H., and Lange, P. (1961). *In* "Regional Neurochemistry" (S. S. Kety and J. Elkes, eds.), p. 190. Pergamon Press, Oxford.

Kaciuba-Uscilko, H., Leggf, K. F., and Mount, L. E. (1970). *J. Physiol. (London) 206,* 229.

Karki, N., Kuntzman, R., and Brodie, B. B. (1962). *J. Neurochem. 9,* 53.

Klosovski, B. N. (1961). *Plzen. Lek. Sb.* Supp. 3, 33.

Klosovski, B. N. (1963). *In* "The Development of the Brain and its Disturbance by Harmful Factors," p. 24. Pergamon Press, Oxford.

Kraml, M. (1965). *Biochem. Pharmacol. 14,* 1684.

Lee, Y. P., and Lardy, H. A. (1965). *J. Biol. Chem. 240,* 1427.

Levey, H. A. (1962). *Endocrinology 71,* 763.

Lynn, R. (1966). *Int. Seri. Monog. Exp. Psychol. 3,* 1-118.

Menckes, J. H. (1966). *Annu. Rev. Med. 17,* 1.

Mitskevich, M. S. (1959). "Glands of Internal Secretion in the Embryonic Development of Birds and Mammals," PST Cat. No. 73. NSF Found.

Money, J., and Lewis, V. (1966). *Bull. Johns Hopkins Hosp. 118,* 365.

Morris, H. G., Jorgenson, J. R., and Jenkins, S. A. (1968). *J. Clin. Invest. 47,* 427.

Mourek, J., Himwich, W. A., Myslivecek, J., and Callison, D. A. (1967). *Brain Res. 6,* 241.

Nadell, B., and Vernadakis, A. (1970). *3rd Annu. Winter Conf. Brain Res.,* Snowmass, Colorado.

Nataf, B., and Sfez, M. (1961). *C.R. Soc. Biol. 155,* 1235.

Osoba, D., and Miller, J. F. (1963). *Nature (London) 199,* 653.

Peterson, N. A., Nataf, B. M., Chaikoff, I. L., and Ragupathy, E. (1966). *J. Neurochem. 13,* 933.

Poczopko, P. A. (1961). *J. Cell. Comp. Physiol. 57,* 175.

Purpura, D. P. (1960). *In* "Inhibition of the Nervous System and GABA" (E. Roberts, ed.), p. 495. Pergamon Press, Oxford.

Rajalakshmi, R., Govindarajan, K. R., and Ramakrishnan, C. V. (1965). *J. Neurochem. 12,* 261.

Ramon y Cajal, S. (1895). *Rev. Med. Cir. Pract. 36,* 479.

Rosenzweig, M. R., Bennett, E. L., Diamond, M. C., Wu, S.-Y., Slagle, R. W., and Saffran, E. (1969). *Brain Res. 14,* 427.

Ruiz-Marcos, A., and Valverde, F. (1969). *Exp. Brain Res. 8,* 284.

Salas, M., and Schapiro, S. (1970). *Physiol. Behav. 5,* 7.

Sawano, S., Arimura, A., Schally, A. V., Redding, T. W., and Schapiro, S. (1969). *Acta Endocrinol. 61,* 57.

Schapiro, S. (1962). *Endocrinology 71,* 986.

Schapiro, S. (1965). *Proc. Soc. Exp. Biol. Med. 120,* 771.

Schapiro, S. (1966). *Endocrinology 78,* 527.

Schapiro, S. (1968a). *In* "Early Experience and Behavior" (G. Newton and S. Levine, eds.), pp. 198-257. Thomas, Springfield, Ill.

Schapiro, S. (1968b). *Endocrinology 82,* 1065.
Schapiro, S. (1968c). *Gen. Comp. Endocrinol. 10,* 214.
Schapiro, S., and Huppert, M. (1967). *Proc. Soc, Exp. Biol. Med. 124,* 744.
Schapiro, S., and Norman, R. (1967). *Science 155,* 1279.
Schapiro, S., and Percin, C. J. (1966). *Endocrinology 79,* 1075.
Schapiro, S., and Vukovich, K. R. (1970). *Science 167,* 292.
Schapiro, S., Salas, M., and Vukovich, K. R. (1970). *Science 168,* 147.
Scheibel, M. E., and Scheibel, A. B. (1964). *Prog. Brain Res. 9,* 6.
Scheibel, M. E., and Scheibel, A. B. (1968). *Commun. Behav. Biol. 1,* 231.
Schlesinger, M., and Mark, R. (1964). *Science 143,* 965.
Scott, J. P. (1962). *Science 138,* 949.
Serota, H., and Gerard, R. (1938). *J. Neurophysiol. 1,* 115.
Shih, J. H., and Eiduson, S. (1969). *Nature (London) 224,* 1309.
Smith, C. G. (1934). *J. Comp. Neurol. 60,* 319.
Sokoloff, L. (1961). *In* "Regional Neurochemistry" (S. S. Kety and J. Elkes, eds.), p. 107. Pergamon Press, Oxford.
Sugita, N. (1918). *J. Comp. Neurol. 29,* 61.
Swanson, H. H., and McKeag, A. M. (1969). *Horm. Behav. 1,* 1.
Valverde, F. (1967). *Exp. Brain Res. 3,* 337.
Van den Berg, C. J., Van Kempen, G. M. J., Schade, J. P., and Veldstra, H. (1965). *J. Neurochem. 12,* 863.
Vernadakis, A., and Woodbury, D. M. (1963). *J. Pharmacol. Exp. Ther. 139,* 110.
Vestal, B. M., and King, J. A. (1968). *Develop. Psychobiol. 1,* 30.
Waterman, A. J. (1959). *In* "Comparative Endocrinology" (A. Gorbman, ed.), p. 351. Wiley, New York.
Wekstein, D. R. (1965). *Amer. J. Physiol. 208,* 1259.
Winick, M., and Noble, A. (1965). *Develop. Biol. 12,* 451.

CHAPTER 18 Encephalization and the Neural Control of Sleep

Dennis J. McGinty

I. INTRODUCTION

The initiation and maintenance of sleep is a complex behavioral activity. In the adult mammal, sleep has many properties in common with appetitive behaviors such as feeding and drinking. In each case, given the accessibility of the objective—food, water, or in the case of sleep, the opportunity to assume and maintain a relaxed posture—the behavior occurs in predictable quantities and with certain temporal patterns. If the objective is not accessible, it will be sought with great intensity. When the deprivation of the objective is terminated, there is usually a rebound increase in its "consumption." These characteristics, which indicate a behavioral regulation of the physiological state of the organism, constitute part of the evidence that sleep is an active appetitive behavior. This approach is in contrast to the older passive theory of sleep which states that sleep represents a lack of behavior in the absence of arousal from sensory stimulation or other drives. While there is general agreement on the inadequacy of the passive theory (see below), there is little consensus on how sleep can be studied and understood. The present discussion will elaborate on the comparison between sleep and other active appetitive behaviors. This point of view provides a framework for understanding the ontogeny of sleep.

It is proposed that the ontogeny of sleep may be viewed as a process of encephalization of behavior. During development, the neural control of sleep appears to shift from a mechanism organized within the brain stem to forebrain mechanisms. This first part of this paper will examine some of the evidence and the problems in the experimental study of this hypothesis, as well as its implications for current theories of sleep. The second section will examine some factors which modulate forebrain influences on patterns of sleep.

335

II. SLEEP IN ADULTS AND IMMATURE MAMMALS

A. Adults

Sleep in adult mammals consists of two basic states: quiet sleep (slow wave sleep) and active sleep (REM sleep, paradoxical sleep). The subdivisions of quiet sleep in man, stages 2, 3, and 4 (Dement and Kleitman, 1957) are grouped together here although they may require separate consideration in some cases. The properties of these basic sleep types have been investigated extensively (Jouvet, 1967a; Kales, 1969). Briefly, adult sleep always begins with quiet sleep, a state characterized by the absence of voluntary motor activity, regular autonomic activity, and a synchronized EEG. Quiet sleep is followed by active sleep, characterized by complete atonia of neck and facial muscles, phasic motor activity including rapid eye movements and muscular twitches, irregular autonomic activity, and desynchronized EEG. A sleep period, such as the night's sleep in man or the equivalent in animals, usually consists of several consecutive cycles, each consisting of an episode of quiet sleep followed by an episode of active sleep. The alternation of the sleep states occurs regularly, defining a quiet sleep-active sleep cycle. It has been found that members of each mammalian species "consume" characteristic amounts of both quiet sleep and active sleep and exhibit a characteristic quiet sleep-active sleep cycle.

This paper will emphasize the *behavioral* aspects of sleep such as the amounts of the sleep states, their temporal patterns, and postural characteristics. Recent research has focused on the electrophysiological correlates and *consequences* of sleep and the differences between quiet sleep and active sleep. Nevertheless, the similarity between these states may be as important as the difference. Indeed, although sleep has long been the subject of scientific curiosity, the existence of two states was not appreciated until quite recently (Aserinsky and Kleitman, 1953).

A distinction between sleep behavior and physiological consequences of sleep may be clarified by a comparison with the behavior associated with feeding. Feeding behavior generally refers to the searching for, selection, and ingestion of food. The consequences of feeding behavior include the digestion of food, distribution of nutrients through the body, and their metabolism. The latter activities are not controlled directly by the neural mechanisms of feeding behavior. Similarly, with sleep we should distinguish between the mechanisms which bring about, maintain, and terminate sleep on one hand, and the *consequential* changes on the brain and body which are correlated with the occurrence of sleep. As with nutrition, the consequential events may be the bases for the physiological requirement for sleep, that is, the restorative processes that are presumed to underly sleep. However, the neural mechanisms that control sleep behavior are distinct from the consequential correlates of sleep just as the neural mechanisms of feeding are distinct from the nutritional changes in cells.

As an example, the equation of behavioral sleep with EEG configurations is misleading. Quiet sleep can occur without EEG synchronization following neo-decortication (Jouvet and Michel, 1958; Kleitman and Camille, 1933), certain pharmacological treatments (Bradley and Elkes, 1953), and most important in the present context, in neonatal animals (see below). The neural mechanisms underlying behavioral sleep must be distinct from those resulting in EEG synchronization. Many instances of EEG synchronization may reflect *passive* changes in forebrain neural networks that occur in the absence of impinging sensory input (Andersson and Wolpow, 1964; Bremer, 1936).

We are greatly hampered by the absence of unambiguous physiological or behavioral criteria for sleep (Jouvet, 1967a). Sleep is defined as a state characterized by a configuration of behavioral or electrophysiological properties. The most compelling criterion, reduced responsiveness to stimulation, is infrequently applied in studies which are concerned with other manipulations of sleep.

B. The Ontogeny of Sleep

The developmental changes in sleep have been described in several species including man, cats, rats, rabbits, and guinea pigs (Delange *et al.*, 1962; Roffwarg *et al.*, 1966; Parmelee *et al.*, 1967; Valatx *et al.*, 1964; Chase and Sterman, 1967; Shimizu and Himwich, 1968; Jouvet-Mounier, 1968). A consistent pattern in the developmental progression of sleep has emerged as shown schematically in Fig. 1. In infant animals, behavioral sleep consists predominantly of active sleep. In the neonatal rat and kitten and in premature human infants, the EEG characteristics of quiet sleep and active sleep are incompletely differentiated. However, some investigators have made judgments of sleep types during this period based on behavioral observations of sleeping postures, eye closure, respiration, and motor activity (Shimizu and Himwich, 1968; Jouvet-Mounier, 1968; Parmelee *et al.*, 1967). Their results suggest that sleep may initially consist exclusively of active sleep. However, this suggestion is only tentative because at very immature states even the differentiation of sleep and wakefulness is unclear. (See Chapter 11 for a further discussion of this point.) Nevertheless, the proportion of the day defined as active sleep is clearly elevated throughout the period of infancy and past the age of weaning.

It may be noted that the proportion of active sleep at birth varies in different species. However, both man, using premature birth (Parmelee *et al.*, 1967; Dreyfus-Brisac, 1967), and guinea pigs, using intrauterine recordings (Astic and Jouvet-Mounier, 1970), have been studied prior to termination of the normal gestation period. These studies are the bases for the extrapolation of the developmental patterns into the prenatal period. The sleep of rats and rabbits, like cats, consists almost exclusively of active sleep at birth (Jouvet-Mounier, 1968; Shimizu and Himwich, 1968).

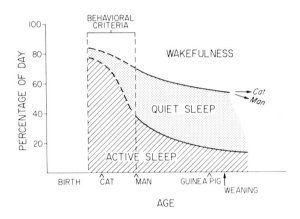

FIG. 1. Schematic representation of the ontogeny of the daily proportions of active sleep, quiet sleep, and wakefulness in the mammal. The figure includes the prenatal period for species such as man and the guinea pig which are more mature at birth than the cat. The age of weaning is suggested as a common anchor point for all species. Prior to the appearance of cortical EEG synchronization, the sleep states are distinguished on the basis of behavioral criteria such as the presence or absence of twitching and rapid eye movements.

During development there is a gradual increase in quiet sleep correlated with the gradual reduction in active sleep. The increase in quiet sleep was based on initially both behavioral and EEG criteria and subsequently on the appearance of EEG synchronization (Parmelee *et al.,* 1967). Jouvet-Mounier (1968) noted that the mammal which is relatively mature at birth, the guinea pig, has at that time large amounts of quiet sleep, while the rat and cat, which are immature at birth, have very little quiet sleep (Fig. 1). Thus, the maturity of the nervous system determines whether or not quiet sleep is established at birth.

The temporal patterns in sleep also exhibit developmental changes. In the infant, active sleep follows directly after wakefulness; but in the adult, active sleep always occurs following quiet sleep, except in certain pathological conditions. Periods of sleep may consist of only one or two quiet sleep-active sleep cycles. The ability to sustain long periods of uninterrupted sleep is acquired gradually coincident with the changing proportion of active sleep and quiet sleep (Parmelee *et al.,* 1964). In addition, a diurnal sleeping and waking pattern begins to emerge during the first few postnatal weeks (Hellbrügge, 1960).

In summary, active sleep is the ontogenetically primitive form of sleep and may initially be the only form of sleep. This sleep state coincides in time with the period of reflexive or instinctive behaviors such as sucking. In the neonate, active sleep onset is rapid and follows directly from wakefulness; it may occur in response to specific interval stimulus conditions. Thus, active sleep appears to exhibit many of the properties of an instinctive reflexive behavior.

Quiet sleep emerges during the period of postnatal maturation and is associated with the development of cortical EEG synchronization. Other evidence, to be reviewed below, indicates that quiet sleep may be controlled by forebrain structures.

III. NEURAL CONTROL OF SLEEP

It is now widely accepted that sleep is controlled by an active neural process. The term "active" implies that onset of sleep is brought about by the activity of discrete brain mechanisms which are specialized for this purpose. This concept is based on the observation that electrical or chemical stimulation of specific sites within the brain can initiate sleep and that lesions of many of these same sites result in the reduction or abolition of sleep. The extensive experimental literature on sleep-inducing systems has been reviewed by several authors (Jouvet, 1967a; Koella, 1967; Sprague, 1967; Clemente and Sterman, 1967). The most significant points are summarized here.

A. Active Sleep

The two phases of sleep are controlled by different brain areas. Jouvet (1962) has shown that a state nearly identical to active sleep can be observed after removal of all neural tissue above the level of the rostral pons. The pontile animal exhibits periodic episodes marked by neck muscle atonia, rapid eye movements, and phasic slow waves in the pontile reticular formation. The cyclicity and overall amount of this state approximates that of the active sleep state of the normal cat (Jouvet, 1962; Villablanca, 1965; McGinty et al., 1970). The atonia of active sleep appears to be abolished by dorsolateral pontine lesions (Jouvet, 1962), while certain components of phasic activity are abolished by lesions of the vestibular nuclei (Morrison and Pompeiano, 1966). Jouvet (1967b) has provided pharmacological evidence that catecholaminergic neurons in the locus coeruleus of the pons (Dahlstrom and Fuxe, 1965) may control active sleep, but a wholly consistent theory is not yet available.

B. Quiet Sleep

There is controversy over the anatomical locations of the mechanisms of quiet sleep. A number of brain areas, including the caudal brain stem (Batini *et al.*, 1959; Magnes *et al.*, 1961), the raphé nuclei of the medial brain stem (Jouvet, 1967b) and medial thalamus (Hess, 1957; Akert *et al.*, 1952), and the preoptic or basal forebrain area (Sterman and Clemente, 1962), have been shown to be important in the induction and maintenance of quiet sleep.

The importance of brain stem mechanisms for quiet sleep was indicated by observations that midpontine transections or hemisections produced diminished forebrain EEG quiet sleep patterns (Batini *et al.*, 1959; Cordeau and Mancia, 1958). This result indicated that brain structures behind the transection normally facilitated EEG synchronization. The localization of this influence was suggested by the finding that electrical stimulation of the region of the solitary tract produced EEG synchronization (Magnes *et al.*, 1961). Jouvet (1967b) proposed an alternative explanation. He showed that localized coagulation limited to the raphé nuclei of the brain stem could suppress sleep. These nuclei contain seotoninergic cell bodies and their destruction produces depletion of brain serotonin (Jouvet, 1969). Pharmacological depletion of serotonin also prevents the occurrence of sleep (Jouvet, 1967b; Koella *et al.*, 1968; Weitzman *et al.*, 1968). Jouvet's interpretations of these data have been questioned (Mancia *et al.*, 1968; Dement, 1969), but a role for one or more brain stem sleep-inducing influences is well documented.

The critical nature of the forebrain in the maintenance of sleep is also well established. Lesions of the basal forebrain area bring about the abolition or suppression of sleep (Nauta, 1946; McGinty and Sterman, 1968) while either electrical or chemical stimulation of the same area can cause the initiation of sleep (Sterman and Clemente, 1962; Hernandez-Peón *et al.*, 1963). The lesions suppress *both* quiet sleep and active sleep. This is a surprising result since active sleep can occur following complete ablation of the forebrain. The lesions appear to release a descending influence which suppresses the initiation of active sleep. When such lesions produce a partial suppression of quiet sleep, active sleep is reduced proportionately. A similar result was obtained by Jouvet (1969) following suppression of quiet sleep after lesions of the raphé nuclei of the brain stem.

The importance of the forebrain in sleep in the adult is further documented in studies of thalamic preparations, that is, after removal of all brain structures above the level of the thalamus. A recent study in the rat in which some animals were observed for more than 50 days showed that the thalamic animal is continuously active except for short periods following feeding (Sorenson and Ellison, 1970). We have confirmed the observation of continuous activity in the cat, although with shorter survival times (McGinty *et al.*, 1970).

The critical forebrain structures for sleep are unknown. Lesions of the basal forebrain destroy a number of ascending and descending pathways as well as cellular groups. A subcortical or paleocortical site is likely since neodecorticate dogs exhibit normal behavioral sleep (Kleitman and Camille, 1933; Jouvet and Michel, 1958). Decorticate animals no longer exhibit the synchronized EEG associated with quiet sleep, but the prolonged periods of behavioral sleep must consist of quiet sleep periods as well as active sleep (Jouvet and Michel, 1958).

In summary, active sleep is controlled by neural mechanisms localized in the lower brain stem. Quiet sleep is influenced by both forebrain and brain stem mechanisms. In the adult mammal, behavioral sleep consists of a sequence of quiet sleep followed by active sleep, the occurrence of the latter depending upon the prior occurrence of quiet sleep.

IV. ENCEPHALIZATION OF SLEEP

A parallel between the developmental changes and the neural control of sleep in the adult is clearly indicated. Active sleep is the ontogenetically primitive form of sleep and is controlled by the lower brain stem. On the other hand, quiet sleep emerges during the period of perinatal forebrain maturation and is associated with forebrain neural mechanisms. Quiet sleep becomes the quantitatively predominant stage of sleep and its prior occurrence is a condition for the onset of active sleep. Other forebrain-controlled activities, to be described below, also become antecedents of active sleep. Thus, *the direction and control of sleep shifts from the brain stem mechanisms of active sleep to forebrain mechanisms underlying quiet sleep.* It is this process that is meant by the phrase "encephalization of sleep." It is proposed that the emergence of quiet sleep and several temporal patterns in sleep are related to the maturation of the forebrain. These forebrain influences are superimposed on the primitive sleep mechanism of the brain stem, active sleep.

The role of forebrain mechanisms in the ontogeny of sleep has been pointed out by several investigators. Jouvet (1967a) has noted that the neocortex is necessary for the occurrence of EEG synchronization, but *not* behavioral sleep. He assigns the latter function to the brain stem. However, the studies reviewed above suggested that paleocortical or subcortical structures may be essential for sleep in the adult. Parmelee *et al.* (1967) have described the development of both EEG and behavioral correlates of sleep states in premature and full-term human infants. They related the emergence of the predominance of quiet sleep over active sleep to the modulation of the medullary sleep center by cortical mechanism.

The preceding investigators have assumed that the forebrain modulates a brain stem quiet sleep mechanism. An alternative hypothesis would be that the quiet sleep mechanisms are organized in the diencephalon, limbic system, and neocortex, with brain stem mechanisms playing a nonspecific modulating role. A model emphasizing the primary role of forebrain mechanisms and regarding sleep as a consummatory behavior was proposed by Parmeggiani (1968). In this model, the limbic system and thalamus served to organize the preparations for sleep, the depression of motor activity in the initiation of sleep, and the integrated depression of sensory responsiveness, visceromotor function, of EEG activation. A similar approach is described here.

A. Encephalized Properties of Sleep

The argument that active sleep and quiet sleep may be viewed as the primitive and encephalized elements in the ontogeny of sleep is a simplification. The forebrain sleep mechanisms provide a number of properties that are essential for the manifestation of sleep in the adult. Some of these properties are suggested in Fig. 2 with the aid of an analogy to the organization of feeding behavior. The occurrence of appetitive behaviors in the normal environment involves a sequence or chain of functional processes which result in the consumption of the goal object. The nervous system must select a behavior, direct the animal to an appropriate site within the environment to obtain the goal, release the required motor behaviors to obtain and consume the goal. Later the behavior must be terminated. This chain of behavioral functions may conveniently be divided into three stages.

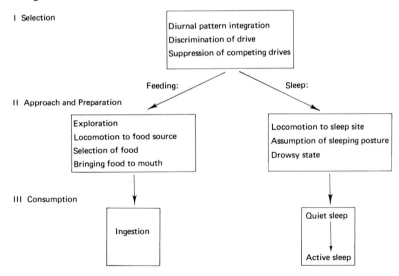

FIG. 2. Appetitive behavior chain in the adult.

1. Selection

The basic needs of the neonatal organism are met by reflexive mechanisms such as sucking, working in combination with maternal activities. With the development of a choice of motivated behaviors, the nervous system is required to discriminate the physiological needs and emit appropriate behaviors in relation to the environmental stimuli. There is evidence that behavioral selection processes are inefficient in the immature organism and that this function is a complex process mediated, at least in part, by the forebrain. A feature of neonatal sleep, the occurrence of sucking or "fussing" within periods of active sleep, may indicate the immaturity of drive selection processes. Two or more driven behaviors seem to occur simultaneously. The inability of children to discriminate hunger, sleepiness, or even elimination needs as sources of irritation may be another example of the immaturity of this mechanism. The capacity of the basal forebrain to perform a drive-selection function has been demonstrated. Electrical excitation of this area suppresses the performance of food-motivated behavior (Sterman and Fairchild, 1966). This brain region may suppress competing drive behavior during sleep.

One aspect of the behavior selection process is integration with diurnal variations in the environment. The diurnal rhythmicity in sleep and waking first appears during the first month in human infants and may reflect the emergence of forebrain control (Hellbrügge, 1960). It has been reported that this rhythm is lost after neodecortication in the dog (Kleitman and Camille, 1933).

2. Approach and Preparation

The role of hippocampal structures in mediating the approach and preparatory phases of sleep has been proposed by Parmeggiani (1968). He observed grooming, yawning, and settling into sleep postures following electrical stimulation of the hippocampus. The suppression of sleep following basal forebrain lesions may involve a deficit in postural preparation for sleep. As indicated in Fig. 3, the residual periods of EEG synchronization may occur while the animal is standing or sitting. The brain has lost the ability to completely suppress alternative behaviors or to initiate sleep postures.

3. Consumption

The identification of both quiet sleep and active sleep as "consummatory" activities is based on observations that sleep is required in certain quantities, like food or water. The amounts of both quiet sleep and active sleep are stable from day to day. A selective rebound increase in active sleep following its deprivation has been observed in several species (Dement, 1960; Siegel and Gordon, 1965; Dement et al., 1967). A selective rebound in quiet sleep is more difficult to document since quiet sleep deprivation also usually produces active sleep deprivation. However, a selective rebound following selective state IV sleep deprivation has been observed in man (Agnew et al., 1964). The bases for the physiological requirement for sleep will be discussed below.

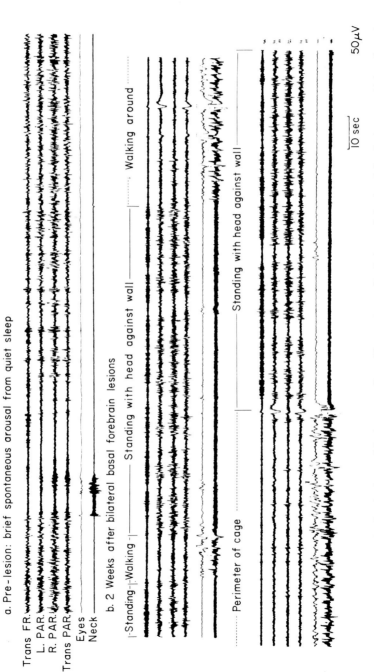

FIG. 3. EEG synchronization is observed during normally waking postures after lesions of the basal forebrain area. Although such lesions suppress sleep, residual sleeplike states may occur without postural relaxation.

V. NEURAL BASIS OF ENCEPHALIZATION

The evidence reviewed above suggests that behavioral aspects of sleep may be organized in several forebrain sites. More generally, sleep, like the behaviors associated with feeding, sex and aggression, may consist of several elements organized at different levels of the neuraxis. These include reflexive or instinctive elements organized in the brain stem, like sucking and swallowing in the case of feeding, and active sleep. The instinctive elements of drive behaviors are in turn regulated by hypothalamic mechanisms which maintain the stability of the "interior milieu" over extended periods. Higher mechanisms modulate both the voluntary behavior that is required to carry out motivated behaviors in the adult and the complex sensory factors that are manifested in the exhibition of preferences and conditioned control of behavior. Our knowledge of the localization and organization of the neural substrate of these functions is scant. However, two functional characteristics of the organization of encephalized behaviors are suggested by recent observations.

A. Suppression and Release of Active Sleep

The suppression of the primitive elements of behavior is a characteristic of the process of encephalization (Peiper, 1963). A descending suppressor influence on active sleep was revealed by the effect of forebrain lesions described above. The existence of this descending influence supports the use of the concept of encephalization to study sleep. However, a new problem is created. In the adult, sleep normally consists of a sequence of quiet sleep followed by active sleep. Thus, during sleep there occurs a functional regression such that the primitive phase of sleep may emerge. Functional regression could be associated with the physiological depression of some forebrain functions.

A functional depression of cortical influences during sleep was observed in the course of study of corticofugal somatomotor influences originating from the orbital gyrus of the cat (Chase and McGinty, 1970). We studied the effects of cortical stimulation on reflex transmission during spontaneous sleep and wakefulness in the cat. During wakefulness, an electrical pulse applied to the surface of the orbital cortex induced excitation in the digastric muscle and inhibition of the masseteric reflex. Figure 4 shows the changes in these descending somatomotor effects during sleep. Both excitatory and inhibitory effects of cortical stimulation gradually declined during quiet sleep episodes preceding active sleep and were greatly reduced or abolished during active sleep. A similar kind of functional decortication may be illustrated by the appearance of the Babinski sign during sleep (Kleitman, 1963). Many regulatory reflexes associated with temperature regulation are also depressed during active sleep (Parmeggiani, 1968). Thus, mounting evidence suggests that during sleep descending control mechanisms are depressed at allow the appearance of active sleep.

A   B

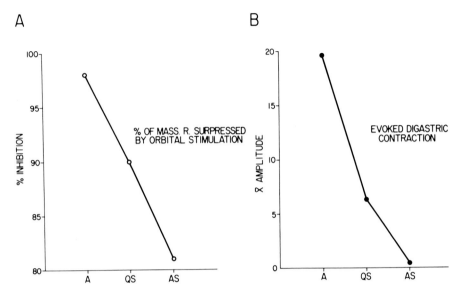

FIG. 4. Both the inhibition of the masseteric reflex (A) and the amplitude of the cortically evoked digastric response (B) were greatest during the alert state and were least during active sleep. The amplitude of the evoked digastric contraction during sleep and wakefulness was, in general, parallel to the degree of inhibition of the masseteric reflex. The masseteric reflex was evoked at the rate of 1/sec and every fourth reflex elicitation was preceded by cortical stimulation (20 msec latency). The percent inhibition for each state was obtained by dividing the mean amplitude of 30 control reflexes by the amplitude of the intervening 100 reflexes which were preceded by orbital stimulation. The mean amplitude of the digastric response (20 trials) is plotted on an arbitrary but relative scale. For each state the mean amplitude of 20 stimulation trials was obtained. A. Orbital stim: 7 V, 0.75 msec, 3 pulses (500 pulses/sec); Mesencephalic Vth nucleus stim: 6 V, 0.5 msec. B. Orbital stim: 7 V, 0.75 msec. (From Chase and McGinty, 1970.)

B. Developmental Changes in Active Sleep

In the adult, the behaviors associated with sleep, feeding, and sex may be described as a chain terminating in a primitive consummatory element. However, the consummatory elements such as the ingestional reflexes, lordosis, or active sleep are modified in the adult when compared with the infant (Beach, 1967). For example, sucking reflexes are replaced by chewing and related activities. These modifications may also reflect the influence of forebrain structures. In the case of active sleep, a modification is seen in reflex modulation. Monosynaptic reflex activity is inhibited during active sleep in the adult cat (Pompeiano, 1967), but is facilitated in the kitten (Iwamura et al., 1968; McGinty et al., 1971). Removal of forebrain influences should restore kittenlike reflex patterns during active sleep. Monosynaptic reflex activity should be augmented during the active sleep phase following rostral brain stem transections. This hypothesis was examined in cats prepared for chronic recording of the masseteric mono-synaptic reflex during sleep (Chase *et al.*, 1968). As shown in Fig. 5, brain stem transections at the level of the rostral midbrain resulted in a regression from the adult pattern to the kitten pattern. The capacity for reflex inhibition in the kitten could be seen during wakefulness. Therefore, the developmental changes in reflex activity during active sleep probably reflect a modulating influence from forebrain structures rather than a direct inhibitory influence on the motoneuron. The functional significance of the modification of the character-istics of active sleep during development is not known.

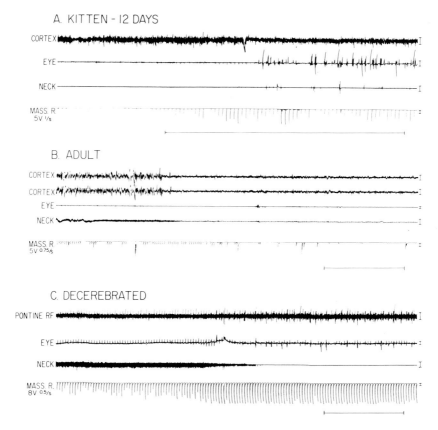

FIG. 5. Modulation of the monosynaptic masseteric reflex during active sleep in the kitten, adult cat, and after midbrain transection. The onset of active sleep is indicated by eye movements, twitches, neck muscle atonia, or EEG desynchronization. Reflex trans-mission is facilitated in the kitten, but inhibited in the adult. Removal of the forebrain restores the modulation pattern of the kitten.

C. Discussion

The concept of encephalization provides an explanation for the finding of neural substrates for sleep at several levels of the neuraxis. Each region may contain elements in a chain of neural mechanisms associated with the complex sleep process. Interruption of the chain at any level can produce a disorganization of the sequence of steps or processes which contribute to sleep. For example, a lesion may disrupt the inhibition of antigravity postural reflexes, depression of autonomic activity, filtering of sensory input to reduce arousal, hypothetical neuroendocrine receptors involved in the regulation of sleep, integration sites for the voluntary postural preparations for sleep, or mechanisms that suppress alternate drives. We have not developed procedures for distinguishing these possibilities; previous studies have leaned heavily on the net effect, the amount of polygraphically defined sleep.

It is notable that the disruption of sleep after lesions of the raphé system or basal forebrain is temporary and followed by restoration of function (Jouvet, 1967b; McGinty and Sterman, 1968). The chronic isolated forebrain also recovers from the initial period of constant synchronization and exhibits regular alternation of states of desynchronization and synchronization (Villablanca, 1962, 1965). A discussion of the several possible mechanisms by which the brain may compensate for disruption of a system is beyond the scope of this paper. However, compensation for the disruption of one component in a complex sleep process may occur in other components. The sleep after recovery may exhibit changes that can shed light on the nature of the function of the area of the lesion. This approach has been profitably applied to the temporary deficits in feeding after lateral hypothalamic lesions (Teitelbaum and Epstein, 1962).

Current reviews of the neural control of quiet sleep stress the role of the brain stem mechanisms (Jouvet, 1967a; Koella, 1967). In the present formulation brain stem mechanisms may control some physiological processes mentioned above that are required for sleep. However, the brain stem mechanisms may be even less specific. The serotonergic neurons of the raphé system appear to be involved in habituation, the inhibition of sexual behavior, aggression, feeding, and social behavior in addition to sleep (Sheard, 1969; Shillito, 1970; Ferguson et al., 1970). This system may normally inhibit behavioral activities which interfere with sleep.

As yet unexplained is the decline in active sleep during development. If this decline is the result of the maturation of descending inhibitory processes, an enhancement of active sleep would be expected after forebrain ablation. However, forebrain ablation usually results in a slight reduction in active sleep (Jouvet, 1962; McGinty et al., 1970). A comparison with other appetitive behaviors suggests another explanation. The time occupied by instinctive ingestional behavior (sucking, etc.) also declines during development, primarily as the result of increased efficiency of ingestion. The decrease in active sleep may reflect increased efficiency in the physiological process that underlies the active sleep.

Roffwarg *et al.* (1966) have proposed that active sleep evolved to provide stimulation to facilitate the development of the immature nervous system. This interesting hypothesis was based in part on the evidence that excitation, at least in sensory pathways, is required for normal development of neural elements and that active sleep is characterized by activation of many elements of the nervous system. However, the function of primitive behaviors cannot necessarily be inferred from their neurophysiological mechanisms. The function of rooting, sucking, and swallowing reflexes is to provide nutrition to the organism, not to stimulate the related musculature.

A problem which has plagued sleep research is that of deciding whether quiet sleep and active represent two distinct sleep processes or a physiological continuum with only superficial changes reflecting levels of activity. The present formulation emphasizes that behaviorally, sleep is a continuum, with relatively variable appetitive states leading toward the more stereotyped instinctive states. The function of the instinctive state may anticipate the needs of the organism just as sucking and swallowing reflexes anticipate the need for nutrition.

VI. SLEEP DRIVE AND SLEEP NEED

The basis of the physiological requirement for sleep continues to elude scientific explanation. The fact that sleep can be regarded as an appetitive behavior directed by forebrain mechanisms does not mean that the need for sleep derives from the forebrain. However, sleep deprivation experiments suggest that the brain suffers some kind of "fatigue." Sleep deprivation in humans reliably produces a number of disturbances in behavior, notably lapses in attention, irritability, feelings of fatigue, disorientation, impaired short-term memory, and slower cognitive operation (although some of these deficits may be caused by the intrusion of brief moments of drowsiness). A small but significant proportion of subjects exhibit definite psychotic episodes (Johnson, 1969). Moreover, prolonged deprivation has been reported to produce visual and occasionally auditory illusions in man (Naitoh, 1969). Such deprivation has been reported to result in death in experimental animals (summarized in Kleitman, 1963). However, except for a single report of deficits in ATP metabolism in red cells (Luby *et al.,* 1960), no proposals have been advanced to account for these phenomena. Thus, practically nothing is known about what is fatigued and restored during sleep. Where the word "fatigue" is used in the following pages, it should be remembered that this term is vague and may refer to any physiological process where some limited rate of synthesis, transport, metabolism, or other mechanism results in a degradation of the performance of the nervous system.

A. Sleep Drive in Immature Animals

Immature animals sleep more than adults. A number of suggestions could be made to account for this increased sleep: (1) It is generally suggested that the immature nervous system is undergoing changes as a result of both growth and experience. Indeed, these two factors seem to be interrelated in some neural pathways (see Chapters 4 and 17). (2) Immature neural mechanisms seem to be more fatigable. Metabolic mechanisms supporting the biochemical processes underlying neuronal firing or synaptic transmission are simply less rapid in the immature nervous system. (3) Increased sleep may reflect the incomplete development of a neural mechanism mediating wakeful behaviors that antagonize sleep. (4) The higher metabolic rate of immature animals may result in greater sleep drive. This list is surely incomplete, but two general types of factors seem to emerge. The first two possibilities are related to the functional activities of the immature brain. The second two possibilities are the result of the immaturity of the brain without regard to the ongoing experience of the organism.

B. Sleep in Isolation-Reared Kittens

Experiments were designed to test the hypothesis that functional activity of the brain associated with immaturity produces an increased drive for sleep and to separate this from the factors of immaturity per se. It was decided to study the amount of sleep in animals where the environmental stimulation was drastically reduced.

It has been shown that animals reared in an impoverished environment exhibit retarded behavioral development (Riesen, 1966). In studies where specific forms of sensory stimulation are reduced, normal neural development is retarded. Thus, this treatment appears to reduce the functional activity of the forebrain, expecially that activity associated with the response to varied experience; at the same time the immaturity of the organism is prolonged.

Half of the kittens from three litters were placed at weaning into individual completely enclosed cages while their littermates were reared in a normal group with frequent handling and complex stimulation. All animals were surgically prepared with chronically implanted electrodes for recording EEG, neck muscle, and eye-movement activity. Twenty-two-hour continuous recordings were obtained to measure sleep during the period of isolation. When the kittens were 23 weeks of age they were taken out of isolation and returned to the normal environment. During this period, these kittens undergo very rapid changes in behavior as a consequence of their exposure to novel environment. The sleep patterns of these animals were studied again 2-4 days after being placed in a normal environment.

The results of the experiment are shown in Fig. 6. Animals living in an isolated impoverished environment sleep much less than their normally raised littermates. Indeed, such animals sleep less than adult animals. The depression of sleep is observed in both quiet sleep and active sleep.

A striking reversal of this result was seen when the isolated animals were placed in a novel environment. Following this period of intense novel stimulation, these animals were sleeping much more than their normal littermates. Indeed, they slept as much as kittens who were several months younger.

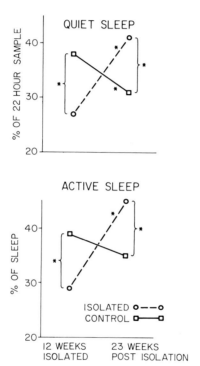

FIG. 6.   Comparison of the amount of quiet sleep and active sleep in kittens reared in an isolated impoverished environment and normally reared littermates. Kittens exhibited reduced sleep during isolation, but augmented sleep following 2 to 4 days exposure to the normal environment. The reduction in sleep in control kittens is the normal developmental change, *, significant, "t" test; $P < 0.05$. (From McGinty, 1971.)

The isolation-rearing experiment was repeated in a second series of kittens with additional precautions against alternative explanations. The 22-hour recordings were completed in the animals' home cages following prolonged adaptation to the recording conditions. This procedure allowed us to rule out the role of novel stimulation or sleep deprivation as various factors in the disturbance of sleep patterns. The results were the same: isolated kittens sleep less.

The depression of sleep in isolated animals is consistent with observations of a high level of behavioral arousal in such animals (Melzack and Burns, 1965). Analysis of the EEG frequency spectrum and evoked potentials in dogs also indicated a high arousal level in response to exposure to the novel environment (Melzack and Burns, 1965). The present data support these findings, but stress that the arousal of isolated animals is reflected tonically by reduced sleep within the familiar home cage.

C. Novel Stimulation and Sleep

The study of isolation-reared animals provided strong suggestive evidence that environmental stimulation was necessary for the elevated sleep drive of immature animals. However, isolation-reared animals are different from the normal animals in a variety of ways. The differences reflect the effect of social stimulation, changes of appetite, in sensory sensitivities, as well as in plastic changes in the nervous system. Therefore, it was decided to do a second kind of experiment where more precise control of the effects of environmental stimulation was possible. Specifically, the amount of sleep was studied following specific "doses" or periods of exposure to novel environmental stimulation. For this purpose, sleep was studied in isolation-reared animals following 4½-hr periods of exposure to a novel stimulating environment. As a control procedure, sleep was measured in the same animals following 4½ hr of sleep deprivation in the animals' home cage. The sleep deprivation control was necessary because animals did not sleep in the novel environment. An additional procedure, employed to control for the "stress" of exposure to novel stimulation, was the restraint of the kittens in a small cubicle. Restraint is known to produce classic stress responses in rats (Brodie, 1962). The results are shown in Fig. 7. Following 4½ hr of novel stimulation, isolation-reared animals exhibited increased sleep when compared with the equivalent amount of sleep deprivation or restraint. Sleep deprivation and exposure to environmental stimulation were not differentially effective in modifying sleep in normal animals. Of course, the environmental stimulation was not novel for the normal kittens. Thus, in this experiment, facilitation of sleep was specifically tied to exposure to a novel stimulating environment.

Taken together, these experiments provide strong support for the hypothesis that sleep is facilitated by exposure to a novel stimulating environment. Furthermore, the elevated amounts of sleep found in immature animals appear to depend upon the effects of the environment. It seems reasonable to hypothesize that a novel stimulating environment is critical because of the complex neural responses to "experience" that it produces in the animal.

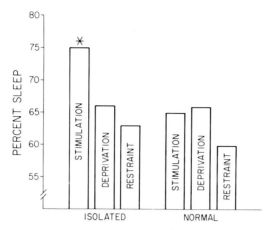

FIG. 7. The percentage of sleep in 18-hr recordings following 4½ hr exposure to a complex environment and control conditions in isolation-reared and normal kittens. The intense novel stimulation provided to the isolated kittens augmented the subsequent sleep more than sleep deprivation or stress caused by restraint. The sleep of normal kittens was not differentially changed by the exposure to the familiar complex environment. The asterisk indicates statistical significance ("t" test, $P < 0.05$).

Hobson (1969) has shown that exercise can reduce the latency of sleep; thus, peripheral fatigue may increase the need for sleep. However, isolated kittens (with reduced sleep) were invariably more active than controls. When isolated kittens were exposed to a new environment, they initially moved more cautiously. Peripheral fatigue does not account for the altered sleep patterns in isolation-reared kittens.

D. Discussion

Sleep was reduced about 40% by prolonged isolation in an impoverished environment and increased about 25% by novel stimulation. The neural response associated with "experience" accounts for a significant fraction of the requirement for sleep. Although "experience" cannot be completely eliminated experimentally, it appears that the neural activity occurring in the absence of specific "experience" may account for a major part of the sleep need. These data suggest that the fatigue associated with "experience" is superimposed on a spontaneous rate of fatigue. This account is consistent with the concept of the spontaneously active nervous system which is repatterned by functional inputs.

In the immature animal, elevated sleep may reflect increased experience or fatigability, or both. The fatigability of the immature nervous system has been noted by several investigators (Scheibel and Scheibel, 1964; Purpura, 1961;

Ellingson and Wilcott, 1960). Further studies will be required to clarify this problem.

These experiments are among the first to test directly the hypothesis that sleep is facilitated following neural activity associated with the experience of the animal. However, there is a good deal of indirect evidence relating sleep to complex or "cognitive" brain functions. Feinberg has correlated the amount of active sleep to functional capacities in several clinical populations in man. In retarded children, the amount of rapid eye-movement activity associated with active sleep is positively correlated with the I.Q. (Feinberg, 1968). At the other extreme, depression of sleep in the aged can be associated with the appearance of other signs of senility (Feinberg et al., 1967). A depression of sleep is also observed during the disorganization of behavior associated with periods of acute illness in depressed and schizophrenic patients (Snyder, 1969).

Some preliminary reports have also appeared relating the amount of "cognitive" function in direct experimental tests. Recently, Zimmerman et al. (1970) have reported that active sleep is greatly facilitated in human subjects after they are required to wear inverting lenses throughout the preceding period of wakefulness. The inversion of the visual field requires difficult behavioral adjustments which are learned after many hours of experience. Some aspect of the neural response to this demand can facilitate active sleep. Other preliminary reports indicate that the selective deprivation of active sleep can interfere with the retention of learned behavior (Fishbein et al., 1969; Stern, 1969).

VII. SUMMARY

As a hypothetical model, sleep was described as an active appetitive behavior similar to feeding. The ontogenetically primitive state, active sleep, may be regarded as an instinctive reflexive function like sucking and ingestion. In the adult, sleep consists of a sequence of behaviors including (1) a behavior selection phase; (2) an approach phase; and (3) a consummatory phase with both quiet sleep and active sleep serving consummatory functions. Evidence was reviewed that showed that most of the elements in the adult sleep chain leading to active sleep are controlled and directed by forebrain mechanisms. Thus, the neural control of sleep is encephalized during ontogenetic development.

This model is supported by five lines of evidence. (1) Behaviorally, sleep exhibits the properties of drive and regulation like appetitive behaviors such as feeding. (2) The neural control of sleep includes elements at several levels of the neuraxis as in other appetitive behaviors. This approach may explain the diffuse anatomical localization of sleep mechanisms. (3) As in other encephalized behaviors, the primitive mechanism, active sleep, is suppressed by a descending forebrain influence. (4) Developmental changes in active sleep are analogous to developmental changes in other instinctive consummatory behaviors. (5) During sleep, the emergence of active sleep is associated with a functional depression of forebrain mechanisms.

The preceding model is concerned with the neural control of sleep behavior, not the basis of the physiological requirement for sleep or the neurophysiological changes during sleep. The model does emphasize the behavioral continuity of quiet sleep and active sleep. As in feeding, the need for sleep cannot be easily inferred from the superficial manifestations of adult or neonatal sleep behavior. The elusive "restorative" hypothesis of the need for sleep is supported by sleep deprivation experiments. The increased sleep in neonates suggests an increased requirement for sleep.

Rearing kittens in an impoverished environment reduces both quiet sleep and active sleep to below adult levels. Thus, increased sleep in immature animals appears to reflect increased functional activity. This hypothesis was supported experimentally by the observation of an augmentation of sleep after exposure to a novel stimulating environment.

ACKNOWLEDGMENT

This research was supported by a grant from the U. S. Public Health Service (MH-10083), and by the Veterans Administration. Bibliographic assistance was received from the UCLA Brain Information Service which is part of the National Institute of Neurological Diseases and Stroke and is supported under Contract No. DHEW PH-43-66-59. The editorial suggestions of Dr. Michael Chase and Barry Jacobs are gratefully acknowledged.

REFERENCES

Agnew, H. W., Webb, W. B., and Williams, R. L. (1964). *Electroencephalogr. Clin. Neurophysiol. 17*, 68-70.

Akert, K., Koella, W. P., and Hess, R., Jr. (1952). *Amer. J. Physiol. 168*, 260-267.

Andersson, S. A., and Wolpow, E. R. (1964). *Acta Physiol. Scand. 16*, 130-140.

Aserinsky, E., and Kleitman, N. (1953). *Science 118*, 273.

Astic, L., and Jouvet-Mounier, D. (1970). *Psychophysiol. 7*, 2.

Batini, C., Moruzzi, G., Palestini, M., Rossi, G. F., and Zanchetti, A. (1959). *Arch. Ital. Biol. 97*, 1-2.

Beach, F. A. (1967). *Physiol. Rev. 47*, 289-316.

Bradley, P. B., and Elkes, J. (1953). *J. Physiol (London) 120*, 14-15.

Bremer, F. (1936). *C. R. Soc. Biol. 118*,1235-1241.

Brodie, D. A. (1962). *Gastroenterology 43*, 107-109.

Chase, M. H., and Sterman, M. B. (1967). *Brain Res. 5*, 319-329.

Chase, M. H., and McGinty, D. J. (1970). *Brain Res. 19*, 127-136.

Chase, M. H., McGinty, D. J., and Sterman, M. B. (1968). *Experientia 24*, 47-48.

Clemente, C. D., and Sterman, M. B. (1967). *Res. Publ., Ass. Res. Nerv. Ment. Dis. 45*, 127.

Cordeau, J. P., and Mancia, M. (1958). *Arch. Ital. Biol. 96*, 374-399.

Dahlstrom, A., and Fuxe, K. (1965). *Acta Physiol. Scand. 62*, Suppl. 232, 1-55.

Delange, M., Caston, P., Cadilhac, J., and Passouant, P. (1962). *Rev. Neurol. 107,* 271-276.

Dement, W. C. (1960). *Science 131,* 1705-1707.

Dement, W. C. (1969). *In* "Sleep: Physiology and Pathology" (A. Kales, ed.), p. 245-265. Lippincott, Philadelphia, Pennsylvania.

Dement, W. C. and Kleitman, N. (1957). *Electroencephalogr. Clin. Neurophysiol. 9,* 673-690.

Dement, W. C., Henry, P., Cohen, H., and Ferguson, J. (1967). In "Sleep and Altered States Of Consciousness" (S. S. Kety, E. V. Evarts, and H. L. Williams, eds.), p. 456-468. Williams & Wilkins, Baltimore, Maryland.

Dreyfus-Brisac, C. (1967). *In* "Regional Development of the Brain in Early Life" (A. Minkowski, ed.), p. 437-457, Oxford: Blackwell.

Ellingson, R. J., and Wilcott, R. C. (1960). *J. Neurophysiol. 23,* 363-375.

Feinberg, I. (1968). *Science 159,* 1256.

Feinberg, I., Koresko, R. L., and Heller, N. (1967). *J. Psychiat. Res. 5,* 107-144.

Ferguson, J., Henriksen, S., Cohen, H., Mitchell, G., Barchas, I., and Dement, W. C. (1970). *Science 168,* 499-501.

Fishbein, W. (1969). *Psychophysiol. 6,* 225.

Hellbrügge, T. (1960). *Cold Spring Harbor Symp. Quant. Biol. 25,* 311-323.

Hernández-Peón, R., Chavez-Ibarra, G., Morgane, P. J., and Timo-Iaria, C. (1963). *8,* 93-111.

Hobson, J. A. (1969). *Science 162,* 1503-1505.

Iwamura, Y., Tsuda, K., Kudo, N., and Kohama, K. (1968). *Brain Res. 11,* 456-459.

Johnson, L. C. (1969). *In* "Sleep: Physiology and Pathology" (A. Kales, ed.), p. 206-220. Lippincott, Philadelphia, Pennsylvania.

Jouvet, M. (1962). *Arch. Ital. Biol. 100,* 125-206.

Jouvet, M. (1967a). *Physiol. Rev. 47,* 117-177.

Jouvet, M. (1967b). *In* "Sleep and Altered States of Consciousness" (S. S. Kety, E. V. Evarts, and H. L. Williams, eds.), p. 86-126. Williams & Wilkins, Baltimore, Maryland.

Jouvet, M. (1969). *Science 163,* 32-41.

Jouvet, M., and Michel, F. (1958). *C. R. Soc. Biol. 152,* 1167.

Jouvet-Mounier, D. (1968). Doctoral Dissertation.

Kales, A., ed. (1969). "Sleep: Physiology and Pathology," Lippincott, Philadelphia, Pennsylvania.

Kleitman, N. (1963). "Sleep and Wakefulness," Univ. of Chicago Press, Chicago, Illinois.

Kleitman, N., and Camille, N. (1933). *Amer. J. Physiol. 105,* 574-584.

Koella, W. P. (1967). "Sleep, Its Nature and Physiological Organization," Thomas, Springfield, Illinois.

Koella, W. P., Feldstein, A., and Czicman, J. S. (1968). *Electroencephalogr. Clin. Neurophysiol. 25,* 481-490.

Luby, E. D., Frohman, C. E., Grisell, J. L., Lenzo, J. E., and Gottlieb, J. S. (1960). *Psychosom. Med. 22,* 182-192.

McGinty, D. J. (1971). In preparation.

McGinty, D. J., and Sterman, M. D. (1968). *Science 160,* 1253-1255.

McGinty, D. J., Sterman, M. B., and Iwamura, Y. (1970). *Psychophysiology 7,* 2.

McGinty, D. J., Chase, M. H., Sterman, M.B., and Iwamura, Y., in preparation.

Magnes, J., Moruzzi, G., and Pompeiano, O. (1961). *Arch. Ital. Biol. 99,* 33-67.

Mancia, M., Desiraju, T., and Chkina, G. S. (1968). *Electroencephalogr. Clin. Neurophysiol. 24,* 409-416.

Melzack, R., and Burns, S. K. (1965). *Exp. Neurol. 13,* 163-175.

Morrison, A. R., and Pompeiano, O. (1966). *Arch. Ital. Biol. 104,* 425-458.

Moruzzi, G. (1966). *In* "Brain and Conscious Experience" (J. C. Eccles, ed.), p. 1-54. Springer, Berlin.
Naitoh, P. (1969). Rep. No. 68-3, Dept. of the Navy.
Nauta, W. J. H. (1946). *J. Neurophysiol. 9,* 285-316.
Parmeggiani, P. L. (1968). *Brain Res. 7,* 350-359.
Parmelee, A. H., Werner, W. H., and Schulz, H. R. (1964). *J. Pediat. 65,* 576.
Parmelee, A. H., Jr., Werner, W. H., Akiijama, Y., Schultz, M. A., and Stern, E. (1967). *Rev. Med. Child Neurol. 9,* 70-77.
Peiper, A.(1963). Cerebral Function in Infancy and Childhood Consultants Bureau, New York.
Pompeiano, O. (1967). *In* "Sleep and Altered States of Consciousness," p. 351-423. Williams & Wilkins, Baltimore, Maryland.
Purpura, D. P. (1961). *Ann. N.Y. Acad. Sci. 94,* 604-654.
Riesen, A. H. (1966). *In* "Progress in Physiological Psychology" (E. Stellar and J. M. Sprague, eds.). p. 117-147. Academic Press, New York.
Roffwarg, H. P., Nuzio, J. N., and Dement, W. C. (1966). *Science 154,* 604.
Scheibel, M. E., and Scheibel, A. B. (1964). *In* "The Developing Brain" (W. A. Himwich and H. E. Himwich, eds.), Vol. IX, p. 6-25. Elsevier, Amsterdam.
Sheard, M. H. (1969). *Brain Res. 15,* 524-528.
Shillito, E. E. (1970). *Brit. J. Pharmacol. 38,* 305-315.
Shimizu, A., and Himwich, H. E. (1968). *Electroencephalogr. Clin. Neurophysiol. 24,* 307-318.
Siegel, J., and Gordon, T. (1965). *Science 148,* 978-979.
Snyder, F. (1969). *In* "Sleep: Physiology and Pathology" (A. Kales, ed.), p. 170-182. Lippincott, Philadelphia, Pennsylvania.
Sorenson, C. A., and Ellison, G. D. (1970). *Exp. Neurol. 29,* 162-174.
Sprague, J. M. (1967). *In* "Sleep and Altered States of Consciousness" (S. S. Kety, E. V. Evarts, and H. L. Williams, eds.), p. 148-188. Williams & Wilkins, Baltimore, Maryland.
Sterman, M. B., and Clemente, C. D. (1962). *Exp. Neurol. 6,* 103-117.
Sterman, M. B., and Fairchild, M. D. (1966). *Brain Res. 2,* 205-217.
Stern, W. C. (1969). Assoc. Psychophysiol. Study of Sleep, Boston, Massachusetts.
Teitelbaum, P., and Epstein, A. N. (1962). *Psychol. Rev. 69,* 74-90.
Valatx, J. L., Jouvet, D., and Jouvet, M. (1964). *Electroencephalogr. Clin. Neurophysiol. 17,* 218-233.
Villablanca, J. (1962). *Science 138,* 44-46.
Villablanca, J. (1965). *Electroencephalogr. Clin. Neurophysiol. 19,* 576-586.
Villablanca, J. (1966). *Electroencephalogr. Clin. Neurophysiol. 21,* 562-577.
Weitzman, E. D., Rapport, M. M., McGregor, P., and Jacoby, J. (1968). *Science 160,* 1361-1363.
Zimmerman, J., Stoyva, J., and Metcalf, D. R. (1970). *Psychophysiology 7,* 2.

CHAPTER 19 Nutritional Deprivation and Neural Development

*Joseph Altman**

I. INTRODUCTION

It was believed for a long time that reserves accumulated in the body of the mother during pregnancy protected or "spared" the fetus from nutritional deficiencies during gestation (Hytten and Leitch, 1964). Furthermore, some evidence was available from animal studies that postnatal nutritional deprivation that led to an appreciable reduction in the weight of the body and most of its organs, "spared" the brain, in the sense that its weight and chemical composition remained unaffected (Donaldson, 1911). The idea that the body and the brain are resistant to undernutrition and malnutrition during development is being gradually abandoned as new evidence is accumulating from human and animal studies that nutritional deprivation during the growth period, both before and after birth, has serious and irreversible effects on the biochemical and morphological maturation of the body and the brain.

A few illustrative examples from human studies may suffice. A survey showed that a long and severe famine during the siege of Leningrad in World War II led to a fall in the birth weight of children ranging from 400 to 500 g (Antonov, 1947). A less severe famine during the same period in Holland led to a reduction by 240 g in the average birth weight (Smith, 1947). A similar decline was recorded in 1944 in Japan (Gruenwald *et al.*, 1967). As economic conditions improved after the war in Japan, there was a conspicuous increase in fetal, birth, and postnatal weights of children, and the recently recorded values surpassed those recorded before the war (Gruenwald *et al.*, 1967). This type of observation

*This research program is supported by the National Institute of Mental Health and the U. S. Atomic Energy Commission.

indicated that in spite of its buffered position, the fetus is not altogether immune to the nutritional status of the mother.

Evidence is also available of the deleterious effects of undernutrition or malnutrition of nursing mothers on the growth pattern of infants, which becomes evident about half a year after birth. The height and weight of children in most economically underdeveloped areas at birth is similar to that of European and North American children, and their growth rates do not differ up to 6 months of age (Sénécal, 1958; World Health Organization, 1965), indicating considerable lactational efficiency which protects the infant from malnutrition. But this favorable situation changes at about 6 months of age, when breast milk no longer suffices and the child requires a supplementary diet. It is during this period that the growth rate of children begins to fall rapidly in most economically disadvantaged societies or socioeconomic groups. The rapid retardation at this time in the growth of height and weight (the most easily measurable indices) was documented in Thailand, Southern India, Malaya, New Guinea, Uganda, Mexico, and Guatemala (Béhar, 1968). While many of these children show only retarded growth and may be healthy otherwise, infantile mortality is high in these societies and there is also a high incidence of diseases related to malnutrition and its complications (Waterlow *et al.*, 1960).

Only a few studies are available on the effects of prenatal or postnatal nutritional deprivation on neural development, and these are restricted to severe cases which led to the death of the children. Thus, in a recent study (Winick *et al.*, 1970) the growth of the brain was studied biochemically in "normal" children who died between birth and 2 years of age as a result of accident, poisoning, or other causes said not to have involved the nervous system, and in children of the same age who died following severe malnutrition (marasmus). In the cerebellum of the normal children there was a twelvefold increase in protein and a tenfold increase in RNA during this period and, during the first 10 months there was a fourfold increase in DNA concentration or "cell number." In the 2-year period the increase in the cerebrum was ninefold in protein, fourfold in RNA and threefold in DNA. In the brain stem, which matures earlier, the increase was eightfold in protein, fivefold in RNA and only twofold in DNA. In marasmic children there was a marked reduction in the protein, RNA, and DNA concentration of these three regions. The reduction in cell number was much higher in the cerebrum and cerebellum than in the brain stem.

There is little information on the effect of less severe undernutrition on the growth of the brain. It is presumed that even in milder forms of undernutrition, retarded body growth is associated with deceleration of brain growth, as indicated by such gross measurements as reduced head circumference (Robinow, 1968; Stoch and Smythe, 1963) and as inferred from studies that suggest retarded mental, particularly motor and intellectual, development (Cabak and Najdanvic, 1965; Cravioto and Robles, 1965; Cravioto, 1968; Dean, 1960; Geber and Dean, 1956; Knobloch and Pasamanick, 1960; Stoch and Smythe, 1963).

The type of data presented regarding the effects of infantile malnutrition in man leave several problems unresolved. The deceleration of the growth of the body commonly seen in economically disadvantaged societies or social groups is only partially the direct effect of malnutrition. The high incidence of death and disease among children in disadvantaged societies is clearly the consequence of the synergistic interaction of malnutrition and infection (Scrimshaw *et al.*, 1959). The isolated effect of dietary deficiency is, accordingly, difficult to establish in studies of human populations. For an analytical study of the consequences of malnutrition and undernutrition, animal studies are needed in which the genetic and environmental variables can be controlled and in which changes in the development of the brain with a variety of biochemical, morphological, and physiological techniques can be investigated. Some of these studies are reviewed in the following pages.

II. NUTRITIONAL DEPRIVATION DURING GESTATION

Animal studies confirmed and extended the observations made in human populations on the deleterious reproductive consequences of dietary deprivation. Some data are available from studies in a uniparous domestic animal, the sheep, and a few multiparous species like the pig and the rabbit (Lodge and Lamming, 1968). The bulk of information comes from experimental studies in the laboratory rat.

Nelson and Evans (1953) reported that the reproductive capacity of female rats was not affected as the protein level of an otherwise balanced diet was dropped from 25, to 20, to 15 and finally 10%. All rats showed 100% implantation, they delivered a normal-sized litter (8 to 10), and the birth weight of the pups was normal (6 gm). When the protein level was decreased to 5%, resorptions (30%), stillbirths (17%), and reduced birth weights (to 5 gm) were noted. There was consistent reproductive failure (90-100%) if the protein-free diet was started on the day of mating, but if it was delayed by 7 days after mating, 90% litters were delivered. In a complementary study, Venkatachalam and Ramanathan (1964) found 100% infant mortality in the offspring of rats fed a 7% protein diet both during gestation and lactation. The mortality was lower (78%) in the offspring of rats that were fed this diet during lactation only and in these there was a lowered weaning weight. If this protein diet was restricted to the gestation period, the birth weights were not appreciably affected. However, the weaning weights of these pups were lower than those of mothers receiving a normal diet (19% mixed protein) during both gestation and lactation and there was an incidence of 40% postnatal mortality. On the basis of these findings, the authors concluded that a 7% protein diet did not affect the reproductive performance of rats but that the postnatal growth of the pups was severely affected.

In a complementary study, Zeman and Stanbrough (1969) studied the effects of a protein-deficient (6% casein) diet in rats during gestation on organ weight, on the concentration of DNA ("cell number") and on RNA/DNA and protein/ DNA ratio ("cell size") in 16- and 20-day old fetuses and in newborn young. When compared with the offsprings of mothers kept on an adequate protein diet (30% casein), the deprived young had smaller organs, and the DNA concentration was significantly decreased in all tissues. In many organs, including the brain, protein/DNA and RNA/DNA ratios were not appreciably changed, suggesting that the reduction in body and organ weights was primarily the result of reduced cell numbers in most tissues. Similar results were obtained by Zamenhof *et al.* (1968). In this study, female rats were maintained on a 8% or 27% protein diet before mating and during gestation. In the brains of newborn rats that were delivered by the mothers fed on the 8% diet there was a 10% reduction in DNA concentration, indicating that this type of dietary restriction can lead to a significant decrease in the cell concentration of the brain.

A gap in our knowledge is the paucity of studies on the effects of prenatal undernutrition on the morphological maturation of the brain at birth and afterward. Biochemical evidence of reduction in "cell number" and "cell size" in total brain samples leaves the question unanswered, whether some brain regions are more affected than others, whether the affected cells are neurons or glia and, also, to what extent the maturation and differentiation of the cells were affected. In a recent study, Shrader and Zeman (1969) reported a reduction in large multipolar neurons in the spinal cord and the brain in newborn rats from malnourished mothers, and also a reduction of cells in the surface layers of the cerebral cortex, and in Purkinje cells and granule cells of the cerebellum. Though reduced in number, these cells appeared to have normal enzymic activity, as determined by histochemical techniques.

III. NUTRITIONAL DEPRIVATION DURING INFANCY

Winick and Noble (1966) found that raising pups in large litters (18 per mother) from birth to weaning resulted in a proportional decrease in the overall weight, protein, RNA and DNA content of all organs, including brain, indicating a reduction in cell number without alteration in cell size. When these animals were re-fed after weaning, they failed to recover normal growth. Rats raised on a restricted diet from weaning to 42 days of age showed a proportional reduction in weight, protein, RNA, and DNA in most organs, except in the lungs and brain. In the latter organs, protein and RNA ratios were reduced, but not total DNA, indicating that the size of cells was smaller but their total number was unaffected. After re-feeding, the organs in which the number of cells was reduced showed no recovery, whereas the lungs and the brain regained normal size. Dietary restriction from 65 to 86 days led to a reduction in protein and RNA concentration without effects on DNA in all organs, except spleen and thymus.

In another study, Winick and Noble (1967) found that the organs of infant rats raised in small groups (3-6 pups per mother) had higher than normal DNA content, but normal protein/DNA and RNA/DNA ratios, indicating that the increased growth rate in these "overnourished" animals was due to the acquisition of more cells. In initially underfed rats nursed up to 9 days in groups of 18 to a mother, which were rehabilitated during the period of active cell proliferation by raising them from then on until weaning in groups of 3, normal recovery was obtained (Winick et al., 1968). These studies suggested that undernutrition affects differentially cell size or cell number, depending on the developmental phase of the affected organs. Early deprivation led to reduced cell number in all organs and to irreversible retardation, presumably because once developmental cell proliferation has stopped, the lost cells could not be replaced. Later deprivation affected irreversibly those organs in which cell acquisition was still in progress. The brain appeared irreversibly damaged only by undernutrition prior to weaning; the cells whose size only was affected (reduced protein and RNA content without DNA change) could recover after re-feeding. This conclusion was corroborated by studies concerned with regional changes in the brain as a consequence of undernutrition.

In a study concerned with regional brain differences in susceptibility to infantile dietary deprivation, Culley and Lineberger (1968) found that of the three brain regions examined (cerebellum, pons-medulla, and mid- and forebrain), restricted feeding affected most severely the weight and DNA content of the cerebellum. Comparable results were obtained by Howard and Granoff (1968) in mice and by Cheek et al. (1969) in rats. In the former study (Howard and Granoff, 1968), experimental mice were intermittently removed from their mothers between 2 and 16 days of age, which led to a 57% reduction in body weight compared with littermate controls. The animals were then fed *ad libitum* up till 9 months of age. At that time, body weight was 17%, cerebrum 7%, and cerebellum 22% below normal. Total DNA was reduced in cerebrum by 8%, in cerebellum by 22%. Chase et al. (1969) compared the effects of nursing rats in groups of 16 or 4 on the development of cerebrum and cerebellum at 18 days of age. They found that the weights of both the cerebrum and cerebellum were significantly lower in the undernourished groups, with a reduction by 9.9% in the cerebrum and 18% in cerebellum. While this difference in the cerebrum appeared to be due to reduction in cell size (with no reduction in DNA), the difference obtained in the cerebellum (reduction by 18%) could be attributed to an appreciable reduction in cell number. In the cerebellum there was also a greater reduction in protein (by 28%) than in the cerebrum (4.6%).

In another study by Fish and Winick (1969), rats that were raised 18 to a mother were killed at intervals between 6 and 21 days, and the weight, DNA, and protein content of the brain stem, cerebellum, hippocampus and cerebrum were compared with control rats of comparable ages. In the early maturing brain stem, in which cell proliferation is relatively low during the postnatal period, malnutrition had no effect on DNA content but there was interference with the normal developmental increase in the protein/DNA ratio. In the cerebellum, where cell proliferation is very brisk during this period (Altman, 1969a), there was a marked reduction in DNA content throughout the time span studied. In the hippocampus and cerebrum the reduction in DNA content was observed between 14 and 21 days and the magnitude of this decrease was much lower than in the cerebellum.

Several reports are also available which were concerned with the effects of infantile malnutrition on the chemical differentiation of the brain. Dobbing and Widdowson (1965) found that nutritional deprivation of suckling rats led to reduced brain cholesterol and phospholipids. This was reported also by Culley and Mertz (1965), who found that brain cerebroside concentration was reduced in the malnourished rats to a greater extent than other brain lipids. These findings suggested interference with myelination, a possibility which was indicated also by the studies of Benton *et al.* (1966) and Guthrie and Brown (1968).

IV. NUTRITIONAL DEPRIVATION AFTER WEANING

Some of the studies reviewed earlier showed that the effects of undernutrition after weaning are different from deprivation sustained before weaning. Thus, the studies of Winick and Noble (1966) indicated that dietary deprivation between weaning and 42 days led to reduction in the size of cells (reduced protein/DNA and RNA/DNA ratios) in the brain rather than to reduction in the number of cells, and that this effect was reversed by putting the animals on an *ad lib* diet. Dickerson and Walmsley (1967) reported that rats that were undernourished from weaning until 11 weeks of age could be rehabilitated if re-fed for 2-8 weeks, and in these animals there was no reduction in DNA-P concentration of the brain. According to Dobbing and Widdowson (1965), when the undernourished 11-week old rats were rehabilitated for 8 weeks they acquired during this period, in a compensatory manner, three times the amount of cholesterol that is typical of well-nourished, control animals.

The studies of Guthrie and Brown (1968) showed that cholesterol levels in the malnourished rats were normal if rehabilitation occurred immediately after weaning, but that they were irreversibly depressed if undernutrition was extended until 5 weeks of age. This indicated that even after weaning, usually at 3 weeks, there is another "vulnerable period" (Dobbing, 1968), one that affects myelination of the brain. After this period of growth the brain becomes resistant to dietary deprivation (Donaldson, 1911). This is illustrated by the observation of Dobbing (1968) that following reduction of the body weight of rats by 45% (as a result of a 5-week starvation diet) the weight of the brain was essentially unaffected. The mature brain, accordingly, unlike the developing brain, is indeed "spared" by severe malnutrition.

However, in contrast to this evidence of "sparing" of the brain, as determined by such gross measurements as brain weight and the concentration of a few chemical constituents, there are some studies in which pathological effects were reported on the basis of histological examination of the brain. In a review of the old literature, Jackson (1925) reported that undernutrition in experimental animals led to chromatolysis, cytoplasmic vacuolation, and the actual loss of cells, while Andrew (1941) described increases in the number of glia cells in mice starved from the sixty-fifth day. It is difficult to determine how well the histological procedures were standardized in the earlier studies. There is a great need for morphological investigations, both qualitative and quantitative, in order to determine the effects of dietary deprivation during the prenatal, preweaning, and postweaning periods on the structural organization of the brain.

V. NUTRITIONAL DEPRIVATION AND THE "VULNERABLE PERIODS" OF BRAIN DEVELOPMENT

The results described indicate unequivocally that nutritional deprivation of mothers during gestation or lactation can have profound effects on the growth of the young. Organs, including the brain, in which cell proliferation is brisk during infancy are affected more than mature organs. In the brain, the early maturing regions (such as the brain stem) are less affected than late maturing regions (such as the cerebellum) and where cell number is reduced rather than cell size, the effect is irreversible.

These studies, valuable as they are, have not cast light on the questions as to whether malnutrition directly affects cell division, cell migration, or cell differentiation (neurogenesis). They provide little evidence as to what cell types (neurons or glia) are particularly harmed, although available knowledge on neurogenesis and gliogenesis in the structures referred to offer some plausible hypotheses. Finally, these biochemical studies are not well suited for providing detailed information about regional alterations in differentiation and maturation of the brain, such as changes in synaptogenesis, regional myelogenesis, and the like, the study of which requires the use of morphological and related techniques (histology, histochemistry, and electron microscopy).

Information that is now becoming available about the chronology of the regional development of the nervous system in lower mammals could serve as the basis of a promising strategy for the study of the effects of nutritional deprivation on the growth of the brain. According to this new evidence (Altman, 1969c, 1970), we may distinguish three critical phases in the development of the mammalian nervous system after birth. These phases are related to the formation of three major classes of cells which arise from three proliferative sources during three successive periods of growth. The three major cell types are macroneurons, microneurons, and neuroglia. The macroneurons are long-axoned nerve cells that form the afferent, relay, commissural, and efferent elements of the peripheral and central nervous system. As such, they are responsible for conveying sensory messages from the receptors to the central nervous system, for relaying afferent impulses from one brain region to another, and for transmitting motor commands from the brain to the effector organs. These macroneurons form the gross circuitry or "coarse wiring" of the nervous system. The microneurons are short-axoned interneurons with regional or local input and output connections. It is presumed that their function is primarily modulatory or associative in nature and thus they represent the "fine wiring" of local brain regions. The neuroglia are supportive elements which are responsible for the myelination of axons (the oligodendrocytes) and for linking the differentiated neurons with the fine capillaries of the brain (astrocytes). As such, they are responsible for the sustenance, protection, and "fixation" of the developed brain circuitry.

The long-axoned nerve cells arise during embryonic development of the nervous system from the primitive ependyma, or neuroepithelium, which surrounds the lumen of the neural tube or brain ventricles. In addition to differentiating macroneurons, stem cells which retain their proliferative capacity also arise from the neuroepithelium and these form secondary germinal matrices such as the subependymal layer of the cerebrum or the subpial, external granular layer of the cerebellum. Short-axoned nerve cells, such as those of the olfactory bulb (Altman, 1969b), of the hippocampal dentate gyrus (Altman and Das, 1965, 1966), and of the cerebellar cortex (Altman, 1966a, 1969a), are formed from cells of these secondary matrices. The secondary germinal matrices also produce "dispersed stem cells" that retain their proliferative capacity. These undifferentiated cells become scattered throughout the brain and are the source of differentiating neuroglia cells (Altman, 1966b).

Macroneurons, microneurons, and neuroglia cells tend to differentiate in any brain region sequentially, and it is possible that a hierarchic, inductive relationship controls their successive regional differentiation. For example, the microneurons of the cerebellar cortex (the basket, granule, and stellate cells) migrate and differentiate after the Purkinje cells, with which they establish synaptic contacts, have begun to differentiate. The differentiation of neuroglia cells, as judged by myelination of the cerebellum, is the last event in the maturation of this brain region.

It is of great practical importance that in altricial mammals (as the mouse, rat, cat, or dog) the macroneurons of the brain differentiate largely during the period of embryonic development; the bulk of the microneurons (at least in the olfactory bulb, hippocampus, and cerebellum) come into existence postnatally during the suckling period; while the bulk of the neuroglia cells are formed during the early postweaning period. Accordingly, dietary deprivation during the suckling period could be expected to inflict less harm on the elements already formed, the long-axoned neurons, but would interfere with the formation of microneurons and, thus, the "fine wiring" of the brain. The great reduction produced in the cell population of the cerebellar cortex by infantile malnutrition, presumably due to decimation of the large population of granule cells, supports this view. Finally, dietary deprivation during the early postweaning period would interfere, by preventing the formation of neuroglia cells, with the final steps in the maturation of the brain, such as myelination.

The maturation of these three basic elements of the brain is not synchronous throughout the nervous system (e.g., the spinal cord matures much earlier than the forebrain), and their formation is not in phase in all mammalian species with the three major periods of development (fetal, infantile, and childhood). Therefore, those brain structures (such as the cerebellar cortex, hippocampal dentate gyrus or olfactory bulb) of mammalian species (such as the mouse, rat, cat, or dog) for which this synchrony holds, would be ideal subjects for experimental study of the effects of nutritional deficiencies on brain development. With these considerations in mind, we have recently examined the effects of undernutrition in rats on the development of the cerebellum and on the maturation of motor skills (Altman *et al.*, 1971a,b; Altman and McCrady, 1971).

REFERENCES

Altman, J. (1966a). *J. Comp. Neurol. 128*, 431.
Altman, J. (1966b). *Exp. Neurol. 16*, 263.
Altman, J. (1969a). *J. Comp. Neurol. 136*, 269.
Altman, J. (1969b). *J. Comp. Neurol. 137*, 433.
Altman, J. (1969c). *In* "Handbook of Neurochemistry" (A. Lajtha, ed.), Vol. II, pp. 137-182. Plenum Press, New York.
Altman, J. (1970). *In* "Developmental Neurobiology" (W. A. Himwich, ed.), pp. 1971-237. C. C. Thomas, Springfield, Illinois.
Altman, J., and Das, G. D. (1965). *J. Comp. Neurol. 124,* 319.
Altman, J., and Das, G. D. (1966). *J. Comp. Neurol, 126,* 337.
Altman, J., and McCrady, B. (1971). *Devel. Psychobiol.,* submitted for publ.
Altman, J., Das, G. D., Sudarshan, K., and Anderson, J. B. (1971a). *Devel. Psychobiol.,* in press.
Altman, J., Sudarshan, K., Das, G. D., McCormick, N., and Barnes, D. (1971b). *Devel. Psychobiol.,* in press.
Andrew, W. (1941). *Amer. J. Pathol. 17,* 421.
Antonov, A. N. (1947). *J. Pediat. 30*, 250.
Béhar, M. (1968). *In* "Malnutrition, Learning and Behavior" (N. S. Scrimshaw and J. E. Gordon, eds.), pp. 30-41. M.I.T. Press, Cambridge, Massachusetts.
Benton, J. W., Moser, H. W., Dodge, P. R., and Carr, S. (1966). *Pediatrics 38*, 801.
Cabak, V., and Najdanvic, R. (1965). *Arch. Dis. Childhood 40*, 532.
Chase, H. P., Lindsley, W. F. B., and O'Brien, D. (1969). *Nature (London) 221*, 554.
Cheek, D. B., Graystone, J. E., and Rowe, R. D. (1969). *Amer. J. Physiol. 217*, 642.
Cravioto, J. (1968). *In* "Environmental Influences" (D. C. Glass, ed.), pp. 3-51. Rockefeller Univ. Press, New York.

Cravioto, J., and Robles, B. (1965). *Amer. J. Orthopsychiat. 35*, 449.
Culley, W. J., and Lineberger, R. O. (1968). *J. Nutr. 96*, 375.
Culley, W. J., and Mertz, E. T. (1965). *Proc. Soc. Exp. Biol. Med. 118*, 233.
Dean, R. F. A. (1960). *Bibl. Paediat. 5*, 111.
Dickerson, J. W. T., and Walmsley, A. L. (1967). *Brain 90*, 897.
Dobbing, J. (1968). *In* "Applied Neurochemistry" (A. N. Davison and J. Dobbing, eds.), pp. 287-316. Davis, Philadelphia, Pennsylvania.
Dobbing, J., and Widdowson, E. (1965). *Brain 88*, 357.
Donaldson, H. H. (1911). *J. Comp. Neurol. 21*, 139.
Fish, I., and Winick, M. (1969). *Exp. Neurol. 25*, 534.
Geber, M., and Dean, R. F. A. (1956). *Courier 6*, 3.
Gruenwald, P., Funakawa, H., Mitani, S., Nishimura, T., and Takeuchi, S. (1967). *Lancet 1*, 1026.
Guthrie, H. A., and Brown, M. L. (1968). *J. Nutr. 94*, 419.
Howard, E., and Granoff, D. M. (1968). *J. Nutr. 95*, 111.
Hytten, F. E., and Leitch, I. (1964). "The Physiology of Human Pregnancy." Blackwell, Oxford.
Jackson, C. M. (1925). "The Effects of Inanition and Malnutrition Upon Growth and Structure." Churchill, London.
Knobloch, H., and Pasamanick, B. (1960). *Pediatrics 26*, 210.
Lodge, G. A., and Lamming, G., eds. (1968). "Growth and Development of Mammals." Butterworth, London and Washington, D. C.
Nelson, M. M., and Evans, H. M. (1953). *J. Nutr. 51*, 71.
Robinow, M. (1968). *In* "Malnutrition, Learning and Behavior" (N. S. Scrimshaw and J. E. Gordon, eds.), pp. 409-424. M.I.T. Press, Cambridge, Massachusetts.
Scrimshaw, N. S., and Gordon, J. E., eds. (1968). "Malnutrition, Learning and Behavior." M.I.T. Press, Cambridge, Massachusetts.
Scrimshaw, N. S., Taylor, C. E., and Gordon, J. E. (1959). *Amer. J. Med. Sci. 237*, 367.
Sénécal, J. (1958). *Ann. N. Y. Acad. Sci. 69*, 916.
Shrader, R. E., and Zeman, F. J. (1969). *J. Nutr. 99*, 401.
Smith, C. A. (1947). *Amer. J. Obstet. Gynecol. 53*, 599.
Stoch, M. B., and Smythe, P. M. (1963). *Arch. Dis. Childhood 38*, 546.
Venkatachalam, P. S., and Ramanathan, K. S. (1964). *J. Nutr. 84*, 38.
Waterlow, J. C., Cravioto, J., and Stephen, J. M. L. (1960). *Advan. Protein Chem. 15*, 131.
Winick, M., and Noble, A. (1966). *J. Nutr. 89*, 300.
Winick, M., and Noble, A. (1967). *J. Nutr. 91*, 179.
Winick, M., Fish, I., and Rosso, P. (1968). *J. Nutr. 95*, 623.
Winick, M., Rosso, P., and Waterlow, J. C. (1970). *Exp. Neurol. 26*, 393.
World Health Organization. (1965). *World Health Organ., Tech. Rep. Ser. 302*, 1.
Zamenhof, S., Van Marthens, E., and Margolis, F. L. (1968). *Science 160*, 322.
Zeman, F. J., and Stanbrough, E. C. (1969). *J. Nutr. 99*, 274.

Author Index

Numbers in italics refer to the pages on which the complete references are listed.

A

Ader, R., 292, *295*
Adey, W. R., 174, *182*
Adolf, A. F., 307, 309, *332*
Aghajanian, G. K., 89, *89*, 97, *107*
Agnew, H. W., 343, *355*
Agrawal, H. C., 65, *69*
Ailion, J., 293, *295*
Airth, J. M., 292, *296*
Akert, K., 340, *355*
Akiyama, Y., 185, *202*, 209, 211, 213, 214, 216, 218, 221, *224*, *226*, 337, 338, 341, *357*
Alexander, F. A. D., 101, *107*
Alman, R. W., 320, *333*
Altman, J., 278, *295*, 364, 365, 366, 367, *367*
Anchel, H., 176, *182*
Anders, T., 206, *225*, *226*
Andersen, P., 31, *40*
Anderson, B. L. R., 331, *332*
Anderson, J. B., 367, *367*
Andersson, S. A., 337, *355*
Andres, V., Jr., 282, *295*
Anokhin, P. K., 308, *332*
Antonov, A. N., 359, *367*
Appel, S. H., 279, *295*
Arimura, A., 310, *333*
Arnason, B. G., 310, *332*
Aschoff, J., 205, *225*
Aserinsky, E., 204, *226*, 336, *355*
Astic, L., *202*, 337, 355
Auerbach, E., 151, *181*
Auerbach, J. H., 281, *296*
Axelrod, J., 282, *295*, 301, *305*
Azar, H. A., 310, *332*

B

Bacharach, A. D. E., 119, *128*
Baldissera, F., 130, 138, *142*
Banks, E. M., 170, *182*
Baptista, M. H., 245, *247*
Barchas, J. D., 293, *295*, 348, *356*
Barker, S. B., 320, *332*
Barnes, D., 367, *367*
Barnes, R. H., 323, 328, *332*
Barnett, S. A., 233, 241, *247*
Barnum, C. P., 205, *226*
Barry, W. F., 67, *69*
Bass, N. H., 94, 98, 105, *107*
Batini, C., 340, *355*
Bauer, J. A., Jr., 64, *69*
Baxter, B., 173, *181*
Baxter, C. F., 94, *107*, 126, *127*
Beach, F. A., 246, *247*, 309, *332*, 346, *355*
Beer, B., 178, *182*
Béhar, M., 360, *367*
Beller, A. J., 151, *181*
Bennett, D. S., 325, *332*
Bennett, E. L., 278, 279, 280, 282, 284, 286, 292, *295*, *296*, 329, *333*
Benton, J. W., 364, *367*
Berger, H., 63, *69*
Berlucchi, G., 158, *181*
Berlyne, D. E., 233, 238, *247*
Bertler, A., 282, *295*
Bevan, W., Jr., 292, *295*
Bishop, E. J., 13, *20*
Bittner, J. J., 205, *226*
Bizzi, E., 130, *142*
Bleyer, W. A., 191, *202*
Blinzinger, K., 253, *263*

369

Subject Index

A

Acetylcholinesterase
  effects of environmental enrichment on, 278, 285, 329
  of thyroxin on, 322
Adrenal steroids, secretion in sleep, 205-206
Alpha-glycerophosphate dehydrogenase, effects of thyroxin on, 321
Androgens, effects on sexual development, 297-304
ATP (adenosine triphosphate), synthesis in developing retina, 122-123
Axon
  collaterals, 256-258
  development of corticofugal, 5-7
  of corticopetal, 7-8
  thalamocortical afferent
    nonspecific, 7-8
    specific, 7

B

Basic rest-activity cycle
  development in gestation, 221-222
  in adult, 211-213
  in cat, 216
    after decerebration, 216, 348
  in fetus, 216-224
  in infant, 213-216
Behavior
  aggression, relation to ludic behavior, 232
  conditioning in infancy, 179-181
  development
    adaptive behavior in rats, 312-315
    blink response, 169
    classical conditioning, 170
    effects of brain lesions, 172
      of cortisol on adaptive behavior, 313

      of thyroxin on adaptive behavior, 313
    motor functions, 140
    startle reflex in rats, 312
  ludic (play) behavior, 229-249
  sexual, 297-305
    effects of neonatal hormone manipulation, 297-305
    relation to ludic behavior, 232
Biogenic amines, 267
Biological cycles, *see also* Basic rest-activity cycle
  circadian rhythms
    effects on norepinephrine content in developing brain, 47
      on serotonin content in developing brain, 47
  in fetus, 216-225
  in infant, 206-210
  in sleep and waking, 205
Brain chemistry, *see also* specific biological compounds
  analytic techniques, 281-282
  effects of enriched housing on acetylcholinesterase, 278, 285
    on caudate, 287
    on cholesterol, 283
    on dopamine, 285, 287-288
    on DNA, 283-284
    on enzyme activity, 285-286, 288-291
    on glia proliferation, 278
    on lipids, 283-284
    on nitrogen, 283
    on norepinephrine, 285, 287-288
    on recovery after rehousing, 290-291
    on regional changes, 287-290
    on RNA, 279, 283-284
    on serotonin, 279
Brain weight, isolation housing, 278, 282

R

Reflex, *see also* Sleep
  modulation in sleep, 129-140
Reticular formation, electrical activity in development, 11-13
Retina
  amacrine cells, 124-125
  catecholamines, metabolism of, 124-125
  dopamine, metabolism of, 124-125
  gamma-aminobutyric acid, metabolism of, 124
  ganglion cells, 124
  horizontal cells, 124
  maturation
    biochemistry, 115-123
    blood supply, 120
    cellular and synaptic morphology, 111-112
    electroretinogram, 108-111
    synaptic transmitters, 123
    visual pigment, 113-114
  serotonin, metabolism of, 124
RNA (ribonucleic acid)
  in developing cerebellar glial cells, 274-275
  effects of cortisol on synthesis, 323-324
    of enriched housing on synthesis, 279, 283-284
    of nutritional deprivation on synthesis, 362-365
  in neurons, 270
  synthesis in retina, 116-117

S

Sensory deprivation, 268, 279
Serotonin, 265
  effects of enriched housing on metabolism, 279
    of isolation rearing on metabolism, 266-268
Sleep
  active 204, 208, 211-224, 336, 339, 346-347, *see also* Sleep, polygraphic patterns in
    cycle, 212-216, *see also* Basic rest-activity cycle
  behavioral regulation, 335

criteria, 337
corticofugal influences on, 345-346
development of, 203-225, 337-339, 346-347
diurnal pattern, 205-210, 338
EEG, 337, 343-344, *see also* Sleep, polygraphic patterns in
effects of environmental enrichment on, 352-353
  of isolation housing on, 350-352
endocrine functions in, 205
influence of maternal sleep on fetus, 223-224
need for, 349
neural control
  basal forebrain mechanisms, 340-341
  encephalization in, 341-349
polygraphic patterns
  adult, 204-205, 336, 340-341
  infant, 129, 131-132, 206-210
  premature, 211, 337-338
preparatory behavior, 343
reflex modulation, 129-140, 346-347
Stress, effects of isolation housing, 284
Synapse
  axodendritic, 76, 95
  axosomatic, 76
  development in cerebellum, 36-39
    in cerebral cortex, 24-25, 30-31, 83-86, 93-96
    in hippocampus, 31
  effects of presynaptic degeneration on, 253-254, 261-263

V

Visual pigment, 113-114, 116
Visual system
  development of visual cliff avoidance, 65
  effects of development deprivation on cortical cell activity, 175
    on cortical volume, 259-260
    on dendritic length, 258-259
    on dendritic spines, 257
    on evoked response, 174-175
    on retinal neurochemistry, 114
  of development enrichment on, 67
  evoked response, 145-168
    effects of anesthesia on, 146-160